THE SPECIAL CONSTABLE'S MANUAL

*To my wife, Isobel,
my raison d'etre*

The SPECIAL CONSTABLE'S MANUAL

A definitive guide for the operational Special

Tom Barron

The Special Constable's Manual

All rights reserved. UK statutory material in this publication is acknowledged as Crown copyright. No part of this publication may be reproduced or transmitted in any form or by any means, or stored in any retrieval system of any nature, without prior written permission, except for permitted fair dealing under the Copyright, Designs and Patents Act 1988, or in accordance with the terms of a licence issued by the Copyright Licensing Agency in respect of photocopying and/or reprographic reproduction. Application for permission for other use of copyright material including permission to reproduce extracts in other published works shall be made to the publishers. Full acknowledgement of author, publisher and source must be given.

Any individuals' names mentioned in this book are fictitious, and any resemblance to actual persons, living or dead, is purely coincidental. Reference to a particular gender in this book is not intended to show bias or discrimination.

© Tom Barron 1999

First edition 1994
Second edition 1997
Police Review Publishing Co

Cover photographs © Hampshire Constabulary
Cover reproduction by Rainbow Reproductions
London E14 7EQ
Printed and bound in Great Britain by
The Cromwell Press, Trowbridge, Wiltshire
Distributed by Brookland Mailing Services, Bristol

To Order
Call ICAL Ltd on 01704515900
Fax 01704515909
Email ical@icalltd.co.uk

Contents

Acknowledgments x
The author x
Introduction xi
Preface to the second editions xiii

Chapt 1: Background

History of the Special Constabulary 2
Identity 3
Differences between forces 3
Rank structure 4
Who are you? 5
The public 6
Section officers 6
Sub-divisional officers 6
Divisional commandant 7
Chief commandant 7
Regular officers 7
Heat or light 8
History of the modern police service 8
Powers and jurisdiction 11
Appointment 11
Attestation of constables 11
Jurisdiction of police constables 11
Jurisdiction of special constables 11
Jurisdiction and powers of arrest 12

Chapt 2: Arrest

Classification of offences 14
Criminal law/common law 14
Arrestable offences 14
Common law powers (citizen's arrest) 14
Powers (police only) 15
Conditions for arrest 15
Serious arrestable offences 15
General arrest conditions 16
Mode of arrest 19
Factors to consider before arrest 19
Information to be given on arrest 19
Caution following arrest 20
Different arrest circumstances 20
Use of force when making arrests 21
Staying alive 22
The Confrontational Continuum 23
Case law 25
    Self-defence 25
    Genuine belief of imminent danger 26
    Honest belief/mistake as to facts 26
Assessment of danger 26
    Officer - personal factors 27
    Special circumstances 27
    Threat recognitions 27
    Signals of submission 28
Reporting the use of force 29

Search and seizure 30
Search after arrest 30
Seizure following search 30

Chapt 3: Search

Police and Criminal Evidence Act 1984 32
Stop and search 32
G O W I S E 32
Where searches may be carried out 34
Conduct of a search 35
Records of searches 36
Entry and search after arrest 37
Entry and search to arrest/save life 38
Search other than at a police station 39
Search warrants 40
Road checks 41
Criminal Justice & Public Order Act 1994 42
Anticipation of violence 42
Terrorism 42

Chapt 4: Crime

Breach of the peace 44
Assaults and woundings 44
Common assault 44
Actual bodily harm 45
Unlawful wounding 45
Wounding with intent 45
Assault on police 46
Attempts 46
Public order 47
Offensive conduct 47
Threatening behaviour 48
Intentional harassment, alarm or distress 49
Affray 49
Violent disorder 50
Riot 50
Trespassory assemblies 51
Racial hatred 52
Aggravated trespass 52
Trespass 53
Raves 53
Litter 55
Noise 56
Offensive weapons 56
Drugs 57
Unlawful possession of a controlled drug 57
Stop and search 58
Sexual offences 59
Indecent assault on a woman 59
Rape 59
Gross indecency 60
Prostitution 60
Kerb crawling 61

Persistent solicitation by men 61
Indecent assault on a man 61
Drink-related offences 62
Drunkenness 62
Driving while unfit 63
Drink driving 63
Breath test powers 64
Administering a breath test 64
Children 66
Offences (by age group) 66
Prevention of cruelty to children 68
Criminal damage 69
Aid and abet, counsel or procure 70
Crime and Disorder Act 1998 .... 70a
Community safety 70a
Youth crime 70a
Orders 70a

Chapt 5: Theft

Theft Act 1968 72
Dishonestly 72
Appropriates 73
Property 73
Land 73
Things growing wild 74
Wild creatures 74
Belonging to another 75
Permanently deprive 75
Taking a conveyance 76
Aggravated vehicle taking 76
Robbery 77
Burglary 78
Aggravated burglary 79
Abstracting electricity 79
Obtaining property by deception 80
Blackmail 81
Handling stolen goods 82
Going equipped for stealing 83
Theft Act 1978 83
Obtaining services by deception 83
Making off without payment 83
Vehicle interference 84

Chapt 6: Motor vehicles

Road traffic accidents 86
Definition 86
Action at the scene of a road traffic accident 87
Driving documents 91
Examining 91
Checking 93
Driving licence 93
Endorsements 94
Insurance certificates 94
MoT certificates 95
Fixed penalty system 96
Vehicle defect rectification scheme 98

Chapt 7: The custody suite

The Codes of Practice 102
Detention officers 103
Main responsibilities 103
Personal requirements 104
Finding your way 105
From arrest to police station 105
Custody officer 106
Custody officer duties 107
Arrival at the police station 107
Grounds for detention 108
Officers at variance 108
Ascertaining property in possession 108
Retention of property by arrested person 108
Arrested person's rights 109
Informing named person 109
Solicitors - free legal advice 110
Urgent interviews 110
Interviews without a solicitor 110
Insufficient evidence to charge 111
Authorising detention 111
Cells 111
Treatment of detained persons 112
Charging 113
Questioning after charge 114
Detention conditions after charge 114
Fingerprints and photographs 115
Reviews of detention 115
Time limits on detention without charge 116

Chapt 8: Interviewing 119

Planning 120
The information 120
The evidence 121
The offence/defence 122
Who's who? 123
The suspect 123
The solicitor 124
Trainees, clerks and legal executives 124
Case law - solicitors and confessions 125
Oppression and inducement 126
Questioning 127
The classification of questions 128
Closed and leading questions -
counterproductive 130
Open questions - productive 132
Art-form questioning 133
Key-word repetition 133
Echoing 134
Supportiveness 134
Summary of questioning technique 135
Recall v process questions 137
Summaries 138
The Bentley case 139
The Y factor 140
Ambiguities 140

Tape recorded interview procedure........ 141	The colour clock code 169
Recording and sealing master tapes................ 141	The counting code 170
Interviews to be tape recorded....................... 141	**Off-duty arrests 170**
The interview... 141	Jurisdiction.. 170
Significant statement or silence 142	When to get involved 171
Ambush defence - special warnings 142	
Statements made - not on tape 143	**Chapt 11: Practical policing 173**
Conclusion of interview 143	
Tape recorded interview procedure model..... 144	**Reporting offenders 174**
	Points to consider 174
Chapt 9: File submission.................145	**Notice of intended prosecution................. 176**
	The warning 176
Preparation, process and submission 146	**Warrants 177**
Manual of Guidance.. 146	**Street collections... 179**
The 10 sections of the *Manual* 147	**Dangerous dogs.. 180**
File submission - time limits 148	**Seizure of stray dogs..................................... 180**
File types 149	**Children - police protection 180**
File unique reference number 151	Care proceedings...181
File content checklist..................................... 152	**Pocket book rules 181**
Custody remand file....................................... 152	**Lost/found property...................................... 183**
Abbreviated file.. 152	**Domestic disputes 186**
Full file... 152	**Domestic violence 188**
Files for summary trial/committal 153	Information to be recorded 188
Case procedures... 154	Children...189
Advance disclosure 154	Other agencies 190
Discontinuance.. 155	Specialist units 190
Mode of trial guidelines................................. 156	**Neighbour disputes.. 191**
Record of tape-recorded interview 158	**Landlord/tenant disputes............................. 191**
	Unlawful eviction 191
Chapt 10: Patrolling a beat 163	Excluded lettings - notice only 192
	Harassment..192
Patrolling a beat 164	Squatters 192
Equipment... 164	Suggested procedure - WRAPPeR...................193
Paperwork... 164	**Actions at the scene of crime 193**
Local knowledge 165	**Index of modus operandi............................. 195**
Hospitals 165	**Crime reports... 195**
Other emergency services.............................. 165	Recording the crime 195
Private emergency services............................ 165	Amendments..196
Vulnerable premises 165	No crime..196
Keyholders... 165	**Victims.. 196**
Public houses 165	Compensation 197
Traffic lights... 166	Civil action.. 197
Neighbourhood Watch....................................166	Criminal Injuries Compensation Board 197
Alarmed premises 166	Motor Insurers' Bureau 198
Garages 166	Victims as witnesses.. 198
Intelligence gathering 167	
Informal intelligence gathering 167	**Chapt 12: PNC and radio procedure**
Plain clothes duty... 168	
Warrant cards 168	**The Police National Computer 200**
Identity 168	Who can use the PNC 200
Assault..168	**Name inquiries.. 200**
Radios 168	CRO number 200
Appropriate clothing 168	Wanted/missing information...........................200
Non disclosure of identity 168	Disqualified driver 201
Special equipment 169	Driving licence number...................................201
Note taking.. 169	Warning signal codes....................................... 201
Arrests 169	**Vehicle inquiries 201**
Target indication system 169	Codes 202

viii   The Special Constable's Manual

Chassis numbers 202
Requests from the public 202
Vehicle report types 203
The Data Protection Act 1984 203
Criminal liability 204
Caution 204
Radio procedure 204
The phonetic alphabet 204
Standard radio codes 205
Personal radios - quick reference guide 205
The ten code 206

Chapt 13: Summary of powers....207

Powers of arrest 208
Arrest - definition 208
Common law - citizen's power 208
Police arrest 208
Arrestable offences 208
General arrest conditions 209
Powers of search 210
Stop/search 210
Prohibited article 210
Procedure 211
Gowise 211
Entry and search leading to arrest 211
Search after arrest 212
Search of prisoner's premises 212
Premises 213
Seizure of property from premises 213
Search in public 213
Powers - traffic 213
Disqualified drivers 213
Documents / name, address date of birth 313
PSV driver and conductor 214
PSV passenger 214
Testing motor vehicles on roads 215
Goods vehicles operator's licence 215
Tachographs 215
Removal of vehicles 215
Traffic regulation 216
Breath test 216
Arrest 216
Powers of entry 217
Road checks 217
Powers - firearms 217
Trespassing with a weapon 217
Carrying in public place 217
Trespassing with firearm 218
Require production 218
Stop and search 218
Production of certificate 218
Powers - miscellaneous 219
Mentally ill people 219
Scrap metal dealers 219
Licensed betting office 219
Licensed premises 219
Drugs - stop and search 219

Fires 220
Public meetings 220
Exclusion orders - football 220
Alcohol at sporting events 220

Chapt 14: Crime prevention 221

Neighbourhood Watch 222
History 222
Setting up a Neighbourhood Watch scheme 222
Success or failure of Neighbourhood Watch 223
Crime prevention 224
Casing the joint 224
Target hardening 224
Target concealment or removal 224
Reducing the pay-off 224
Dwelling security 225
Property marking and identification 227
Intruder alarm systems 228
Security lighting 228

Chapt 15: Path to promotion (Supervisors) 229

Post profile 230
Responsibilities 230
Skills required 231
Seeking promotion 232
Mentors 233
Personal development 233
Setting up a section 233
The individual 234
The team 235
The organisation 235
Conflict 236
Supervision of files 236
Assessment reports - a model 237
Availability and duties worked 237
Recruiting 238
Disqualified categories 238
Requirements for selection 239
Conditions of service 241
Disciplinary procedure 242
Past and present 242
The Police (Conduct) Regulations 1999 243
Code of Conduct 243
Working Group recommendations 245
Legal representation 245
Complaints and discipline - the law 242
Dismissal 246
Suspension or retirement 247
Operation orders 248
IIMAC 250
Specialist units 252
Criminal Investigation Department (CID) 252
Road Traffic Department 254
Support Group (Task Force) 255
Lower profile units 256

Chapt 16: Evidence 257

Statements of evidence 258
    Statement taking................................. 258
    Witness statement 259
    Hearsay evidence 261

Chapt 17: Staff appraisal...............263

Preparing reports 264
Assessment criteria 264
Ratings..265
    Potential gradings 265
    Rating criteria 266
    Supervisory ranks - rating criteria.....................270

Chapt 18: Stress and burnout.......273

Introduction to stress 274
    The fight or flight response 275
    Vulnerability.......................................275
Recognising stress 276
    Signs of tension..................................276
    Change in lifestyle 276
    Stress indicators 277
Minimising burnout and stress 277
Seeking help..279
    Self help 279
Burnout 280
    Structured programmes......................280
    Tutor constables 289
    Assessments.......................................280
    Solo patrol..281
    Training programme 281
    Final assessment 283
Special to regular 283
    Gaining insight...................................283
    Improving position.............................283
    The unsuccessful candidate 284
    Best advice 284
Post-traumatic stress.............................. 285
    Post traumatic stress disorder 286
    Characteristics....................................286
    General symptoms..............................287
    Defusing 288
    Critical incident stress debriefing.............. 289

Chapt 19: Useful information........291

Expenses 292
    Basic allowances.................................292
    Other allowances/expenses................293
Sick pay/pensions 293
    Death or permanent disability 293
    Permanent partial disability................293
    Injuries 294
Pay for specials...................................... 295
Uniform and equipment........................ 296

The Ferrers trophy 297
Associations and further sources
  of information.......................................300
    The Black Police Association 300
    European Police Information Centre
        EPI-centre) 300
    International Police Association (IPA) 301
    Magazines 301
        Special Beat...................................301
        Police Review................................301
    Further reading...................................302

Chapt 20: Changes to terms and conditions of service 305

Recommendation and implementation....306
Home Office Working Group
    Recommendations............................. 307
    Role and purpose............................... 307
    Retention.. 307
    Leave of absence................................ 308
    Transfers 308
    Employer support............................... 308
    Grading structure 309
    Promotion 310
    Special Constabulary insignia.............311
    Eligibility for appointment................. 312
    Age 312
    Requirement to retire 313
    Ineligible occupations 313
    Recruitment....................................... 315
    Training.. 317
    Representation 318
    Complaints and discipline................. 318
    Resignation 320
IMPORTANT NEW CONDITIONS
Health and safety 321
    Hours of work 321
    Rest periods..322
Compensation for injury........................322
Legal representation..............................323
Complaints and discipline 324
Transfers 324
Other conditions of service 334

Appendix A: Skills and abilities 335
    Desired character traits 336
    Monitoring and performance.............337
    Communication and relationship with
        others..338
    Investigation 339
    Decision making, problem solving
        and planning..................................340
    Practical effectiveness.........................341
    Written reports 341
    Knowledge..342

Index 343

Acknowledgments

The author is particularly indebted to **Ian MacQuillin** for the invaluable contributions he has made to this book. At the time Ian was the editor of *Special Beat* and a special constable in the City of London Police. It was he who cajoled, encouraged, shaped, managed and disciplined the production of the book. He set it away at the right speed and direction, pre-determined left and right turnings, resulting in its arrival at the right time with the right information for the right audience. Ian himself has made a number of contributions to the book, too many to mention. In the absence of Ian, frankly, the book may never have had an existence.

Other contributors are: **David Harris**, Inspector, 'Custody Officers'; **Christine Stevens** BSc, Senior Welfare Officer, 'Stress and burnout'; **Paul Crockett**, Special Section Officer, 'First Aid'; **Mary Piper**, Former Special Constable, 'Neighbourhood Watch'; **Clive Wellbelove**, Senior Communications Officer, 'The PNC and radio procedure'; **Stephen Baggs**, Inspector, 'Criminal Justice and Public Order Act 1994'; **Robin Ford**, Home Office, 'Changes to terms and conditions of service'.

About the author

Born in Glasgow in 1945, Tom Barron joined the army, aged 15, as a boy soldier. He subsequently served in Germany, Cyprus (United Nations), Singapore, Malaya and in Borneo where he saw active service with the Royal Corps of Transport (Air Despatch).

Tom joined the police service in 1969 where he served 25 years in many operational and training posts, retiring in 1996. Two years were spent teaching crammer courses for officers taking the sergeants' and inspectors' exams, followed by 10 years prosecuting in magistrates' courts in the west country. He was also in charge of the Force Interview Technique training unit. Throughout the whole of his service he has been closely associated with the Special Constabulary, in particular, being responsible for initial induction training. It was during the course of this training that the need for a book which addressed the need of the special constable germinated.

Tom presently teaches constable and sergeant promotion courses. Also, in addition to teaching and writing books, he has had a number of articles published, most notably in the *Daily Telegraph*, and an exclusive in the *Daily Mail*. He enjoys lecturing in various colleges and universities in the South West.

Correspondence is invited from interested parties who may have ideas for the improvement of the book. All ideas are welcome and should be addressed to The Publisher, Special Constable's Manual c/o Brookland Mailing Services (see page 304 for address details) or E-mail; tombarron1033@yahoo.co.uk

Introduction

During the course of the last 25 years I have enjoyed a close relationship with specials of all ranks, shapes and sizes. I have been especially enriched by your insatiable appetite for knowledge, which I have been fortunate enough to help feed. No one is more conscious of the fact that knowledge is strength than the special, and I am forever left gasping at the sponge-like ability to absorb information that I constantly witness when teaching specials, be it during the course of induction weekends or to seasoned section officers. I often privately wish that regular officers showed the same degree of curiosity that I find in specials.

It has always been a worry to me that there is no one source of reference, one book, one publication, that singularly addresses the specific needs of the special. I recently ran a weekend induction course where I was asked over and over again: 'Is there a book for the Special Constabulary?' To my lasting shame I had to answer 'No'.

I have finally been overtaken by the realisation that if you want a book badly enough, then you have to write it yourself. Well, I have sat at my typewriter, opened a vein, and given birth to the beast - a book for the special constable. By way of reinforcing my singularity of purpose, it is entitled the *Special Constable's Manual*.

This manual is not burdened by being couched in judicial parlance, no semantic somersaults, no linguistic limbo dancing; in short, straightforward talk. Too many law books fall into the category of 'judicial nightmare', due to the language employed. Too much time is wasted in trying to unstitch the language that attends Acts of Parliament, which is counterproductive and self-defeating. We often fail to discover what mischief the Act is seeking to control - the law tends therefore to shoot itself, not in both feet, but comprehensively and sometimes fatally, in the head. Too often we have to abandon a book because it fails to make its point in any meaningful way, or because it just doesn't make sense. This happens to both regulars and specials alike. I have tried to make this manual pertinent, simple to read and easily referenced, in order that you can extract from it the maximum benefit in the shortest time.

It seems incredible, does it not, that no single book exists which addresses your needs? Why is that, how can this be? Surely you are held in sufficiently high esteem to merit, nay warrant, your own publication - I believe so. So I hope this book goes some way in redressing the imbalance in your favour.

The scope of this book is designed to cover all those day-to-day matters that you, the special, are likely to encounter, when going about your duties, both on the streets and in the police station. Whatever problem you encounter, a quick reference to this book will give you not only the stated law on the subject, but also an understanding of why that law was enacted and what mischief the law was created to deal with. This book does not cover those matters that can best be described as being specialist. It does not, for example, deal with such things as Construction and Use Regulations, which are only understood by traffic officers, nor does it deal with liquor laws, which really would be a judicial nightmare to try to deal with in a few pages. These matters are best left to the specialist.

What we will touch on, in some detail, are the 'bread and butter' offences that you are likely to be faced with on a day-to-day basis - theft, criminal damage, assault and wounding, drugs, sexual offences, drink/drive laws, offensive weapons, drunks and the like. Procedures will also be looked at - pocketbook rules, cautions, warrants, statement taking, interviewing and questioning techniques, what is expected of you in the custody suite, handling prisoners, breath test procedures, fixed penalty tickets, issue of HO/RT ls, VDRS, etc.

I have especially incorporated a section devoted to the custody officer, designated police stations, limitations on detention, reviews of detention, the review officer, and all those other matters that touch on the Police and Criminal Evidence Act, so far as it relates to arrest, detention, questioning and treatment of persons, and the Codes of Practice. Too often I have seen specials in custody suites at police stations, listening to conversations between regular officers, which the special does not always fully understand. The section on custody officers will help you through the laws and procedures in an easy to understand way, so that you will be able to comprehend the rationale behind the decisions made in the custody suite.

We will also look at the question of promotion in the special constabulary, how to prepare yourself for it, and, having achieved it, what then? What new responsibilities will you then have? Might you be asked to prepare, for example, an operation order... if so, how? All these questions will be looked at, and answered. We'll also look at the regulations that govern the workings of the Special Constabulary, at discipline, expenses, injury benefits, and much more.

Light, more light . . .

Tom Barron
1994

Preface

To the second edition

This second edition of the *Special Constable's Manual* has been re-shaped by many of my special constable colleagues and by letters I have received by the readership. It necessarily incorporates new legislation, in particular the Criminal Justice and Public Order Act 1994 plus consequential amendments, and the Police Act 1996. A new section on 'staying alive' has been added and also a chapter is devoted to the proposed changes to the Special Constabulary, as recommended by the Home Office Working Group.

Tom Barron

1997

To the revised second edition

The significant revision to this edition is in chapter 20 which now includes the latest information on the recommendations and regulations governing terms and working conditions within the Special Constabulary.

Elsewhere in the book minor revisions have been incorporated to keep the Manual completely up-to-date. Examples of this would be where provisions of the Criminal Justice and Public Order Act 1994, The Crime and Disorder Act 1998 and the Police (Conduct) Regulations 1999 have been brought into force since the publication of the second edition. (Chapt 2 'Arrests' has also been re-structured.)

However, the bulk of the Manual remains largely unchanged and, for the purposes of study, the original and revised editions can be used side-by-side.

Tom Barron

July 1999

CHAPTER 1

BACKGROUND

Chapter contents

A short history of the Special Constabulary 2
Identity 3
    Differences between forces 3
    Rank structure 4
        Who are you? 5
        The public 6
        Section officers 6
        Sub-divisional officers 6
        Divisional commandant 7
        Chief commandant 7
        Regular officers 7
    Heat or light 8
A short history of the modern police service 8
Powers and jurisdiction 11
    Appointment 11
    Attestation of constables 11
    Jurisdiction of police constables 11
    Jurisdiction of special constables 11
    Jurisdiction and powers of arrest 12

A short history of the Special Constabulary

When the Saxons settled in this country they formed societies which observed unwritten rules known as norms. At first, the head man of each society or community and all its members were responsible for each other's conduct. When the country became united under one king, he would promise to maintain peace and security. This was in return for his subjects' allegiance and promise of good conduct. This state of good order was known as the King's peace. A local policing system was then evolved. All males above the age of 12 years joined their local peace-keeping group. Each acted as security for the other's conduct, and when one committed a crime the others were required to produce him to the court, or the whole group was penalised. Eventually this led to the groups appointing one of their members as a peace officer with a full time responsibility for supervising the conduct of the group.

After the Norman conquest, the system of policing began to change and those responsible for policing were given the title of constable. In fortified communities, a watch and ward system evolved where all male inhabitants were liable to be called upon to guard the gates at night under the supervision of a constable. You can probably see the analogy between then and now. Nowadays we have community constables together with special constables living within the community. As time progressed, the constable became answerable to a justice of the peace, rather than to the community. However, during the 18th century the system began to break down, due to the constables not fulfilling properly their policing role, resulting in law enforcement falling into disrepute.

Towards the end of that century the cities were growing at a startling rate, due to the industrial revolution. The methods of policing previously discussed were unable to cope. Although the Bow Street runners had been established in the capital, the larger towns and cities were facing major problems with violence and disorder reaching unacceptable levels. On a number of occasions the militia were used to quell such disturbances but, due to their frequent use of excessive force, they became unpopular with the people.

After the Napoleonic Wars, determined efforts were made to re-establish a system of policing. It was appreciated that for it to be in any way acceptable to the people, it would have to be a civilian body. Therefore, in 1829 when Sir Robert Peel created the Metropolitan Police, a non-military uniform was designed and its officers carried no weapons other than a wooden staff. After initial unpopularity, the force was soon supported by the public. This led to the Municipal Corporations Act of 1835 which required every borough to appoint sufficient paid constables to police it properly. In the meantime, the Special Constables Act of 1831 gave to justices the power to conscript men as special constables on the occasion of a riot or a threat of a riot. In 1856 Parliament compelled counties to establish police forces and, by 1862, the whole of England and Wales were being policed by paid officers.

The Special Constables Act of 1914 permitted the recruiting and the appointment of special constables for the duration of World War One. After the war it was appreciated how well this force had worked and so in 1923 another Act was passed which allowed for the continued existence of this wartime force. Thus, the basis for today's Special Constabulary was established. In 1962 a Royal Commission Report made recommendations about the whole area of police administration and organisation. As a result, the Police Act 1964 laid down the law governing the administration of provincial police forces in England and Wales. It also established the Special Constabulary in its present form, giving chief constables the power to appoint, direct and control special constables. In 1996 it was replaced by the Police Act of that year - also the Police and Criminal Evidence Act 1984 made further provision in relation to the powers and duties of the police. These two Acts, and the Police and Magistrates' Courts Act 1994, are the principal pieces of legislation governing the police service today.

Some of Sir Robert Peel's first commissioners issued a set of instructions which recruits had to learn and included in which was this edict, which is as true today as it was then:

'Therefore the constable will be civil and obliging to people of every rank and class. He must be particularly cautious not to interfere idly or unnecessarily in order to make a display of his authority; when required to act he will do so with decision and boldness . . . There is no qualification so indispensable to a police officer as perfect command of temper, never suffering himself to be moved in the slightest degree by any language or threat; if he does his duty in a quiet and determined manner, such conduct will probably excite the well-disposed of the bystanders to assist him if he so requires them.'

Identity

Differences between forces

Before looking at the question of who you are, and your relations with the public, with supervisory and management ranks in the special constabulary and with regular officers, it is important at the beginning to understand that each force differs in many respects. The differences are not only in the quantity and quality of uniform issued but also in rank structures and other matters relating to what powers are exercisable by you. It is best not to look at these differences as being negative or divisive. For the most part, the differences result from historic, and in some cases financial, reasons. Let us look first at the rank structure in the Special Constabulary.

Rank structure

Grade	Insignia	Area of responsibility
Special constable	The words 'Special Constabulary' sewn on uniform Metal tag on epaulette with words 'Special Constabulary' in it or letters 'SC' surmounted by a crown. (In Devon and Cornwall, the words 'Special Constabulary Police Reserve'.)	At the direction of the special section officer, or regular sergeant.
Section officer	One bar	To organise and administer a section of specials reporting to the sub divisional officer.
Sub-divisional officer	Two bars	To oversee section officers and to liaise with divisional commandant.
Divisional commandant	Three bars	Overall responsibility for the Special Constabulary in his area reporting to the chief commandant.
Chief commandant	Four bars	The chief commandant acts as a figurehead and focal point for the special constabulary. He will no doubt have the ear of the chief constable and may well be a retired senior regular officer.

Note. These are known officially as 'grades'. There are no ranks in the Special Constabulary.

These grades are not constant in each force. Indeed some grades go under different names and insignia, while whole grades are missing in some forces. Many, for instance, do not have a chief commandant. Later in this chapter I deal with the grades of section and sub-divisional officers in detail because these are the the people who actually make the organisation work in terms of administration and organisational ability. The remaining ranks, divisional commandant and chief commandant are, in many ways, political creatures who act in the widest regard for the interests of the Special Constabulary, but who in fact are not 'hands on' people who face the demands of the streets.

Over the years there has been a great debate as to whether supervisory grades are needed at all. Many supervisory grade officers believe they are - grades are needed for administrative purposes, they say. A regular shift sergeant could never know the strengths and weaknesses of specials in the way that a fellow volunteer could. Ranks are also needed, they argue, if specials are to undertake operations on their own initiative. The argument was well advanced by Neville Jones, former Chief Commandant of Cheshire, when he said it would place too much of an administrative burden on regular officers to have to liaise with 30 individual specials. He said that each division has to have someone accountable to the regular commander to help provide support. An individual is needed who can draw together 20 or 30 specials - you cannot rely on 30 individuals to respond to something themselves - someone has to pull it together.

Scotland's forces are the only ones in the UK without any hierarchy in the Special Constabulary, this is because specials always patrol with a regular officer and do not carry out projects on their own as they do down south, so there is really no need for ranks. But, if specials are to take on policing initiatives themselves, there has to be some kind of rank structure with some officers taking responsibility.

Whatever view you may hold on the rank structure, it must be remembered that the holders of 1, 2 or 3 bars did not arrive there by accident. In the main, these are men and women who have spent many years in the Special Constabulary and have a wealth of experience and knowledge, and have shown an aptitude for command. They are not just light weights who bask in the reflected glory of the special constable on the ground, they have been forged on the hard anvil of reality. Where there are individual and collective initiatives policed solely or in the main by specials, then clearly there is a need for a hierarchy.

Who are you?

On joining the Special Constabulary, most specials undergo an identity crisis - who am I? Where do I fit into the organisation? What is my status? How am I expected to behave? These questions are asked by anyone on first joining a new organisation. Equally, you will undergo a mobility crisis, you won't know if you are coming or going. Regular officers feel much the same during the course of their probationary period. You will constantly be asking yourself questions like: How do you do this? How do you do that? Where am I expected to be and when? These are normal teething problems and will quickly evaporate.

The real question that arises is that of the perception of others. How do members of the public see me and what do they expect from me? What about my bosses in the Specials, section officers, sub-divisional officers and the rest. What about regular supervisors (sergeants) and managers (inspectors and above). What do they think of me? What do they expect me to know and to do? And the most important question: What do regular constables think of specials? Do they hold them in high, or low, esteem? Do they see them as 'hobby bobbies' or professionals like themselves? The question of perception really is very important and needs to be looked at in some detail. By understanding how everyone else sees you, you will stand less of a chance of being at a disadvantage in dealing with them. Let us look at each in turn.

The public

The first thing to understand is that members of the public generally speaking cannot distinguish you, the special, from regular officers. Substantially you now wear exactly the same type of uniform, helmets included for many, and for all intents and purposes you are a constable. It needs a sharp-eyed member of the public to pick out the shoulder flash 'special constable', and then he needs some knowledge of the organisation to know that you are not a full-time regular.

In any case, your powers are the same as the regular officer - a fact that the public takes for granted - so that making a distinction between special and regular is purely academic. Most members of the public on seeing you will say to themselves - police officer.

So far as the public are concerned, you, like regular officers, are the eyes and ears of the community, you are its executive arm, you are the teeth of the law.

Section officers

Your immediate supervisor is the section officer, who, while his grade is an administrative one, in reality is perceived by the regular officers as your sergeant. If you look upon the section officer as a sergeant, you will not go far wrong.

The section officer has immediate responsibility for all matters of administration, discipline and welfare. He, or she, is your first line supervisor and all matters concerning you should properly be addressed to him. He will have responsibility for a group or section of specials, numbering up to 10. To my mind this is the most important 'rank' in the special constabulary and certainly the hardest to attain.

Your section officer sees you as a resource to employ as each need arises. Depending on your experience, your knowledge and how you handle yourself in the police station and on the streets, he will decide what jobs he will entrust you with. Clearly, as you improve with service you become a more valuable commodity which will be reflected in the quality of job, or area of responsibility he tasks you with.

The section officer is the team builder, and you represent a cog in the wheel that is his responsibility. Remove any cog, however small, and the wheel will eventually grind to a halt. Always look to your section officer for advice.

Sub-divisional officers

The next 'rank' up from the section officer, is the sub-divisional officer, usually known as the SDO. He represents management in the Special Constabulary and is perceived by regular officers as an inspector. Many will deny this, but their behaviour is such that the SDO is an inspector in fact.

The SDO has massive responsibility. Usually he commands a sub-division, or district, and can be in charge of as many 30 specials. He is usually in close liaison with the regular inspector, as their jobs are in many ways similar.

You are unlikely to see him on a regular, day-to-day basis. He is much in evidence at events, shows, rallies, marches and the like, and often has the responsibility of policing the event in its entirety. Any problems you have that cannot be resolved by your section officer will be referred by him to the SDO.

The SDO has many years of experience and has been 'promoted' twice. He is held in high esteem by regular officers and he has the necessary influence to be able to make things happen. As a special constable, the SDO sees you as reflecting the quality of the Special Constabulary on the ground. Look to the SDO for management.

Divisional commandant

The divisional commandant is the local territorial commander and is responsible for all special constables within the division or district. Sub-divisional officers report directly to him on the state of health and morale in each of their sub-divisions and it is he who is most aware of the state of affairs in his district by keeping a eye open for any problems.

It is important to remember that he has a responsibility for advising the regular local commander on matters relating to welfare, discipline, promotion, recruitment, postings and all other important issues governing or touching on the specials immediately under his command.

This officer can actually shape policy and bring about important change because he has the ear of the local regular decision-maker.

Chief commandant

The chief commandant is the top special in the force area. He acts as a focal point for the whole of the Special Constabulary in your force and has the ear of the chief constable and the attendant assistant chief officers of police - a man to be reckoned with. He will deal with all important matters of policy as they affect the Special Constabulary.

This is the person who can bring about real change and it is to him that important issues should be addressed, through section officers, sub-divisional officers and divisional commandants.

Such matters as the issue of helmets to specials can best be resolved by the chief commandant who, don't forget, is in direct contact with the chief constable. Look to your chief commandant therefore for serious change in your force area.

Regular officers

The most important area is the relationship that exists between specials and regular officers, of whatever rank. The SDOs and regular inspectors tend to gravitate towards one another on the basis of job identity, as do section officers and regular sergeants. They are in many ways kindred spirits and enjoy a meeting of minds. Equally, the special constable and his regular counterpart have much in common and on that basis they are thrust together. This can produce heat, or light.

This is an area of concern to special constables who are very sensitive to the question of their relationships with regular officers. There is a basic psychological premise which states that relationships, of whatever description, must be rewarding. If they are unrewarding, then one party or more will distance himself from it.

A rewarding relationship is productive and binds the parties together. To put yourself in the most advantageous position in your relations with the regular officer, it is as well to bear in mind that behaviour breeds behaviour. If you behave responsibly, professionally, are user-friendly and willing to make a contribution, then regular officers will behave accordingly, reflecting your behaviour.

Equally, the cocky, brash, loud, 'designer' special does nothing to endear himself to the regular officer. His behaviour results in reciprocal behaviour from the regular officer who will distance himself from that type of special.

Heat or light

There is no doubt that in the 1960s and '70s, there was an undercurrent of unrest between the specials and regular officers. This was at a time when regulars' wages were miserly and many regular officers took the view (usually wrongly), that specials took away their overtime. 'How would you feel if I came to your place of work and worked alongside you - for nothing?' This created heat, which is always counter-productive.

During the 1980s and certainly now at the end of the '90s, the position has completely changed. Specials are welcomed on duty, indeed they are actively sought out and invited to carry out a joint duty by regulars, of whatever rank. Most specials I know go on duty with the same shift or section, and are seen by that group of regulars as belonging to the group family. There is a sense of bonding and the specials enjoy participation in all events, both on duty and off - light, more light.

A short history of the modern police service

The Metropolitan Police was created by Act of Parliament in 1829, by the then Home Secretary, Robert Peel. Justices, now known as Commissioners, were empowered to appoint constables to police the capital (but not the City of London). Three thousand officers were appointed in the ranks of superintendent, inspectors, sergeants and constables.

Prior to this time there was little control of the populace, and this new 'control' was not well-received. Great care was taken in appointing constables, as they had to be seen to be representative of ordinary people. For the first time, a uniform was issued, and again, Parliament was anxious that the new uniform was as far removed as possible from the military style. The new police force had to be seen to be civil and not military in nature.

Part of the effect of creating this force, was that many London criminals moved into the shires to operate, where they were undisturbed by the activities of the police. This was one of the reasons for the creation of Borough Police under the Municipal Corporations Act 1835. One hundred and seventy eight boroughs in England and Wales appointed constables to police their respective boroughs, making accountability of the police local, ie to the borough to which they were appointed.

As a result of national unrest by the working classes, Parliament sought to gain greater control of the population by creating the County Police Act 1839. This did not compel counties to establish police forces and as a result, some counties remained unpoliced. This prompted Parliament to create the County and Borough Police Act 1856, which compelled every county and borough to establish a police force, which they did.

Central government sought to gain greater control of the provincial forces by the use of a number of devices, including the appointment of inspectors of constabulary. These inspectors would report to central government on the state of efficiency of each police force and those found to be efficient were awarded grants towards the cost of uniform and pay.

Smaller forces were encouraged to amalgamate by withholding financial assistance to those which served populations of fewer than 5,000. Further control was gained by the increase of central funding to 50 per cent of the cost of each police force. The Police Act 1946 again required smaller forces to amalgamate to a point where we find ourselves today, with 43 police forces in England and Wales, and eight in Scotland. Some say that this is still too many, and moves are currently afoot to reduce numbers further.

Prior to the Second World War, chief constables were responsible for the training of constables in their own force areas. This changed soon after the war and central government established police training centres to cope with the large number of recruits. Again funding by the Home Office was 50 per cent of costs, which had the effect of increasing their control.

In 1962 the Royal Commission on the police reported on a number of important factors. It covered such questions as national control, funding, complaints, organisation of police authorities, police areas, appointment of officers and jurisdiction of constables - resulting in the Police Act 1964. This Act struck a balance between central and local government in their exercise of control of police forces. Operational management of police forces, however, was left in the hands of chief constables.

The Police Act 1964 (now repealed and replaced by the Police Act 1996) defines the meaning of police area.

Police area

Police area	Police authority	Chief officer	Funding
City of London	Common Council	Commissioner	The City Purse
Metropolitan Police District	Secretary of State	Commissioner	Metropolitan Police Fund
Relevant counties (duplicating existing forces)	Police Authority	Chief constable	Police Fund

The next Act that sought fundamentally to affect the workings of the police was the Police and Criminal Evidence Act 1984, which came into force on January 1, 1986. In the mid-'60s, the Home Office asked the Criminal Law Revision Committee to inquire into the rules of evidence in criminal cases. There followed an eight-year study resulting in the ill-fated report made to government in 1972. A storm of protest arose because the committee recommended, among other things, that the right of silence at police stations should be abolished. The furore that followed was such, that the whole report was shelved. In 1977, another Royal Commission was set up by the then Labour government. The Commission was asked to examine the issues:

'. . . having regard both to the interests of the community in bringing offenders to justice and to the rights and liberties of persons suspected or accused of crime and taking into account also the need for the efficient use of resources.'

The Royal Commission's findings reached the report stage in the Commons when a general election brought the Bill to a halt. In October 1983 the new Home Secretary unveiled the new Bill which attracted so much attention during the committee stage that it broke all records for the highest number of sittings.

The Bill finally emerged as the Police and Criminal Evidence Act 1984 - the most important Act to date governing the activities of the police. This Act deals with:

Powers to stop and search.
Powers of entry, search and seizure.
Entry and search without search warrant.
Seizure.
Arrest.
Detention.
Questioning and treatment of persons by police.
Codes of practice.
Documentary evidence in criminal proceedings.
Other evidence in criminal proceedings.
Convictions and acquittals.
Police complaints and discipline.

The Act runs to 122 sections and touches upon every aspect of police behaviour. The Act is attended by the Codes of Practice, as is required by section 66 of the Act, which are:

A   Code of Practice for the exercise by police officers of statutory powers of stop and search.
B   Code of Practice for the searching of premises by police officers and the seizure of property found by police officers on persons or premises.
C   Code of Practice for the detention, treatment and questioning of persons by police officers.
D   Code of Practice for the identification of persons by police officers.
E   Code of Practice on tape recording of interviews with suspects.

This is, without doubt, the most important piece of legislation to affect the police since Robert Peel's initiative in 1829.

The Police and Magistrates' Courts Act 1994 amended the 1984 Act, most importantly in relation to membership and function of police authorities, the requirement of local policing plans and reports, the abolition of the rank of deputy chief constable, the setting of objectives and performance targets and changes to the system of funding police forces. The relevant sections of the 1994 Act have now been replaced by the Police Act 1996.

Powers and jurisdiction

Appointment

Under section 27 of the Police Act 1996, the chief officer of police is empowered to appoint special constables in accordance with the regulations made under section 51 of the Act. Appointment therefore is the sole prerogative of the chief constable.

Attestation of constables

Under section 29 of the Police Act 1996, every member of a police force maintained for a police area and every special constable appointed for a police area shall, on appointment, be attested as a constable by making the following declaration:

> 'I "........" of "........" do solemnly and sincerely declare and affirm that I will well and truly serve Our Sovereign Lady the Queen in the office of constable, without favour or affection, malice or ill will; and that I will to the best of my power cause the peace to be kept and preserved, and prevent all offences against the persons and properties of Her Majesty's subjects; and that while I continue to hold the said office I will to the best of my skill and knowledge discharge all the duties thereof faithfully according to law.'

Jurisdiction of police constables

By virtue of section 30(1) of the Police Act 1996 a police constable may exercise all the powers and privileges of a constable throughout England and Wales and adjacent United Kingdom waters. Section 136 of the Criminal Justice and Public Order Act 1994 gives a power of arrest for arrestable offences across the border in Scotland and Northern Ireland (and vice versa).

Jurisdiction of special constables

The powers of a special are more geographically constrained. By virtue of section 30(2) of the Police Act 1996, a special constable may exercise all the powers and privileges of a constable in the police area for which he is appointed and, where the boundary of that area includes the coast, in the adjacent United Kingdom

12 The Special Constable's Manual

waters. Section 30(3) adds that a special may also exercise the full powers and privileges of a constable in any other police area which is contiguous to his own police area. For specials in the City of London, this is further extended to the Metropolitan police district and in any area which is contiguous to that district.

Basically this means that special constables have the same powers as regular officers in the force area in which they are appointed and in surrounding force areas which touch on the boundaries of the parent force. In the case of the City of London Police, specials appointed to that force can operate with full police powers in the Metropolitan area as well as the surrounding forces which touch on the Metropolitan police boundaries.

Mutual aid and collaboration - In addition to the above, section 30(4) of the Act caters for special constables who, for the time being, are required to serve with another police force under mutual aid or collaboration agreements. In this situation the special may exercise, in the host force area, all the powers and privileges of a special appointed in that area

Jurisdiction and powers of arrest

It is important to remember that the powers of arrest afforded to a regular officer are not extended to special constables when they are outside their areas of jurisdiction as defined above - and illustrated below.

When you are outside these areas you have the same common law powers of arrest which are enjoyed by every citizen in the land. You have to be especially careful if you are employed to travel into other force areas on escort duties. Once you have passed beyond your jurisdiction, you leave behind at the border the powers you enjoy as a constable and have to rely solely on your 'any person' common law powers. Common law powers are much more restricted than your powers as a constable, therefore you have to know both sets of powers very well indeed.

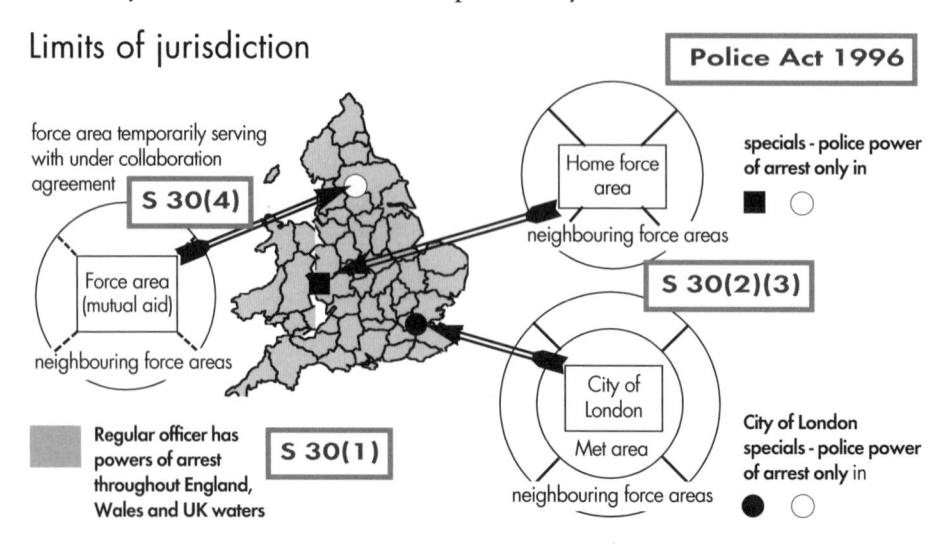

Limits of jurisdiction

Police Act 1996

force area temporarily serving with under collaboration agreement — S 30(4)

Home force area — neighbouring force areas

specials - police power of arrest only in ■ ○

Force area (mutual aid) — neighbouring force areas

S 30(2)(3)

City of London Met area — neighbouring force areas

City of London specials - police power of arrest only in ● ○

Regular officer has powers of arrest throughout England, Wales and UK waters — S 30(1)

CHAPTER 2

ARRESTS

Chapter contents

Classification of offences 14
Criminal law/common law 14
    Arrestable offences 14
    Common law powers (citizen's arrest) 14
    Powers (police only) 15
Conditions for arrest 15
    Serious arrestable offences 15
    General arrest conditions 16
Mode of arrest 19
    Factors to consider before arrest 19
    Information to be given on arrest 19
    Caution following arrest 20
    Different arrest circumstances 20
Use of force when making arrests 21
    Staying alive 22
    The Confrontational Continuum 23
    Case law 25
        Self-defence 25
        Genuine belief of imminent danger 26
        Honest belief/mistake as to facts 26
    Assessment of danger 26
        Officer - personal factors 27
        Special circumstances 27
        Threat recognitions 27
        Signals of submission 28
    Reporting the use of force 29
Search and seizure 30
    Search after arrest 30
    Seizure following search 30

Classification of offences - Offences are classified in order to identify which offence is triable at the higher Crown court, or the lower magistrates' court. Schedule 1 to the Interpretation Act 1978 defines the classes of offences as follows:

- (a) **Indictable offences** - if committed by an adult, are triable on indictment (whether exclusively so triable or triable either way) (Crown court).
- (b) **Summary offences** - if committed by an adult, are triable only summarily (magistrates' court).
- (c) **Offences triable either way** - if committed by an adult, are triable either on indictment or summarily (Crown court or magistrates' court).

Criminal law/common law

Arrestable offences

> S 24(1) PACE

Section 24(1) of the Police and Criminal Evidence Act 1984 (PACE) defines what an 'arrestable offence' is, and confers the power of summary arrest as follows:

- (a) Offences for which the sentence is fixed by law (murder).
- (b) Offences for which a person of 21 years of age or over (not previously convicted) may be sentenced to imprisonment for a term of five years or more (eg theft - 10 years).
- (c) Other offences specified by section 24(2) of the Act.
    The most notable of these is taking a conveyance without the consent of the owner (six months' imprisonment) (s12(1) Theft Act 1968), or going equipped for stealing (s25(1) Theft Act 1968).
- (d) Attempting, aiding or abetting, or conspiring to commit any of the above offences.

Note that powers of arrest for section 24 arrestable offences are exercisable without reference to the conditions imposed on the general conditional police power of arrest offered by section 25 (post).

Common law powers (citizen's arrest)

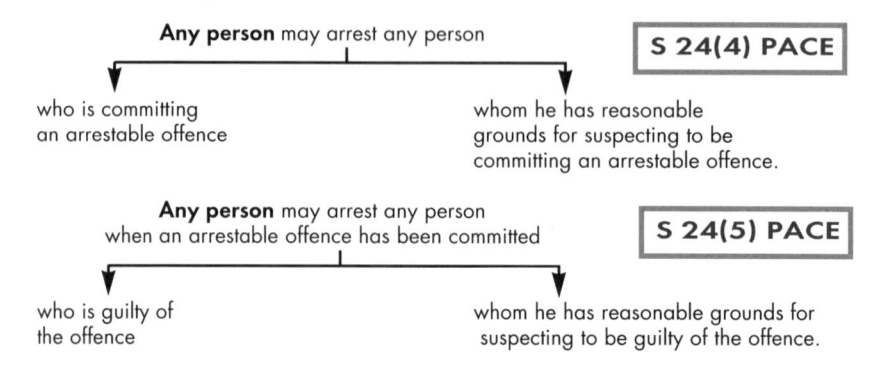

Any person may arrest any person

> S 24(4) PACE

- who is committing an arrestable offence
- whom he has reasonable grounds for suspecting to be committing an arrestable offence.

Any person may arrest any person when an arrestable offence has been committed

> S 24(5) PACE

- who is guilty of the offence
- whom he has reasonable grounds for suspecting to be guilty of the offence.

It is important that you are familiar with the common law power of arrest. When you go beyond the force area for which you were appointed and its neighbouring areas (unless by special mutual aid or collaboration agreement) (see Chapter 1 'Jurisdiction of special constables'), then the only power of arrest that you possess is the common law power. This power is much more restrictive than the full police powers you enjoy within your jurisdiction. Be aware that on escort duties you may find yourself armed only with common law powers.

Powers of arrest (police only)

Having given a restricted power of arrest to citizens, the common law recognises that police officers should enjoy a greater power than that of the ordinary citizen and therefore gives us these added powers.

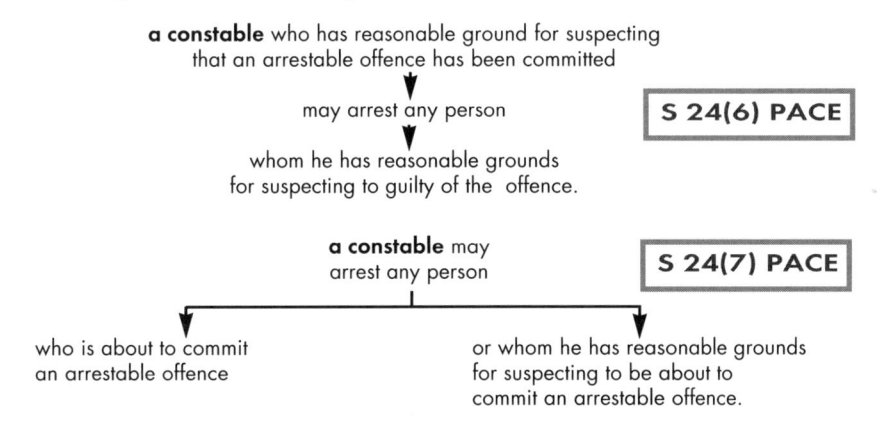

a constable who has reasonable ground for suspecting that an arrestable offence has been committed
▼
may arrest any person
▼
whom he has reasonable grounds for suspecting to guilty of the offence.

S 24(6) PACE

a constable may arrest any person

S 24(7) PACE

who is about to commit an arrestable offence

or whom he has reasonable grounds for suspecting to be about to commit an arrestable offence.

Conditions for arrest

Serious arrestable offence

If a serious arrestable offence has been committed, the Police and Criminal Evidence Act gives the police greater powers in order to combat such offences: ie road checks, authority to detain without charge for up to 36 hours, delay in allowing notification of a person's arrest, delay in allowing access to legal advice, authority to take intimate samples, authority to take samples without consent.

The serious arrestable offences that are most noteworthy are:
 (a) Serious harm to the security of the state or to public order.
 (b) Serious interference with the administration of justice.
 (c) The death of any person.
 (d) Serious injury to any person.
 (e) Substantial financial gain to any person.
 (f) Serious financial loss to any person.

General arrest conditions

S 25 PACE

Section 25 of the Police and Criminal Evidence Act 1984 (PACE) is designed to cope with the lesser type of offence which does not fall into any other category - flashing, litter, obstruction etc. This section of the Act is highly conditional and must be understood fully. It is the single most important section of any Act that the special needs to know, and it is the section under which most arrests are made by patrolling officers on their beats.

In subsequent sections of the Manual, where an offence is cited which is subject to the section 25 general power of arrest it will be indicated by this motif....

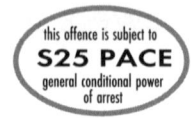

this offence is subject to
S25 PACE
general conditional power of arrest

General arrest conditions

When **a constable** has reasonable grounds for suspecting that an offence

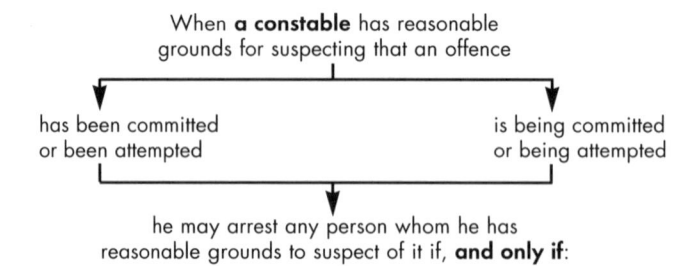

- has been committed or been attempted
- is being committed or being attempted

he may arrest any person whom he has reasonable grounds to suspect of it if, **and only if**:

1. the service of a summons appears to be

- impracticable
- inappropriate

because

- the person's name is not known and it cannot be ascertained, or there are reasonable grounds to believe it to be false
- he failed to give a satisfactory address to enable a summons to be served, or there are reasonable grounds for believing the address is unsatisfactory;

Note:

For the purposes of this section, an address is a satisfactory address for service of a summons if it appears to a constable
(a) that the person will be at the address for a sufficiently long period for the service of the summons; or,
(b) that some other person specified will accept the service of the summons on behalf of the offender

OR

2. there are reasonable grounds for believing that an arrest is necessary to prevent that person

- causing physical injury to himself or another
- causing loss of, or damage to, property; or, committing an offence against public decency
- causing an unlawful obstruction of the highway.
- or there are reasonable grounds for believing that arrest is necessary to **protect** a child, or other vulnerable person, from that person

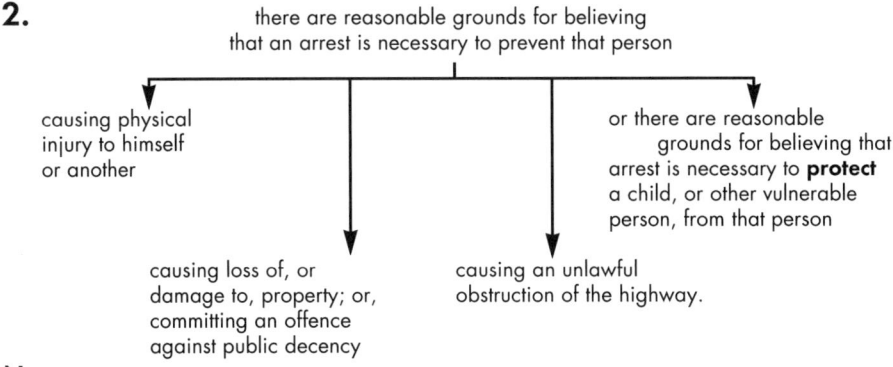

Note:
So far as public decency is concerned, the power can only be exercised if members of the public, going about their normal business, cannot avoid the person.

Section 25 of PACE is your bread and butter, day-to-day power which you will use during the course of most of the incidents you deal with, and from which an arrest arises. Let us look closely at what each part of the section really means.

A constable. This means both regular officers and special constables, on or off duty, except that it does not apply to a special when he is outside his area of jurisdiction (see 'Jurisdiction').

Reasonable grounds. This means that the grounds for arrest may not actually exist in reality. However, if, in all the circumstances you reasonably believe that they do exist then an arrest is lawful.

An offence. This covers all offences that are not arrestable offences, serious arrestable offences, etc. It means any offence, so that riding a pedal cycle inconsiderately, dropping litter, simple drunkenness and offences of this nature come within the ambit of the section.

Summons. There are two ways to get offenders before the courts - by arrest or by the service of a summons. You will see below that the service of a summons is often impracticable or inappropriate.

Impracticable. The person's name is not known and it cannot be ascertained or there are reasonable grounds to believe it to be false. The first part of this sub-section has in mind the person who wilfully fails to give you his name notwithstanding your request for it. The second deals with the man who tells you his name is Mickey Mouse, or Donald Duck . . . which you believe to be false. Clearly therefore if you are unable to put a name on the summons it would be impracticable to serve it. Who would you serve it on?

Impracticable. The person failed to give a satisfactory address to enable a summons to be served or you have reasonable grounds for believing the address to be unsatisfactory. You have to be careful here. It is easy enough if the offender simply refuses to give his address after request.

However, he may give you an address which you consider to be unsatisfactory.

What if he is a foreigner on holiday in this country with a perfectly satisfactory address? If he is about to return home in two or three days' time then you may consider that he will not be at the address for a sufficiently long period for the service of a summons.

Equally, for the long-distance lorry driver about to leave the country who gives you the address of his transport firm, this can amount to a satisfactory address, just as with the homeless person who gives you the address of his solicitor or the like, which can amount to a satisfactory address. Be careful when dealing with addresses.

Impracticable. It may be that the offender is known to you. You know his full name and his address. There are times when he may still be arrested. If he will not stop committing the crime that he is doing, then what use is a summons? If a man is exposing himself in the street, then a summons is of no value, he would have to be arrested because the service of a summons would be inappropriate.

So here, we are dealing with the belief that there are reasonable grounds for believing that an arrest is necessary to prevent certain social evils.

Causing injury. Causing physical injury to himself or another. Where 'X' is laying hands on 'Y', resulting in injury, and will not stop the assault, then it is necessary to make the arrest to prevent the continued assault, as it would be inappropriate to serve a summons. This applies equally well to the person who is causing harm to himself. He may be arrested to prevent the situation continuing.

Property. Causing loss or damage to property has to be prevented and, if we are unable to stop the loss or damage other than by arrest, then this section will bring the offender to book.

Indecency. Committing an offence against public decency has to be looked at carefully. It only becomes arrestable if members of the public going about their normal business cannot reasonably be expected to avoid the person to be arrested.

This then would protect members of a nudist colony, walking about naked, in their own private and protected property, from the member of the public who happens on them by mistake. Equally, if a member of the public has to climb a 20 foot ladder in order to peer into your private garden, to see you naked, this would be no offence on your part.

This part of the section is intended for the public 'flasher'.

Obstruction. Causing an unlawful obstruction of the highway. 'Highway' includes both the road and the pavement.

The man who is parked so badly that he is causing an obstruction and who wilfully refuses to move after being asked to do so may be arrested under this section even though the Police National Computer (PNC) may have given you his name and address.

Layabouts on the pavement, lying with their legs sprawled across the footpath, causing persons to leave the safety of the pavement and venture onto the road, should be asked to desist. If they refuse, then they offend against this section and are liable to be arrested.

Child or vulnerable person. There are reasonable grounds for believing that an arrest is necessary to protect a child or other vulnerable person. An example of this is the parent who is so drunk that he or she is quite unable to look after a small child, or a drunken social worker who is incapable of looking after a retarded person in his care.

Mode of arrest

The Royal Commission which resulted in the Police and Criminal Evidence Act 1984, was at pains to stress the necessity principle when making arrests, in particular powers exercised under section 25 of the Act. When an offender refuses to give his name or his address, it does not necessarily follow that he should at once be arrested. An explanation of the consequences of his refusal should be spelled out to him, in order that he might reflect on the matter. If he continues to refuse, then arrest will almost certainly be inevitable; but in any case, always ask yourself the question: **Is arrest necessary?**

What factors should you consider before making an arrest? What if, having arrested an individual, he then gives the information you first requested, which he earlier refused? What if you have made up your mind that, although you have not told him he is under arrest, you do not intend letting him go until he has complied with your instructions, or answered your questions?

Factors to consider before arrest

(a) Having regard to all the circumstances of the case, is the arrest really necessary?
(b) Is there a power of arrest?
(c) Is the behaviour just offensive, or does it amount to an offence known to law?
(d) Are there sufficient grounds to exercise the power? Did he act dishonestly? Did he knowingly do the act? Are your grounds for suspicion reasonable in all the circumstances?
(e) Is it prudent in the circumstances to effect an arrest which might have disastrous results for you? You may need assistance - should delay be considered?

Information to be given on arrest

You are obliged by law to tell the person that he is under arrest and also the grounds for the arrest. Section 24 of PACE makes the arrest unlawful if he is not told the grounds of arrest either at the time or immediately afterwards, even if it is obvious why he is being arrested. This information must be given as soon as possible after arrest unless the offender makes it impossible for you to do so (by assault or escape). The true reason must be given to him in straightforward words. Remember, communication is not so much what is said, it is what is received. Telling someone that you are arresting him because he has breached PACE means nothing to Joe Public. Tell him how it really is:

> **'I am arresting you on suspicion of theft of this pedal cycle which was reported stolen an hour ago.'**

Reinforce what you say by taking hold of the person's arm. Leave him in no doubt that he is under arrest.

Caution following arrest

Anything that is said by the arrested person will be excluded in evidence as having been obtained by unfair means (even though it is true), if the person has not been cautioned. Only after caution do things said become evidence that can be put before a court. The caution currently prescribed by the Detention Code (Code C of PACE Codes of Practice) is:

> **'You do not have to say anything. But it may harm your defence if you do not mention when questioned something which you later rely on in court. Anything you do say may be given in evidence.'**

(Minor deviations do not constitute a breach of this requirement provided the sense of the caution is preserved.) If the caution is not understood by the arrested person then explain it to him. Also note any reply he may make. The two exceptions to the delivery of an immediate caution are that:
- (a) it is impracticable to do so by reason of his condition or behaviour at the time of arrest, or
- (b) he has already been cautioned immediately prior to being arrested.

Different arrest circumstances

Plain clothes arrests

Members of the public must be aware that they are dealing with a police officer. When in plain clothes you must identify yourself as a police officer and be prepared to show your warrant card. Failure to do so will probably result in your not acting in the execution of your duty and any subsequent assault that may follow may not be seen as an assault upon the police, although other offences might have been committed.

Use of tactical batons

Tactical batons should only be used as a remedy of last resort and when violence is being used against you or another. They should never be used as a means of punishment. If all other means have failed, then you may use your baton:
- (a) for your own protection when dealing with a violent person, or
- (b) to prevent the escape of a violent prisoner, if you, or another person who is assisting you, are being overpowered.

(See 'Use of force when making arrests', opposite. Both Acts emphasise **'reasonable'**.)

If it is necessary to use a baton under whatever circumstances when dealing with a violent person, you must:
- (a) make a pocket book entry as soon as is practicable, and
- (b) inform the custody officer immediately on arrival at the police station.

Delay in returning to the police station

The general rule is that there should be no delay in returning to the police station with an arrested person. There are however exceptions to the rule:

'If his presence elsewhere is necessary in order to carry out such investigations as it is reasonable to carry out immediately.'

Section 30(10) of the Act envisages the need for an immediate search, say, for stolen property which might be lost if not searched for and recovered at once. Remember, any delay in returning to the police station with the arrested person must be reported to the custody officer upon arrival and he will record the fact of the delay and reason for it in the custody record (section 30(11)).

Release before arrival at police station

Prior to the Police and Criminal Evidence Act 1984, an arrested person had to be taken back to the police station, even though, following arrest, it was discovered that he was in fact innocent. The procedure then was for the custody officer to book the 'prisoner' in and then refuse the charge against him. Section 30(7) of the Act now recognises that this is unjust and sets the matter right by stating that:

'A person arrested by a constable at a place other than a police station shall be released if a constable is satisfied, before the person arrested reaches a police station, that there are no grounds for keeping him under arrest.'

A constable who releases a person under the above subsection shall record the fact that he has done so. If you discover that there are no grounds for holding the arrested person when you have arrived at the police station, then the only person who can release the person is the custody officer.

Use of force when making arrests

Two Acts of Parliament deal with the use of force when making an arrest, and both use the word 'reasonable'. .

S 3 Criminal Law Act 1967

'**A person** may use such force as is **reasonable** in the circumstances in the prevention of crime, or in effecting or assisting in the lawful arrest of offenders or suspected offenders or of persons unlawfully at large.'

S 117 PACE

'Where any provision of this Act confers a power on **a constable**; and does not provide that the power may only be exercised with the consent of some person, other than a police officer, the officer may use **reasonable** force, if necessary, in the exercise of the power.'

Notice that the Criminal Law Act empowers **any person** to use reasonable force, whereas the Police and Criminal Evidence Act empowers **a constable** to use reasonable force. Again this should be remembered should you find your powers as a constable evaporating because you are leaving your own force area or neighbouring force areas. Upon leaving these areas you leave behind both your enhanced common law powers of arrest and your powers to use reasonable force under the Police and Criminal Evidence Act - so be conscious that you still enjoy the basic powers of citizen's arrest and the protection of the Criminal Law Act 1967 should you be required to use reasonable force.

The following set of guidelines is designed to help you understand the psychology of force and how to **stay alive**.

Staying alive

Police use of force in this country is centred on the word **reasonable**. The main thrust of an encounter on the streets with persons who are hostile is to control the situation and remain free from injury. The goalposts can be set out as follows:
'We enjoy good negotiating skills,
augmented by physical alternatives;
but all we **want** to do is talk.'

An arrest is the taking or restraining of a person from their liberty and the three principles that govern a successful arrest are:
(a) control;
(b) the 50/50 proposition;
(c) choice of force option.

Control during the course of an arrest is incomplete until the arrested person has accepted his state of arrest. If that person is refusing to accept his arrest then clearly he is not under control and the arrest is both incomplete and represents a danger to you the arresting officer.

Arresting officers should never enter a 50/50 proposition. The arresting officer must have an advantage so that he can exercise control, and to that end he must consider his force option based on control versus injury. When there is an increased danger of injury to the officer he must look to his physical alternatives in order to maintain an advantage. This is best understood by looking at the confrontational continuum.

The confrontational continuum is a model designed to help the officer judge his force options in relation to the behaviour of his assailant. On the left of the model is a line representing the assailant. Based on a sliding scale of one - five (one being minor disorder and five representing the most serious threat to the officer), one can be found at the bottom of the vertical line and five at the top.

The confrontational continuum

Police officers generally deal with three types of people when making arrests, yes people, no people and maybe people. The yes people are those who will always accept their state of arrest and go quietly with the arresting officer. Equally the no people are those who, no matter what the circumstances, will never accept a state of arrest and will violently oppose the arresting officer. There are people in the middle whom we call maybe people, it may be that they will be yes people or it may be that they will be no people. These maybe people respond to our personal style and our negotiating skills. Based on the premise that behaviour breeds behaviour, it is the maybe people we can influence most by personal style and negotiating skills. The graph of the Confrontation Continuum is set out on page 18.

Assailant level of threat - level 1

This level of threat is at the lowest end of the scale and the officer's reaction when considering his force options should be appropriate in all the circumstances. The appropriate force option at this level will probably be **persuade/dialogue**. In cases like this which, by way of example, we can consider rowdy youths on a street corner, our very presence is likely to bring them back to a state of order. Our uniformed presence together with the 'persuasion/dialogue' option would appear to the appropriate force option.

Assailant level of threat - level 2

This level of threat is greater than level 1. The assailant is beginning to climb the vertical ladder of threat to the officer who must now consider another force option. It may be that the example of rowdy youths who have not been susceptible to **persuade/dialogue** should now be be met with the **compliance/escort** force option. This would mean that the officer gains compliance by escorting the youths from the scene.

Assailant level of threat - level 3

This level of threat is greater than level 2. The assailant is now continuing to climb the vertical ladder of threat to the officer who must now consider another force option. To continue with the example of the rowdy youths, it may be that an arrest must now be made having regard to the level of threat to the officer. **Compliance/pain** might be the appropriate level of response that has to be made. **Compliance/pain** may take the form of taking hold of the assailant in a body lock (goose neck, thumb lock etc) in order to negate the threat level.

The Confrontational Continuum

ASSAILANT LEVEL OF THREAT

- level 1
- 2
- 3
- 4
- level 5

see descriptions of assailant levels of threat

OFFICER REACTION

FORCE OPTIONS

- PERSUADE/ DIALOGUE
- COMPLIANCE/ ESCORT
- COMPLIANCE/ PAIN
- COMPLIANCE/ MECHANICAL
- IMPEDE/ BATON

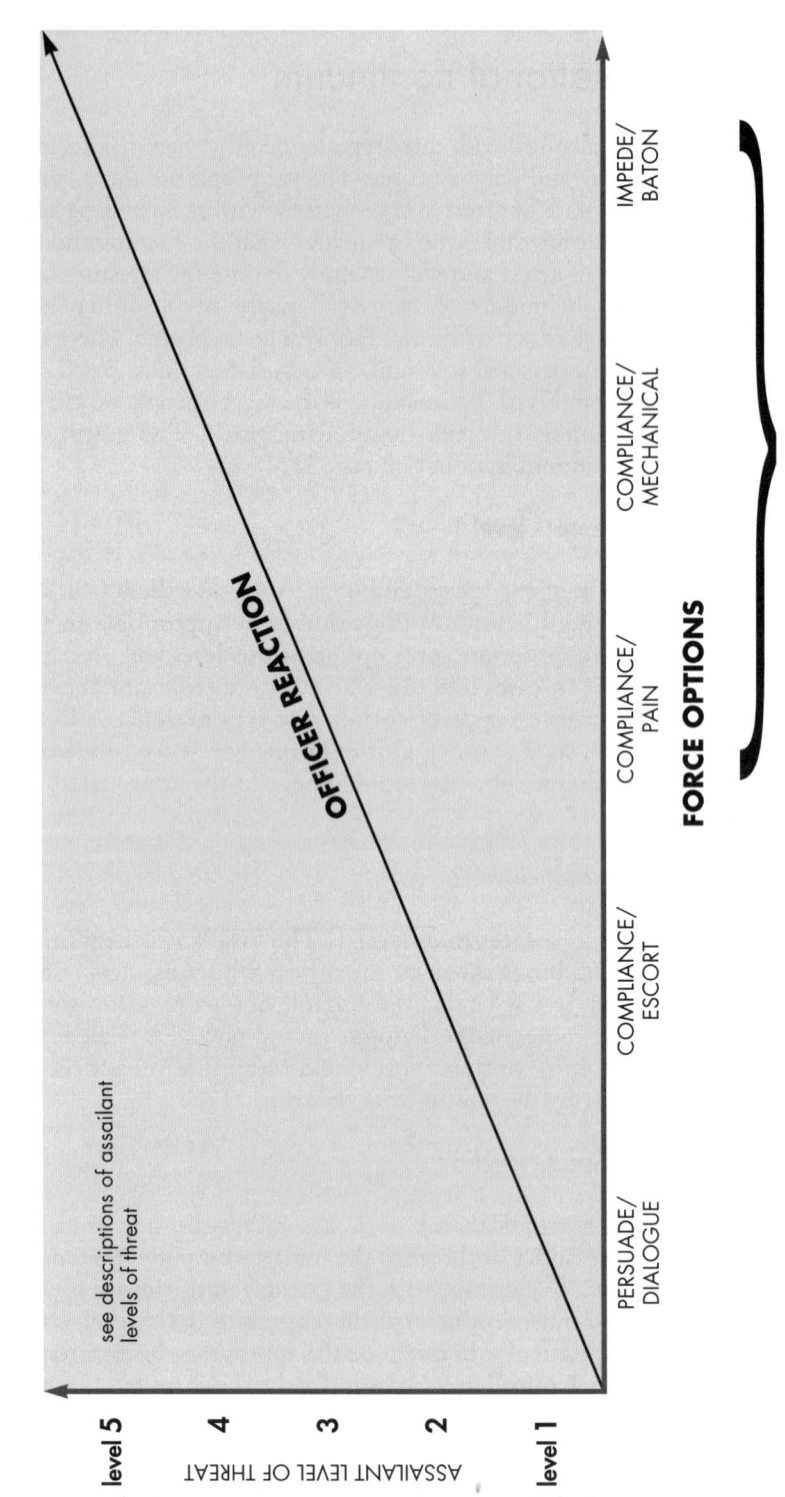

CS spray is a remedy which depends on the immediacy of the situation and the level of perceived threat

Assailant level of threat - level 4

This level of threat is greater than level 3. The assailant is continuing to climb the ladder to a threat level which is immediate and even desperate to the well being of the arresting officer. The force option that the threatened officer should now consider to be appropriate is that of **compliance/ mechanical**. In order to control the assailant it is now time to consider handcuffs/quickcuffs/ speedcuffs. Having placed the cuffs on the assailant, officers should always remember to double-lock.

Assailant level of threat - level 5

This level of threat is greater than 4. The assailant has now climbed to the top of the ladder to a threat level which, if left without intervention by the officer, will result in him being injured or killed. The force option that the threatened officer should now consider to be appropriate is that of **impede/ baton**. The officer now needs to take measures to control the assailant by the use of the tactical baton. The baton should be used until the threat is reduced and/or the assailant is brought under control by the use of **compliance/mechanical**.

The pre-emptive strike

If you have an honestly held belief that you or another are in imminent danger, then you may use such force as is reasonable and necessary to avert that danger.

Case law relevant to the use of force

Self defence

In applying the use of force to the question of self-defence, Lord Griffith said:
'The common law has always recognised as one of these circumstances the right of a person to protect himself from attack and to act in defence of others, if necessary to inflict violence on another in so doing. If no more force is used than is reasonable to repel the attack such force is not unlawful and no crime is committed. Furthermore, a man about to be attacked does not have to wait for his assailant to strike the first blow or fire the first shot. Circumstances may justify a pre-emptive strike.'

R v Beckford 1988

Genuine belief of imminent danger

In Northern Ireland a police officer on duty had fired a baton round from a riot gun at short range. This struck the victim on the chest and caused injury to his heart which proved fatal. The defence was based on the fact that the victim had been seen to be about to strike other officers from behind with a stave during a riot. The defendant explained that he fired at the man because he thought that two police officers were in danger of serious injury from him. The prosecution argued that the weapon was fired without an order to do so, it was not aimed as directed by the force instructions and it was at a distance of less than the minimum 20 metres.

Held: The judge came to the conclusion that it was probable that the defendant acted almost instinctively to defend his comrades, without having time to assess the situation in the light of his knowledge of the police regulations relating to the use of riot guns and without having time to balance the nature of the injury which might be caused to the deceased against the nature of the injury which might be caused to one or other of the two police officers.

R v Hegerty 1986

Honest belief/mistake as to facts

Lord Lane, the Lord Chief Justice, said:
> 'In a case of self-defence, where self-defence or the prevention of crime is concerned, if the jury come to the conclusion that the defendant believed, or may have believed that he was being attacked or that a crime was being committed and that force was necessary to protect himself or to prevent the crime, then the prosecution have not proved their case. If however, the defendant's alleged belief was mistaken and if the mistake was an unreasonable one, that may be a powerful reason for coming to the conclusion that the belief was not honestly held and should be rejected. Even if the jury come to the conclusion that the mistake was an unreasonable one, if the defendant may genuinely have been labouring under it, he is entitled to rely on it.'

R v Williams 1984

Assessment of danger

In determining the level of danger an officer is facing he must have regard to the totality of circumstances in order to make the right decision in relation to his force option ranging from **persuasion/dialogue** to **impede/baton**. The totality of circumstances touches on matters relating to officer - subject factors and special circumstances. In making his determination, the officer facing the confrontation will enjoy a higher sense of self-preservation if he is able to correctly assess threat recognition by having regard to such matters as warning signals, danger signs and signals of submission.

Officer - personal factors

Age - The officer may be in his late 40s and facing two fit young men in their 20s.

Gender - A female officer would almost certainly be at a disadvantage when facing a hostile man having regard to the usual size/weight difference.

Size - While there is much truth in the saying 'it's not the size of the dog in the fight it's the size of the fight in the dog', the prudent officer will view a weight advantage of the opposition to be a disadvantage to himself.

Skill level - Where an officer is new to the concept of hostility, or has a skill level which needs improvement, then the officer may well be at a disadvantage. Equally when faced on the streets by a hostile man adopting martial arts poses suggesting he has a black belt in nokando then again, the officer may well be at a disadvantage.

Multiple subjects - An individual officer who is facing multiple subjects will clearly be disadvantaged as the physical and psychological strength lies with the opposition.

Special circumstances

Close proximity to weapon - Where an officer is dealing with a hostile who suddenly produces a weapon then the appropriate response to this new situation would be to adopt a greater force option.

Special knowledge - Where the officer is dealing with a known hard man who is known for his violent behaviour then this knowledge should be used by the officer in determining his force option.

Injury or exhaustion - An officer who becomes injured during the course of an arrest or who simply becomes exhausted may have to choose a different force option.

Ground - Who holds the high ground and therefore the advantage? Is it the villain at the top of the stairs throwing furniture at the officer? If so, a new force option may have to be chosen.

Imminent danger - Where an officer finds himself suddenly confronted with imminent danger, his force option choice may be greater than it would had he been prepared for the danger.

Threat recognition

If a threat is to be correctly assessed in order to respond properly with the appropriate force option then it is important to recognise warning signals, danger signals and submission signals. They can be recognised thus:

Warning signals

> Head and shoulders back;
> facial colour dark/red;
> breathing is fast and shallow;
> belligerent, challenging, shouting;
> exaggerated movements;
> hands held on or above the waist;
> direct uninterrupted eye contact;
> kicking nearby objects.

Danger signals

> Head down;
> eyebrows move down into a frown;
> facial colour pales;
> lips tighten over teeth;
> breathing becomes rapid and deep;
> stance changes from square to bladed;
> fists clench and unclench;
> dropping centre of gravity and lowering body stance;
> target identification.

So far as target identification is concerned, (where the assailant glances at a target, eg the officer's testicles), this is the last danger signal that the officer will be aware of prior to attack. It is important therefore, when the danger signals manifest themselves, that the officer should consider the option of **separate** and **escalate**, ie, move away from the assailant and consider a force option which is appropriate in all the circumstances.

Signals of submission

Recognising warning and danger signals helps the officer to respond appropriately to his assailant. It is just as important to recognise submission signals as it means that the assailant wishes to disengage. Where this is recognised early, the officer will be at an advantage as the hostilities directed toward him have now come to an end.

Submission signals

> Putting hands up in front of body - palms out;
> reduction in large movements;
> lowering tone and volume of voice;
> standing still;
> looking down at the ground;
> falling down;
> lifting eyebrows (showing fear/anxiety);
> backing away.

When an assailant shows these submission signals, the officer should now consider whether the assailant is in need of first aid, and all should now be done to help him as he is now controllable.

Reporting the use of force

> **Remember**
>
> > Your statement is an account of what happened in a confrontation.
> > Many individuals (complaints, juries, senior officers) may read your statement.
> > Be certain to indicate the causes for your action including all reasonable suspicion.
> > Quote the subject directly if possible.
> > Quote your statements as accurately as possible.
> > Be chronological.
> > Show the totality of the circumstances.
> > List all factors that contributed to the incident.
> > Specify the care that was rendered to the subject after control was effected.
> > State your perception at the time of the incident based upon your experience.
>
> Be specific in justifying your chosen force option based on:
> > > assailant's actions;
> > > level of threat experienced;
> > > officer - subject factors;
> > > special circumstances;
> > > warning signals;
> > > danger signals;
> > > submission signals.   If you were frightened - say so.

Police officers are accountable to the courts and the Police Complaints Authority, but they also have a duty of care both to arrested persons with whom they come into conflict, and to themselves. So far as the officer himself is concerned, it is fundamentally important to report fully any use of force. The report must be factual and, above all, honest. If an officer was frightened during the confrontation then he should say so. Report the encounter in fine grain detail in order to expose the totality of the circumstances of the case. This is especially important as the case might not come to court for a year or indeed the officer may be sued in the civil courts for damages. Civil lawsuits may go on for years and for that reason the more comprehensive the report, the fewer the problems later encountered with ailing memories of the event. A report that is glib and touches only on the barest of facts will excite the sense of curiosity of any lawyer who will claw at it in the hope that it becomes unstitched. The more detail contained in a report the fewer are the loose ends to unravel. Too often a report on the use of police force is summarised thus:

'At 0200 hours on Sunday, 5th May, 1996, I attended 28 High Street where I saw Ricky Allen. He was drunk and aimed a blow at me. A violent struggle ensued and he was restrained. He was brought to the police station and placed in cells.'

A report as brief as this suggests that much more happened. A barrister or solicitor will take this type of report apart and, during cross examination, attempt to fill in the missing detail themselves putting the officer on the defensive. If the report is full of fine grain detail there will be little to pick holes in or elaborate on. Take time to examine the model on the previous page for reporting the use of force.

Search and seizure

Search after arrest

A constable may search an arrested person in any case when the person to be searched has been arrested at a place **other than at a police station**:
 (a) if the constable has reasonable grounds for believing that the arrested person may present a danger to himself or others;
 (b) to search for anything which the person might use to assist him to escape from lawful custody;
 (c) to search for anything which might be evidence relating to an offence.

Restrictions on search after arrest

The search must be restricted to a search to the extent that is reasonably required for the purposes of discovering any of the above articles. There will be a fuller search at the police station, so this search should be immediate and if possible, out of the public view. A search in public following arrest does not allow you to remove any clothing except **outer coat, jacket or gloves**.

If the person does not agree to be searched, then you may use reasonable force to conduct the search. It is as well to remember that **behaviour breeds behaviour**. Most people will submit to a search. If however, your behaviour is such that you are creating heat, not light, then you may find yourself in difficulty.

Seizure following search

A constable searching a person in the exercise of the power may seize and retain anything he finds if he has reasonable grounds for believing that:
 (a) the person may use the article to injure himself or another;
 (b) he may use the article to escape from custody;
 (c) the article is evidence of an offence;
 (d) the article has been obtained through committing another offence.

CHAPTER 3

SEARCH

Chapter contents

Police and Criminal Evidence Act 1984 32
    Stop and search 32
        G O W I S E.. 32
        Where searches may be carried out 34
        Conduct of a search 35
        Records of searches... 36
    Entry and search after arrest 37
    Entry and search to arrest/save life............................ 38
    Search other than at a police station 39
    Search warrants 40
    Road checks 41

Criminal Justice and Public Order Act 1994 42
    Anticipation of violence 42
    Terrorism 42

Police and Criminal Evidence Act 1984

Stop and search

Prior to the Police and Criminal Evidence Act 1984 (PACE), the most contentious issue to afflict both the police and the public was what was then known as the 'sus' laws, whereby police officers often stopped people 'on suspicion' of something or other and searched the individual for evidence which would justify the suspicion. These were often 'fishing trips' carried out by police officers on the off-chance of detecting crime.

However laudable an enterprise this may have been it was, very often, unlawful in that the reasonable suspicion the officers relied upon were things like hunches, they 'just knew', or there was a 'better than evens chance' of detecting crime by concentrating on certain elements of the community.

The Police and Criminal Evidence Act 1984 redressed this imbalance in favour of the right of the individual not to be harried by over-zealous police officers. Section 2 of the Act deals with the checks and balances that now operate upon the police in order to make them accountable to society. It enacts safeguards for the man in the street who, if he feels aggrieved by police behaviour, has an avenue of complaint which he may pursue.

GOWISE

> S 2 PACE

Before looking closely at the law governing the matter, there is one golden thread which permeates through the whole of stop and search philosophy which can be summed up in a word:

Gowise.

When a constable **contemplates** a search (other than a search of an unattended vehicle) he **shall** take reasonable steps **before** he commences the search, to bring to the attention of the appropriate person:

- **G** Grounds for the proposed search.
- **O** Object of the proposed search.
- **W** Warrant card, documentary evidence that he is a constable (if not in uniform).
- **I** Identification of officer.
- **S** Station to which the officer is attached.
- **E** Entitlement to a copy of the search record.

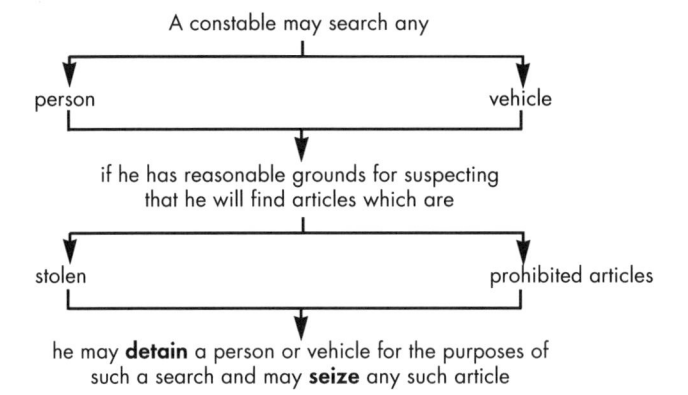

Stop and search

> **S 1 PACE**

```
                A constable may search any
                    ↓              ↓
                 person         vehicle
                    └──────┬───────┘
                           ↓
             if he has reasonable grounds for suspecting
                  that he will find articles which are
                    ↓              ↓
                 stolen       prohibited articles
                    └──────┬───────┘
                           ↓
         he may detain a person or vehicle for the purposes of
           such a search and may seize any such article
```

Search. Does not authorise a constable to remove any of the person's clothing in public other than an outer coat, jacket or gloves, or authorise a constable not in uniform to stop a vehicle.

Vehicle. Includes vessels, aircraft and hovercraft, and includes anything which is in or on the vehicle.

Reasonable grounds. Powers of stop and search should be used responsibly and sparingly.

If a police officer has reasonable grounds to suspect that a person is in innocent possession of stolen or prohibited articles (which includes bladed and pointed instruments), the power of stop and search continues to exist, although there is no power of arrest.

Every effort should be made to **secure the voluntary** production of the article before the power is exercised. Whether reasonable grounds for suspicion exist will depend on the circumstances in each case, but there must be some objective basis.

An officer will need to consider the nature of the article suspected of being carried in the context of other factors such as the time and the place, and the behaviour of the person concerned or those with him.

Reasonable suspicion may exist, for example, when information has been received, such as a description of an article being carried or of a suspected offender; a person has been seen acting covertly or warily or attempting to hide something or a person is carrying a certain type of article at an unusual time or in a place where a number of burglaries or thefts are known to have taken place recently.

The decision to stop and search must be based on all the facts which bear on the likelihood that an article of a certain kind will be found.

Not reasonable grounds. Reasonable suspicion can never be supported on the basis of personal factors alone.

For example, a person's colour, age, hair style, or manner of dress, or the fact that he is known to have a previous conviction for possession of an unlawful article, cannot be used alone or in combination with each other as the sole basis on which to search that person.

Neither may it be founded on the basis of stereotyped images of certain persons or groups as more likely to be committing offences.

Stolen articles. This is not defined and should therefore be given its ordinary meaning under the provisions of the Theft Act 1968.

Prohibited articles. A prohibited article is an offensive weapon; which is any article made or adapted for use for causing injury, or intended by the person having it with him for such use by him or by some other person, or any article made or adapted for use in the course of or in connection with an offence of burglary, theft, taking a motor vehicle or other conveyance without authority and obtaining property by deception, or intended by the person having it with him for such use by him or by some other person.

Innocent possession. Where a police officer has reasonable grounds to suspect that a person is in innocent possession of a stolen or prohibited article or other item for which he is empowered to search, the power of stop and search exists notwithstanding that there would be no power of arrest. However every effort should be made to secure the person's co-operation in the production of the article before resorting to the use of force.

Where searches may be carried out   S 1 PACE

A constable may exercise these powers

- in any place to which at the time the public or any section of the public has access, on payment or otherwise, as of right or by virtue of express, or implied, permission
- in any other place to which people have ready access at the time when he proposes to exercise the power but which is not a dwelling

if the place is

- a garden
- a yard
- other land

occupied with and used for the purposes of a dwelling, or on other land so occupied and used. The search may not be carried out unless the constable has reasonable cause for believing in the case of

a person
that person does not reside in the dwelling and is not in the place with the express or implied permission of a person who resides there

a vehicle
that the person in charge of the vehicle does not reside in the dwelling or that the vehicle is not in the place with the express or implied permission of a person who resides there

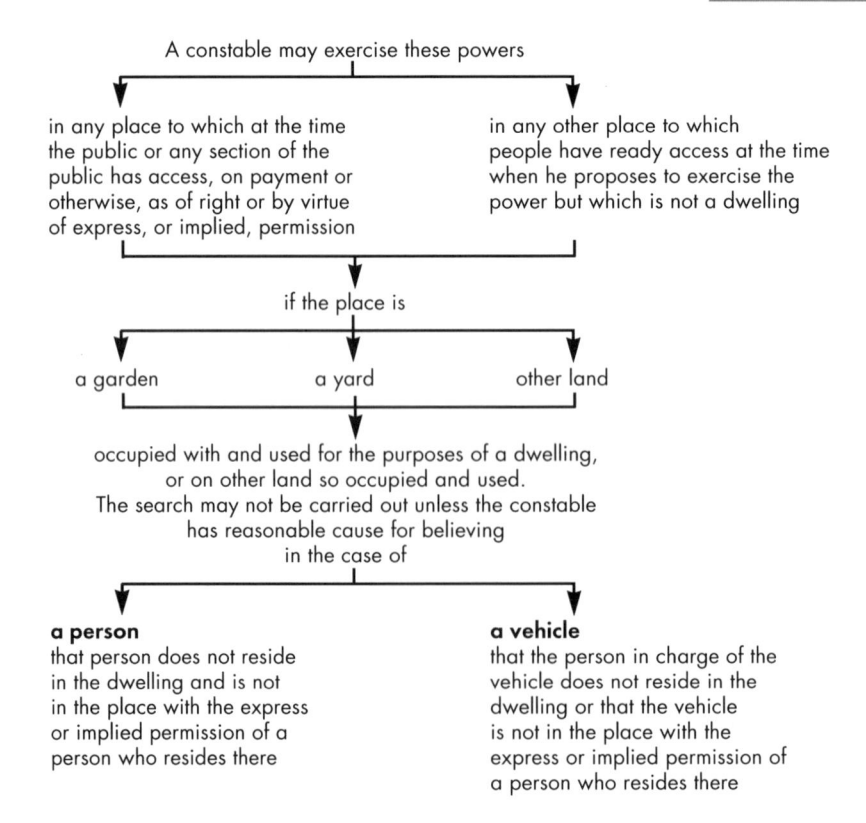

Conduct of a search

S 2 PACE

If a constable contemplates, under any power, a search of a **person** or **vehicle**, before he commences the search he must take reasonable steps to bring to the attention of the appropriate person

- the constable's name and police station
- the object of the search
- the grounds for making it
- (if it is not practicable to make a record of the search) that the person is entitled to a copy of any record made in the following 12 months

Search. Cannot require the removal of clothing in public other than outer coat, jacket, gloves.

Vehicle. Includes vessels, aircraft and hovercraft.

Appropriate person. Means the person searched, or, in the case of a vehicle, the person in charge of it.

Unattended motor vehicle. In the case of an unattended motor vehicle, a notice shall be left inside the vehicle, unless not practicable to do so without damaging it, stating:

> That the constable has searched it.
> That an application for compensation for any damage caused may be made to that police station.
> That the owner of the vehicle and person in charge at the time of the search will be entitled to a copy of the record or the search for up to 12 months.
> The constable's police station.

Copy of search records. Copies of search records do not automatically go out to the searched person, or the person in charge of the vehicle. There must be an application made by the appropriate person.

Plain clothes searches. Any officer about to carry out a search should identify himself to the suspect before the search is carried out. If the officer is in plain clothes then he should produce his warrant card, and, even if in uniform, if identity is sought then the warrant card should be produced.

Records of search

S 2 PACE

Where a constable has carried out a search he shall make a record of it in writing (unless it is not practicable to do so) recording

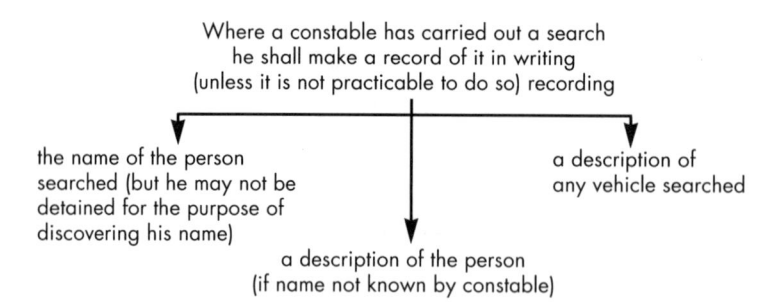

- the name of the person searched (but he may not be detained for the purpose of discovering his name)
- a description of the person (if name not known by constable)
- a description of any vehicle searched

In making the search record the constable shall state:

(a) object of the search;
(b) grounds for making search;
(c) date and time made;
(d) place made;
(e) whether anything was found, and if so, what;
(f) any injury to a person or damage to property which appears to the constable to have resulted from the search;
(g) the identity of the constable.

When impracticable...

If it could be made, but it is not practicable to make it on the spot, he shall make a record as soon as practicable afterwards.

Copy record...

A record will be available, on request for a period of 12 months, and will be available to:

(a) the person who was searched;
(b) the owner of the vehicle;
(c) the person in charge of the vehicle when it was searched.

Entry and search after arrest

S 2 PACE

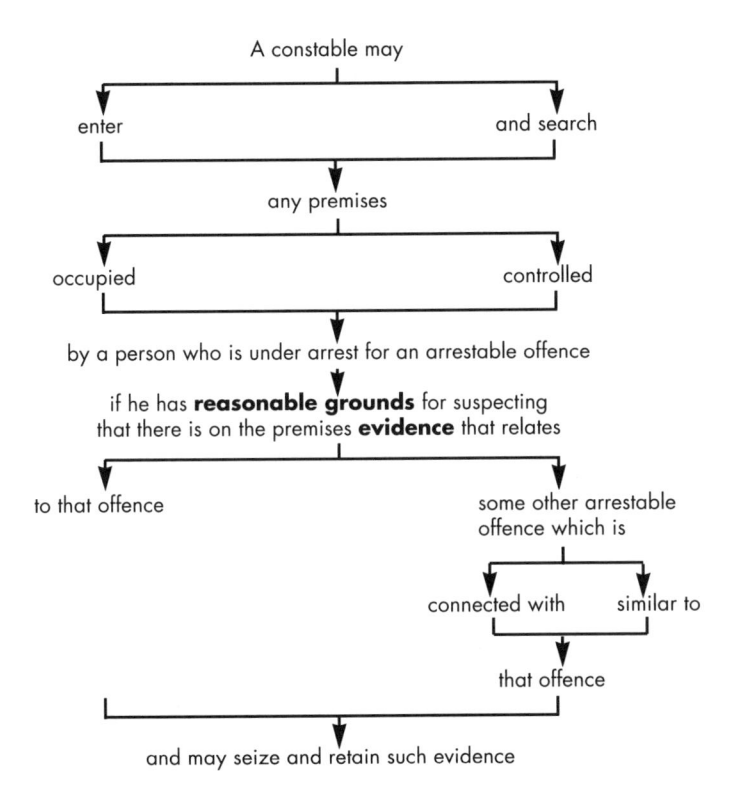

```
                        A constable may
                   ┌───────────┴───────────┐
                   ▼                       ▼
                 enter                 and search
                   └───────────┬───────────┘
                               ▼
                         any premises
                   ┌───────────┴───────────┐
                   ▼                       ▼
                occupied                controlled
                   └───────────┬───────────┘
                               ▼
        by a person who is under arrest for an arrestable offence
                               ▼
                if he has **reasonable grounds** for suspecting
                 that there is on the premises **evidence** that relates
                   ┌───────────┴───────────┐
                   ▼                       ▼
             to that offence       some other arrestable
                                    offence which is
                                   ┌────────┴────────┐
                                   ▼                 ▼
                              connected with      similar to
                                   └────────┬────────┘
                                            ▼
                                       that offence
                   ┌────────────────────────┘
                   ▼
           and may seize and retain such evidence
```

Authority. If authorised to do so in writing by an officer of the rank of inspector or above. This authority is not necessary before taking a person to the police station if his presence elsewhere is necessary for the effective investigation of the offence. (An inspector, or above, must be informed as soon as practicable afterwards.)

Search. The search must be directed at the purpose of discovering evidence.

Premises. Includes any place and any vehicle, vessel, aircraft, hovercraft, tent or moveable structure.

Seizure. Evidence found that relates to that offence or some other arrestable offence which is connected with or similar to that offence may be seized and retained.

Entry and search to arrest/save life `S 17 PACE`

A constable may
- enter
- and search

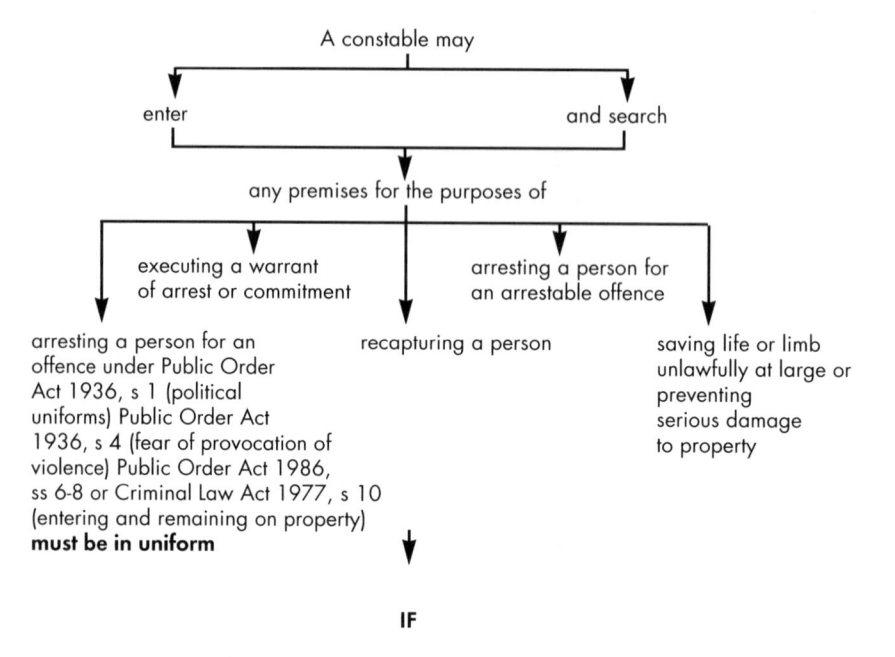

any premises for the purposes of
- executing a warrant of arrest or commitment
- arresting a person for an arrestable offence

- arresting a person for an offence under Public Order Act 1936, s 1 (political uniforms) Public Order Act 1936, s 4 (fear of provocation of violence) Public Order Act 1986, ss 6-8 or Criminal Law Act 1977, s 10 (entering and remaining on property) **must be in uniform**
- recapturing a person
- saving life or limb unlawfully at large or preventing serious damage to property

IF

the constable has reasonable grounds for believing the person sought is on the premises

(the proviso does not affect the saving life sub-section)

Premises. Includes any place and in particular includes any vehicle, vessel, aircraft, hovercraft, tent or moveable structure.

Where the premises consist of two or more separate dwellings, in those parts in common use, and where the constable reasonably suspects the person to be.

Breach of the peace. The power of entry to deal with a breach of the peace or prevent a breach of the peace is not affected by this section.

Search other than at a police station $\boxed{\text{S 32 PACE}}$

A constable may search the **arrested person** if he has reasonable grounds for believing that the person may present

- a danger to himself
- a danger to others

for anything which might

- assist his escape
- be evidence relating to an offence

if the constable believes such articles are concealed on him

a constable may search **any premises**

- where he was arrested
- where he was **immediately before** arrest

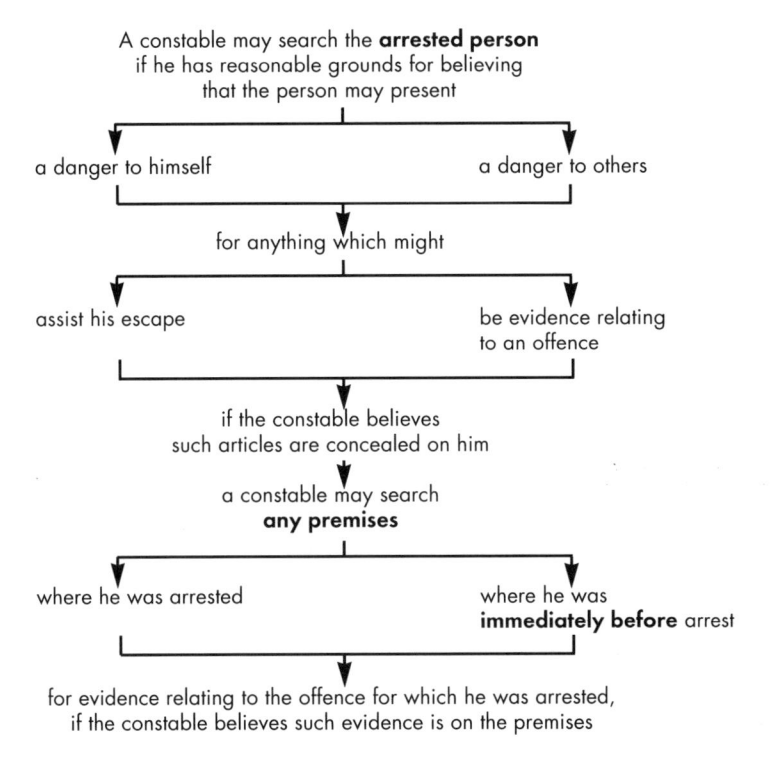

for evidence relating to the offence for which he was arrested, if the constable believes such evidence is on the premises

Clothing. A constable may not remove clothing in public other than outer coat, jacket or gloves.

Seizure. A constable may seize and retain anything found if he believes that the person arrested might use it to cause injury. He may also seize and retain anything found (other than items subject to legal privilege) if he believes it might be used to assist escape or that it is evidence of or obtained in consequence of the commission of an offence.

Premises. Any premises where he was arrested or where he was immediately before his arrest, means that if these consist of two or more separate dwellings only that part where he was when he was arrested, or where he was before his arrest, or used in common with other occupiers.

Used in common. Used in common with other occupiers means those parts of the premises such as kitchens, bathrooms lounge areas, hallways and the like, so long as they have common usage.

Extent of search. The premises may only be searched to the extent that is reasonably required for that purpose. It would be unreasonable to search a kitchen area for a stolen car, or a chest of drawers for a chainsaw. It would clearly be unreasonable, and therefore unlawful, to use these search powers as a vehicle of mischief to conduct a search of the whole of a premises on a 'fishing expedition', in the hope of finding stolen goods.

Arrested person. Ideally, when practicable, the arrested person should be present during the course of the search, to ensure fairness and to note any replies he may wish to give.

Search warrants $\boxed{\text{S 8 PACE}}$

If on application made by a constable, a justice of the peace is satisfied that there are reasonable grounds for believing

(a) that a serious arrrestable offence has been committed; and
(b) that there is material on premises specified in the application which is likely to be of substantial value to the investigation of the offence; and
(c) that the material is likely to be relevant evidence; and
(d) that any of the conditions specified below applies,

he may issue a warrant authorising a constable to enter and search the premises, and the constable may seize and retain anything for which a search has been authorised. The conditions that apply are

- that it is not practicable to communicate with any person entitled to grant entry to the premises
  - that it is practicable to communicate with a person entitled to grant entry to the premises but it is not practicable to communicate with any person entitled to grant access to the evidence
- that the purpose of the search may be frustrated or seriously prejudiced unless a constable arriving at the premise can secure immediate entry to them
  - that entry to the premises will not be granted unless a warrant is produced

General power. Section 19 provides that a police $\boxed{\text{S 19 PACE}}$ officer lawfully on premises may seize anything which he has reasonable grounds for believing:
(a) has been obtained as a result of the commission of an offence;
(b) is evidence in relation to an offence;
(c) and it is necessary to seize it to prevent it being lost, hidden or destroyed.

Material. This means material other than items subject to legal privilege, excluded material or special procedure material.

(This section of the law is complicated and requires further reading before being party to the execution of a warrant.)

Reasonableness. The warrant must be executed at a reasonable hour unless the purpose may be frustrated by doing so.

Duration. The warrant must be executed within one month of issue.

Copy warrant. Where the occupier or person in charge of the premises is present the constable must identify himself and produce the warrant and supply him with a copy. If no such person is present then a copy must be left in a prominent place on the premises.

Records. A constable executing a warrant shall make an endorsement on it stating:
(a) whether the articles or persons sought were found; and,
(b) whether any articles were seized, other than the articles sought.

Inspection. Warrants (which are usually kept for 12 months from their return) may be inspected by the occupier of the premises to which they relate, for that period.

Road checks

S 4 PACE

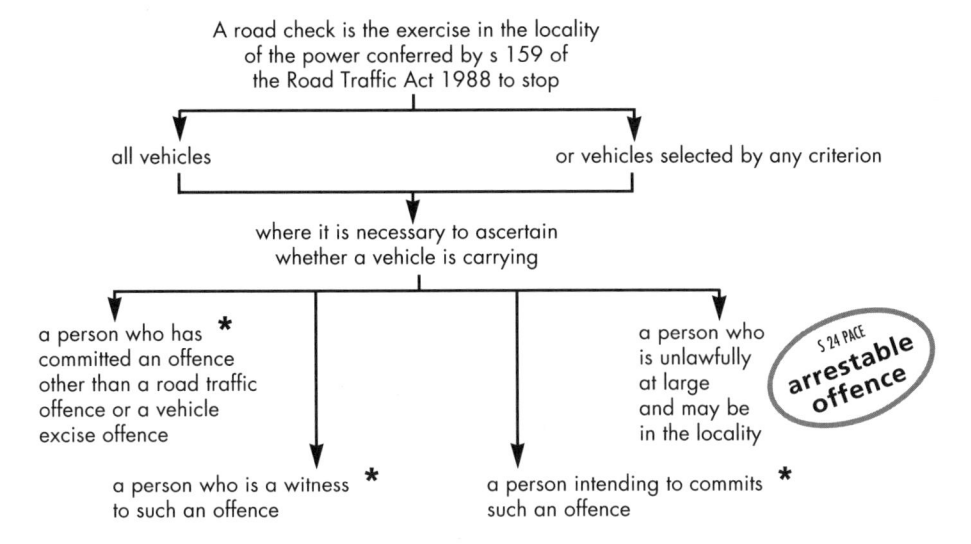

A road check is the exercise in the locality of the power conferred by s 159 of the Road Traffic Act 1988 to stop

- all vehicles
- or vehicles selected by any criterion

where it is necessary to ascertain whether a vehicle is carrying

- a person who has committed an offence other than a road traffic offence or a vehicle excise offence *
- a person who is a witness to such an offence *
- a person who is unlawfully at large and may be in the locality
- a person intending to commits such an offence *

S 24 PACE arrestable offence

* serious arrestable offices

Authorisation. A road check must be authorised, in writing, by an officer of the rank of superintendent and above. However it may be authorised by any officer in a matter of urgency, in which case, as soon as practicable, he must make a written record of the time he gives it and cause an inspector, chief inspector or superintendent to be informed.

Locality. The locality in which the road check is to be carried out must be specified.

Duration. The superintendent or above must specify a period not exceeding seven days during which it may take place (this is renewable in writing). He may direct that the road check be continuous or conducted at specific times.

All vehicles. This means precisely what it says. Causing all vehicles to stop with a view to establishing any of the selected criteria amounts to a road check.

Vehicles selected by any criterion. This means that while an officer may wish to conduct a check of vehicles (but not all vehicles), say, of a particular make or colour or with numbers of people aboard then this would amount to a road check. An example is stopping all blue Ford Escorts, carrying three white men.

Not a road check. Nothing in section 4 of the Act affects the exercise by police officers of any power to stop vehicles for purposes other than those specified in the Act.

Written statements. When a vehicle is stopped in a road check, the person in charge of the vehicle at the time when it is stopped shall be entitled to obtain a written statement of the purpose of the road check, if he applies for such a statement not later than the end of the period of 12 months from the day on which the vehicle was stopped.

Reasonable grounds. When authorising a road check, the authorising officer (of whatever rank) must have reasonable grounds for believing that where an offence has been committed, or there is a witness to such an offence, or a person is intending to commit an offence, the offence, amounts to a serious arrestable offence. However, when a person is believed to be unlawfully at large, then a serious arrestable offence does not figure in the reasonable grounds, but there should be grounds for believing that the suspect may be in the locality.

Criminal Justice and Public Order Act 1994

Anticipation of violence

S 60

If a police officer of the rank of inspector or above reasonably believes that incidents 'involving serious violence' may take place in any locality in his area and it is expedient to do so to prevent their occurrence, then he may authorise (in writing) the stopping and searching of persons and vehicles within that locality for a period not exceeding 24 hours, with a possible 24-hour extension.

The search must be for offensive weapons or dangerous instruments, but a constable in uniform may - in the exercise of these powers - stop any person or vehicle and make any search he thinks fit, whether or not he has any grounds for suspecting that person or vehicle to be carrying weapons. If any weapon is found it may be seized.

A driver or pedestrian stopped by a constable acting under this section shall be entitled to obtain a written statement that the stop was carried out under the powers of this section if he applies for such a statement within 12 months of the stop being carried out.

Terrorism

S 81

A new section 13A has been added to the Prevention of Terrorism (Temporary Provisions) Act 1989 empowering ACPO officers, in order to prevent acts of terrorism, to authorise stopping and searching of vehicles and persons for a period of 28 days. The power is to search for articles which could be connected with terrorism but a constable in uniform may exercise the stop and search powers, whether or not he has grounds for suspecting that the vehicle or person is carrying articles of that kind.

The person stopped is entitled to a written statement if he applies for it within 12 months.

The Prevention of Terrorism (Additional Powers) Act 1996 has added a new section, 13B, to the 1989 Act which empowers ACPO officers, in order to prevent acts of terrorism, to authorise any constable in uniform, for a period of 28 days, to stop and search any pedestrian.

CHAPTER 4

CRIME

Chapter contents

- Breach of the peace 44
- Assaults and woundings 44
    - Common assault 44
    - Actual bodily harm 45
    - Unlawful wounding 45
    - Wounding with intent 45
    - Assault on police 46
- Attempts 46
- Public order 47
    - Offensive conduct 47
    - Threatening behaviour 48
    - Intentional harassment, alarm or distress 49
    - Affray 49
    - Violent disorder 50
    - Riot 50
    - Trespassory assemblies 51
    - Racial hatred 52
    - Aggravated trespass 52
    - Trespass 53
    - Raves 53
    - Litter 55
    - Noise 56
    - Offensive weapons 56
- Drugs 57
    - Unlawful possession of a controlled drug 57
    - Stop and search 58
- Sexual offences 59
    - Indecent assault on a woman 59
    - Rape 59
    - Gross indecency (indecency between men) 60
    - Prostitution 60
    - Kerb crawling 61
    - Persistent solicitation by men 61
    - Indecent assault on a man 61
- Drink-related offences 62
    - Drunkenness 62
    - Driving while unfit 63
    - Drink driving 63
    - Breath test powers 64
    - Administering a breath test .. 64
- Children 66
    - Offences by age group 66
    - Prevention of cruelty to children 68
- Criminal damage 69
- Aid and abet, counsel or procure 70
- Crime & Disorder Act 1998 ... 70a
    - Community safety 70a
    - Youth crime 70a
    - Orders 70a

Breach of the peace

The Queen's peace, or, 'the peace', is the normal state of society and any interruption to that state of society is a breach of the peace. This broad definition has been handed down to us since the enactment of the Justices of the Peace Act 1361. This has evolved at common law to a point whereby, where there is a threat or an act which:
  (a) causes harm to persons or property; or,
  (b) creates fear in the minds of ordinary citizens or is likely to do so; or,
  (c) is likely to cause harm to persons or property;
an offence is committed at common law.

Power of arrest. Any person may arrest without warrant where:
(a) a breach of the peace is committed in the presence of the person making the arrest; or,
(b) a breach of the peace has been committed and it is reasonably believed that a renewal of it is threatened; or,
(c) where the person making the arrest reasonably believes that such a breach will be committed in the immediate future by the person he has arrested.

Public or private. This offence can be committed anywhere, be it public or private, and includes anywhere where the public have access by payment.

Threats, real or idle. To be considered under this section, any threats made must be real and not idle. They should operate on the minds of others creating in them a belief in what is being said.

Binding over. A magistrates' court has the power to bind over a person to keep the peace or be of good behaviour. This is usually done for a period of one year. A monetary condition may be imposed or imprisonment for up to six months, or until he complies with the order.

Assaults and woundings

Common assault

> S 39 Criminal Justice Act 1988

Common assault is an act by which the suspect causes another to sustain or fear the infliction of immediate, unlawful violence. Physical contact is not necessary, so a threatened or intended blow which misses would suffice for an assault. The harm need not be directed towards the actual victim. The suspect must intend to cause the victim to fear immediate and unlawful violence or be reckless as to whether such apprehension would be caused. Where the assault is on a police officer, see 'Assault on Police'. If injury is caused then unless it is minor (a scratch or black eye) the suspect should be charged with actual bodily harm.

Defences.
  (a) Lawful correction (parent on child).
  (b) Consent (boxing match).
  (c) Reasonable defence of property.
  (d) Self-defence.

S 24 PACE arrestable offence

Actual bodily harm (ABH)

S 47 Offences Against the Person Act 1861

Actual bodily harm is an act by which the suspect intentionally or recklessly causes another to sustain unlawful personal harm. While physical contact is not necessary, some actual bodily injury which causes hurt or psychiatric injury is necessary. This need not be visible or permanent, for example minor fractures (undisplaced nasal fracture), extensive bruising or abrasions. The harm need not be directed towards the actual victim.

Defences
(a) Lawful correction (parent on child).
(b) Consent (boxing match).
(c) Reasonable defence of property.
(d) Self-defence.

S 24 PACE arrestable offence

Unlawful wounding

S 20 Offences Against the Person Act 1861

Whosoever unlawfully and maliciously wounds or inflicts grievous bodily harm upon any other person, whether with or without any weapon or instrument, shall be guilty of an offence.

Maliciously. Maliciously means where the suspect intends to cause the injury as well as cases where the suspect is aware that his act might result in some physical harm to another, albeit of a minor character. It is enough that the defendant foresaw that his actions would cause some harm.

Wound. This offence should be charged for injuries involving permanent disability or loss of sensory function, substantial loss of blood or lengthy treatment or incapacity. Small cuts and minor fractures should not result in a charge under this section, but rather one under section 47 (ABH).

Defences. Defences of consent, lawful chastisement, self-defence and reasonable defence of property become increasingly difficult to advance when the injury is more serious.

Wounding with intent

S 18 Offences Against the Person Act 1861

Whosoever shall unlawfully and maliciously, wound or cause any grievous bodily harm to any person, with intent to do grievous bodily harm to any person or with intent to resist or prevent the lawful apprehension or detainer of any person, commits an offence.

Grievous bodily harm. This means really serious bodily harm, but need not be permanent.

With intent. The intent to wound or cause grievous bodily harm is what distinguishes this offence from a section 20 offence, not the seriousness of the injuries. This offence may be committed against any person, so that if 'A' fires a gun at B intending to do 'B' grievous bodily harm, but hits 'C', then the offence is complete.

Defences. Defences of consent, lawful chastisement, self-defence and reasonable defence of property become very much more difficult to advance when this offence is committed.

Assault on police

S 89 Police Act 1996

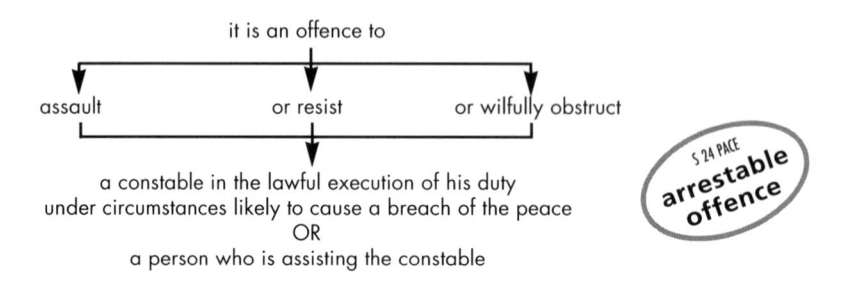

it is an offence to

assault | or resist | or wilfully obstruct

a constable in the lawful execution of his duty
under circumstances likely to cause a breach of the peace
OR
a person who is assisting the constable

S 24 PACE arrestable offence

Lawful execution of duty. Any assault on a police officer who is not acting in the execution of his duty is a common assault.

When a constable is off-duty or in plain clothes he should make his office known to the suspect by telling him he is a police officer and producing his warrant card. Any minor assault on the officer by a suspect who is unaware of his office will be regarded as a common assault.

When a constable is acting beyond his powers, eg; remaining on premises after being required to leave and is subject to a minor assault, again, the offence is probably common assault.

Wilful obstruction. The wilful obstruction of a constable in the execution of his duty must be both deliberate and intentional. There must be a real obstruction which makes it more difficult for the officer to carry out his duty and that obstruction must be done wilfully. An accident, mistake or misunderstanding by the accused would certainly benefit him.

Assisting a constable. This offence protects any person who is assisting a constable, where that constable is acting in the lawful execution of his duty, so that where a constable is in the act of arresting a violent prisoner and members of the public who are assisting the officer are assaulted by the prisoner, then a charge under this section should be brought.

Attempts

Attempting to commit an offence

S 1 Criminal Attempts Act 1981

If, with intent to commit an offence, a person does an act which is more than merely preparatory to the commission of the offence, he is guilty of attempting to commit the offence. The penalty for an attempt is the same as that for the actual offence.

Intent. Foresight of consequences might be something from which a court may infer intent. Recklessness is not acceptable as an alternative to intent.

Preparatory acts. Providing a false name and address on a form used for credit-worthiness inquiries does not make a person guilty of attempting to obtain services by deception, he must actually do something more.

It is a question of fact whether the defendant has gone beyond mere preparation and embarked on the commission of the offence, but it must be something which, if not interrupted, would result in the actual commission of the offence.

Impossible acts. If on the facts as the defendant believed them to be, an offence would have been committed, but on the true facts the commission of the offence was impossible, the defendant may nevertheless be convicted of an offence under section 1 of the Act. For instance a pickpocket attempting to steal from a bag which is actually empty.

Drugs. When a person believes that he is dealing in prohibited goods, namely drugs, and analysis shows that they are in fact harmless vegetable matter, he may rightly be convicted under the Act.

Public order

Offensive conduct

S 5 Public Order Act 1986

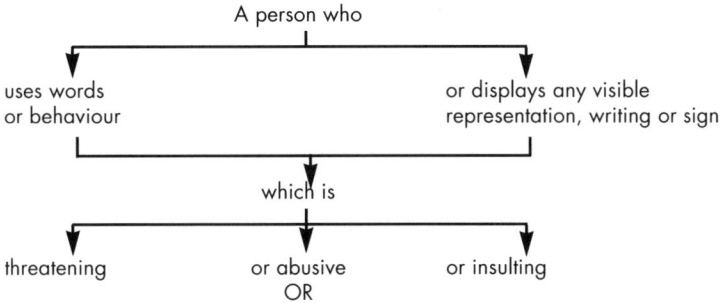

A person who
- uses words or behaviour
- or displays any visible representation, writing or sign

which is
- threatening
- or abusive
- or insulting

OR uses disorderly behaviour within the hearing or sight of a person, which is likely to cause harassment, alarm or distress, commits an offence

A person. There is no requirement that the conduct should be directed towards any person.

Dwelling. This offence may be committed in public or private. However, if it is committed from within a dwelling, then the person who is alarmed or distressed must be outside that dwelling and any other dwelling.

Defences. If a defendant can prove that:
> his conduct was reasonable; or,
> he had no reason to believe anybody was within sight or hearing; or
> he was in a dwelling and did not think he or any display could be seen or heard outside the dwelling;

then he will have a defence to the charge.

Arrest. A constable may arrest for this offence any person who ignores a warning to stop his offensive conduct. The continued offensive conduct does not have to be of the same nature. Be careful when dealing with large groups of people to ensure that they all hear your warning to stop.

Evidence. Informants of offensive conduct or those alarmed or distressed do not necessarily have to appear in court. It may be enough for the police officer to say that another person was distressed.

Mental element. You must prove that the offender intended his actions to be, or he was aware that those actions were, threatening or abusive or insulting.

Your decision. The effect of this section is to make socially undesirable behaviour a criminal offence. Before exercising powers under the Act try persuasion, it is often successful. What exactly is offensive conduct will be up to you to decide on the spot. The government has given the example of youths pestering people at bus stops or in cinema queues. In New Zealand and South Australia, where similar powers exist, the courts have said that 'disorderly conduct involves conduct which offends right-thinking members of the public'. Remember, there is a distinction between disorderly conduct and youthful high spirits.

Escalation. One of the problems with a situation of public order is that it can quickly escalate from a small incident to a major confrontation. A good knowledge of your powers will help you deal confidently and lawfully with any situation and prevent escalation. Knowledge of the law is not always enough, the use of tact, humour, common sense and also discretion, may help defuse a situation which, if dealt with inappropriately, may escalate to a point whereby it becomes threatening behaviour, affray, violent disorder or riot. Section 5 is the least serious of the Act, but the one which requires most tact.

Threatening behaviour [S 4]

This offence will be committed when a person

- uses words or behaviour
- or displays or distributes any visible representation, writing or sign

which is

- threatening
- or abusive
- or insulting

towards another person, and which is intended, or is likely to cause that person to believe

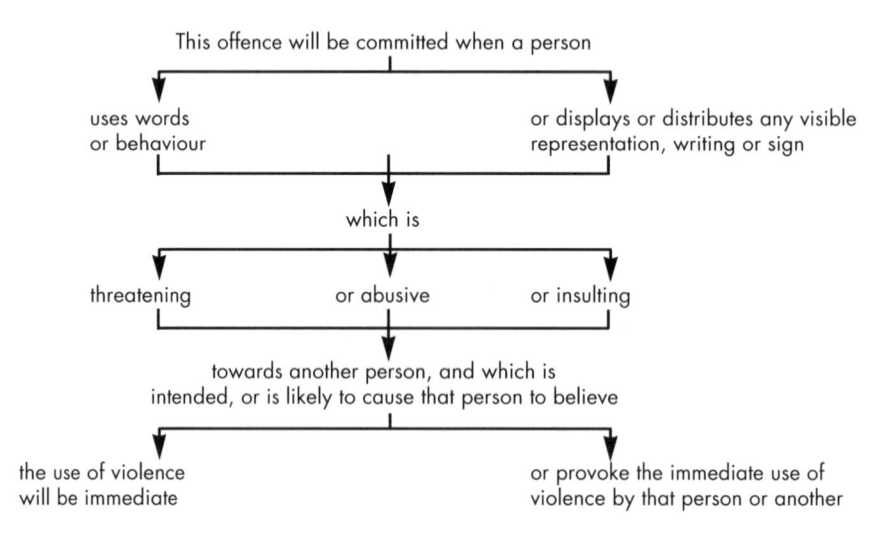

- the use of violence will be immediate
- or provoke the immediate use of violence by that person or another

Dwelling. This offence may be committed in public or private, however if it is committed from within a dwelling, the person to whom the threatening or abusive behaviour is directed must be outside the dwelling.

Mental element. You must prove that a person intended his actions to be, or was aware that those actions were, abusive, threatening or insulting.

Arrest. The offence carries a specific power of arrest, you may arrest any person you reasonably suspect is committing this offence.

Entry. The section gives you a specific power to enter any premises to arrest a person for this offence.

Police. The offence is complete even when the only person present is a police officer.

Intentional harassment, alarm or distress `S 4A`

A person shall be guilty of an offence if with intention to cause a person harassment, alarm or distress, he

- uses, threatening, abusive or insulting words or behaviour
- or displays any writing, sign or other visible representation which is threatening, abusive or insulting

thereby causing that or another person harassment, alarm or distress

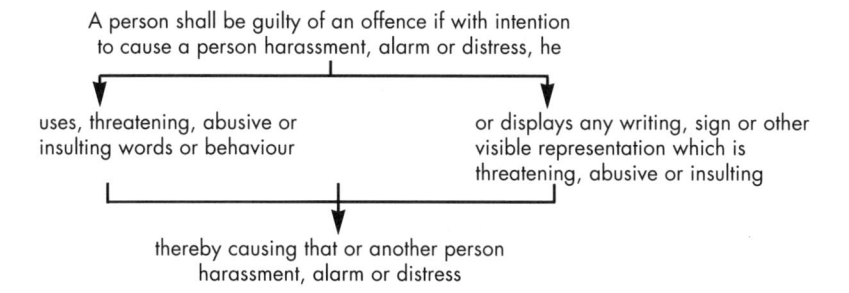

Note: This new offence was created by the Criminal Justice and Public Order Act 1994.

Dwelling. The requirements are the same as those for a section 4 offence.

Arrest. You may arrest without warrant upon reasonable suspicion.

Affray `S 3`

This offence is committed where one, or more, persons

- use
- or threaten violence

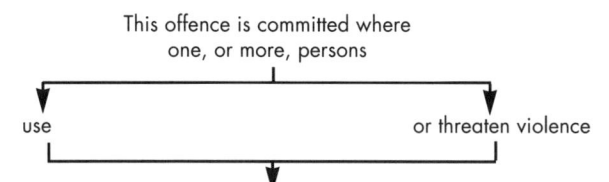

towards another so that their conduct would cause a person present, of reasonable firmness, to fear for his personal safety

Two or more. If the conduct involves more than one person, it is the conduct of the group as a whole that must be looked at.

Public or private. This offence may be committed in a private or a public place.

Words alone. Words alone cannot constitute a threat of violence, there must also be conduct.

Property. Any threat made must be made towards a person, not property. Threats against property may be dealt with under the Criminal Damage Act 1971.

Arrest. You may arrest without warrant anyone you reasonably suspect is committing this offence.

Reasonable firmness. It is not necessary to prove that there was any person of reasonable firmness present, merely that had someone been present he would have feared for his personal safety.

Intention. You have to prove the intention in the mind of the suspect or an awareness.

Personal safety. The Act does not define the meaning of 'personal safety' but it should be given its everyday meaning.

Violent disorder. One person alone can commit the offence of affray, however, if a number of persons are involved then consider violent disorder.

Violent disorder

S 2

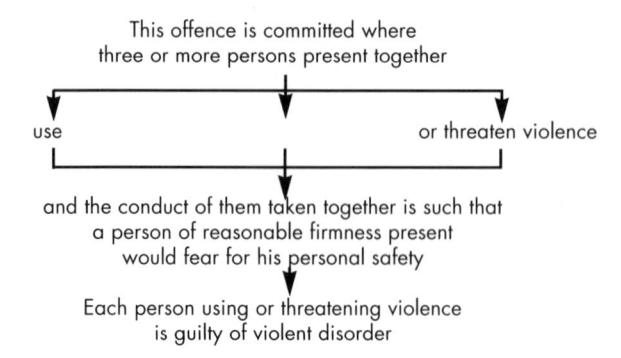

```
              This offence is committed where
              three or more persons present together
         ↓              ↓              ↓
        use                      or threaten violence
              ↓
  and the conduct of them taken together is such that
       a person of reasonable firmness present
           would fear for his personal safety
              ↓
    Each person using or threatening violence
              is guilty of violent disorder
```

Reasonable firmness. As with affray, no person of reasonable firmness need actually be present or is even likely to be present.

Threats. Persons who only threaten violence, and this may be by words only, are also guilty of this offence.

Public or private. The offence may be committed in public or in any private place.

Arrest. This is an arrestable offence.

Intention. Again, as in the previous offences, you must prove his intention or awareness of the nature of his actions.

The group. It need not be shown that the group (three or more) used or threatened violence simultaneously.

Scope. The scope of this offence is particularly wide and it must be looked at together with the offence of threatening behaviour. Apart from the requirement that three or more be involved, the two offences are very similar.

Which one to charge may be the cause of some difficulty. It has been suggested that this particular offence may be suited to incidents of missile throwing, an all too frequent occurrence at football matches.

Riot

S 1

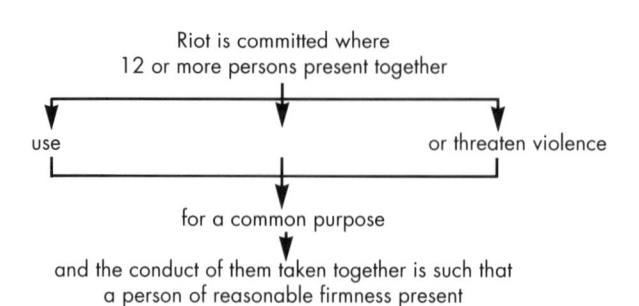

```
              Riot is committed where
              12 or more persons present together
         ↓              ↓              ↓
        use                      or threaten violence
              ↓
              for a common purpose
              ↓
  and the conduct of them taken together is such that
       a person of reasonable firmness present
           would fear for his personal safety

    Each person using the violence for the common purpose
                is guilty of this offence
```

Use or threaten. It does not matter if the 12 or more use or threaten violence simultaneously.

Common purpose. A common purpose may be inferred from the conduct of the group, eg they may charge a football queue, using violence to enter the ground without paying.

Public or private. This offence may be committed in a public place as well as a private place.

Reasonable firmness. It is not necessary to show that any person of reasonable firmness was actually present.

Arrest. This is an arrestable offence.

Who is guilty. It should be emphasised that only those persons in the group using unlawful violence for the common purpose are guilty of riot. Those who only threaten violence may be guilty of the lesser offence of violent disorder.

Trespassory assemblies S 14A Public Order Act 1986

If a Chief Officer of Police reasonably believes an assembly of

20 or more persons

at a place on land in open air to which public have

- limited access
- no right of access

is likely to be held

- without permission of occupier of the land
- likely to exceed limits of his permission
- limits of public right of access likely to be exceeded

and may result in

- serious disruption to the life of the community
- damage to land or buildings which is of
  a) historic
  b) architectural
  c) archeological or
  d) scientific importance

he may apply for an order **prohibiting assembly**

Note:

The application shall be made to the local authority, it shall not exceed four days and cover an area not exceeding five miles radius.

This section is aimed at disruption of national monuments, eg Stonehenge.

Offence. It is an offence to comply with the direction not to proceed.

Arrest. A constable may arrest without warrant.

Police powers. A constable in uniform may stop persons proceedings to trespassory assemblies (section 14c Public Order Act 1986).

Racial hatred

Ss 17-23 Public Order Act 1986

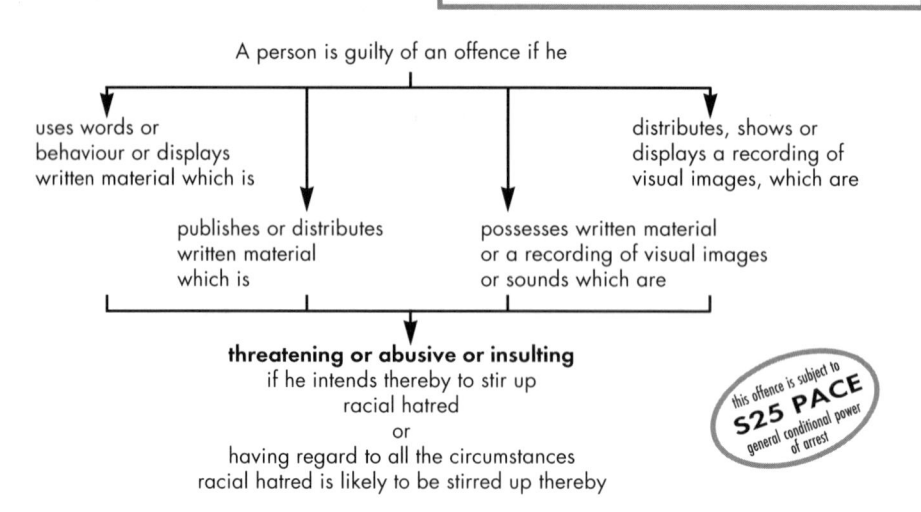

A person is guilty of an offence if he

- uses words or behaviour or displays written material which is
- publishes or distributes written material which is
- possesses written material or a recording of visual images or sounds which are
- distributes, shows or displays a recording of visual images, which are

threatening or abusive or insulting
if he intends thereby to stir up racial hatred
or
having regard to all the circumstances racial hatred is likely to be stirred up thereby

this offence is subject to S25 PACE general conditional power of arrest

Racial hatred. Racial hatred is hatred against a group of persons in Great Britain, defined by reference to colour, race, nationality (including citizenship), or ethnic or national origins.

Broadcasts etc. It is also an offence to broadcast, produce or direct a programme of visual images or sounds, or present or direct a public performance of a play which involves words or behaviour which are threatening, abusive or insulting.

Aggravated trespass

S 68 Criminal Justice and Public Order Act 1994

The Criminal Justice and Public Order Act 1994 creates an offence of aggravated trespass (aimed mainly at hunt saboteurs) and provides powers to deal with 'raves'.

A person commits the offence if he trespasses on land in the open air and

in relation to any lawful activity which persons are engaging in or are about to engage in on that or adjoining land, does there anything intended to have the effect of

- intimidating those persons so as to deter them from engaging in that activity
- obstructing that activity
- disrupting that activity

Land. Does not include highways and roads but does include footpaths and bridleways.

Trespass

> **S 61 Criminal Justice and Public Order Act 1994**

Where a senior police officer present believes that two or more persons have entered land **as trespassers** with a common purpose of residing there and have

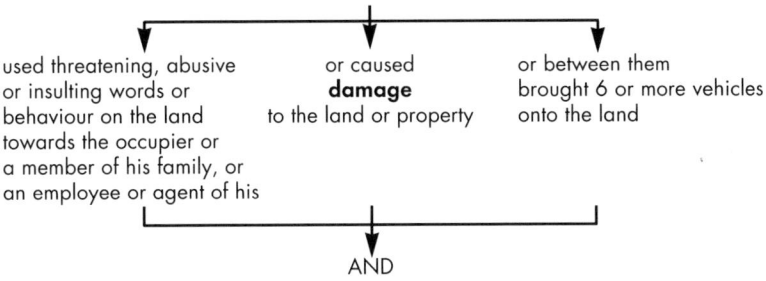

- used threatening, abusive or insulting words or behaviour on the land towards the occupier or a member of his family, or an employee or agent of his
- or caused **damage** to the land or property
- or between them brought 6 or more vehicles onto the land

AND that reasonable steps have been taken on behalf of the occupier to ask them to leave and remove their vehicles

the police officer may direct them or any of them to leave
IF
persons so directed fail to leave as soon as practicable or, having left, again enter within three months, they commit an offence

Vehicle. Vehicle includes caravan. If not removed a vehicle may be seized, s 62 Criminal Justice and Public Order Act.

Land. Includes agricultural buildings

Arrest. There is a power of arrest for a constable in uniform.

Damage. Includes depositing potentially polluting material.

Raves

> **Ss 63-66 Criminal Justice and Public Order Act 1994**

Sections 63 to 66 of the Criminal Justice and Public Order Act 1994 give powers to remove persons attending or preparing for a rave, which is defined as a gathering on land in the open air of 100 or more people (whether or not trespassers) at which amplified music is played during the night which by reason of its loudness, duration and the time at which it is played is likely to cause serious distress to the inhabitants of the locality. Other new powers include the right to enter any land (if authorised by an officer of at least the rank of superintendent) and to seize vehicles and sound systems, and the power to stop people proceeding to a rave and to arrest without warrant any person who fails to obey a direction not to proceed.

Music. Means sounds wholly or predominantly characterised by the emission of a succession of repetitive beats.

Preparing for a rave

S 63(2) CJPOA 1994

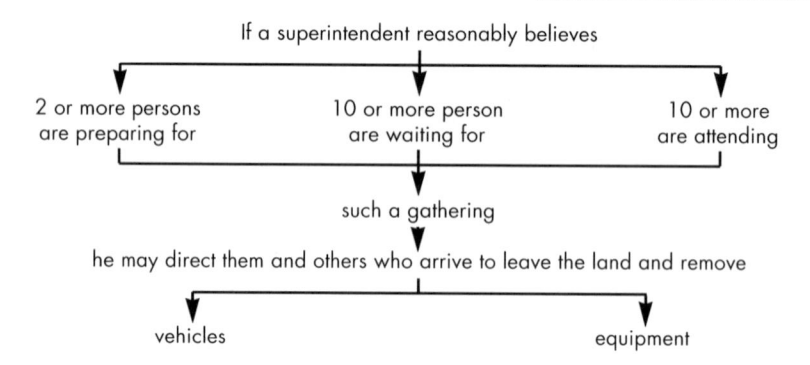

If a superintendent reasonably believes

- 2 or more persons are preparing for
- 10 or more person are waiting for
- 10 or more are attending

such a gathering

he may direct them and others who arrive to leave the land and remove
- vehicles
- equipment

Offence. To fail to leave as soon as reasonably practicable. To return to the land again within seven days.

Constable. A superintendent may authorise a constable to enter land to ascertain if an offence is being committed.

Arrest. A constable in uniform may arrest any person he suspects is committing an offence.

Defence. This section does not apply to an occupier, family, agent, employee or resident.

It is a defence to show reasonable excuse for not leaving or returning to land.

Raves - entry and seizure

S64 CJPOA 1994

If a superintendent reasonably believes that a direction under s 63 may be justified in respect of land

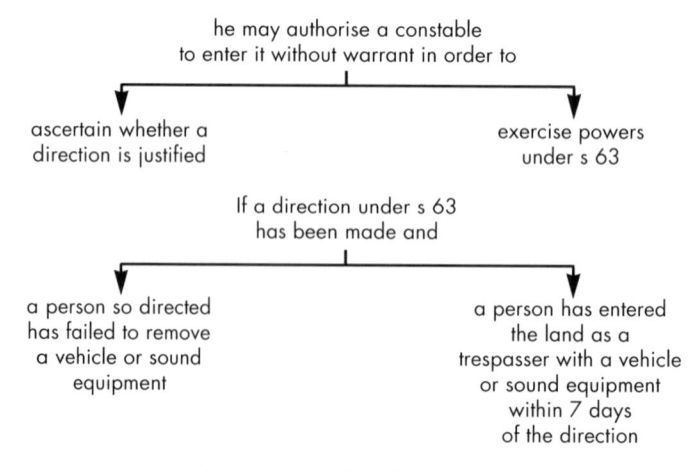

he may authorise a constable to enter it without warrant in order to
- ascertain whether a direction is justified
- exercise powers under s 63

If a direction under s 63 has been made and
- a person so directed has failed to remove a vehicle or sound equipment
- a person has entered the land as a trespasser with a vehicle or sound equipment within 7 days of the direction

a constable may **seize** the vehicle or equipment

Defence. This section does not apply to an occupier, family, agent, employee or resident.

Chapt 4: Crime 55

Power to stop rave attenders

S 65 CJPOA 1994

If a constable in uniform
is within 5 miles of the boundary of a rave
and reasonably believes
a person is en route to a gathering
to which a S 63 direction has been given
he may
▼
stop that person and
direct him **not to proceed** in the direction of the rave

Offence. It is an offence for a person so directed not to comply.

Defence. This section does not apply to the occupier, family, agent, employee or resident.

Arrest. A constable may arrest on reasonable suspicion of the offence being committed.

Litter

Litter Act 1983

It is an offence to **throw down**
▼   ▼   ▼
in   or into   or from
▼
any place
AND
leave anything whatsoever in such circumstances as to cause, contribute to,
or tend to lead to **defacement** by litter of any place in the open air

this offence is subject to **S25 PACE** *general conditional power of arrest*

Litter bins. It is an offence wilfully to remove or otherwise interfere with any litter bin or notice board provided or erected under this section or section 185 of the Highways Act 1980.

Throw down. This includes dropping or to otherwise deposit.

Any place. This means any place in the open air to which the public are entitled or permitted to have access without payment.

And leave. This offence is not complete until the discarded litter is left behind, so that an individual who accidentally drops an item must be given time to recover it.

Evidence. It is good evidence to be able to say that you alerted the culprit to the offence and invited him to recover the article which he failed to do.

Arrest. If the culprit fails to give you his name and address for the service of a summons, consider arrest under section 25 of the Police and Criminal Evidence Act 1984.

Noise

S 62 Control of Pollution Act 1974

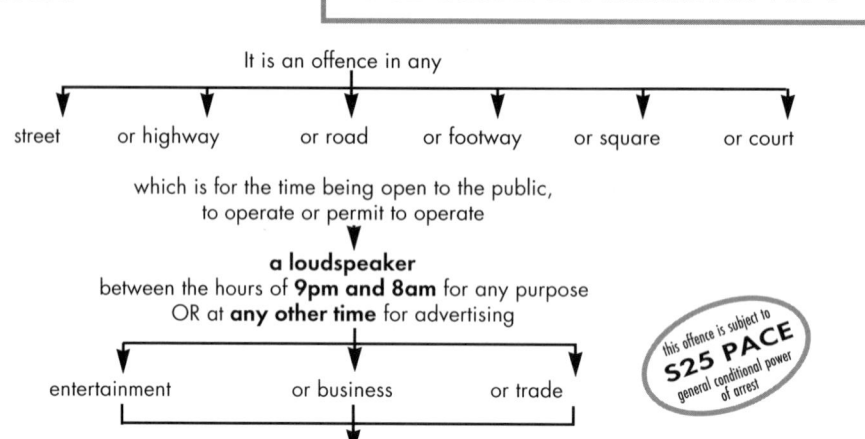

It is an offence in any **street** or **highway** or **road** or **footway** or **square** or **court** which is for the time being open to the public, to operate or permit to operate **a loudspeaker** between the hours of **9pm and 8am** for any purpose OR at **any other time** for advertising **entertainment** or **business** or **trade** except between **12 midday and 7pm** provided the loudspeaker is fixed to a vehicle carrying perishable goods for human consumption and the loudspeaker is used only for the purpose of advertising those goods in a manner which does not cause annoyance. Words may not be used

this offence is subject to S25 PACE general conditional power of arrest

Does not apply to: Emergency services, vessel movement, public telephone, passenger announcements, showmen, emergencies.

Offensive weapons

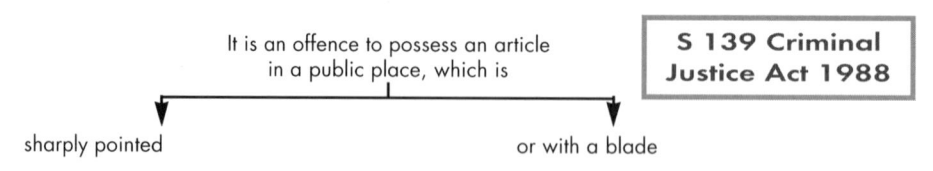

S 139 Criminal Justice Act 1988

It is an offence to possess an article in a public place, which is **sharply pointed** or **with a blade**

Pocket knives. The Act exempts folding pocket knives providing the cutting edge of the blade does not exceed three inches.

Defence. It is a defence to prove lawful authority or good reason for possession, so that articles being carried for work (eg a skinner's knife), or for religious reasons or as part of a national dress would be exempt.

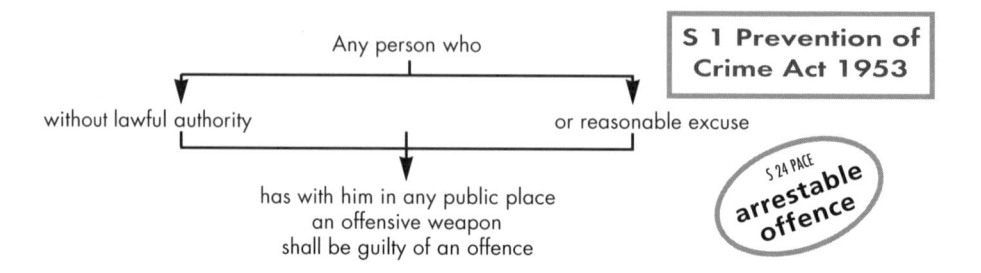

S 1 Prevention of Crime Act 1953

Any person who **without lawful authority** or **reasonable excuse** has with him in any public place an offensive weapon shall be guilty of an offence

S 24 PACE arrestable offence

Proof. The onus of proving that he had the weapon with him with lawful authority or reasonable excuse lies with the defendant, not the police.

Offensive weapon. Offensive weapon is defined as any article made or adapted for causing injury to the person, or intended by the person having it with him for such use by him or by some other person.

Made. Articles which are made to cause injury would include knuckle-dusters, flick knives, gravity knives and swordsticks. These articles have no other purpose in life, than to cause injury and are therefore offensive per se.

Adapted. Articles which are adapted to cause injury are those articles which have had their use changed. So a baseball bat spiked with nails, a broken bottle, a motor cycle chain, which has been sharpened and bound partially in masking tape to make a handle, are all adapted from their original use to become offensive.

Intended. Any other article, however inoffensive, a chair, stick, crutch, spanner, anything whatsoever, if intended for use as an offensive weapon becomes such. You have to be careful here. If I take into immediate use, say, a hammer which I am working with, and bash someone over the head with it because of a spontaneous disagreement, then this hammer would not be an article intended to be used as an offensive weapon, because I intended to use it to drive in nails. If however, I carry a walking stick for 'self-protection' then this would be intended for causing injury. When dealing with intent, you have to look into the mind of the defendant by asking him the right questions.

Lawful authority. Lawful authority covers such 'offensive' articles as a truncheon carried by a policeman, or weapons carried by members of the armed forces.

Reasonable excuse. Reasonable excuse for carrying an offensive weapon is a rare defence and usually is advanced by defendants who say they were carrying it for 'self-protection'. This is not reasonable excuse.

Public place. A public place is any place to which the public are admitted whether on payment or otherwise and would therefore cover cinemas, hospital waiting rooms etc.

Drugs

Unlawful possession of a controlled drug

S 5 Misuse of Drugs Act 1971

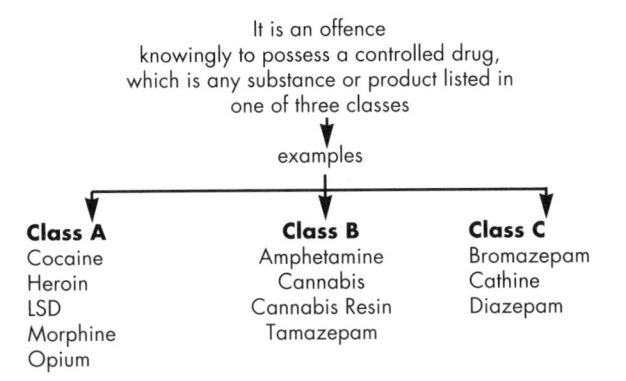

It is an offence knowingly to possess a controlled drug, which is any substance or product listed in one of three classes

examples

Class A
Cocaine
Heroin
LSD
Morphine
Opium

Class B
Amphetamine
Cannabis
Cannabis Resin
Tamazepam

Class C
Bromazepam
Cathine
Diazepam

Possession. This can be proved by the physical presence of the drug on the suspect's person but also by showing that the drug was in someone else's custody but subject to the suspect's control.

A drug which has been digested would not be a drug for the purposes of prosecution but evidence of digestion might go towards proving possession prior to consumption.

It is not necessary to prove possession of a usable quantity of drug, any quantity is sufficient, however minute, providing it amounts to something, eg, visible, tangible and able to be measured, rather than merely detectable upon laboratory analysis.

Knowingly. Knowledge of possession is required - a person cannot possess something of which he is ignorant. But ignorance or mistake as to the quality of the substance in question does not prevent the suspect being in possession of it, provided the substance is a controlled substance.

Defences. The defences to possession are:
(a) taking possession to prevent another from committing an offence, provided that he takes all reasonable steps to destroy it or deliver it to a person lawfully entitled to take it as soon as possible after taking possession of it;
(b) taking possession to deliver it into the custody of a person lawfully entitled to take it,
(c) being authorised under regulations to possess it;
(d) neither knowing or suspecting, nor having reason to suspect the existence of any fact which the prosecution must prove if the suspect is to be convicted - for example, where the suspect says he did not know the substance was a controlled drug.

Proof. The onus of proof so far as the defences are concerned lies with the suspect.

Arrest. Possession of Class A and Class B drugs is arrestable. For Class C use section 25 PACE.

Drugs - stop and search

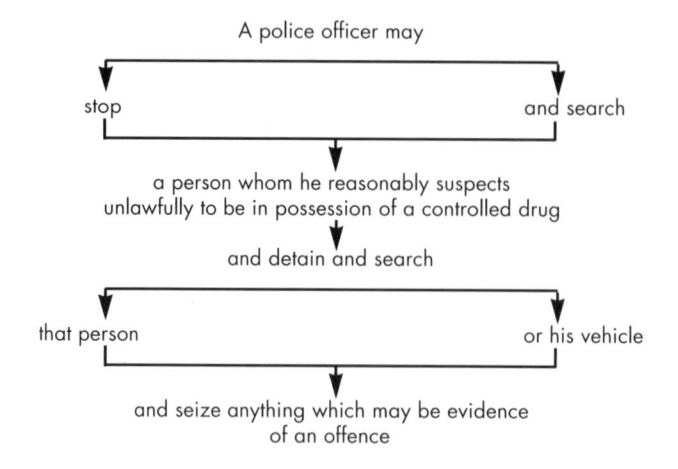

A police officer may
↓   ↓
stop   and search
↓
a person whom he reasonably suspects unlawfully to be in possession of a controlled drug
↓
and detain and search
↓   ↓
that person   or his vehicle
↓
and seize anything which may be evidence of an offence

Sexual offences

Indecent assault on a woman

> **S 14 Sexual Offences Act 1956**

It is an offence to commit an indecent assault on a woman.

S 24 PACE arrestable offence

Assault. An act by which the suspect intentionally or recklessly causes another to sustain unlawful personal violence or to apprehend unlawful violence.

Indecent. It must be shown that the assault was accompanied by a gesture of indecency, the act itself must be indecent per se.

Woman. Woman includes girl.

Intent. The suspect must intentionally assault the victim or be reckless as to whether he assaulted her or not and must intend the assault to be indecent.

Consent. Consent of the victim is a defence except if obtained by force or fraud. A person under the age of 16 years or a mental defective are incapable in law of consenting. It is not a defence for the suspect to say that he reasonably believed the victim to be over the age of 16 years.

Defence. It is a defence for the suspect to say that he did not know and had no reason to believe that the victim was a mental defective.

Note. For Unlawful Sexual Intercourse with a Girl Under 16 see 'Children' (post).

Rape

> **S 1 Sexual Offences Act 1956**

A man commits rape if

- he has sexual intercourse (whether vaginal or anal) with a man or woman who at the time of the intercourse does not consent to it
- and at that time he knows the person does not consent to the intercourse or he is reckless as to whether that person consents to it.

S 24 PACE arrestable offence

Person. Prior to 3 November 1994 when section 141 of the Criminal Justice and Public Order Act 1994 amended the Sexual Offences Act, rape could only be committed by a man against a woman. The change in wording recognises the offence of rape of a man by another man.

Proof. Proof that penetration of the vagina or anus occurred is necessary for the offence of rape. However, the prosecution do not have to prove that seed was emitted. In the absence of penetration, consider the offence of indecent assault.

Consent. If consent is obtained by fear, force or fraud, then it is not consent.

Corroboration. In practice, though not in law, corroboration is required to prove the offence. Evidence that there was an immediate, or recent complaint would be helpful, just as is evidence of bruising, torn clothing and the like.

Boys. Previously, boys under 14 years could not commit rape, being deemed physically incapable of doing so. The Sexual Offences Act 1993, s 1 abolished this presumption for acts of rape carried out on or after 19 September 1993. A child under 10 is deemed incapable of forming the necessary criminal intent.

Indecency between men (gross indecency)

S 13 Sexual Offences Act 1956

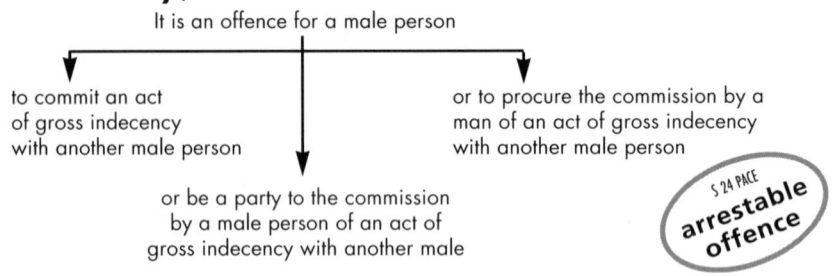

It is an offence for a male person

- to commit an act of gross indecency with another male person
- or be a party to the commission by a male person of an act of gross indecency with another male
- or to procure the commission by a man of an act of gross indecency with another male person

S 24 PACE arrestable offence

Defences. It is not an offence for a man to commit a homosexual act with another man if:
(a) the act is committed in private, and
(b) both parties consent, and
(c) two persons only are present, and,
(d) both parties have attained the age of 18. *

Private. An act of gross indecency committed in a locked cubicle of a public toilet is not protected by this Act and would therefore be an offence.

* Parliament intends to reduce this age to 16

Prostitution

S 1 Street Offences Act 1959

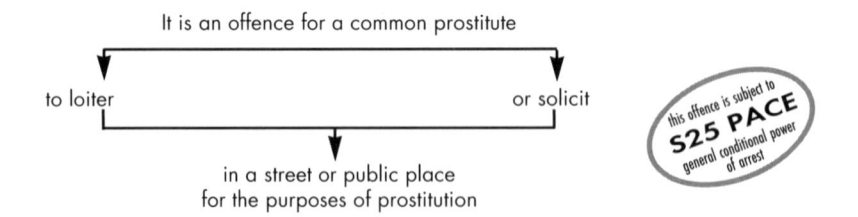

It is an offence for a common prostitute

- to loiter
- or solicit

in a street or public place for the purposes of prostitution

this offence is subject to S25 PACE general conditional power of arrest

Common prostitute. The proof that a woman is a common prostitute can be deduced from the fact that she has been cautioned by a constable for this behaviour and that she has persisted with it. The conduct or behaviour is defined as 'who for reward offers her body commonly for sexual intercourse or for acts of lewdness'. The object of the legislation is to prevent loitering and soliciting in the street and the habitual use of premises for sex.

Loiter or solicit. The prostitute does not have to make an approach to a prospective client by words or gesture. Behaviour which is alluring or tempting may be enough.

Street or public place. Street includes being on a balcony or at a window looking onto the street. A public place is any place to which the public have access whether on payment or otherwise.

Practice. In practice, a common prostitute is a woman who is either
(a) a convicted prostitute, or
(b) who has been cautioned by police twice.

The Home Office recommend that: 'where a woman has not previously been convicted of loitering or soliciting for the purposes of prostitution, she should be cautioned as to her conduct on two occasions, and such formal cautions should be recorded, before she is charged with this offence.' Where a woman complains about a caution and it appears that the constable who administered it was mistaken, the caution shall be expunged, or she may apply within 14 days to a magistrates' court for an order expunging the caution.

Kerb crawling

S 1 Sexual Offences Act 1985

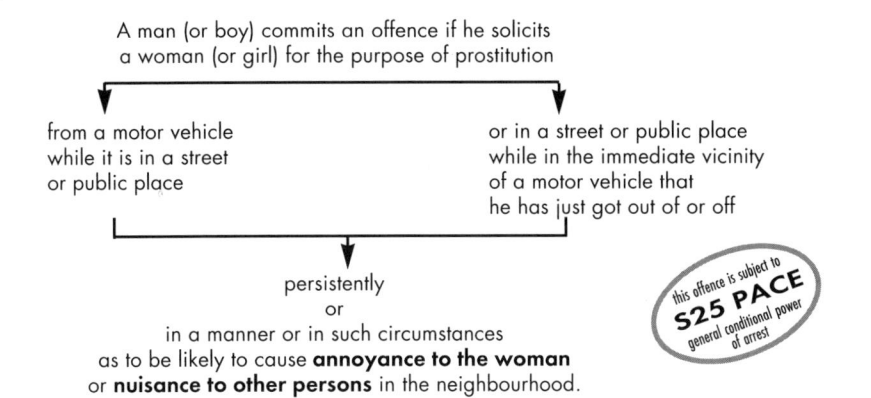

A man (or boy) commits an offence if he solicits a woman (or girl) for the purpose of prostitution

- from a motor vehicle while it is in a street or public place
- or in a street or public place while in the immediate vicinity of a motor vehicle that he has just got out of or off

persistently
or
in a manner or in such circumstances as to be likely to cause **annoyance to the woman** or **nuisance to other persons** in the neighbourhood.

this offence is subject to S25 PACE general conditional power of arrest

Note:

It is common practice for many forces to deal with the matter of kerb-crawling by way of a written letter to the private address of the registered keeper of the vehicle alerting him to the effect of the legislation.

Persistent solicitation by men

S 2 SOA 1985

A man commits an offence if, in a street or other public place, he persistently solicits a woman, or different women, for the purposes of prostitution.

Note:

This offence differs from kerb-crawling in that there is no mention here of a motor vehicle.

Persistent. Persistent means repeated behaviour, a 'one-off' attempt therefore would not amount to an offence under this section.

Indecent assault on a man

S 15 Sexual Offences Act 1956

It is an offence for a person to make an indecent assault on a man.

Consent. As with offences against women, a boy under 16 or a mentally defective man cannot give a valid consent.

this offence is subject to S25 PACE general conditional power of arrest

Drink-related offences

Drunkenness

Simple drunkenness

> S 12 Licensing Act 1872

Any person found drunk in any highway or other public place, whether a building or not, or on any licensed premises, commits an offence.

In charge

> Licensing Act 1872

Any person who is drunk while in charge on any highway or other public place of a carriage (this includes a bicycle whether being ridden or pushed, but not usually a motor car, see section 4 of the Road Traffic Act 1988) or a horse, cattle or a steam engine or who is drunk in possession of any loaded firearm, commits an offence.

Drunk and incapable

> S 1 Licensing Act 1902

Any person found drunk in any highway or other public place, whether a building or not, or on any licensed premises, and who appears to be incapable of taking care of himself, commits an offence.

Drunk in charge of a child

> S 2 Licensing Act 1902

Any person found drunk in any highway or other public place, whether a building or not, or on any licensed premises, while having the charge of a child apparently under the age of seven years, commits an offence.

Drunk and disorderly

> S 91 Criminal Justice Act 1967

Any person, who in any public place, is guilty, while drunk, of disorderly behaviour, commits an offence. Public place for these sections of the Act, includes any place to which the public have access, whether on payment or otherwise.

Licensed premises

> S 174 Licensing Act 1964

The holder of a justices' licence, may refuse to admit to, or expel from, the licensed premises, any person who is drunk, violent, quarrelsome or disorderly, or whose presence in the licensed premises would subject the the licensee to a penalty under the Act.

Permitting drunkenness

> S 172 Licensing Act 1964

Selling to, or permitting drunkenness of, a drunken person.

Role of constables

Any constable shall, on demand by the licensee, agent or servant, **help** expel any person offending under section 174 (above), and may use such force as is required.

Driving while unfit

S 4 Road Traffic Act 1988

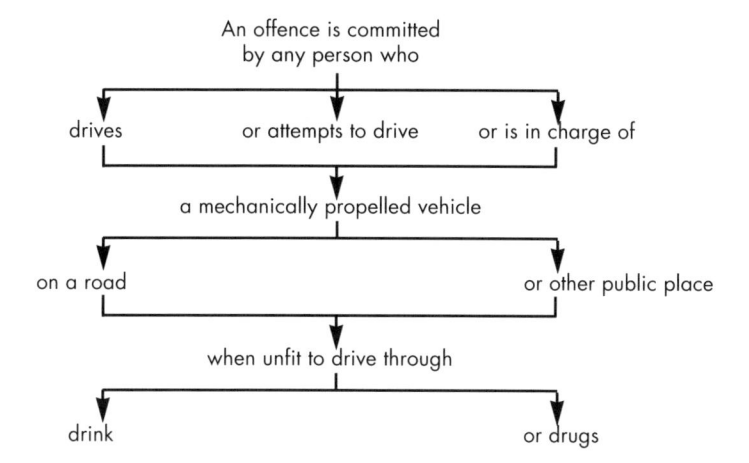

An offence is committed by any person who
- drives
- or attempts to drive
- or is in charge of

a mechanically propelled vehicle
- on a road
- or other public place

when unfit to drive through
- drink
- or drugs

Road. Any highway and any other road to which the public has access and includes bridges over which roads pass.

Public place. Any place to which the public has access at the material time.

Unfit. A person is unfit if his ability to drive is for the time being impaired.

Drink. Alcoholic drink.

Drugs. Includes any intoxicant other than alcohol, and includes any medicine taken to cure, alleviate or assist an ailing body.

Defence. A person shall be deemed not to be in charge of a motor vehicle if he proves that at the material time the circumstances were such that there was no likelihood of his driving it so long as he remained unfit to drive, or while the proportion of alcohol in his breath, blood or urine remained likely to exceed the prescribed limit. In determining whether there was such likelihood a court may disregard any injury to the person and any damage to the vehicle.

Drink driving

S 5 Road Traffic Act 1988

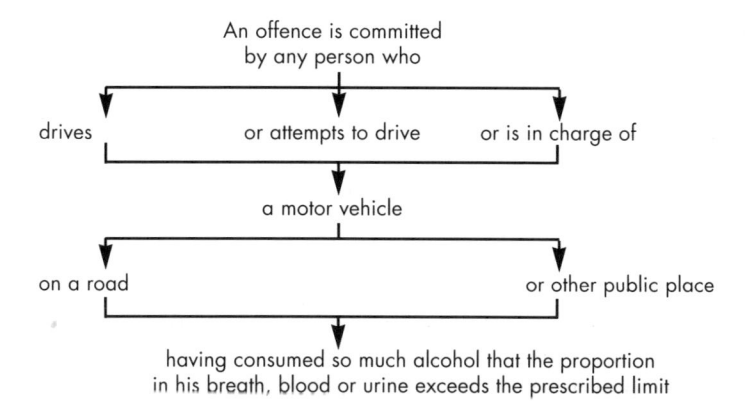

An offence is committed by any person who
- drives
- or attempts to drive
- or is in charge of

a motor vehicle
- on a road
- or other public place

having consumed so much alcohol that the proportion in his breath, blood or urine exceeds the prescribed limit

Prescribed limit. 35 microgrammes of alcohol in 100 millilitres of breath, 80 milligrammes of alcohol in 100 millilitres of blood, or 107 milligrammes of alcohol in 100 millilitres of urine.

Defence. A person shall be deemed not to be in charge of a motor vehicle if he proves that at the material time the circumstances were such that there was no likelihood of his driving it so long as he remained unfit.

Breath test powers

S 6 Road Traffic Act 1988

A constable **in uniform** may require a person to provide a specimen of breath for a breath test if he has reasonable cause to suspect

- that a person driving or attempting to drive or in charge of a motor vehicle on a road or public place has alcohol in his body or has committed a traffic offence while the vehicle was in motion

- that a person **has been** driving or attempting to drive, or **been in charge** of, a motor vehicle on a road or public place with alcohol in his body and that he still has alcohol in his body

- that a person **has been** driving or attempting to drive or **been in charge** of a motor vehicle on a road or public place and has committed a traffic offence while the vehicle was in motion

When an accident has occurred owing to the presence of a motor vehicle on a road or other public place a constable in uniform may require any person whom he has reasonable cause to believe was driving or attempting to drive or in charge of the vehicle at the time of the accident to take a breath test.

Arrest. A person who, without reasonable excuse, fails or refuses to provide a specimen of breath is guilty of an offence and may be arrested if the constable has reason to believe that he has alcohol in his body, unless the person is in hospital as a patient.

Administering a breath test

There are two types of breath test devices. The hand-held Lion Alcolmeter S-L2A, used by officers on the streets, and the Lion 3000 Intoximeter used by custody officers at police stations. The special constable on patrol may be required to use the hand-held device and therefore needs to be proficient in its use.

> While reading these instructions it is useful to have a device to hand. To check the device press the 'READ' button and hold down for 10 seconds and observe the display. Only the green 'BAT' and 'READY' lights should come on. If the amber light comes on, depress and lock the 'SET' button and wait two minutes before checking the device again.

> To set the device, depress and lock the 'SET' button. Now attach a mouthpiece to the device ensuring a firm connection. To take a sample of breath explain the procedure to the subject.

> The subject should fill his lungs and blow one continuous breath through the lipped-edge, wide bore end of the mouthpiece. He must blow strongly enough to bring on light A and long enough to bring on light B. If he fails to do this then he has failed and may be subject to arrest.

> When light B is illuminated, press the 'READ' button and tell the subject to stop blowing. Now observe the reading.

> Observe the display lights as they rise to a maximum reading after approximately 30 seconds and then interpret them.

Interpretation of display

The highest level shown on the display indicates the blood alcohol level of the subject to be as follows:

RED	Blood alcohol above 80mg per 100ml	POSITIVE TEST
RED/AMBER	Blood alcohol between 70 and 80mg per 100ml	NEGATIVE TEST
AMBER	Blood alcohol between five and 70mg per 100ml	NEGATIVE TEST
GREEN	Blood alcohol less than five mg per 100ml	NEGATIVE TEST

Each test must be preceded by a satisfactory READY CHECK. Twenty minutes should elapse between the consumption of alcohol and the use of the device. Don't allow the subject to hold the device or blow tobacco smoke through it. Store the unit with the 'SET' button depressed. Avoid extremes of temperature.

Children

Numerous Acts of Parliament deal with the care, supervision, custody, employment, education, etc, of children. Before looking in detail at these Acts it is important to have an understanding of the ages that are fixed by law:

Under five years

> S 5 Children and Young Persons Act 1933

Any person who gives, or causes to be given to any child under the age of five years, any intoxicating liquor, except upon the order of a medical practitioner, or in case of sickness, shall be guilty of an offence.

Five years and over

> S 10 CYPA 1933

If a person habitually wanders from place to place and takes with him any child who has attained the age of five, and if it is proved that the child or young person is not receiving efficient full-time education suitable to his age, ability and aptitude, and to any special educational need he may have, that person shall be guilty of an offence.

Under seven years

> S 2 Licensing Act 1902

Any person found drunk in a public place with a child apparently under seven years of age shall be guilty of an offence.

Under 10 years

> S 50 CYPA 1933

It shall be conclusively presumed that no child under the age of 10 years can be guilty of any offence.

Under 12 years

> S 11 CYPA 1933

Any person who has attained the age of 16 years, having the responsibility for any child under the age of 12 years, allows the child to be in any room containing an open fire grate, or any heating appliance liable to cause injury, with insufficient protection against the risk of being burnt or scalded, resulting in the child being killed or suffering serious injury, shall be guilty of an offence.

> S 24 CYPA 1963

No person under the age of 12 years shall be trained to take part in performances of a dangerous nature, and any person who causes or procures him to be so trained shall be guilty of an offence. A local authority may grant a licence for such training when a person has attained the age of 12 years but is under 18.

> S 3 Pet Animals Act 1951

If any person sells an animal as a pet to a person whom he has reasonable cause to believe to be under the age of 12 years, he shall be guilty of an offence.

Under 13 years

S 18 CYPA 1933

No child shall be employed under the age of 13 years:
(a) before the close of school hours on any day which he is required to be at school;
(b) before seven am or after seven pm on any day;
(c) for more than two hours on any day on which he is required to attend school;
(d) for more than two hours on any Sunday; or
(e) to lift, carry or move anything so heavy as to be likely to cause him injury. Local authorities may make bye-laws governing this subject.

Under 14 years

The common law rule that a child **Common Law** under the age of 14 was presumed not to have a guilty intent unless it could be shown that he knew his act was seriously wrong was found to be obsolete in the March 1994 case of *C v DPP.*

Between 10 and 14 years - It must be shown that the child knew the act was wrong.

A licensee shall not allow a person under **S 168 Licensing Act 1964** the age of 14 years to be in the bar of licensed premises during permitted hours **unless** the child is:
1. the licencee's child;
2. a resident's child and so lives in the building;
3. a child passing through to another part of the building;
4 in a railway rest room;
5. there is a child certificate in force.

Under 16 years

It is an offence for a person to **S 7 CYPA 1933** sell to a person apparently under the age of 16 years any tobacco or cigarette papers. A constable must seize any tobacco or cigarette papers from a person apparently under 16 who is found smoking in a public place.

The Fireworks (Safety) Regulations 1986

Gunpowder shall not be sold to a person apparently under the age of 16 years. It is also an offence to sell fireworks to a person under 16 years.

Any person having responsibility for of a child who has attained the age **S 3 CYPA 1933** of four years and is under the age of 16 years who allows that child to reside in or frequent a brothel shall be guilty of an offence.

Any person who causes or **S 4 CYPA 1963** procures a person under the age of 16 years in any street, premises or place to beg or receive shall be guilty of an offence.

Persons under the age of 16 years are disqualified from driving motor vehicles by reason of age.

It is an offence for a man to **S 6 Sexual Offences Act 1956** have unlawful sexual intercourse with a girl under 16 years of age.

Defence - A man is not guilty of this offence if he is under 24 years of age - and has not previously been charged with a like offence - and believed the girl to be over 16 years of age - and had reasonable cause for his belief.

Under 17 years

No person under the age of 17 years of age [CYPA 1963] may be employed in street trading; local authorities may pass by-laws allowing employment by their parents.

A person under arrest at a police [S 38(1) PACE] station who has not attained the age of 17 years shall be bailed unless he ought to be detained in his own interest.

[House to House Collections Act 1939]

No person may be employed in street or house to house collections until he has attained the age of 16 years or is a member of a youth organisation.

Under 18 years

It shall be an offence to tattoo a person under the age of 18 except when the tattoo is performed for medical reasons by a qualified medical practitioner or by a person working under his directions. [S 1 Tattooing of Minors Act 1969]

[Licensing Act 1964]

It is an offence for a licensee or his servant, on licensed premises, to sell intoxicating liquor to a person under 18 or to knowingly allow him to consume intoxicating liquor in a bar. [S 169]

Note - it is permitted for a person of 16 to consume or buy beer, porter, cider or perry for consumption with a table meal.

Section 170 prohibits the employment of someone under the age of 18 behind a bar when it is open for the sale of intoxicating liquor. [S 170]

Prevention of cruelty to children [S 1 CYPA 1933]

Section 1 of the Children and Young Persons Act 1933, as amended, deals with offences in connection with children. For the purposes of the Act:

A child - is a person under the age of 14 years.

A young person - is a person who has attained the age of 14 years and is under 17 years.

An adult - is a person who, in the opinion of the court, has attained the age of 17 years.

Offences. If any person who has attained the age of 16 years, having the **custody, charge or care** of any child or young person under that age, wilfully **assaults, ill-treats, neglects, abandons, or exposes** that child in a manner likely to cause him unnecessary suffering or injury to health (including injury to or loss of sight, or hearing, or limb or organ of the body, and any mental derangement), that person shall be guilty of an offence.

Assault. An assault can be caused by a genuine lack of understanding through stupidity. Ignorance or personal inadequacy is a defence.

Ill-treats. If a child is under the control of both parents and there is no evidence to point to which one has ill-treated the child, then the inference may be drawn that they were jointly responsible.

Neglects. Failure to provide adequate food, clothing, medical aid or lodgings.

Abandons. Abandons means to leave the child to its fate.

Exposes. The exposure need not consist of the physical placing of the child somewhere with the intention of injuring it. Intent is not necessary.

Criminal damage

S 1(1) Criminal Damage Act 1971

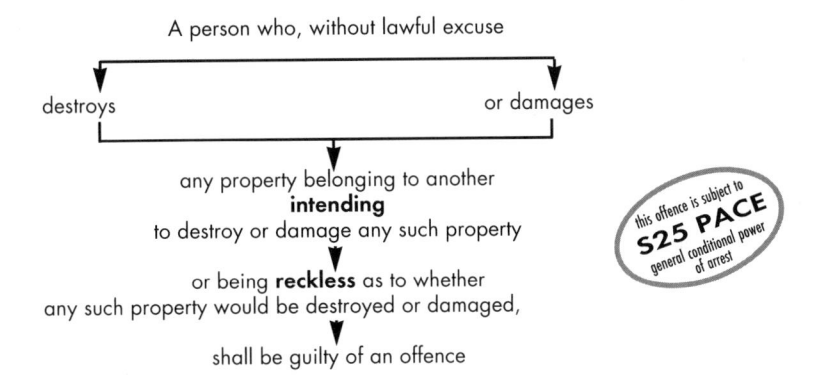

A person who, without lawful excuse
destroys or damages
any property belonging to another
intending
to destroy or damage any such property
or being **reckless** as to whether
any such property would be destroyed or damaged,
shall be guilty of an offence

this offence is subject to S25 PACE general conditional power of arrest

Without lawful excuse. Having a lawful excuse actually excuses many acts of damage, eg police officers entering premises under the authority of a warrant, fire officers who are engaged in making forceable entry into premises where there is fire or suspected fire, recovery vehicles putting right a disabled car following an accident, forced entry into a house by ambulance personnel to recover an ill or injured person. Lawful excuse is honestly held by such people behaving in this manner.

Where, however, there is no lawful excuse and the damage done is intentional then this becomes an offence under the Act. If there is no intent see 'recklessness'.

Destroys. A distinction has to be made between destruction and damage. So far as destroys or destruction is concerned, this imports the notion of laying to waste, depriving of life, reducing to nominal value. A broken window is therefore destroyed.

Damage. Damage, while still offensive, is something less in tangible terms than the notion of destroys or destruction. It is the idea of reducing a property's value, such as the cost of putting right paint splashed on a car, or dents to the bodywork, or even letting all four tyres down on a vehicle whereby the wheel-rims are slightly bent. These would amount to damage, so long as there is a reduction in value.

Damaging own property. Damaging or destroying property one owns, for example during a domestic dispute, is a matter for the owner and does not amount to an offence.

Be careful when attending domestic disputes because if, following an arrest, usually of a man, it is discovered that he actually owns or jointly owns the property, the charge will be refused.

Animals. While there is other legislation to deal with cruelty to animals, animals may be destroyed or damaged under the provisions of this Act. To kill a dog belonging to someone else is an offence because it has been destroyed. If the animal is injured to a point whereby it needs the attention of a vet, then clearly its value is reduced and therefore it is damaged.

This equally applies to wild creatures which have been tamed or are ordinarily kept in captivity. A pet snake therefore, or an animal ordinarily kept in a zoo, may be damaged or destroyed.

Where there is destruction of or damage to a wild animal, you will need to look at other legislation.

Belonging to another. Property shall be treated for the purpose of the Act as belonging to any person:

(a) having custody or control of it;
(b) having a proprietary right or interest in it; or,
(c) having a charge over it. Note that section 1(2) provides for the offence of damaging or destroying any property (which includes the offender's property) either intentionally or recklessly but with the additional intention of endangering the life of another (or being reckless as to its endangerment).

Recklessness. Recklessness is the idea of shutting one's eyes to the risks embarked upon, and nevertheless going on to take the risk. So that if I throw a brick at a man standing in front of a shop window and he ducks, resulting in the brick breaking the window, then my act could be seen as being reckless. The mind of each person must be considered because, what is obvious to the average person may not be obvious to someone who is, say, intellectually disadvantaged.

Possessing items to cause damage. Any person who has anything in his custody or under his control intending, without lawful excuse, to use it or cause or permit another to use it:

(a) to destroy or damage any property belonging to another; or,
(b) to destroy or damage his own or the user's property in a way which he knows is likely to endanger the life of another,

commits an offence. This section should be borne in mind during the course of stop searches; items such as spray paint, metal punches and the like may well be being carried for illicit purposes.

Arson. Offences of causing damage or destruction to property if caused by fire should be charged as arson.

To aid and abet, counsel or procure

If a person aids, abets, counsels or procures another to commit a crime, then he is liable to be tried and punished as though he were a principal to the commission of the offence. These terms mean:

Aid and abet. To give support or help to someone to do something to assist or encourage in wrongdoing.

Counsel. To talk over, giving advice or guidance.

Procure. Take steps to ensure that a crime is committed.

> S 44 Magistrates' Courts Act 1980, S 8 Accessories and Abettors Act 1861

Crime and Disorder Act 1998

The main focus of the Crime and Disorder Act is young offenders and community safety. The Act came into force (in part) on October 1, 1998.

Community safety

The community safety element of the Act stems from the 1991 Morgan Report, *Safer Communities - the local delivery of crime prevention through the partnership approach*. The Act requires the police to develop strategies alongside local authorities to create safer environments and reduce crime. Many specials will rightly say that they have spent much of their duty time involved in just such projects. However, the difference now is that all parties have a statutory responsibility to implement a joint policy to reduce crime. In theory these joint strategies will help reduce the workload of officers in the long term, but it would seem unavoidable that additional time and training will be required in getting them up and running.

Youth crime

The stated object of the Act is crime prevention. A Youth Justice Board will have an inspectorate role to identify good practice throughout the country. It will have the power to call for reports from any local authority. Each local authority area is to set up its own multi-agency 'youth offending team'.

It is also intended that the Crime and Disorder Act will replace police cautions with a system of reprimands and final warnings. Any young person receiving a final warning will be set a programme of 'intervention and diversion' by the local 'youth offending team'- and reprimands and final warnings will be cited with convictions. Only in exceptional circumstances can a young person receive a second warning and the use of conditional discharges by the youth court are to be virtually abolished.

Significant new orders introduced by the Act

Parenting Order

The purpose of the Parenting Order is to recognise and reinforce the importance of the family in providing a positive influence.

It requires the parents of a young offender to attend weekly guidance sessions for up to three months and any other requirements placed upon them by the court for up to 12 months. The onus is on the court to make an order for all 10- 16-year-olds it convicts - or to explain why such an order is not required.

Child curfew scheme

The curfew can be imposed by the local authority on a child under 10 years of age. The Scheme is designed to be used to exclude children of this age group from defined public places and during specified hours unless they are under the effective control of a person aged 18 or over

Child Safety Order

Again for children under 10 years of age, the purpose of the Child Safety Order is to impose supervision upon children who, but for their age, would be convicted of an offence or subjected to an Antisocial Behaviour Order. It can also be imposed upon a child who has broken the requirements of a curfew notice. The order may run for three or 12 months.

Reparation Order

A Reparation Order enables the court, subject to the wishes of the victim, to direct a youth to undertake up to 24 hours' work - for an individual or the community - in reparation for his offence. Supervision Orders will be amended to take this order into account.

Action Plan Order

The Action Plan Order, which has the authority of a court order, provides for more than mere reparation. It enforces a three-month regulatory plan of action to improve the role of offenders in the community. The Action Plan regulates where they go, whom they contact and what they do.

Detention and Training Order

The purpose this Order is to divert young offenders away from prison. It is generally designed for those aged 15 years and over but may be used for children:
a. under the age of 15 years if they are persistent offenders; or
b. under 12 years if a custodial sentence would be the only alternative.

Drug Treatment and Testing Order

This provides the court with an alternative to sentencing an offender if it is satisfied he is dependent upon or misuses drugs. However the offender must be a person whom it is believed is 'suitable' and who will be susceptible to treatment. The Order may then specify a treatment and testing period of from six months up to three years.

Antisocial Behaviour Order

This Order is designed to deal with the problem of, for example, gangs of nuisance youths, or harassment from neighbours. The Order can be obtained by way of complaint by the police and local authority to the magistrates. If heard in a magistrates' court the usual penalties apply as for breach of the peace. In an upper court the Order carries a maximum of five years' imprisonment and an unlimited fine.

Sex Offender Order

A Sex Offender Order, which is effective for five years, can be obtained in a magistrate's court on the evidence of a police officer. The officer must identify a known sex offender and, on behalf of the chief officer of police, explain why the order is necessary to protect the public.

CHAPTER 5

THEFT

Chapter contents

Theft Act 1968 72
    Dishonestly 72
    Appropriates 73
    Property 73
        Land 73
            Things growing wild 74
            Wild creatures 74
    Belonging to another 75
    Permanently deprive 75
    Taking a conveyance 76
    Aggravated vehicle taking 76
    Robbery 77
    Burglary 78
    Aggravated burglary 79
    Abstracting electricity 79
    Obtaining property by deception 80
    Blackmail 81
    Handling stolen goods 82
    Going equipped for stealing 83
Theft Act 1978 83
    Obtaining services by deception 83
    Making off without payment 83
Vehicle interference 84

Theft Act 1968

A person is guilty of theft if he

dishonestly appropriates property belonging to another with the intention of permanently depriving the other of it;

and 'thief' and 'steal' shall be construed accordingly.

S 24 PACE arrestable offence

`S 1`

Dishonestly...

`S 2`

A person's appropriation of property belonging to another is not to be regarded as dishonest:
- (a) if he appropriates the property in the belief that he has in law the right to deprive the other of it, on behalf of himself or of a third person;
- (b) if he appropriates the property in the belief that he would have the other's consent if the other knew of the appropriation and the circumstances of it; or
- (c) if he appropriates the property in the belief that the person to whom the property belongs cannot be discovered by taking reasonable steps.

A person's appropriation of property belonging to another may be dishonest notwithstanding that he is willing to pay for the property.

Belief in law. Where there is an honest and subjective belief that he has in law the right to deprive the other of it, then this may not be dishonest. Where an individual mistakenly takes property belonging to another then so long as his mistake is genuine and reasonable the taking would not amount to being dishonest under this section.

The other's consent. It would not be a defence in law to remove a stranger's property in the 'hope' or somehow 'just knowing' that he would have consented if he had known all the facts. But where, say, a friend removed property in the absence of the owner, there would be a strong case to say that he believed the owner would have consented had he known who took it and all the circumstances.

Reasonable steps. It is not dishonest to appropriate property if there is a belief that the owner cannot be discovered by taking reasonable steps. So if a purse is found and the owner's name and address is contained therein, then it should be returned to the owner or to the police station. If however, a 20p piece is found at, say, a football match, then it would clearly be unreasonable to take the steps necessary to find the owner and so pocketing the money would not amount to an offence.

appropriates... `S 2`

Any assumption by a person of the rights of an owner amounts to an appropriation, and this includes, where he has come by the property (innocently or not) without stealing it, any later assumption of a right to it by keeping or dealing with it as owner.

Where property or a right or interest in property is or purports to be transferred for value to a person in good faith, no later assumption by him of rights which he believed himself to be acquiring shall, by any defect in the transfer's title, amount to theft of the property.

Assumption of ownership. When property comes into possession, without a theft taking place, eg found property, borrowed property and the like, the moment the possessor deals with that property as though he is the owner then he is guilty of theft. So where an individual borrows a ladder from a friend, and subsequently sells it without permission, then the appropriation is complete. Where a shopkeeper makes a mistake in giving change, so that the purchaser finds himself say £5 up, if the purchaser is aware of the mistake but nevertheless continues to keep the change then the appropriation is complete.

Good faith. Where a person comes into possession of property for value in good faith then he is not guilty of appropriation. For value means in exchange or something, usually money, and good faith means an honest belief.

property... `S 4`

Property includes money and all other property, real or personal, including things in action (in law a 'chose in action' is a right over property which can only be enforced by court action, not by physically taking possession of it, eg a debt) and other intangible property.

Land

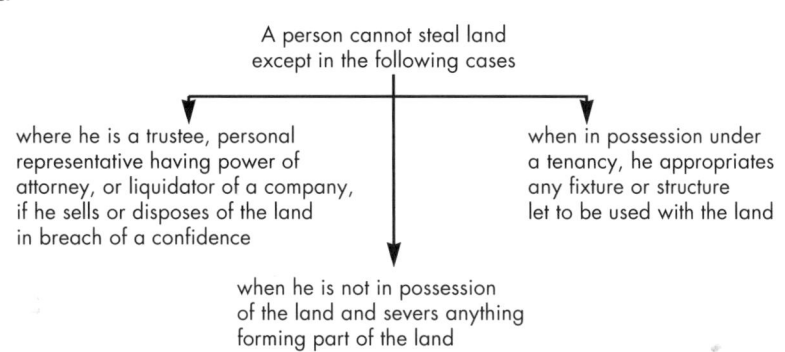

A person cannot steal land except in the following cases

- where he is a trustee, personal representative having power of attorney, or liquidator of a company, if he sells or disposes of the land in breach of a confidence

- when he is not in possession of the land and severs anything forming part of the land

- when in possession under a tenancy, he appropriates any fixture or structure let to be used with the land

Things growing wild

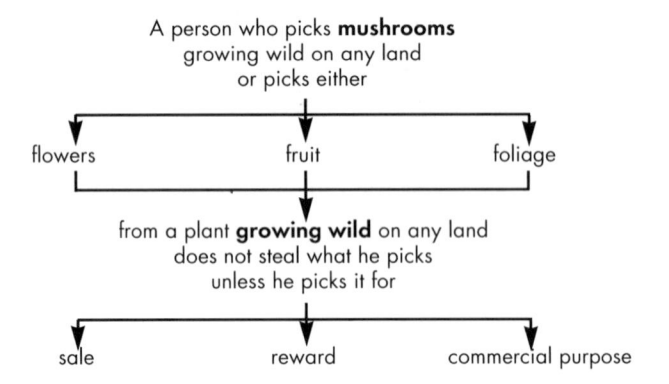

```
         A person who picks mushrooms
              growing wild on any land
                 or picks either
    ┌──────────────────┼──────────────────┐
    ▼                  ▼                  ▼
 flowers             fruit             foliage
    └──────────────────┼──────────────────┘
           from a plant growing wild on any land
                does not steal what he picks
                   unless he picks it for
    ┌──────────────────┼──────────────────┐
    ▼                  ▼                  ▼
   sale             reward         commercial purpose
```

Things growing wild. So long as the mushrooms, flowers, fruit or foliage are actually growing wild, on any land, then the picker commits no offence even if the land does not belong to him. He must not however, sever, ie dig into the sub-soil to remove the whole plant as this would amount to theft. By picking only part of the plant it will be able to recover and grow.

If the picker is making some kind of business out of the plants then this becomes an offence and he is guilty of theft.

So people walking in the forest picking bluebells which are growing wild, commit no offence. If they subsequently decide to go from door to door with a view to selling the bluebells, then the picking becomes an act of theft.

Wild creatures

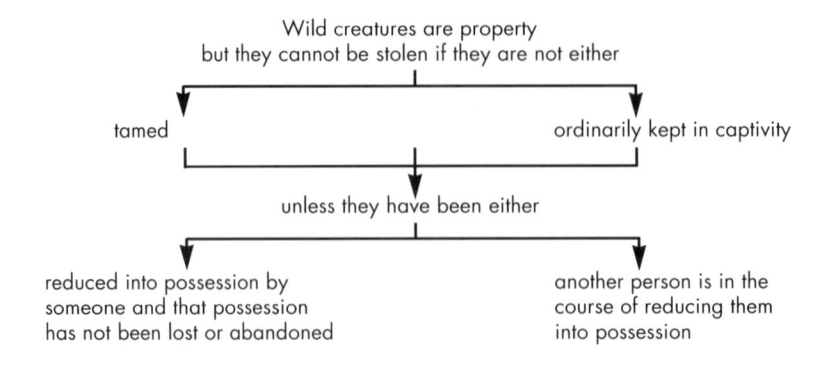

```
             Wild creatures are property
     but they cannot be stolen if they are not either
    ┌──────────────────┼──────────────────┐
    ▼                                     ▼
  tamed                          ordinarily kept in captivity
    └──────────────────┼──────────────────┘
               unless they have been either
    ┌──────────────────┼──────────────────┐
    ▼                                     ▼
 reduced into possession by        another person is in the
 someone and that possession       course of reducing them
 has not been lost or abandoned    into possession
```

Wild creatures. Animals kept in zoos clearly are kept in captivity and can therefore be stolen just as can any domestic creature, dogs, cats etc.

Reduced into possession. Where a wild creature has been shot, netted, captured or in any way taken into possession, then it belongs to the captor, so long as he does not lose or abandon his catch.

Belonging to another... **S 4**

Property cannot be stolen unless it belongs to another. Property shall be regarded as belonging to any person having

- possession
- control
- proprietary right or interest

Possession. Possession lies usually with the owner so that all your worldly possessions are capable of being stolen as they belong to you.

There may come a time when you part with your property or even abandon it (to the dustbin) when the question of ownership becomes increasingly vexed.

Possession (as contrasted with ownership) may be given temporarily to another in circumstances whereby the other acquires a 'pecuniary interest' in the property. So that a car being serviced is in the possession of the garage proprietor and any unauthorised removal by the owner with a view to avoiding payment of the bill will be theft.

Control. While a person may not be in physical possession of his property, he nevertheless maintains control over it, rather like leaving a car in a car park. A person employed as a storeman will, of course, possess all goods in the store, but the employing company controls those goods and any theft would be against either the storeman, the possessor, or the company with control. If the company chairman comes to the store and removes goods, unknown to the storeman, with a view to the storeman making up the loss then he is guilty of theft.

Theft by finding. Where property of value is left unattended and there is no evidence of its having been abandoned, then its removal amounts to theft. This 'defence' is often advanced by pedal cycle thieves.

With the intention of permanently depriving another of it **S 6**

A person appropriating property belonging to another without meaning the other permanently to lose the thing itself, is nevertheless to be regarded as having the intention of permanently depriving the other of it - if his intention is to treat the thing as his own to dispose of regardless of the other's rights. A borrowing or lending of it may amount to so treating it if, but only if, the borrowing or lending is for a period and in circumstances making it equivalent to an outright taking or disposal.

Borrowing/lending. Whenever there is a borrowing or lending there are expressed or implied conditions as to the return of the property.

So that if you say to a neighbour 'can I borrow your car to pop into town', but then keep the car for a month - although intending to return the car sooner or later, you cannot rely on that as a defence because you have treated it as your own, regardless of the owner's rights. The borrowing or lending is for a period and in circumstances which make it equivalent to an outright taking.

Consumed value. Were you to ask a friend at the beginning of the football season if you could borrow his season ticket as you knew he could not see the match because of work commitments, and then you kept hold of the ticket and used it throughout the season to see all the matches - then the value of the ticket decreases with the passing of each weekend. Clearly you would be treating the thing as your own to dispose of quite regardless of the other's rights and would therefore be guilty of theft.

Conditional parting. Where a person parts with someone else's property under a condition for its return which he may not be able to perform, then this amounts to treating the property as his own. So if you borrowed a friend's new bike and lent it to a total stranger who promised its return and failed in that promise, then you would be liable under this section.

Taking motor vehicle or other conveyance without authority

S 12

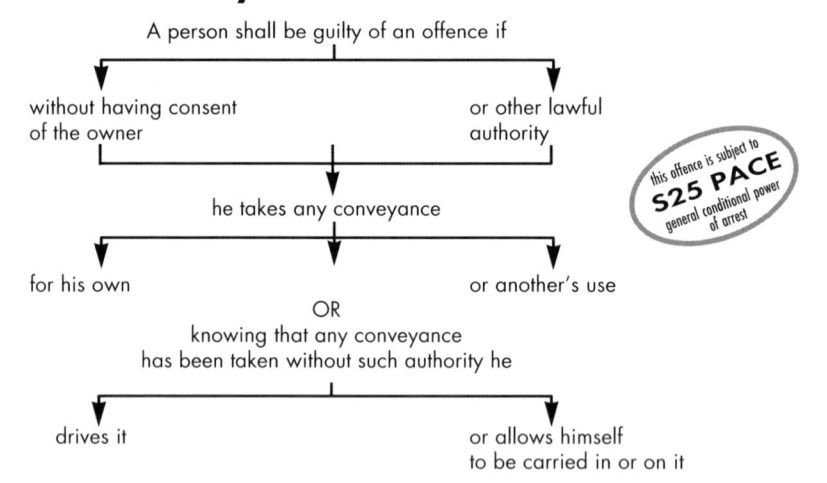

```
                A person shall be guilty of an offence if
                                  |
        ┌─────────────────────────┴─────────────────────────┐
        ▼                                                   ▼
   without having consent                            or other lawful
   of the owner                                      authority
        └─────────────────────────┬─────────────────────────┘
                                  ▼
                        he takes any conveyance
        ┌─────────────────────────┴─────────────────────────┐
        ▼                                                   ▼
    for his own                                      or another's use
                                  OR
                        knowing that any conveyance
                  has been taken without such authority he
        ┌─────────────────────────┴─────────────────────────┐
        ▼                                                   ▼
     drives it                                    or allows himself
                                                  to be carried in or on it
```

this offence is subject to **S25 PACE** *general conditional power of arrest*

Theft or taking. If on a trial for theft the jury are not satisfied that the accused is guilty of theft, but it is proved that the accused committed this offence, then he may be convicted of taking.

Defence. A person does not commit an offence under this section by anything done in the belief that he has lawful authority to do it, or that he would have the owner's consent if the owner knew of his doing it and the circumstances of it.

Conveyance. Conveyance means any conveyance constructed or adapted for the carriage of a person or persons whether by land, water or air, but not a pedestrian controlled vehicle.

Aggravated vehicle taking

On April 1, 1992, a new offence was created of an aggravated form of the offence under section 12 of the Theft Act 1968. Any person committing an offence under section 12, of taking, or being carried, is guilty of the aggravated offence if any of the following circumstances occurs after the taking of the vehicle but before its recovery:
    (a) the vehicle was driven dangerously on a road or other public place; or,
    (b) owing to the driving of the vehicle, an accident occurred causing injury to any person, including the driver; or,

(c) owing to the driving of the vehicle, an accident occurred causing damage to any property other than the vehicle; or,
(d) damage was caused to the vehicle.

It is sufficient for the aggravated offence, to prove that the offence under section 12 was committed and that an aggravated circumstance occurred. It is not necessary to establish that a particular defendant was directly responsible for the aggravated circumstance.

> S 12A

Note:

The offence carries obligatory disqualification.

Time. This offence is not subject to a time limit on prosecution.

Defence. There is a defence if the aggravating circumstance occurred before the defendant committed the basic offence under section 12 or if he can prove that he was neither in or on, nor in the immediate vicinity of the vehicle when the aggravated circumstance occurred. If a defence is successful, the defendant can still be found guilty of an offence under section 12.

Robbery

> S 8

This offence is usually described by the public and media as mugging

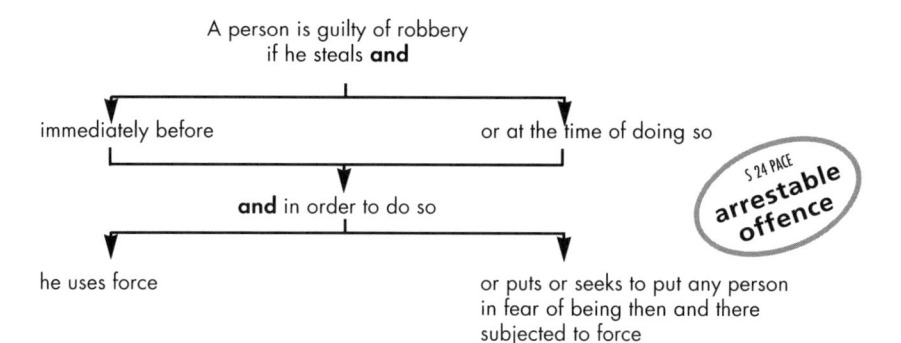

A person is guilty of robbery if he steals **and**

- immediately before
- or at the time of doing so

and in order to do so

- he uses force
- or puts or seeks to put any person in fear of being then and there subjected to force

S 24 PACE arrestable offence

Steals. Steals has the same meaning as theft so steal and thief shall be construed accordingly.

Immediately before. Force used immediately before the theft must be in order to commit the theft.

If 'A' punches 'B' in the mouth and then, as an after-thought, decides to take B's wallet, this would be both theft and ABH, not robbery. If however the motive for the assault is theft, then this would be robbery.

Uses force on any person. The force used to commit the theft (thereby making it robbery) need not necessarily be against the loser of the property. So if a man stops a mother and daughter in the street and holds the daughter, calling on the mother to hand over her purse, this is robbery.

Putting any person in fear. Again, to threaten 'B' that if 'A' does not hand over his wallet then 'B' will become a casualty will amount to robbery.

Burglary

S 9

A person is guilty of burglary if he enters

- a building
- or part of a building

as a trespasser and with intent

- to steal anything in the building or part of the building
- to inflict on any person therein grievous bodily harm
- to rape any person therein
- to do unlawful damage to the building or part of the building

S 24 PACE arrestable offence

or having entered

- a building
- or part of a building

as a trespasser

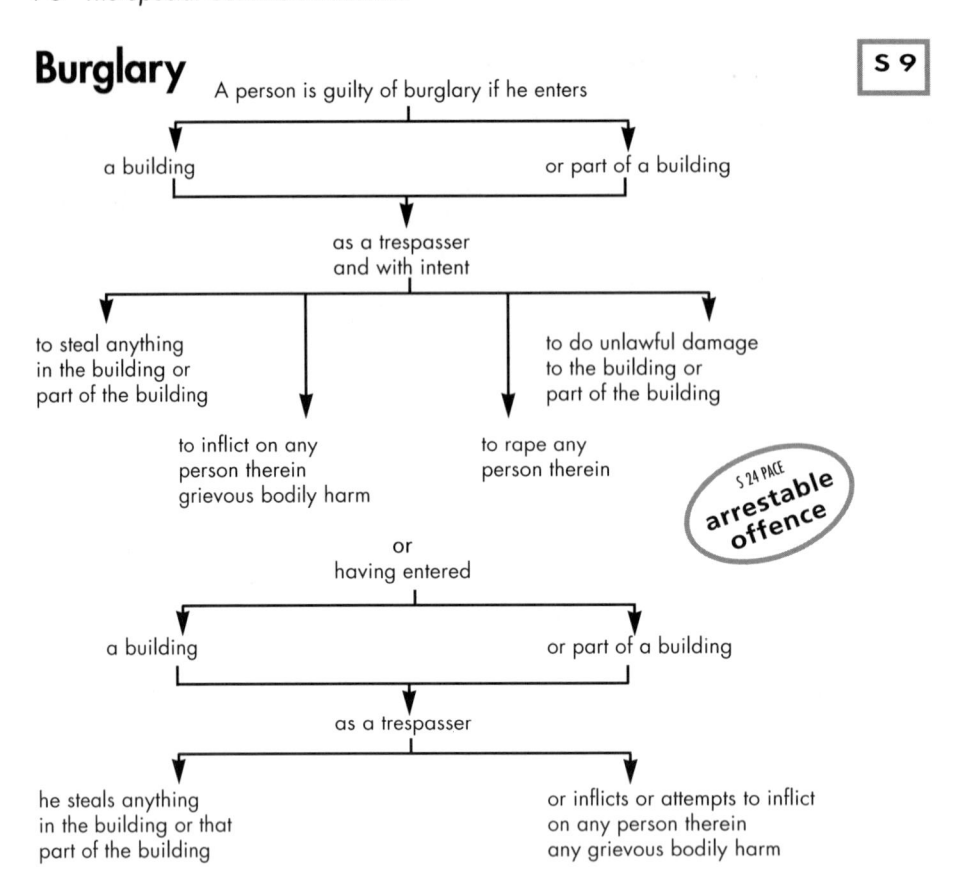

- he steals anything in the building or that part of the building
- or inflicts or attempts to inflict on any person therein any grievous bodily harm

Building. Building shall apply also to an inhabited vehicle or vessel, and shall apply to any such vehicle or vessel at times when the person living in it is not there, as well as when he is.

Enters. The whole body of the burglar need not enter the building. It is enough that a would-be thief puts a hand through a window in order to steal or, possibly, a hook through a letter box, so long as the entry is effective

Part of a building. The phrase part of a building is intended to protect the parts of buildings that are not intended for use by the public. So a thief in Woolworth's would become a burglar the moment he entered the private staff quarters of the building with a view to theft.

Trespasser. A man who mistakenly enters a part of a building will usually be a trespasser, but for the purposes of burglary one must be able to prove a guilty state of mind. Equally, the individual who gains entry by consent, that consent being obtained by deception (say a bogus gas official), is a trespasser and if he has the necessary intent then he is guilty of burglary.

The intent. The first part of the section touching on (a) theft, (b) GBH, (c) rape and (d) damage, requires that the burglar intends to commit one or more of these offences.

The second part of the section dealing with (a) theft and (b) GBH, deals with those persons who find themselves in buildings or parts of buildings with no specific intent, but nevertheless commit one or both offences, so that if intent cannot be proved then theft or GBH has to be proved before the offence is classified as burglary.

In the case of rape, this offence may be charged separately and attracts life imprisonment. This would still be the case if the prosecution was unable to prove that the entry as a trespasser was for that purpose, so that nothing is lost.

Aggravated burglary $\boxed{\text{S 10}}$

Aggravated burglary is a more serious offence than burglary and carries a maximum sentence of life imprisonment - as opposed to 14 years for burglary of a dwelling. A person is guilty of aggravated burglary if he commits any burglary and at the time has with him any:

Weapon of offence; or
Imitation firearm; or,
Firearm; or,
Explosive.

(S 24 PACE arrestable offence)

These terms are further defined:
(a) **weapon of offence** means any article made or adapted for use for causing injury to or incapacitating a person, or intended by the person having it with him for such use;
(b) **imitation firearm** means anything which has the appearance of being a firearm, whether capable of being discharged or not;
(c) **firearm** includes any air gun or air pistol;
(d) **explosive** means any article manufactured for the purpose of producing a practical effect by explosion, or intended by the person having it with him for that purpose.

Before charging the offence of aggravated burglary it is essential to prove that the offence of burglary has been committed. There is no need to prove that the burglar took any of the above items into the building with him. What has to be proved is that the burglar had one or more in his possession at the time when he committed or attempted to commit the offence.

Abstracting electricity $\boxed{\text{S 13}}$

Any person who dishonestly
— uses without due authority
— or causes to be wasted or diverted
any electricity commits an offence

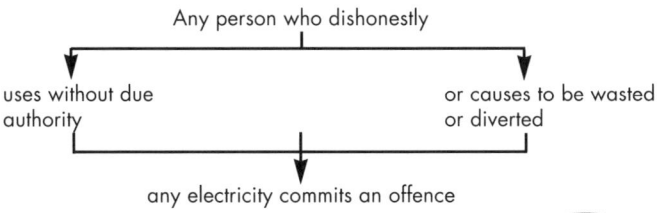

(S 24 PACE arrestable offence)

Uses without due authority. This would apply to the employee who dishonestly uses his employer's electrical goods or machinery without permission, or a householder who, having been disconnected by his supplier, dishonestly re-connects it, or by-passes the meter. Squatters, if they have no means or intention to pay for consumed electricity, would offend against this section.

Telephones. While the dishonest use of public telephones is dealt with in the Telecommunications Act 1984, the dishonest use of telephones, both public and private, may be dealt with under this section of the Theft Act. This would make criminal the use of private calls from, say, a place of work by an employee where it is expressly forbidden. In any case private telephones subject to this abuse would have to be dealt with under this section.

Consumption. The terms use, waste and divert, all presuppose that there is an actual consumption of electricity. It would appear therefore that the prosecution would have to prove that the owner actually suffered a loss as a result of dishonest behaviour.

Obtaining property by deception   S 15

A person who by any deception dishonestly obtains property belonging to another with the intention of permanently depriving the other of it commits an offence.

S 24 PACE arrestable offence

Deception. Deception means any deception (whether deliberate or reckless) by words or conduct as to fact or as to law, including a deception as to the present intentions of the person using the deception or any other person.

Obtaining property. A person is to be treated as obtaining property if he obtains ownership, possession or control of it, and 'obtain' includes obtaining for another or enabling another to obtain or to retain.

False statements. When a false statement is used in order to obtain property, it must be proved that the statement actually operated on the mind of the loser before the offence is complete. If the loser knows that the statement used is false and continues nevertheless to part with the goods, then he has not been deceived. In cases like this a charge of attempt may be considered.

Machines cannot be deceived. Deceptions can only work on people. Where foreign coins are fed into a machine and the machine gives up its contents, there is no deception because no human mind was deceived. In cases like this consider theft or making off without payment.

By words or conduct. When words are spoken resulting in an owner being duped into parting with his goods, then this is enough to satisfy this part of the section, ie where a false name and address is furnished in order to hire equipment which is subsequently sold on.

Conduct implies express action on behalf of the offender, eg dressing as a postman in order dishonestly to collect parcels from a sub-post office, or producing a false identity card in the name of the gas or electricity company in order to collect monies.

Deliberate or reckless. Where a statement is made which is known to be false (deception) then the author of the statement is clearly acting deliberately. So that if a prospective car owner parts with money for a car on the grounds that it only had one previous owner, which the seller knows to be false, then this would be a deliberate deception.

Being reckless is easier to prove, in that if the seller of the car, without knowing how many previous owners there were, and knowing that the buyer was only interested in the car if it had had only one owner, stated (without any knowledge as to its truth or otherwise) that the vehicle had but one previous owner, resulting in money being exchanged for the car, then this would be reckless.

Deception as to present intentions. This part of the section is designed to outlaw making promises as to future intentions which are never in fact fulfiled but nevertheless result in deposits being paid out.

It was commonplace prior to the 1968 Theft Act to escape prosecution in cases in which a man received a deposit for work to be completed when in fact it was never his intention to carry out the work. This section now makes that behaviour a criminal offence.

However, it is important to prove that he never intended to carry out the work. It may be that he did intend to do it but subsequently found it impossible to do so, which is not an offence.

Blackmail

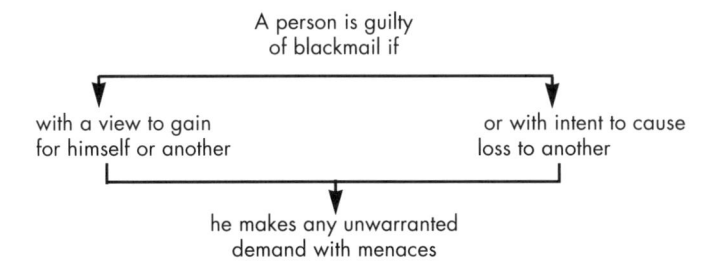

S 21

A person is guilty of blackmail if

- with a view to gain for himself or another
- or with intent to cause loss to another

he makes any unwarranted demand with menaces

S 24 PACE arrestable offence

Defence. That the person making the demand does so in the belief that he has reasonable grounds for making the demand and that the use of the menaces is a proper means of reinforcing the demand.

A distinction is therefore made between the individual who is seeking to trade on the position of someone who has been compromised by demanding say, money in order to pay for the blackmailer's silence, and the daily threats people receive through the post, eg if you don't pay your gas bill then you'll be cut off.

In the latter case there are reasonable grounds for making the demand and the use of the menaces (to be cut off) is the proper means of reinforcing the demand.

Gain or loss. Gain and loss are to be construed as extending only to gain or loss in money or other property, but this includes any such gain or loss whether temporary or permanent.

Gain. Includes a gain by keeping what one has, as well as a gain by getting what one has not.

Loss. Loss includes a loss by not getting what one might get as well as a loss by parting with what one has.

Menaces. Would include an action to be carried out by another.

Handling stolen goods

S 22

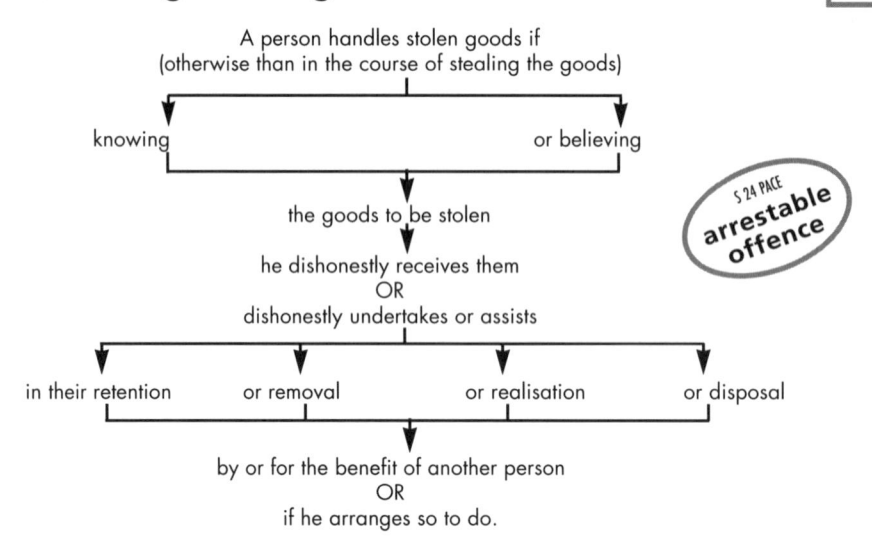

A person handles stolen goods if (otherwise than in the course of stealing the goods)

knowing or believing

the goods to be stolen

he dishonestly receives them
OR
dishonestly undertakes or assists

in their retention or removal or realisation or disposal

by or for the benefit of another person
OR
if he arranges so to do.

S 24 PACE arrestable offence

Otherwise than in the course of stealing. When an individual actually steals the goods, then the proper charge should be one of theft.

The handling offence is applicable to those people who subsequently undertake or assist in retention, removal, disposal or realisation.

Knowing or believing. This is the mental element of the crime. Where the handler has been told that the goods are stolen he has knowledge. 'Believing' amounts to where the handler says to himself: 'I believe these goods are stolen.'

When goods cease to be stolen. No goods shall be regarded as still being stolen after they have been restored to the person from whom they were stolen, or to other lawful possession or custody, or after that person and any other person claiming through him have otherwise ceased, as regards those goods, to have any right to restitution in respect of the theft.

Clearly then, where goods have been restored to the owner they are no longer stolen goods, but equally when they are recovered by the police they are no longer stolen. So if the police keep observation on stolen property and arrest persons who come to collect it, the proper charge would be theft and not handling.

Receiving. Receiving means what it says. Where there is reception of the goods from the thief by the handler then the transaction is complete.

Undertaking or assisting. The dishonest undertaking or assisting is either the agreement to help dispose of the stolen goods or the actual physical helping in their disposal.

Retention. Retention is where the handler accepts the stolen goods and retains them for the time being, say in a lock-up garage.

Removal. Removal is actual physical 'movement' of the goods. It could mean actually helping load the goods, or perhaps supplying a vehicle for their movement.

Disposal. Disposal is the idea of actually offloading the goods, say to a third party, or perhaps to the eventual buyer or fence.

Realisation. Realisation could cover the individual who arranges the deal to convert the stolen goods (say cigarettes) into cash.

Theft or handling. Where the above arrangements are made prior to the theft, consider theft rather than handling because the receiver must know or believe the goods to be stolen.

Going equipped for stealing `S 25`

A person shall be guilty of an offence if, when not at his place of abode, he has with him any article

- for use in the course of
- or in connection with any

burglary, or theft, or cheat

S 24 PACE arrestable offence

Evidence. Where a person is charged with an offence under this section, proof that he had with him any article made or adapted for use in committing a burglary, theft or cheat shall be evidence that he had it with him for such use.

Theft. For the purposes of this section theft shall include the offence under section 12(1) of the Act of taking a conveyance without authority.

Cheat. Cheat means an offence under section 15 of the Act, ie obtaining property by deception.

For example marked playing cards, forged documents, bogus identity cards.

In practice. During the course of stop-checks - especially at night - be aware that items that seem innocuous might well be for use in burglaries, items such as masking tape, torches, bunches of keys and the like. If an individual is stopped in mid-summer and is found in possession of say, gloves, it is right to ask the question why. Check all documents against the name of the suspect, they are often different.

Theft Act 1978

Obtaining services by deception `S 1`

The 1978 Act was implemented to check with offences which did not always fit comfortably within the wording of the 1968 Act. Section 1 of the Act creates the offence of obtaining services (as opposed to property) by deception. The type of behaviour covered by this section includes obtaining car hire or a surveyor's report by using a worthless cheque or a stolen credit card.

Making off without payment `S 3`

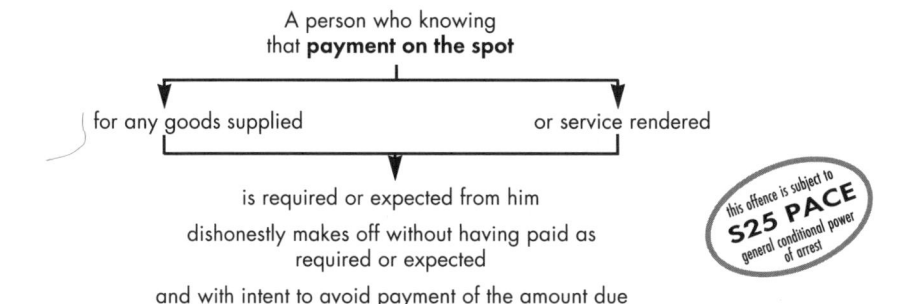

A person who knowing that **payment on the spot**

- for any goods supplied
- or service rendered

is required or expected from him

dishonestly makes off without having paid as required or expected

and with intent to avoid payment of the amount due commits an offence

this offence is subject to S25 PACE general conditional power of arrest

Payment on the spot. Includes payment at the time of collecting goods on which work has been done or in respect of which service has been provided.

Unlawful acts. This section shall not apply where the supply of the goods or the doing of the service is contrary to law, or where the service done is such that payment is not legally enforceable.

Bilking. This offence is known as bilking, eg driving off from a self-service filling station without paying. It is usually committed by an 'opportunist' who sees a chance to avoid paying.

Account or bill. Where there is a standing account between a firm and a wholesaler/retailer, then there is no requirement to pay on the spot for goods supplied or services done; payment is by agreement between parties. A bill such as that of a taxi-driver, restaurateur or garage where payment is to be made then and there must be settled on the spot otherwise an offence under this section may be committed

Dishonestly. Dishonest intention must be proved to exist at the time of making off. An honest and genuine mistake would be a defence.

Vehicle interference   S 9 Criminal Attempts Act 1981

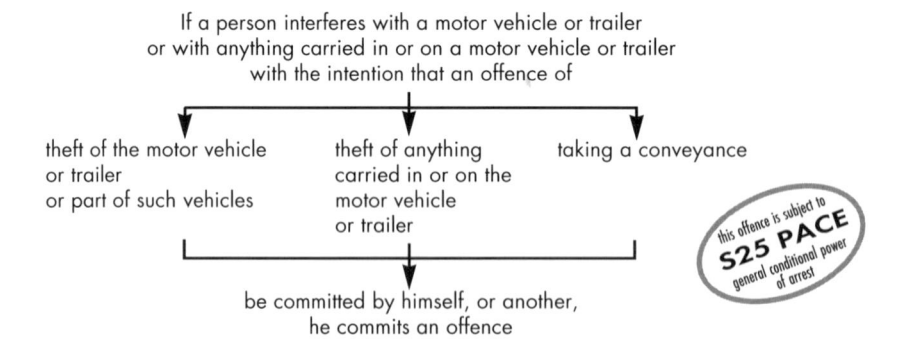

If a person interferes with a motor vehicle or trailer or with anything carried in or on a motor vehicle or trailer with the intention that an offence of

- theft of the motor vehicle or trailer or part of such vehicles
- theft of anything carried in or on the motor vehicle or trailer
- taking a conveyance

be committed by himself, or another, he commits an offence

this offence is subject to S25 PACE general conditional power of arrest

Interferes. This section was enacted to outlaw the preparatory acts of stealing vehicles and/or things from vehicles as well as the 'taking a conveyance' offence, wrongly named as joy riding.

The intention. The intention which must be proved is that there was to be a theft of the motor vehicle or trailer or part of such vehicle or of anything carried in or on the motor vehicle or trailer or a taking of the conveyance. Persons seeking to cause damage to a vehicle would not be caught by this section although they would be guilty of criminal damage.

By himself or another. When an individual interferes with a car, his intention should quickly become obvious. However he may be in the process of doing a preparatory act in order to allow another to complete the act. In this case both parties are equally guilty of the offence.

CHAPTER 6

MOTOR VEHICLES

Chapter contents

Road traffic accidents 86
    Definition 86
    Action at the scene of a road traffic accident 87
Driving documents 91
    Examining 91
    Checking 93
    Driving licence 93
    Endorsements 94
    Insurance certificates 94
    MoT certificates 95
Fixed penalty system 96
Vehicle defect rectification scheme 98

Road traffic accidents

Definition

S 170 Road Traffic Act 1988

If owing to the presence of a motor vehicle on a road, an accident occurs whereby personal injury is caused to a person other than the driver of that motor vehicle, or damage is caused to a vehicle other than that motor vehicle or a trailer drawn by that motor vehicle, or to an animal other than to an animal in or on that motor vehicle or trailer, or to any other property constructed on, fixed to, growing in or otherwise forming part of the land on which the road in question is situated, or land adjacent to such land, then the driver of the motor vehicle shall stop, and, if so required to do so by any person having reasonable grounds for so requiring give:
  (a) his name and address;
  (b) the name and address of the owner of the vehicle; and
  (c) the identification marks of the vehicle.

If, for any reason, such a driver does not give his name and address to any such person he shall:
  (a) report the accident to a police station; or,
  (b) to a constable,

as soon as reasonably practicable and in any case, within 24 hours.

Presence. The vehicle need only be present on a road for an accident to occur, the vehicle does not have to be in motion. So that a pedal cyclist who collides with a stationary car would be involved in an 'accident'.

Motor vehicle. Defined by section 185 of the Act as a mechanically propelled vehicle intended or adapted for use on the roads'. There are further sub-definitions into different classes of vehicle (to which different weight and function specifications apply): heavy locomotive, light locomotive, heavy motor car, motor car, invalid carriage, motor cycle, tractor.

Injury or damage to self. The personal injury discussed in the section must happen to someone else and does not include injuries to the driver of the vehicle. It would however, include injuries to any passengers. Equally, damage to the vehicle is not included but damage to any other vehicle would be.

Animal. An animal in this section of the Act means any: horse, cattle, ass, mule, sheep, pig, goat or dog. A circus vehicle which crashes causing no injury to any other person, or damage thereto, but has the effect of injuring wild creatures carried on its trailer, would not come within the ambit of the section, nor do cats.

Other property. Other property constructed on, fixed to, growing in or otherwise forming part of the land on which the road in question is situated, or land adjacent to such land, which is damaged, comes within the section and includes roadside 'furniture', eg telephone boxes, walls, hedgerows, telegraph poles, in fact anything capable of being damaged.

Driver to stop. Stop means stop now. It does not mean drive on to the next village and then stop.

The driver should stop in order to fulfil his statutory obligations. These include giving his name and address, the name and address of the owner of the vehicle and the vehicle identification mark to any person having reasonable grounds for requiring it.

Supplying information. If the driver stops at the scene of the accident and supplies the stipulated information to a person having reasonable grounds for requiring it, then he has discharged his duty under the Act and does not therefore have to report the matter to a police station or a constable.

Reporting to police. Where a driver stops at the scene of an accident and there is no one present to require his 'details' then he shall report the matter to a police station or to a constable as soon as reasonably practicable, and in any case within 24 hours.

'As soon as reasonably practicable' comes before and in any case within 24 hours. So that after an accident a driver would commit an offence of failing to report if he left the matter unreported for 24 hours, without first trying, 'as soon as practicable' to report the matter to a police station or to a constable.

Insurance. Where there is personal injury to someone other than the driver of the motor vehicle involved, then the driver has to produce insurance details to any person having reasonable grounds for so requiring or he must produce them to a police station or a constable within 24 hours.

Action at the scene of traffic accidents

Whether a road traffic accident is 'reportable' (see the definition), or not reportable, does not affect the action taken by police officers at the scene. The main duty of police officers is to protect life and property, and this duty is never more evident than at the scene of a road traffic accident.

First action at scene

Protect yourself from danger. Wear highly conspicuous clothing so that other road users can see you. If the accident occurs at night, illuminate the scene, use blue flashing lamps and bring to the notice of other road users that an accident has occurred.

Protect

In order to protect people who may be injured and to safeguard property, take immediate measures to protect the scene of the accident. Place

'POLICE SLOW'

and 'POLICE ACCIDENT'

signs some distance from the scene, on both sides of the road, so that other road users have some advance warning that there is an obstruction or danger ahead. The further from the scene the signs can be placed, the better.

Do not hesitate to employ passing members of the public to help you to protect the scene. Having set out signs, consider placing cones next, they are of high luminosity and especially useful at night. Cones can be placed near and around the disabled vehicles in order to protect them from further damage.

The injured

In cases involving injury, summon an ambulance immediately. People may be trapped in which case the fire service should be called out. As these emergency services begin to arrive further protection of the scene is secured by the use of their flashing lamps.

During the course of an accident, fractures may occur to those parts of the vehicles which contain petrol, oil and lubricants. Do not allow naked lights near the scene and ensure that you know if the police vehicle contains a fire extinguisher and also its location. Be especially careful about the prospects of fire if persons are trapped.

Names and addresses

Before ambulances leave the scene with the injured, make every effort to obtain names and addresses. Also note which hospital the injured are being taken to. It may be that where there are a number of ambulances they will take the injured to different hospitals, be in a position to ask your control room to arrange for the injured to be met at the hospital if there is a need.

Possible fatalities

When there is a fatality, or you suspect that injuries are so serious that the injured may die, it is important to have someone, ideally a police officer at the scene, to go with that person in the ambulance in order to maintain continuity of evidence.

Offences

It is quite easy to overlook offences at the scene of a road traffic accident, due to the enormous responsibility that is placed on the shoulders of the first officers at the scene.

Nevertheless, constantly ask yourself questions: 'Is this a stolen vehicle?' 'Has the driver been drinking alcohol?'

Be conscious of the fact that there may be a need to ask the control room to arrange a hospital breath test.

The hidden injured

As an accident occurs people tend to be propelled from the location of the impact. Try and establish from the people present if everyone is accounted for. There may be telltale signs present which suggest someone is lying injured in a field or over a wall - the unattended pedal cycle for example.

In cases like this, call out a dog handler with a view to establishing that you have accounted for everyone. If the vehicle is stolen the driver and passengers may have escaped on foot.

First aid

On arrival at the scene of an accident the first person to protect from injury is yourself. Having established a safe zone, the injured must be examined and helped.

Consciousness can be checked by speaking loudly, eg, 'What happened?' 'Open your eyes'. A casualty in an altered state of consciousness may respond by groaning, mumbling or even by moving slightly. A fully unconscious casualty will make no response.

Where a casualty becomes unconscious the airway may become blocked. This often happens as a result of the tongue falling back and blocking the throat. In this event open the mouth, remove any obstruction (vomit), place two fingers under the point of the chin, lift the jaw at the same time with the other hand tilt the head to the back thus opening the airway.

Breathing can be checked by looking closely for chest movements. Listen for sounds of breathing. Feel for breath on your cheek. This needs to be continued for about five seconds before deciding that the casualty is not breathing.

Circulation (or pulse) can be checked by checking the Adam's apple with two fingers (not thumb) and feeling for a pulse. Again, this should be continued for about five seconds before deciding that the pulse is absent.

If both breathing and pulse are absent it is essential to have an ambulance attend the scene as soon as possible. In the meantime artificial ventilation (mouth to mouth) should be attempted.

When there is breathing and pulse the casualty's level of consciousness can be checked more fully by assessment of responsiveness.

Is the casualty:

- A   Alert?
- V   Responsive to voice?
- P   Responsive to pain?
- U   Unresponsive?

Any casualty who is not fully conscious should be put in the recovery position ie, placed on their side.

Serious bleeding is best dealt with by putting direct pressure onto the wound, if nothing is in the wound, eg glass. If possible elevate the injured limb.

Fractures are best not moved but where movement is necessary, try to support the fracture in a comfortable position.

Note: These notes are not exhaustive and special constables are strongly recommended to attend a first aid course which is available in colleges and through voluntary organisations.

Remember the five basis principles and you will save lives:

- S   Safety;
- R   response;
- A   airway;
- B   breathing;
- C   circulation.

Witnesses

As early as is possible establish who witnessed what and write their fresh memories in your pocket book. Secure names and addresses and arrange for the witnesses to be seen as soon as possible.

Other witnesses

Evidence of what happened in giving rise to the accident can often be found in skid marks on the road, make a note of them. It is often easy to miss skid marks at night. The scene may have to be revisited during daylight hours.

Position of vehicle

On arrival at the scene of an accident, establish if the vehicles have been moved. If the answer is yes, then little can be done about locating their position at the time of the accident.

When they have not been moved, use yellow waterproof chalk to mark the road showing the position of each vehicle. This is particularly important if the vehicles have to be moved suddenly.

Ideally marks made on roads and measurements taken should be done with the help of, or in the presence of, the drivers involved.

Scenes of crime

If accident is serious or fatal - or even a multiple accident - consideration should be given to having the scene photographed. When the scenes of crime officer attends the scene, tell him what angles you wish the photographs to be taken from, at the same time listening to his advice as he has no doubt done this in the past.

Accident book

Throughout the whole of your attendance at the accident you will be in the process of writing-up the accident book. Remember that these are original notes and you will be expected to give evidence from them. Remember also that they may be subject to scrutiny by court officials and also the defence.

Hit and run

When attending a hit and run accident remember that the vehicle which has failed to stop, if in actual collision with vehicles found by you at the scene, will have left evidence at the scene as to its identity.

Paint samples will be left in any vehicle damaged. Broken glass and other debris may be found. Anything which appears to have come from the other vehicle may be seized and submitted for forensic examination if the case is serious enough in all the circumstances.

This type of evidence gathering calls for special skills and you may wish to call on the services of a scenes of crime officer.

Disabled vehicles

Where disabled vehicles are left at the scene, owners should be asked who should recover them. If they do not know, then offer recovery from the call-out system held at the police station. Control room staff will want to know the manner of recovery, ie, suspended tow, rigid tow, etc.

Specialist traffic officers

Where the accident is serious, early thought should be given to calling to the scene specialist traffic officers. These officers are highly trained and are able to give expert evidence on such matters as speed of travel before the accident based on skid marks.

They are also trained in preparing detailed sketches of the scene of an accident with great precision. Many are trained as vehicle examiners and can give expert evidence on matters of braking systems, tyres and the like.

From the above you will see that the prospect of attending an accident can be quite daunting. What is of paramount importance at the scene of an accident is the speed at which the officer carries out his duties. He has to be professional; his skills and knowledge will be tested when he is under the most pressure. The public, by and large, will simply stand and look on. It is important to remain calm, and to remain alive to what is happening all around. Do not hesitate to call for assistance and remember that members of the public, if asked, will do all they can to help; use them. Whatever panic you may feel do not allow it to show on your face.

Documents

Examining driving documents

Minimum age

Before examining driving documents it is important to know the minimum age for driving certain classes of motor vehicles and police powers to demand the production of documents and the provision of information. The minimum ages for driving motor vehicles on a road are:

16 years
- (a) moped;
- (b) mowing machine;
- (c) invalid carriage;
- (d) pedestrian controlled vehicle.

17 years
- (a) motor cycle;
- (b) small passenger vehicle;
- (c) small goods vehicle;
- (d) road roller.

18 years
- (a) medium sized goods vehicles;
- (b) certain large passenger vehicles.

21 years
other motor vehicles.

Police powers

> Ss 164-5 Road Traffic Act 1988

A constable has the power to demand the production of driving licence, insurance and test certificate from any person:
- (a) driving a motor vehicle on a road; or,
- (b) whom a constable has reasonable cause to believe to have been the driver of a motor vehicle at a time when an accident occurred owing to its presence on a road;
- (c) whom a constable has reasonable cause to believe to have committed an offence relating to the use of a motor vehicle on a road; and
- (d) supervising a driver in category (a), (b) or (c) above.

Any person who fails to produce any of these documents commits an offence.

HO/RT 1

Any person required to produce these documents and who fails to do so at the time commits an offence, however it is a defence and a person shall not be convicted of the offence if he shows that:
- (a) within seven days after the production was required, he produced the document at a police station requested by him. In the case of a driving licence this must be done in person in order that his signature can be checked; or,
- (b) it was produced there as soon as was reasonably practicable to do so; or,
- (c) it was not practicable for it to be produced before the day on which the proceedings were commenced.

Seven days: In calculating the seven days, the day on which the demand was made should not be included.

The Form HO/RT 1 should be issued to the driver in order to facilitate his production of driving documents at a police station requested by him. The driver should be given the original copy, the second copy is posted to the police station where he elects to produce his documents and the third copy is kept by the officer (but note that some forces have only two copies). The HO/RT 1 has no place in law, it simply facilitates ease of production. Where the demand is made for production of driving documents and an HO/RT 1 is not issued, the documents must still be produced.

Date of birth

When there is a demand by a constable for a driving licence and:
  (a) the person fails to produce the driving licence forthwith; or,
  (b) there is reason to suspect that the licence was not granted to that person, or it was granted to him in error, or it contains an alteration made with intent to deceive, or contains a driver number which has been altered or defaced;

then the officer has the power to demand that person's date of birth.

Provisional driving licence

This licence is issued to persons who have not passed a driving test and places conditions on the driver who must:
  (a) be supervised by a person who has a full licence to drive vehicles of the same class;
  (b) display 'L' plates to the front and rear of the vehicle;
  (c) not drive a vehicle drawing a trailer;
  (d) not ride a solo motor cycle while carrying on it any other person; the solo motor cycle shall not exceed 125 cc (and if registered after January 1, 1982 be of a special learner type); or shall be electrically powered.

Supervisor

The person supervising the provisional licence holder must:
  (a) have attained the age of 21 years; and,
  (b) have held a full driving licence for a period of at least three years, for the same class of vehicle which he is supervising.

New driver

Note, that as from June 1997, newly qualified drivers have a two-year 'probationary' period from the date of passing the driving test during which the licence may be revoked if six penalty points are accumulated. If the licence is revoked, the driver must re-take a driving test, (Road Traffic (New Drivers) Act 1995).

Driving licence offences

Offences which may be committed in relation to driving licences are:
(a) driving a motor vehicle on a road and not holding a driving licence for that class of vehicle;
(b) causing or permitting a person to drive a motor vehicle on a road who is not the holder of a driving licence for that class of vehicle;
(c) driving a motor vehicle on a road whilst being disqualified by reason of age or by a court from holding or obtaining a licence;
(d) failing to comply with the conditions of a provisional licence;
(e) failing to sign the driving licence in ink;
(f) failing to notify a change of address forthwith.

Checking driving documents

Driving licence

When checking driving licences take care and time to examine the licence in detail. Officers often feel under pressure when checking documents resulting in their missing important detail. Make a check list of details which are important:
(a) Type of licence (full or provisional).
(b) Serial number (on the new European Communities model of driving licence, this can be found in the top left corner).
(c) Driver number, this number discloses both the sex of the holder and his/her date of birth. Suppose the driver number is:

MITCH 455294 IA9XT

The first five letters contain part or the whole of the holder's name, in this case MITCHELL;
The following six figures tell you the date of birth. The first and last figures are the year of birth, in this case 1944;
The second and third figures tell you the sex and month of birth, in this case, a female born in May. Had this been a male person then the second and third figures would have been 05, 5 is always added to the second figure for a female;
The fourth and fifth figures tell you the date in the month, in this case 29;
The next two letters tell you the person's initials, in this case I A (Isobel Agnes). If the holder has only one forename then the second space will show the figure 9:

The holder of this driving licence therefore is:

ISOBEL AGNES MITCHELL, born May 29, 1944:

(d) Name of holder of licence, (where this has been changed check the driver number).

(e) Dates of issue and expiry.
(f) Categories of vehicles entitled to drive.
(g) Signature of holder. (This signature can be checked against the signature in HO/RT 2).

Endorsements

Endorsements can be found on the driving licence under the head 'Endorsements as supplied by convicting court' and comprise the following information:
- (a) code of convicting court;
- (b) date of conviction;
- (c) offence code;
- (d) date of offence;
- (e) fine;
- (f) disqualification period; and
- (g) penalty points.

The penalty points system is standardised by Schedule 2 to the Road Traffic Offenders Act 1988, as amended, and indicates national guidelines to the courts when awarding penalty points in relation to the endorsements of a licence, periods of disqualification or other punishments. Examples of these are:

Driving
(a) Careless or inconsiderate driving	3 - 9 points
(b) Failing to provide a breath test specimen	4 points
(c) Causing death by dangerous (obligatory disqualification)	3 -11 points
(d) Failing to comply with traffic signs	3 points

Accidents
(a) Failing to stop after an accident	5 - 10 points
(b) Driving without insurance	6 - 18 points

Other offences
(a) Motor racing on highways, (this offence also carries obligatory disqualification)	3-11 points
(b) Leaving vehicle in dangerous position	3 points
(c) Driving with defective eyesight	3 points

In each case the Act has to be consulted so an officer may determine the number of penalty points awarded for each offence, and also when the officer is seeking to determine whether the penalty points are on a sliding scale, obligatory or conditional.

Checking insurance certificates

Insurance of motor vehicles being driven on roads is obligatory under the provisions of s 143 of the Road Traffic Act 1988 which states that:
(a) it is an offence for any person to use a motor vehicle on a road unless there is in force in relation to the use of the vehicle by that person a

policy of insurance or such a security in respect of third party risks as complies with the Act; and,
(b) it is an offence for any person to cause or permit any other person to use a vehicle as outlined in (a) above.

Use. Use means leaving a vehicle on a road (parked) as well as driving the vehicle.

Cause. Cause suggests that the person causing the use of the vehicle has some power or authority to do so. There must be an order for the vehicle to be used.

Permit. The permitting offence in relation to the use of motor vehicles on a road without insurance or security is much wider in scope than the offence of Causing.

Permitting a vehicle to be used with no insurance would occur where A (the owner of a vehicle) knowing the vehicle not to be insured, lends the vehicle to B.

Defence. A person charged with using a vehicle with no insurance shall not be convicted if he proves that the vehicle did not belong to him and was not in his possession under a contract or loan, and that he was using the vehicle in the course of his employment and that he neither knew, nor had reason to believe, that there was not in force an insurance policy or security.

Check. When an insurance certificate is produced a record should be made of the following:
(a) Serial number;
(b) Dates commenced/expires;
(c) Name of insurance company;
(d) Vehicles entitled to drive;
(e) Limitations as to use; and
(f) Persons entitled to drive.

Checking MoT certificates

Motor vehicles require an MoT test certificate three years from the date of first registration or manufacture. Certain passenger vehicles require a certificate after one year. Goods vehicles are exempt but they require a goods vehicle test certificate. MoT testing stations issue test certificates where the vehicle has passed a test in relation to:
(a) audible warning instruments;
(b) bodywork/suspension; points;
(c) brakes;
(d) exhaust system;
(e) lighting system;
(f) road wheels;
(g) seat belts and anchorage
(h) steering;
(i) tyres; and
(j) windscreens; washers and wipers.

Check

When checking MOT certificates a record should be made of the following points:
(a) the serial number;
(b) date of issue/expiry;
(c) testing station number;
(d) testing station name and address (this information is embossed on the certificate); and
(e) registration number of the vehicle.

Defence. It is a defence to a charge of using a motor vehicle on a road without an MOT certificate where:
(a) the vehicle was going to or from a pre-arranged test; or
(b) it was being driven by an authorised examiner who was testing it; or
(c) a certificate having been refused, the vehicle was going to or from a pre-arranged place of repair or being towed away to a breaker's yard.

Fixed penalty system

> **Road Traffic Act 1988**

The fixed penalty system enables a motorist who commits certain specific offences to avoid prosecution for the offence by electing to pay a fixed sum of money. Alternatively, he may, if he wishes, elect not to pay the sum and appear in court instead.

Schedule 3 to the Road Traffic Offenders Act 1988 specifies which offences are 'fixed penalty offences'. The Act also specifies which of those offences are to be regarded as endorsable offences and which are not.

Endorsable offences - are those where, following conviction, the court would order obligatory endorsement of penalty points providing certain conditions are met.

There is no room here to list all endorsable and non-endorsable offences. A comprehensive list can be found in any police station and the list should be consulted before contemplating issuing a fixed penalty notice. Each fixed penalty notice contains the address of the clerk of the court where the fine can be paid.

Endorsable

The following are examples of endorsable offences:
- (a) provisional driving licence offences;
- (b) using a vehicle with defective brakes, steering or tyres;
- (c) speeding;
- (d) contravening red traffic lights, stop signs, double white lines and a constable's signal when engaged in traffic regulation; and
- (e) leaving a vehicle in a dangerous position.

Non-endorsable

The following are examples of non-endorsable offences:
- (a) failing to exhibit excise licence;
- (b) no speedometer or defective speedometer, no mirrors, no windscreen wipers/washers or defective windscreen wipers, no horn, no seat belts;
- (c) failing to stop for a police constable, contravening give way sign or no entry sign, driving the wrong way in a one-way street, parking without lights;
- (d) breaching no waiting or limited waiting restrictions, unnecessary obstruction and stopping on a clearway.

Driver present. If, on any occasion, a constable in uniform has reason to believe that a person he finds is committing - or has on that occasion committed - a fixed penalty offence, the constable may give him a fixed penalty notice in respect of that offence.

A fixed penalty notice should only be issued at the time of, or immediately after, the offence. The notice should be issued for the most serious offence where there is more than one offence. Other offences should be dealt with by way of verbal caution. Alternatively all offences may be reported for summons. The decision lies solely with the constable.

Driver not present. Where on any occasion a constable has reason to believe in the case of any stationary vehicle that a fixed penalty offence is being or has on that occasion been committed in respect of it, he may fix a fixed penalty notice in respect of the offence to the vehicle unless the offence appears to him to involve obligatory endorsement.

Removal of notice. A person is guilty of an offence if he removes or interferes with any notice fixed to a vehicle under this section, unless he does so by or under the authority of the driver or person in charge of the vehicle or the person liable for the fixed penalty offence.

Obligatory endorsement. Where the offence appears to the constable to involve obligatory endorsement, the constable may only give a fixed penalty notice if:
(a) the driver produces his driving licence for inspection by the constable;
(b) the constable is satisfied, on inspecting the licence, that he would not be liable to be disqualified by reason of penalty points if he were convicted of that offence; and,
(c) he surrenders his licence to the constable to be retained and dealt with.

When a licence is so retained, the 'receipt' part of the fixed penalty notice should be completed and given to the driver who may produce it to police subsequently (*in lieu* of the licence).

In cases in which the offence would take the driver over 12 penalty points the licence should not be seized and a summons should be issued instead (see penalty points below).

Failure to produce licence. When the offence appears to the constable to involve obligatory endorsement, and the person concerned does not produce his licence for inspection by the constable, the constable may give him a notice stating that if within seven days after the notice is given he produces the notice together with his licence in person to a constable or authorised person at the police station specified in the notice and:
(a) the constable or authorised person is satisfied, on inspecting the licence, that the driver would not be liable to be disqualified by reason of penalty points if he were convicted of that offence; and,
(b) he surrenders his licence to the constable or authorised person to be retained and dealt with;

then he may be given a fixed penalty notice in respect of that offence.

Notices. Where a notice is issued prior to the driving licence being produced for inspection, this notice is known as a provisional notice. The notice becomes full after the driving licence has been produced.

Driving licence. Where a driver produces his driving licence for inspection, it is a matter for him to surrender the licence if he so chooses, there is no power of seizure under the Act.

Authorised person. An authorised person is a constable or a person authorised by or on behalf of the chief officer of police for that area. This could mean a civilian counter clerk if he or she is so authorised.

Penalty points. When 12 penalty points are accumulated within a period of three years by a person, he must be disqualified for at least six months, unless the court thinks fit to disqualify for a shorter period or not at all. This is known as the 'totting-up' procedure. If the court does not disqualify a person or does so for a shorter period for special reasons, the reasons must be stated in open court.

Vehicle defect rectification scheme

The vehicle defect rectification scheme (where it applies), is a scheme which allows the drivers/owners of motor vehicle which have been found to be defective, to possibly avoid prosecution for the offence in relation to the condition of the vehicle by taking certain action to rectify the defect. Examples of the defects which might escape prosecution when rectified are:

(a) lights/reflectors not properly maintained;
(b) indicators or stop lights not maintained;
(c) defective tyre(s);
(d) no number plate fitted;
(e) offending number plate (obscured/not the right size, etc);
(f) inefficient brakes;
(g) inefficient exhaust;
(h) exhaust not fitted;
(j) audible warning instrument offences;
(k) no audible warning instrument.

Where the police are prepared to issue a vehicle defect rectification notice (VDR) the driver can avoid possible prosecution for the offence if he takes the following action:

(1) make immediate arrangements for repair of the vehicle; and,
(2) present the vehicle, together with the (VDR) notice, to an MoT garage for examination and certification on the form by the examiner that the defects have been repaired; and,
(3) after certification at an MoT garage, or when written evidence of disposal is obtained, the driver must send it to the Central Ticket Office within 14 days of being stopped for the offence.

When the certification is made by the authorised examiner it does not preclude the driver being prosecuted for this defect at any subsequent examination of the vehicle.

Insurance policies

Drivers who continue to use their vehicles with the defects which have been specified and are involved in an accident, may have their insurance policy wholly or partially invalidated. It is therefore in the driver's interest to have the defect repaired as soon as possible..

Disposal of vehicle

When the vehicle is disposed of and a certificate is produced to that effect then the driver may escape prosecution. . .

Form type

The VDR issued to the driver contains the following information:

(a) name, address, date of birth;
(b) signature (only on request);
(c) location, date and time of stop;
(d) owner's name and address;
(e) a list of the defects to be rectified;
(f) the vehicle registration mark;
(g) make, type, use, class;
(h) reason for stop;
(j) details of issuing officer; and
(k) address to which the form should be sent when the defects have been rectified.

The MoT testing station garage which rectifies the defects is required to issue a form stating that the defects listed have been repaired. The form usually looks like this:

Certification of Vehicle Defect Rectification

This is to certify that Vehicle Reg No
was produced at   am/pm on
at Vehicle Testing Station number
with the defects listed satisfactorily repaired.
Examiner
Signature

Official stamp

CHAPTER 7

THE CUSTODY SUITE

Chapter contents

The Codes of Practice	102
Detention officers	**103**
Main responsibilities	103
Personal requirements	104
Finding your way	**105**
From arrest to police station	105
Designated police stations	105
Custody officer	106
Custody officer duties	**107**
Arrival at the police station	107
Grounds for detention	108
Officers at variance	108
Ascertaining property in possession	108
Retention of property by arrested person	108
Arrested person's rights	109
Informing named person	109
Solicitors - free legal advice	110
Urgent interviews	110
Interviews without a solicitor	110
Insufficient evidence to charge	111
Authorising detention	111
Cells	111
Treatment of detained persons	112
Charging	113
Questioning after charge	114
Detention conditions after charge	114
Fingerprints and photographs	115
Reviews of detention	115
Time limits on detention without charge	116

The Codes of Practice

Section 66 of the Police and Criminal Evidence Act 1984 was introduced the Codes of Practice which attend the Act, and which came into force on January 1, 1986. These Codes (though not the Notes for Guidance) have the same force as the Act itself, and any breach of the Codes by regular police officers constitutes a disciplinary offence.

The Codes have been amended (most recently following the enactment of the Criminal Justice and Public Order Act 1994) and additions made since first being published, following extensive public consultation which sought to enhance the Codes as clear and workable guidelines for the police, balanced by strong safeguards for the public.

There are four main Codes plus a Code on tape recorded interviews. The main areas covered by the Codes are:

Code A

The exercise by police officers of statutory powers of stop and search.

Code B

The searching of premises by police officers and the seizure of property found by police officers on persons or premises.

Code C

The detention, treatment and questioning of persons by police officers.

Code D

The identification of persons by police officers.

Code E

Tape recording of interviews with suspects.

Under each section in the Codes there are specific actions laid down, which have to be followed by police officers. The Codes also contain Notes of Guidance which provide a uniform structure for the behaviour of the police.

While special constables are not subject to the Police Discipline Regulations, any special who contravenes the provisions of the Codes of Practice could well find himself subject to a civil law suit. It is important that you should have a copy of the Codes. If they are not issued personally to you by your force, then a copy can be found in each custody suite. Alternatively, they are available through HMSO at a reasonable price.

Detention officers

Custody officers discharge their duties in relation to persons in custody under the provisions of the Police and Criminal Evidence Act 1984, and the attendant Codes of Practice. It is often the case that the custody officer is helped with these duties by a civilian detention officer, a regular officer and in many cases by a special constable. This person is usually referred to as a 'goaler' and helps to relieve the custody officer of the more mundane and non-contentious tasks, thus freeing the custody officer to address the more important issues. In many ways the detention officer is the eyes and ears of the custody officer, his executive arm, his 'right arm'.

Main responsibilities of the detention officers

While the detention officer will engage in all manner of activity at the behest of the custody officer, his duties regularly fall into six main areas, all of which are governed by the Codes of Practice. Before engaging in detention officer duties it is essential that the person doing so makes himself very familiar with the Codes of Practice. This is particularly so for special constables as the detainees will perceive that they are being dealt with by a police officer and not a member of the public. The main areas of responsibility are:

Security

Opportunity for escape must not arise and to that end, not only should detainees be kept in cells or detention rooms, they should also be visited regularly and inquiry made into their welfare.

Treatment

The Codes of Practice lay down very firm rules concerning the treatment of detainees, their welfare and comfort. They touch on all matters governing the basic rights of the individual - including heating and lighting, feeding, washing and shaving.

Supervised visits

While in custody detainees receive visits by official and non-official persons. These include legal advisors and lay visitors as well as family and friends. The detention officer will be responsible for supervising such visits (except where they are required by law to be private) and must be alert to the practice of prohibited articles being smuggled in to detainees, ie drugs, weapons, mobile 'phones, etc.

Movement of detainees

While in police custody detainees often have to be transferred from station to station and from station to court, as well as being moved within the custody suite complex. It is at such times that detention officers should be most alert to the prospect of escape.

Court escorts

Detention officers, in company with regulars, are responsible for the safe escort and custody of the detainee when he is required to appear before a judge or magistrates. The court escort must ensure that any order made by the court be acted upon without delay, be it an order for further detention, release on bail or otherwise.

Documentation

All matters affecting the detainee are recorded on the custody record and, ideally, should be made by the person involved. Where the detention officer is responsible for an activity, eg feeding, welfare check or whatever, he should make an entry in the record which truly reflects his involvement with the detainee. It is essential that entries be made in the custody record as soon as the activity is complete and not left until later as the matter may be overlooked or a subsequent entry be made by another officer, thus exposing to view a late entry. All matters should be accurately recorded at the time as they cannot be put right retrospectively.

These six main areas of responsibility of the detention officer are vital to the smooth and efficient running of the custody office, whether it be a 10-cell complex with one sergeant or a 50-cell complex with two or more sergeants. The contribution made by the detention officer cannot be exaggerated in that he is the link between all persons in the custody suite: detainees, doctors, lay visitors, family and friends, as well as police officers.

Personal requirements

Detention officers need to be keen, fit, alert and, above all, employ a sense of dignity when dealing with detainees, who, in many cases, are simply at a disadvantage and find themselves in police stations as a result of circumstances which are not always of their making. Detention officers should be no strangers to confrontation and their communication and negotiating skills should be such that they should never be at a disadvantage.

Avoid judgmentalism

A fatal flaw which detention officers must at all costs avoid is in being judgmental when dealing with detainees. Whatever wrong a detainee may be thought guilty of he should be shown equality signals and treated with dignity.

Different cultures have different values and this should be respected.

Discipline

The checks and balances that operate on the detention officer are the same as those which govern the activities of the custody officer. PACE prohibits behaviour which does not comply with the Codes of Practice and officers who transgress are subject to disciplinary action. In addition to disciplinary action, officers who fail to comply with the Act or Codes of Practice may be liable to a civil law suit where they will bear individual responsibility for their actions.

Finding your way

As a special constable you will quickly find yourself in the custody suite with an arrested person whom you want to have booked in by the custody officer. Custody officer duties are an exact science and when there is a flaw in procedure or the law is not strictly followed then the case is usually fatally flawed and will not proceed to court. It is essential that the special constable is as aware of the custody officer procedures as his regular counterpart because the courts will not make a distinction in favour of any party to the proceedings. Custody officers are highly specialised people and enjoy a thorough understanding of the Police and Criminal Evidence Act 1984 (PACE) and in most cases undergo specialist training. PACE actually came into being on 1 January 1986 and has several Codes of Practice which have recently been amended. We will deal now with the procedures involved from arrest, through the complexities of the custody suite, to charge and appearance before a court.

From arrest to police station

Warrant | S 117(3) Magistrates' Courts Act 1980, s 47(8) PACE

If the arrest is on **warrant for non-payment backed for bail**, then the arrested person may be released on bail to the court by you. This is known as doorstep bail. The warrant need not be in your actual possession but must be in existence. Each force uses its own forms for this purpose.

Delay | S 30(7) & (8) PACE

When there is a **delay in taking the arrested person to a police station** as his presence elsewhere is necessary in order to carry out such investigations as it is reasonable to carry out immediately, ie search, then this is allowed.

Release before arrival | S 30(10) PACE

If you wish to **release before arrival** at a police station because you are satisfied before arrival that the arrested person is no longer subject to grounds for keeping him under arrest then he should be **de-arrested**.

Designated police station

Arrested persons must be taken as soon as practicable to a designated police station. Certain police stations are designated by the chief officer of police and are more usually stations where there is a proper custody suite, a custody officer, and where there are to be found an inspector and superintendent. A list is held in each force showing which stations are designated for the purposes of the Act.

The exceptions - non-designated station

When an officer is working in a locality covered by a non-designated police station then he may take the arrested person to a non-designated police station **unless** it appears to the officer that it may be necessary to keep the arrested person for **more than six hours**. `S 30(3) & (4) PACE`

The rationale for this **six-hour rule** is that an inspector has a duty to review the arrested person's detention after six hours and it is rare to find an inspector at a non-designated police station. If it appears that the arrested person may be detained for more than six hours then it is better to take him to a designated police station.

If any officer **arrests on his own**, or takes into custody on his own from a person who is not a constable - and in either case, no other officer is available to assist AND it appears to him that he will be unable to take the person to a designated police station without him injuring himself, the constable or some other person - then he may take the arrested person to **any** police station. `S 30(5) PACE`

If an arrested person is **not released within six hours** he should be taken to a designated police station. `S 30(6) PACE`

It is important for you to discover which police stations are designated and which are non-designated in order that you take your arrested person in the first place to a designated police station. The circumstances outlined above are exceptions and not the rule.

The custody officer

Who the custody officer is depends whether the police station is a designated police station or a non-designated police station. Designated police stations have all the facilities to deal with arrested persons, ie: a custody suite, a custody officer who is specially trained, an inspector at hand to carry out reviews of detention and a superintendent who is called upon from time to time for certain authorities required in law and to resolve problems where there is a dispute between the custody officer and the review officer (a rare occurrence).

Designated police stations

At a designated police station the first choice of custody officer shall be the appointed custody officer. `S 36(4)`

Invariably such an officer is readily available to carry out these duties.

However, if the appointed custody officer is not readily available, then the second choice shall be a sergeant - except one involved in the investigation of an offence for which the person is in detention. `S 36(4)`

When no such sergeant is readily available, then the third choice is any officer. In the rare event of this occurring then the superintendent has to be informed and will provide a superintendent's authority to cover the emergency.

[S 36(4) & (5) PACE]

Non-designated police stations

At non-designated police stations the first choice of custody officer shall be a sergeant - except one involved in the investigation of an offence for which the person is in detention. Where no such sergeant is readily available then the second choice is any officer.

[S 36(7)(b) PACE]

If the officer who is employed as custody officer is the same officer who took the arrested person to the police station then he shall inform an inspector or above attached to a designated police station as soon as is practicable.

[S 36(9) & (10) PACE]

Custody officer duties

This section is designed in order to enable you, the special constable, to have a basic understanding of custody procedure which will allow you to follow the action while on duty in a custody suite and also to enhance your knowledge of the law. It does not aim to train or give sufficient information for you to act as a custody officer. The custody officer is perhaps the most important individual in the police force and it is certainly true that he shoulders enormous responsibility. This section is by no means exhaustive and touches on:

(a) arrival at the police station;
(b) grounds for detention;
(c) officers at variance;
(d) ascertaining property in possession;
(e) retention of property by arrested person;
(f) arrested person's rights;
(g) named person to be informed of arrest;
(h) delay in informing named person;
(j) solicitors - free legal advice;
(k) urgent interviews;
(l) interviews without a solicitor;
(m) insufficient evidence to charge;
(n) authorising detention;
(o) cells;
(p) treatment of detained persons;
(q) charging;
(r) questioning after charge;
(s) detention after charge;
(t) fingerprints and photographs;
(u) reviews of detention/representations;
(v) time limits on detention.

Arrival at police station

[S 31 PACE]

When an arrested person is brought to a police station in the custody of a constable or any other person, having been arrested for an offence either without warrant or on warrant not backed for bail, then he must be seen by the custody officer who shall start a custody record. If the arrested person is surrendering to bail, then he must be seen by the custody officer who will continue with the original custody record. The arrested person should be arrested for all offences for which he is liable to arrest.

If grounds for detention cease `S 34(2) (3) (4) PACE`

If grounds for detention cease and no others apply and the arrested person is not unlawfully at large, then only the custody officer can authorise release. This makes a distinction between 'de-arrest' on the streets by the arresting officer and 'refused charge' at the police station by the custody officer.

Officers at variance `S 39(6) PACE`

If an officer of higher rank than the custody officer gives directions at variance with any decision or action taken or to be taken by the custody officer, then the matter must be referred to the superintendent. It is clear from this section that the custody officer commands great power in the exercise of his duties in the custody office. Where an inspector or chief inspector requires a certain course of action which is at odds with the proposed course the custody officer wishes to take, the custody officer usually prevails. It is rare indeed for decisions to be taken at variance.

Ascertaining property in possession `S 54(1) PACE`

The custody officer is responsible for ascertaining what property a detained person has with him when he comes to the police station, whether on arrest, re-detention on answering to bail, commitment to prison custody, lodgement at a police station with a view to his production in court, lodgement at a police station on transfer from one station to another, or if he is detained under the Mental Health Act. The custody officer has to ascertain what property he might have acquired for an unlawful or harmful purpose while in custody. It is for the custody officer to ensure the safekeeping of any property which is taken from the arrested person. To this end the custody officer may search him or authorise his being searched to the extent that the custody officer considers necessary (providing that a search of an intimate part of the body or involving the removal of more than outer clothing is made in accordance with the special permissions laid down in the Codes of Practice). A search may only be carried out by an officer of the same sex as the person searched.

Retention of property by arrested person `Code C`

A detained person may retain clothing and personal effects at his own risk unless the custody officer considers that he may use them:

(a) to cause harm to himself or others; or,
(b) to interfere with evidence; or,
(c) to damage property; or,
(d) to effect an escape; or,
(e) they are needed as evidence.

In this event the custody officer may withhold such articles as he considers necessary. If he does so he must tell the arrested person why. Personal effects are those items which a person may lawfully need or use or refer to while in detention but do not include cash and other items of value.

Arrested person's rights

> Code C

Upon arrival at a police station the custody officer shall read the rights leaflet to the arrested person, provide him with a copy and obtain a signature on the custody record, and also supply a legal aid notice.

If juvenile

Read in presence of appropriate adult if present. If not, repeat on arrival of appropriate adult. For these purposes a juvenile is anyone who appears to be under the age of 17 years.

If deaf or does not understand English

Call an interpreter.

If blind

Ensure a relative, solicitor, appropriate person, adult, or person with an interest in the detainee, is available to assist with documentation etc.

If mentally handicapped.

Read in presence of appropriate adult if present. If not, repeat on arrival of appropriate adult.

Named person to be informed

> S 56 and Code C

An arrested person is entitled to have someone informed of his arrest and he is entitled not to be held incommunicado. Any person arrested and held in custody at a police station or other premises may, on request, have one person known to him, or who is likely to take an interest in his welfare, informed at public expense as soon as practicable of his whereabouts. If the person cannot be contacted, the person who has made the request may choose up to two alternatives. If they too cannot be contacted, the person in charge of detention or of the investigation has discretion to allow further attempts until the information has been conveyed.

Delay in informing named person or solicitor

> Code C, Annex B

The above rights may be delayed if the person is in police detention in connection with a serious arrestable offence, has not yet been charged with an

offence and an officer of the rank of superintendent or above has reasonable grounds for believing that the exercise of the right:
- (a) will lead to interference with or harm to evidence connected with a serious arrestable offence or interference with or physical injury to other persons; or,
- (b) will lead to the alerting of other persons suspected of having committed such an offence but not yet arrested for it; or,
- (c) will hinder the recovery of property obtained as a result of such an offence.

When the named person is informed - or there is a superintendent's authority to delay the intimation - then the custody record will be written up accordingly and the arrested person informed.

Solicitors - free legal advice

> S 58 PACE and Code C

The arrested person should be told of his right to free legal advice. He should signify on the custody record whether he wants legal advice at this time. No police officer shall at any time do or say anything with the intention of dissuading a person in detention from obtaining legal advice.

Urgent interviews

> Code C, Annex C

If, and only if, an officer of the rank of superintendent or above considers that delay will involve an immediate risk of harm to persons or serious loss of, or serious damage to, property:
- (a) a person heavily under the influence of drink or drugs may be interviewed in that state; or,
- (b) an arrested juvenile or a person who is mentally disordered or mentally handicapped may be interviewed in the absence of an appropriate adult; or,
- (c) a person who has difficulty in understanding English or who has a hearing disability may be interviewed in the absence of an interpreter.

Questioning in these circumstances may not continue once sufficient information to avert the immediate risk has been obtained. A record shall be made of the grounds for any decision to interview a person under this power.

Note for guidance. The special groups referred to above are all particularly vulnerable. The provisions of this power, which overrides safeguards designed to protect vulnerable people and to minimise the risk of interviews producing unreliable evidence, should be applied only in cases of exceptional need.

Interviews without a solicitor

> S 56 PACE & Code C

If at any time the arrested person wants legal advice then he may not be interviewed until he has received it unless:

(a) the rules concerning delay in informing a named person or solicitor apply ante; or,
(b) a superintendent believes delay will involve immediate risk of harm to a person or loss of or damage to property, or that awaiting the arrival of a solicitor would cause unreasonable delay to the investigation; or,
(c) the solicitor nominated or selected cannot be contacted, does not wish to be contacted, or declines to attend and the duty solicitor has been offered and has refused to attend or is unavailable; or,
(d) he has given agreement in writing or on tape;
(e) where a person who wanted a solicitor changes his mind and no longer requests a solicitor, before an interview can take place the authorisation of an officer of the rank of inspector or above, is required. The officer must satisfy himself as to the reason for the person's change of mind and be satisfied that it is proper to continue the interview.

Insufficient evidence to charge

S 37(11) PACE

When there is insufficient evidence to charge an arrested person then the custody officer may refuse the charge, or, may bail him to a police station. If the arrested person first arrives at a police station and at that time there is insufficient evidence to charge, there are times when the custody officer may detain long enough to consider matters.

Authorising detention

Ss 37 and 56 PACE

When a detention condition applies to a person, ie:
(a) the need to secure and preserve evidence; or,
(b) to obtain such evidence by questioning him; or,
(c) he is unlawfully at large;

then the custody officer shall inform the detained person of the detention condition and record it in his presence, unless the detained person is:
(a) incapable of understanding; or,
(b) violent or likely to become so; or,
(c) in urgent need of medical attention.

The right to have someone informed of the place of detention applies to every transfer.

Cells

Code of Practice, Code C

After detention has been authorised, adults may then be placed in cells. A juvenile, however, should not be placed in cells unless there is no other secure accommodation available, and the custody officer considers it is not otherwise practicable to supervise him. Juveniles should never share a cell with an adult.

Treatment of detained persons

Medical treatment [Code C]

The custody officer must immediately call the police surgeon (or, in urgent cases, send the person to hospital or call the nearest available medical practitioner) if a person brought to a police station or already detained there:
(a) appears to be suffering from physical illness or disorder; or
(b) is injured; or,
(c) does not show signs of sensibility and awareness; or,
(d) fails to respond normally to questions or conversation (other than through drunkenness alone); or,
(e) otherwise appears to need medical attention.

This applies even if the person makes no request for medical attention and whether or not he has recently had medical treatment elsewhere (unless brought to the police station direct from hospital).

If a detained person requests a medical examination the police surgeon must be called as soon as is practicable; he may in addition be examined by a medical practitioner of his own choice, at his own expense.

Deaf or does not understand English [Code C]

Most local authority social services departments can supply a list of interpreters who have the necessary skills and experience to interpret for the deaf at police stations.

The local community relations council may be able to provide similar information in cases where the person concerned does not understand English.

Blind or seriously visually handicapped [Code C]

If a person is blind, or seriously visually handicapped, or is unable to read, the custody officer should ensure that his solicitor, relative, an appropriate adult or some other person likely to take an interest in him (and not involved in the investigation) is available to help in checking any documentation. Where the Code requires written consent then the person who is assisting may be asked to sign instead if the detained person so wishes.

Mentally ill or mentally handicapped [Code C]

If a person is mentally handicapped or is suffering from a mental disorder, then the custody officer must, as soon as practicable, inform an appropriate adult of the grounds for his detention and his whereabouts, and ask the adult to come to the police station to see the person.

Persons arrested under the Mental Health Act [Code C]

It is imperative that a mentally disordered or mentally handicapped person who has been detained under s 136 of the Mental Health Act be assessed as soon as possible. An approved social worker and a registered medical practitioner should be called to examine the person. Once he has been examined and suitable arrangements made for his treatment or care he can no longer be detained under section 136. He should not be released until he has been seen by both the social worker and the registered medical practitioner.

Juveniles

If the person is a juvenile, the custody officer must, if it is practicable, ascertain the identity of a person responsible for his welfare. That person may be his parent or guardian (or, if he is in care, the care authority or voluntary organisation) or any other person who has for the time being assumed responsibility for his welfare.

That person must be informed as soon as practicable that the juvenile has been arrested and where he is detained. If the juvenile is known to be the subject of a supervision order, reasonable steps must also be taken to notify the person supervising him.

Notice of entitlements   `Code C`

The notice of entitlements provided to detained persons is intended to provide them with brief details of their entitlements over and above their statutory rights which are set out in the notice of rights. It should list:

(a) rights to have visits and contact with outside parties;
(b) reasonable standards of physical comfort;
(c) adequate food and drink;
(d) access to toilets and washing facilities;
(e) clothing;
(f) medical attention;
(g) exercise where applicable;
(h) the conduct of interviews;
(j) the circumstances in which an appropriate adult should be available to assist the detained person; and,
(k) his statutory rights to make representation whenever the period of his detention is reviewed.

The Codes of Practice

Arrested persons are entitled to consult the Codes of Practice and must be told of this when they are seen by the custody officer.

The Codes must be readily available at all police stations for consultation by police officers, detained persons and members of the public.

Charging

When there is sufficient evidence to charge a detained person and he is fit to be dealt with, then he should be charged or reported for summons. (He may of course be cautioned in line with force policy.) If he is a juvenile or is suffering from mental illness or is mentally handicapped, then the charge, reporting for summons or caution should be in the presence of an appropriate adult.

At the time of charging, the detained person should be given a written notice showing particulars of the offence with which he is charged and including the name of the officer in the case, his police station and the reference number for the case. So far as possible the particulars of the charge shall be stated in simple terms, but they shall also show the precise offence in law with which he is charged. The notice shall begin with the following words:

'You are charged with the offence(s) shown below.

You do not have to say anything. But it may harm your defence if you do not mention now something which you later rely on in court. Anything you say may be given in evidence.'

If the person is a juvenile or is mentally disordered or mentally handicapped the notice shall be given to the appropriate adult.

Questioning after charge   `Code C`

Questions relating to an offence may not be put to a person after he has been charged with that offence, or informed that he may be prosecuted for it, unless they are necessary for the purpose of:
- (a) preventing or minimising harm or loss to some other person or to the public; or,
- (b) clearing up an ambiguity in a previous answer or statement; or,
- (c) where it is in the interests of justice that the person should have put to him, and have an opportunity to comment on, information concerning the offence which has come to light since he was charged or reported for it;

he should, however, be cautioned first.

Detention conditions after charge   `Ss 38 & 40 PACE`

An arrested person cannot be detained in custody after charge unless a detention condition applies. There are currently only four conditions:
1. name and address not ascertained or believed to be false; or,
2. necessary for his own protection or to prevent him injuring another or causing loss or damage to property; or,
3. he will fail to appear, interfere with witnesses or obstruct justice; or,
4. he ought to be detained in his own interest (applies only to juveniles).

If detention is to be authorised by the custody officer then he shall inform the detained person of the detention condition and record the fact in his presence unless the detained person is:
- (a) incapable of understanding; or,
- (b) violent or likely to become so; or,
- (c) in urgent need of medical attention.

Section 28 of the Criminal Justice and Public Order Act 1994 amends S 38 PACE to provide additional grounds for police detention after charge:
1. if arrested for an imprisonable offence, that it is necessary to prevent him committing an offence;
2. for his own protection;
3. to prevent him interfering with the investigation of an offence.

When a detention condition applies and therefore a person has been detained in police custody after being charged with an offence, he must be brought before a magistrates' court as soon as is practicable.

Fingerprints and photographs `S 61 PACE & Code D`

Fingerprints and photographs may be taken of persons aged 10 years and over charged with, or reported for, recordable offences. A list of recordable offences is held by the custody officer.

Fingerprints include palm prints. Reasonable force may be used to take fingerprints if necessary. Fingerprints of a person and all copies of them taken in that case must be destroyed as soon as practicable if the person is prosecuted for the offence concerned and cleared, or is not prosecuted (unless he admits the offence and is cautioned for it) - retention of fingerprints and samples in certain cases. He should be informed beforehand that his prints may be the subject of a speculative search against other fingerprints.

Reviews of detention `Ss 34 and 40 PACE`

When a person is in detention for an offence, then his conditions for detention must be reviewed constantly to ensure that the police are dealing with the matter diligently and expeditiously. To that end PACE requires that a review officer be appointed at each designated police station. The identity of the review officer depends on whether or not the arrested person has been charged. Before charge the review officer shall be an inspector or above, not directly involved in the investigation. After charge the review officer shall be the custody officer.

If a detention condition ceases at any time the detained person shall be released with or without bail unless he is unlawfully at large.

Reviews may be conducted by telephone if it is the only practical way.

First review. Not more than six hours from time of first authorisation of detention.

Second review. Not more than nine hours after first review.

Subsequent reviews. Are not to be at more than nine-hour intervals.

Postponement of review. A review may be postponed beyond the latest time due and carried out as soon as practicable afterwards if:
(a) having regard to all the circumstances prevailing at the latest time specified for it, it is not practicable to carry out the review at that time; or,
(b) at that time the person in detention is being questioned by a police officer and the review officer is satisfied that an interruption of the questioning for the purposes of carrying out the review would prejudice the investigation in connection with which he is being questioned; or,
(c) at that time no review officer is readily available.

Representations to review officer

S 40 PACE

Before determining whether to authorise continued detention, the review officer **shall give** the following persons an opportunity to make representations, either orally or in writing:

The detained person - unless asleep or unfit by reason of his condition or behaviour. If asleep then his review should be brought forward.

His solicitor - if he is available at the time of the review.

The responsible adult - if available at the time.

The following **may** make representations at the **review officer's discretion**:

Any other person - having an interest in the detained person's welfare. Any representation made in writing should be retained. Oral representations should be recorded in the custody record and responded to in writing by the review officer.

Review officer's detention conditions

With or without charge

Ss 37, 38 & 40 PACE

After charge

See the conditions set out on p114.

Not charged

A person may be detained without charge **by an inspector or above** if:
(1) detention is necessary to secure and preserve evidence of the offence; or,
(2) to obtain such evidence by questioning.

If a **detention condition applies** then the person should be so informed unless:

S 38 PACE

(a) he is incapable of understanding; or,
(b) he is violent or likely to become so; or,
(c) he is in urgent need of medical attention.

If a **detention condition does not apply**, then:
> if charged he should be released with or without bail following charge and - if bailed - to a court with or without conditions;
> if not charged, he should be released without bail or on bail to a police station.

Ss 37 & 38 PACE

Time limits on detention without charge

The general rule concerning time limits on detention without charge is that an arrested person cannot be held in police detention longer than **24 hours** after arrest. The first question that arises is at what time was he arrested, this is known as 'the relevant time'.

If arrested in your own force area

The relevant time starts at the time of arrival at the first police station to which he is taken after arrest, or, if arrested at a police station, then at the time of arrest.

If arrested in another force area in England or Wales `S 41`

The relevant time starts either 24 hours after his arrest, or at the time of arrival at the first police station in the force area in which the offence is being investigated, whichever happens first. However, the time will start on arrival at a police station in the arresting force area if he is questioned about the offence.

If the arrested person is arrested in another force area and he is in detention there for any offence, then the relevant time is the earlier of 24 hours after leaving the place where detained, or the time of arrival at the first police station in the force area in which the offence is being investigated.

When arrested on behalf of another force `S 41`

If you make an arrest for another force, inform the other force that they must collect the detainee. The relevant time will begin either 24 hours after arrest or at the time of arrival at the second force, whichever is the earlier.

Do not put any questions to the arrested person in order to obtain evidence in relation to the offence for which the person has been arrested unless asked by the other force to do so, otherwise time in detention begins to run from when you commence questioning.

If removed to hospital `S 41`

When in detention, any time when the person is questioned by a police officer on the way to or from, or at hospital for the purposes of obtaining evidence is included in the time in detention before charge.

If detained after reporting on bail to a police station `S 47`

Any time in police detention prior to being granted bail is to be included in the time in detention before charge.

Arrested outside England and Wales `S 41`

Where a person is arrested outside England and Wales, the relevant time starts at the earliest time of 24 hours after entry into England and Wales, or, the time of arrival at the first police station in the force area where the offence is being investigated.

Further detention `Ss 42, 43 & 44`

Arrested persons can be detained beyond 24 hours in special circumstances. In the first instance the detention may be extended to 36 hours by the use of a superintendent's authority and in the second by obtaining a warrant from the magistrates' court. These procedures should be discussed with your custody officer.

CHAPTER 8

INTERVIEWING

Chapter contents

Planning **120**
    The information 120
    The evidence 121
    The offence/defence 122
Who's who? **123**
    The suspect 123
    The solicitor 124
    Trainees, clerks and legal
    executives 124
Case law - solicitors and confessions **125**
    Oppression and inducement 126
Questioning **127**
    The classification of questions 128
    Closed and leading questions - counterproductive ..130
    Open questions - productive 132
    Art-form questioning 133
        Key-word repetition 133
        Echoing 134
        Supportiveness 134
    Summary of questioning technique 135
    Recall v process questions 137
Summaries **138**
    The Bentley case 139
    The Y factor 140
    Ambiguities 140
Tape recorded interview procedure **141**
    Recording and sealing master tapes 141
    Interviews to be tape recorded 141
    The interview 141
        Significant statement or silence 142
        Ambush defence - special warnings 142
        Statements made - not on tape 143
        Conclusion of interview 143
    Tape recorded interview procedure model 144

Planning

When did you last launch a bottomless ship, build a garden wall without foundations, drive onto the motorway without first checking your fuel gauge, or consider putting the washing out without first checking the weather? We don't do we? Because we would be planning to fail.

When considering the question of preparation and planning for an interview, much has to be considered. What is the information, is it good, does it come from a reliable source, or is it gossip which has taken on the mantle of gospel? From the information, where do we look for evidence, what evidence are we looking for? Having gathered the evidence, does it amount to an offence known to law, or is it just offensive? If it is an offence known to law, who committed it. Who is the offender, can he be identified? Having identified the offender, when is it best to interview him, and where? How do we cope with his solicitor if he has one? What defences are open to the offender? Quite apart from having to prove *actus reus* (that he physically committed the offence), we also have to prove *mens rea* (he knew what he was doing and that it was wrong). What defences exist?

The days are gone when, following a crime which fitted a particular *modus operandi* used by a particular villain, he was 'nicked' because he was 'favourite' and the interview was down to what police called 'a cough to nothing'. Everything relied on the belief that if we went at him long and hard enough, he would admit it. We salved our consciences by having him admit things only the offender would know or by recovering property from a location given to us by the offender.

The better the game-plan before the interview, the more disadvantaged the interviewee will be. The ideal to find yourself in as an interviewer, is to interview for two reasons only - to allow the suspect to play his 'Y' card and to negate any defences to the offence.

The information

The bearer of information must know that what he says will be incorporated into a written Criminal Justice Act statement, which will be subjected to scrutiny and acted upon, and that the information might subsequently be tested in court. I accept that certain registered informers and the anonymous information that comes our way, by definition, cannot be tested in this way, but, as a general rule - no representation without taxation. The person who volunteers information, but will not back it up with a degree of moral courage, in many ways is not unlike the gossipmonger we find in any organisation, including the police force.

How often has canteen gossip disadvantaged someone you know, maybe even yourself? To act on poor information is the road to ruin. Information that is accepted at face value, without check or probe, is the basic building block of offending natural justice. You may have been on the wrong end of this denial of natural justice. Take for example, the last time you were overlooked for a post. Was it because the 'whispering gallery' suggested your name was linked with something it ought not to be. You find yourself found guilty of an offence which is not known to law, you have not heard the charge (to which you may have a complete answer), punitive measures may be taken against you (denial of the post), and there is no right of appeal. This is the classic denial of natural justice. We suffer from this in our daily lives. Let us ensure that we check ourselves when dealing with others, in the same way that we wish that our masters would check themselves when dealing with us.

Also, if we act on information that is not checked, not tested, probed and prodded, then we lend ourselves to civil proceedings for wrongful arrest, false imprisonment and worse. Increasingly, police forces are paying out large sums of money to litigants who sue successfully because the police acted, albeit in good faith, prematurely, and unwisely. So tread carefully. If informants will not commit their information to paper, then ask yourself why.

The evidence

Substantially, evidence comes in two parts; the allegation, and the real (physical) evidence which tends to corroborate the allegation. A suspect should be left in no doubt that it is not the police who are creating a charge, but the victim's allegation, witnessed by Y and Z, and evidenced by injuries, property, forensic, finger prints, etc.

We must distance ourselves from the idea that the evidence will flow from the interview. Too often we have to adjourn an interview and rush out and gather more evidence - another statement, visit the scene or whatever. This is done, not because the suspect has given us more information, but because he hasn't. If we adjourn the interview to gather more information, then why did we fail to gather it before the interview? We really have to be prepared for the suspect to tell us nothing so, go into the interview room fully prepared. By adjourning an interview you disadvantage yourself. The detention clock continues to tick away and you have signalled to the suspect that you were poorly prepared.

When an adjournment is necessary time is being lost, if not squandered. The 24 hours allowed by PACE are slowly being eroded, and every hour that passes favours the suspect. The only way to extend the 24 hours is by using section 47(3), bail. If you use this section for anything other than forensic results, ID parades, or protracted inquiries, then you probably went into the interview badly prepared. We often hear that someone has been arrested on suspicion of a section 47(3)! The more evidence you have available in the interview room, the stronger your hand. Let the suspect know that you have been busy, seen all the witnesses, collected the real evidence, and have a complete understanding of what has occurred. If he is guilty, then his position is much weakened.

The offence/defence

If we have received information or an allegation, we gather what evidence there is to hand. We must now look at what we have and decide if this is an offence known to law. Smashing a window is not an offence if the window belongs to the vandal. Taking a conveyance is not an offence if it is taken with the permission of the owner or other lawful authority, and obtaining money by the use of menaces is not blackmail if the menace is the proper way of reinforcing the demand (eg if you don't pay this last reminder for your electricity bill - we will cut you off). In short, we have to know the law, we have to know definitions and also the points to prove. We have to prove, in nearly every case, the two main constituents of every crime, the *actus reus* and *mens rea* - the guilty act and the guilty state of mind.

Is there a a remedy available to the victim, other than the criminal courts? If the answer is yes, talk him through the civil remedy as well as the criminal course of action. Litigation, compensation, restitution, insurance or even apology may be appropriate. Equally, ask yourself if the police are the proper authorities to instigate proceedings. Offences by military personnel can in many cases be tried by the military power. Is it a case of, say, noise pollution, in which the local authority are responsible for gathering evidence?

If the matter is a criminal offence, and the police are the proper authority for instituting proceedings, then before interview we have to look carefully at the law. I recall prosecuting a summary offence at a magistrates' court in the West country in the mid 1970s. It was a case of a man owning two dogs without dog licences and I was surprised to find that the case was defended by one of the better solicitors in town. My case was on first and the court was packed with solicitors awaiting their cases. After the charge was read out and a not guilty plea entered by the clerk, I rose to my feet and asked the defendant if it was right that on a certain date he was the owner of two large dogs. He agreed that he was. I asked him if he had dog licences on that date: he said he hadn't. I told the magistrates that that was the case for the prosecution and sat down. His solicitor rose and in rather too loud a voice said: 'Mr Green, would you explain to the court why you don't need dog licences?' Well, he did. He said, in something of a whisper: 'They're sheep dogs, aren't they!'

What was left of my memory quickly convinced me that I had read somewhere that sheep dogs were exempt from the requirements of a licence. I was facing total humiliation in front of about 10 solicitors, all of whom were known to me. What to do . . . ? I rose to my feet as slowly as decency permitted, thinking, just a few obligatory questions, a spirited challenge, then collapse. I asked a few questions about the size of his farm. Finally, only by way of a closing broadside, I asked: 'How many sheep do you actually have?' Answer: 'Two.' 'Two?' I repeated. 'Two,' he confirmed. I could smell success. I said: 'Are you really asking this court to believe that your two sheep are so undisciplined, so fractious, so recalcitrant, as to require a dog apiece?' He shamefacedly repeated: 'Yes.' He was acquitted.

I had been guilty of not ensuring that the defence had been negated. For most offences, there is a defence. When the defence is negated, we have a substantive offence. Can you recall when you last reported a motorist for a defective light? Did you ask him when he last checked his lights? If not, then you failed to negate the defence, because it is a defence to show that it happened on the journey. How may times have the decision-makers sent prosecution files back marked, 'no further action' because the defence has not been negated? Just a few I suspect. Before going into the interview room, prepare for yourself something, anything, so long as it acts as a reminder of what has to be proved:

INFORMATION	Jones was found driving a stolen car, Smith was the front seat passenger.	S 12(1) Theft Act 1968
EVIDENCE	Mr Green secured his car at 11pm and found it missing at 8am. No one had permission to take it. PC Russel found both Smith and Jones in the car at 4am.	
OFFENCE	(1) Jones – taking a vehicle without authority. (2) Smith – being carried.	
DEFENCE	No offence if done in the belief that he has lawful authority or the owner's consent.	

Who's who?

The suspect

Who is the suspect? Is he known? What do we know about him? Has he had previous experience of dealing with the police, if so, with whom? What can the officer who has dealt with him in the past tell us about him? What previous convictions, if any, has he? Is it his modus operandi? What can we discover about him from any previous antecedents?

The more we know about the suspect, the better prepared we are to deal with him. He may be known to be a strictly no-reply merchant, or, when presented with real evidence, be prepared to admit to the crime. The more we know, the less we are likely to be surprised by his behaviour. If we know his address, his habits, his associates, his workplace etc, then we are better positioned to arrest him on our terms. We can choose the time and the place to our best advantage.

Always remember the detention clock that starts to tick the moment we arrive at the police station, or when questioning begins. If we know that he is the sort of man always to ask for a solicitor and that his solicitor usually takes three hours to come to the police station, then it would be counter-productive to make the arrest at 4am, in the knowledge that his solicitor cannot be contacted until 9am, and then wait until 12 noon for him to attend the police station. Eight wasted hours - not his hours, our hours. Only 16 hours left; if the inquiry is a difficult one, or serious, then we disadvantage ourselves by not picking the time to arrest that suits us most. The more we know about the suspect the better we are able to exercise good and sound judgement.

The solicitor

Solicitors tend to breeze into police stations with an authoritative air that suggests that they have some sort of advantage over the police officer - they have not. They are professional consultants. Just as we are seeking the truth, so they are present at the interview to look after their clients' interests.

> 'If a person has been permitted to consult a solicitor and the solicitor is available... he must be allowed to have his solicitor present while he is interviewed.'

Code C

Most solicitors, if treated properly, will respond responsibly. It is important to treat them as equals, professional people working towards a common goal - the truth of the matter. If they are treated as the enemy then they may behave like the enemy. Behaviour breeds behaviour.

The removal of a solicitor from an interview room is a very serious step. It requires the authority of a superintendent, who will only act if the solicitor's conduct is such that the investigating officer is unable to put questions to the suspect properly. This has never happened in my experience. The matter is considered so serious that the superintendent should consider whether or not the matter should be reported to the Law Society. The sort of reasons which might give rise to this expulsion are where the solicitor himself answers all the questions on his client's behalf, or perhaps if he hands written answers to his client to all the questions put by the police. If expulsion of the solicitor does take place, the suspect will be given the opportunity to consult another solicitor before the interview continues and that solicitor will be given an opportunity to be present at the interview.

All this grief is best avoided. Where the police officer behaves professionally, the chance of this situation developing is, frankly, nil. Where there are difficulties of this nature during the interview the police do not always find that they are wholly blameless. The expulsion of a solicitor from the interview should be as rare as Roman coins dated 53 BC.

Trainees, clerks and legal executives

Under the revisions to para 6.12 of Code C, the term 'solicitor' includes a trainee, a clerk or a legal executive accredited in accordance with the Law Society's Scheme. Where a solicitor chooses to send a non-accredited or

probationary representative to the police station to act for his client then he shall be admitted to the police station, unless an inspector (or above), considers that such a visit will hinder the investigation of crime and directs otherwise. In the exercise of this power the inspector may take into account:
- (a) the non-accredited representative's identity and status;
- (b) the suitability of his character to provide legal advice (a person with a criminal record is unlikely to be suitable unless the conviction was for a minor offence and is not of recent date).

It seems to me, that the less fuss there is in the interview room, the more attention can be paid to the reason for the attendance of all parties.

Case law - solicitors and confessions

'Perhaps the most important right given (or rather enacted) to a person detained by the police is his right to obtain legal advice.
R v Samuel (1988)

'However strongly and however justifiably the police may feel that their investigation and detection of crime is being hindered by the presence of a solicitor… they are nevertheless confined to the narrow limits imposed by section 58(8) on their right to delay access.' Conviction for robbery not quashed despite breach of section 58 and old Code C because the defendant had been properly cautioned and was well able to cope with the police interviews. **R v Alladice (1988)**

'Any officer attempting to justify his decision to delay the exercise of this fundamental right of a citizen will, in our judgment, be unable to do so save by reference to specific circumstances including evidence as to the person detained or the actual solicitor sought to be consulted… Duty solicitors will be well known to police, and we think it will therefore be very difficult to justify consultation with the duty solicitor being delayed. If the duty solicitor has the reputation, deserved or not, for advising persons detained to refuse to answer questions that would of course be no reason for delaying consultation.' Conviction for armed robbery quashed because refusal by police of access to solicitor prior to interview had not been justified. **R v Samuel (1988)**

'The wrongful denial of access coupled with other breaches of the Codes were held to be sufficient to render the ensuing confession unreliable, notwithstanding… that there was later evidence that it was true.' Conviction for manslaughter quashed because defendant was of limited intelligence, had been aged 19 at the time and was six months' pregnant, her request for a solicitor had been refused and no contemporaneous note had been taken of her confession. Held, the confession evidence should have been excluded. **R v McGovern (1991)**

A defendant, aged 18 at the time of the Broadwater Farm disturbances in October 1985, had his conviction for the murder of PC Blakelock quashed. The only evidence against him had been his admission to hitting 'a young policeman' with an iron bar. Held, that had he known the circumstances the trial judge would have excluded the interviews. Other factors which influenced the Court of Appeal were the fact that the second defendant was not arrested until 121 days after the murder; there were no grounds for attacking the professional integrity of the second defendant's solicitor; the age of the defendant; the denial of access to a solicitor, a liaison officer or an appropriate person despite a specific request; the extent of the interviews (about 12 hours out of 30.5 hours); the fact that in the eighth, ninth and tenth interviews in the presence of a solicitor the second defendant did not make any reply.

R v Silcott, Braithwaite and Raghip (1991)

At the police station the defendant agreed to be interviewed in the absence of a solicitor because the solicitor she nominated was unavailable. She was not told of the duty solicitor scheme. Held, as the defendant had not been told of the duty solicitor scheme her consent to be interviewed in the absence of a solicitor was given under a misapprehension.

R v Vernon (1988)

The defendant was interviewed twice on the day of his arrest in the absence of a solicitor, the police having wrongfully refused him access. The following day he was again interviewed in the absence of a solicitor, the police having informed him that his rights had been reinstated. Held, all three interviews would be excluded. Even if it could be said that the third interview was untainted, it was vitiated by the previous breaches.

R v Cochrane (1988)

If [a] challenged confession is to be admitted [in evidence], the prosecution must prove to the court beyond reasonable doubt that the confession was not... obtained in consequence of anything said or done which was likely to render it unreliable. Conviction quashed because the defendant was questioned before the police allowed him access to a solicitor, his admissions were not recorded contemporaneously, when a note of the interview was subsequently made it was not shown to the defendant and his solicitor was not told of its existence.

R v Chung (1990)

Oppression and inducement

Oppressive questioning or behaviour by the police can render an admission or confession inadmissible and the lower the mental age of the detainee the more likely this is to become an issue. A confession secured by an inducement (eg a promise of bail) is likely to be found to be unreliable and therefore excluded.

Questioning

So far as questioning is concerned, this is the area in which the police interviewer has much to learn from lawyers and judges. The checks and balances that operate on lawyers in court, operate in prospect and not in retrospect. When a lawyer breaches a rule of evidence by asking an injudicious question, he will be challenged at once by the other side.

> Take, for example, the rule on leading questions:
> 'In direct examination (in court), the general rule is that witnesses shall not be asked leading questions, or in other words questions framed in such a manner as to suggest to the witness the answer required from him. The answers to leading questions are not *per se* inadmissible, although the weight which can be properly attached to them may be substantially reduced.'

Any barrister or solicitor breaching this rule would expect to be challenged. Why is it then, that police officers, as a matter of routine, continue to ask leading questions not always because it is appropriate (though it often is) but by choice?

Questioning techniques applied by lawyers in court, so far as the broad rules are concerned, are highly professional and just as highly polished. Why then are police officers apparently so clumsy in this field? Is this not our bread and butter? Do we not interview suspects, witnesses and victims on a daily basis?

Until the introduction of tape-recorded interviews, brought about by the Police and Criminal Evidence Act 1984 and the attendant Codes of Practice, the *police v suspect* interview was a mystery to everyone, except the combatants.

The Judges' Rules (the forerunner of PACE), were observed more in the breach than in the observance. The closed door of the interview room, housing a suspect and two police officers - without the checks and balances that could be operated on a 'then and there' basis - allowed oppression to rule (the hard man) or inducements to take their insidious toll (the soft man). So that what we had was not so much a voluntary confession, but what villains call a straight 'fit-up' or, as others described it, 'noble-cause corruption'. Most people in the know accepted this as a matter of routine. Noble-cause corruption was shaped by historical factors, the police culture and nurture; everyone did it, therefore it was the norm. People who did not conform were ostracised, and generally shunned, but in any case, went into involuntary exile. You either conformed or perished. Most conformed.

Convictions began to be put aside under the heading 'unsafe and unsatisfactory'. The difficulty for the police was that the numbers of these cases were increasing out of manageable and explainable proportions. It was no good asking the public to make subtle distinctions between 'unsafe and unsatisfactory' and not guilty because he had not done it. So the cold wind of change brought about new rules.

To put this in perspective - everyone knew that villains did not queue up at police station enquiry desks saying: 'Officer, lock me up for I have done wrong.' They had to be captured and confessions extracted, that was the real world. Following the villain's 'full and frank' confession, the police officers in the case would often adopt a siege mentality until the prosecution process was complete and the villain banged up.

I once heard a detective chief inspector giving evidence at a Crown court in the 1970s. Clearly he had acted beyond his powers and the matter had been exposed by defence lawyers. He was invited to offer an explanation for his behaviour. There was a long silence - the jury leaned forward, the judge peered over his half-moon specs, even the court usher looked slightly anxious. When the DCI had everyone's attention he said, and I can still hear this ringing in my ears: 'For the greater good.' The jury smiled in agreement - the defendant was convicted. *1970s' justice might have been right for the '70s, but no longer.*

Police officers are now exposed to retrospective criticism because interviews are tape recorded. This means that we must be professional in prospect. To repeat what was said in the introduction, to be ethical, we have to be seen to be fair and just. During interview we must take the view that the trial judge, barristers, jury members *et al*, are present in the interview room. This will affect your attitude, which in turn will control your behaviour. If, after the interview, all parties agree that it was fair, that it was just, then you have behaved ethically, and defence criticism will be unsustainable. Remember, no longer is the police interview an enigma, shrouded in mystery.

The classification of questions

The classification of questions will be dealt with in some detail. This is a subject mastered by lawyers and little understood by police officers, however competent. Police officers see the classification of questions as something of a legal nightmare. There are two main ideas to start, the counter-productive question, and the productive question. The difficulty is, not only do the goal posts move halfway through the match, but after the match you are likely to be told that the game was not rugby at all, it was football - red card! *So tread carefully, know the rules, be professional.*

Closed and leading questions - counterproductive

Closed questions are generally counter-productive. The closed question takes us only a short way along the road of the interview. Think of a closed question as a question which is framed in such a manner as to suggest to the suspect that the answer must be yes or no. Were you to ask a suspect only closed questions concerning his address, you probably would not have enough of your life left to establish the full facts.

Question:	'Do you live in Warwick?'
Answer:	'No.'
Question:	'Do you live in Swindon?'
Answer:	'No.'
Question:	'London?'
Answer:	'No.'
Question:	'Glasgow?'
Answer:	'No.'

Clearly, closed questions in this case do nothing to advance the cause of the interviewer. Closed questions here are wholly inappropriate. The question that should be asked is: 'Where do you live?' This will either produce the desired answer, or at least an address that can be checked.

When closed questions may be productive

However, there are times when closed questions are appropriate. Think of questions as gearing in a car. Closed questions are first or second gear. If, during the course of an interview, you find yourself saying, 'This is an uphill struggle', then first or second gear is appropriate. We engage low gearing in a car when the going gets tough. If an individual needs bump-starting, or would benefit from jump-leads, then first or second gear is appropriate. Closed questions are productive in this case and may freely be used, however, once started, move quickly up the gears.

Examples of closed questions

'Did you go out last night?'	(closed yes/no)
'Which hand was it in?'	(closed identificatory)
'Did you walk or drive to the pub?'	(closed option)
'Did you walk to the pub or… ?'	(dangling option)

Examples of leading questions:

'You went out last night, didn't you?'	(leading simple)
'You don't go out with that cow Stella, do you?'	(leading critical)

The leading critical question, often begets a reverse leading answer:

Question:	'You didn't vote Tory, did you?'	(leading critical)
Answer:	'Christ, would you?'	(reversed leader)

The last answer told us nothing. Reversed leading answers should be ignored, and the question repeated.

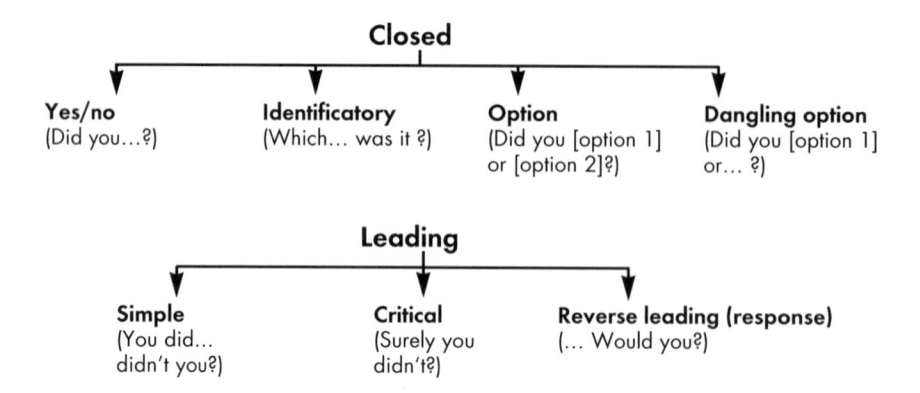

Closed and leading questions

Closed
- **Yes/no** (Did you...?)
- **Identificatory** (Which... was it ?)
- **Option** (Did you [option 1] or [option 2]?)
- **Dangling option** (Did you [option 1] or... ?)

Leading
- **Simple** (You did... didn't you?)
- **Critical** (Surely you didn't?)
- **Reverse leading (response)** (... Would you?)

Such questions may be appropriate when dealing with silences, no-replies, resistance and when suspects need to be jump or bump-started. They are also appropriate when probing expanded topics. The general rule, however, is that open questions are always to be preferred.

Why the police use closed and leading questions

Let us look at the reasons why police officers have asked closed and leading questions. If you understand the reasons why this happens, then your techniques will improve. The three main reasons the police ask closed and leading questions turn on the mechanics employed to record conversations. They are:
(1) pocket book notes (verbals);
(2) contemporaneous notes;
(3) taped summaries.

Unlike solicitors and barristers operating in court, when questions are put and answers given - duly noted first-hand by the bench or the jury (requiring little note taking) - police officers suffer from and are seriously handicapped by the doctrine of remoteness. The bench or jury have to rely on police records made at the time of interview, which they then hear second-hand.

This is where defence lawyers begin to unstitch the police case. Had the bench or the jury been present at the interview, had they witnessed the exchange, there would be little doubt as to exactly what had occurred. The remoteness of the second-hand account lends itself to being tinkered with by the defence in order to create some doubt in the jurors' minds.

Why then, should the defence claim that the police officer's account of what was said differs from the account the suspect says he gave? Because where there is variance, there is a 'not guilty' plea.

Perceived benefits and associated dangers of closed and leading questions

In the real world, what is actually said is not actually recorded verbatim. It is impossible to do so. The problem is that good open questions invite long descriptive answers. Closed leading questions invite short 'manageable' answers.

Here is an example of a good open question:

Question: 'David, tell me what happened leading to your arrest yesterday?'

Answer: 'Buggered if I know, it was nothing to do with me, these two idiots came over and started giving me these bad verbals, and that was that.'

But a rambling answer, however potentially informative, is impractical to record - so we interrupt with a mind-focusing question, a closed question, and stay in that vein, to keep the **subject on course** and make for a manageable recording.

Police officers know perfectly well that they are not going to write down every single word spoken by the suspect, it is too time-consuming, so we close down by asking closed questions. The difficulty here, is that it is often argued that it is the interviewer's course that is travelled, and not the course of the interviewee. Again, the open invitational question:

Question: 'Tell me, why did you steal the purse?'

Answer: 'My Giro got nicked, didn't it? The Social wouldn't pay me no more money, so I went down my mum's house, didn't I? No one in so I waited. I was bloody starving and there was only beer in the fridge, so I had some, then on my way home I found this purse…'

Interruption by the interviewer with

Question: 'Can we summarise that by saying, I don't know what came over me, it must have been the beer?'

Answer: 'Yeah, ok.'

Increasingly, especially in serious cases, such records of interviews are being discredited because linguistic experts are showing that alleged replies attributed to defendants were not couched in the defendant's linguistic mode and are therefore unsafe.

If the defendant did not say the words, who did, who else could?

When interviewing on tape, we have one eye on the suspect and the other on the interview room clock. We are ever mindful of the written tape summary which necessarily has to be compiled. So much writing! So we tell ourselves to keep this more to the point - of course the way to keep to the point is by asking closed and leading questions!

The problem with this is the point that is being kept to is ours, and not necessarily the defendant's. This might be fine from a police perspective, but defendants feel cheated, the judiciary 'know' that the written records are, shall we say, lightweight; this gives rise to 'not guilty' pleas; suggestions of doubt being seeded into the magistrates' minds followed by not guilty verdicts.

It is no good berating ourselves and crying 'foul'. In the past we may have taken shortcuts, always for what we have seen as being the best possible reasons, but shortcuts equal not guilty verdicts.

Let each be the author of what they have to say, however inconvenient.

In many ways contemporaneous note-taking did wonders for conversation management, but not a great deal for free expression.

Open questions - productive

Open questions give rise to open answers. They allow the suspect to introduce the topics for mutual discussion. In the gearing sequence, we are now motoring along in third gear. When police officers give their evidence in chief at court, they are left uninterrupted to give an account of the evidence. The police officer introduces the topics for discussion and, having been introduced, the topics are then looked at in fine-grain detail by the defence, who ask for expansions of particular topics, which are then probed.

We must start with open questions. The use of open questions during the interview of a suspect will not give rise to criticism. There is nothing hidden, no ambush, because the suspect opens the can of worms himself. Open questions were described in a Kipling poem:
'I kept six honest serving men,
They taught me all I knew,
Their names were,
How and **What** and **When**
and **Why** and **Where** and **Who**.'

Any journalist will tell you that if any of the **'WH?'** ingredients are missing from a story, then there is no story. These are known as the interrogatives. While they are probing questions, they are also **invitational**. They are definitive, in that they set out their own parameters, so the suspect knows where the goalposts are. The suspect himself, when asked an interrogative question, will answer with more topics for discussion, each one of which can be expanded and probed. But first, use the power of the open question to introduce the topics. The open interrogatives are global in their implications.

How? In what way, by what means, to what extent, inquiry, what is the meaning. The way a thing is done, the 'how?' of it.

What? A determiner, a request for further information, identity, categorisation, the purpose, 'the what' of it.

When? To state when an action is to be stopped or begun. A time, a period, a delimiter or parameter.

Why? A question as to the cause of something.

Where? At, in, or to what place, location, relativity. A question as to the position, direction or destination of something.

Who? Identification - which person, what person.

Good openers are:
 (a) 'How do you explain... ?'
 (b) 'Talk me through what happened.'
 (c) 'When you say you... tell me what you mean by that.'
 (d) 'Where did you go after you left the pub?'
 (e) 'Who can assist us in verifying what you say?'

No problems for the interviewer here, we are in third gear. Good open questions are not in any way restrictive, leading or suggestive, the answer lies solely in the mouth of the suspect. By now you may be wondering when we can get down to the really searching questions that the suspect does not want to answer. Remember the elephant eater's recommendation, one piece at a time. First we must deal with fourth gear and art-form questioning.

Art-form questioning

Art-form questioning is the notion of flying downhill in your car in fourth gear. Coasting in top gear requires very little effort from the driver (interviewer), a touch of acceleration here, a slight directional change there, even 'look, – no hands', the thing (suspect) practically drives itself. We ask a good open question, then we keep the momentum going by using very simple devices.

Key-word repetition

Statement: 'Last week[1] I went to Scotland[2] on a train[3] to see the match[4].'

Question: 'You went to Scotland[2]?'
Answer: 'Yeah, I had a few days off[5], thought I'd kill two birds with one stone[6] so I had a day in Glasgow[7] and a day in Edinburgh[8].'

Question: 'Two birds with one stone[6]?'
Answer: 'Yeah, my parents live in Glasgow[9] so I had a real beano there[10] and then travelled to Edinburgh for the match[11].'

Question: 'A real beano[10]?'
Answer: 'It was great, had a few jars[12], saw uncle David[13] - didn't get home until four[14].'

Question: 'A few jars[12]?'
Answer: 'Well, quite a few[15]. We went into town[16]. It was my pal's birthday[17] and we got smashed[18].'

Question: 'His birthday[17]?'
Answer: '… '

Who is conducting this interview? The interviewee (or suspect) is in full flow. He started with four topics from the open question and by using the gentlest possible persuasion, and key word repetition; he was nudged, cajoled and teased into producing 18 topics, anyone of which the interviewer could pick up for expansion and subsequent probing. Anyone charged with the duty of finding fault with your questioning technique will have to report that no questions were in fact asked.

By asking no questions how then do we receive the greatest possible benefit? The key word that is repeated to the interviewee provokes him to give an expanded version of his story. Repetition of the key words gives the interviewee the impression that the questioner simply wants more information, or that he is thick - this will cause him to give more information. Try some key word repetition with the next person you speak to. It works a treat and is great fun.

Echoing

We subconsciously use the echo each day of our lives. Echoing, if it is to meet with success, should be practiced at appropriate moments in conversations. The echo is the **repetition of the last word** used by the other party.

Statement:	'I fancy a pint.'
Echo:	'Pint?'
Question:	'Yeah, shall we go down the Swan?'
Echo:	'The Swan?'
Answer:	'I know it's a bit tacky, but there's a competition.'
Echo:	'Competition?'
Answer:	'Yeah, its the darts final.'
Echo:	'Final?'
Answer:	'The Black Bear against the Swan.'
Reply:	'OK.'

The echo, like the key word repetition, must be used sparingly, otherwise the suspect will think you are mocking him. The echo is another device used to keep the conversation in fourth gear. No questions are actually asked, therefore there can be no criticism of your questioning technique. The suspect, however, knows that if you echo his last word then you are asking for more information, and duly discloses. When the echo and key word repetition are used together, the results can be quite breathtaking. There's more...

Supportiveness

This technique is, perhaps, the overdrive of the mechanised questioning skill. This is a true art-form skill showing the professional at his sparkling best. This can be used on the suspect, any interviewee; or even on the person standing next to you in the bus queue. By using supportiveness skillfully, it is quite possible to keep him talking to a point of exhaustion, without ever actually asking a question.

Get into your supportiveness mode, sit, looking at the suspect; lean forward with open hands, be close enough to lay on the notional touch; speak quietly using reinforcers (nods), etc. Do not interrupt, let him do all the talking, act as though you are listening to a man who is telling you a tale of woe. He is your friend and has chosen to disclose to you alone, on a strictly non-attributable basis, behind closed-doors, if you like. You are on his side, he is looking for sympathy and support. Show him empathy... feel for him.

Statement	**Support**
'I'm pissed off.'	'Oh... ?'
'She stood me up.'	'She did... ?'
'The bastard.'	'Right!'
'I love her really.'	'I see... '
'But...'	'Yes... ?'
'I think she's seeing Bob.'	'Really... ?'

'She and him... '	'Go on...'
'They've been seen together.'	'Oh dear... '
'I had a word with her last night.'	'and... ?'
'She denied it.'	'Uh huh... '
'But they are seeing each other.'	'You said.'
'I don't know what to do.'	'Difficult.'
'I think I'll...'	'Yes... ?'
'Have a word with him on his own.'	'And... ?'
'See if I can sort it all out.'	'Right.'

The word 'And... ?' is especially powerful when used in the support mode. Doctors and nurses are seriously into the role of the supportive professional. They have to be. Their patients need to feel that they can disclose their inner-most thoughts, their fears and anxieties, they have to know that the interviewer, be he doctor or nurse, will not judge them, but will show them understanding, empathy, the interviewer will stand in the shoes of the interviewee. It is easy to disclose information of the most personal nature, if you know that the other party will understand - be supportive.

Let us pull all these ideas together now. Remember; you can always tell the quality of an interviewer by the **questions he does not ask.**

Summary of questioning technique

> Only use closed and leading questions when absolutely necessary - when it is a serious uphill struggle - when the interviewee would benefit from a jump-start, just to get him going.
> Move quickly into open questions - these are productive and will allow the interviewee to create topics for discussion.
> Use the interrogatives - the 'How?' the 'What?' the 'When?' the 'Why?' the 'Where?' and the 'Who?'.
> Use good openers - 'Tell me... Talk me through... Why do you suppose... ? Where did you go... ? Who can assist... ? What do you mean... ? How do you explain... ?'
> Now continue into art-form questioning; nudge, cajole, tease, using key word repetition, echoing and supportiveness.

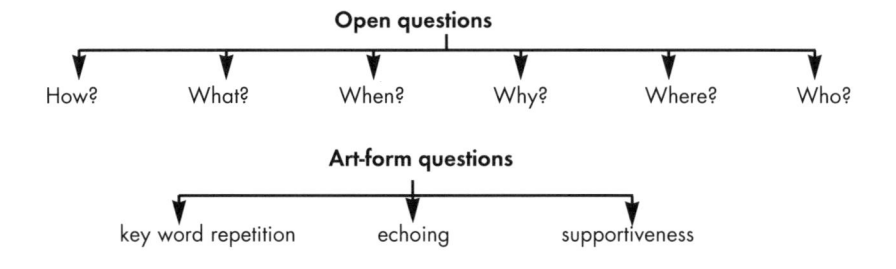

Open questions

How?   What?   When?   Why?   Where?   Who?

Art-form questions

key word repetition   echoing   supportiveness

Let us see what this looks like...

	Dialogue	Questioning technique
Question: Answer:	'Talk me through what happened last night Bob.' 'Damn all.'	**OPEN** Up-hill struggle
Question: Answer:	'Did you go out?' 'For you to find out pal!'	**CLOSED** Resistance
Question: Answer:	'You did go out, didn't you?' 'So, what if I did?'	**LEADING** Co-operation
Question: Answer:	'Tell me about it.' 'I went down the pub that bastard Jason was there so he had some.'	**OPEN** Topic 1 Topic 2 Topic 3
Question: Answer:	'You went down the pub?' 'Yeah, the Pig and Whistle.'	**Key word repetition** Topic 1 expanded
Question: Answer:	'Go on.' 'Like I said, I saw that bastard Jason.'	**Support** Topic 2 expanded
Question: Answer:	'Jason.' 'Jason Mitchell, he's overdue for some.'	**Echo** Topic 3 expanded
Question: Answer:	'Is he?' 'Yeah, we had an argument.'	**Support** Justification
Question: Answer:	'And…' 'I gave him some.'	**Support** Vague
Question: Answer:	'Gave him some?' 'I gave him a smack in the gob, he went down like a stuck pig.'	**Key word repetition** Admission
Question: Answer:	'Why?' 'Because he's been paying too much attention to my girl-friend.'	**OPEN** No defence
Question: Answer:	'So what you're saying then, is that you went to the Pig and Whistle pub last night where you saw Jason Mitchell, and as a result of his paying too much attention to your girlfriend, you punched him in the mouth- is that right?' 'Yeah.'	**Summary** **Offence**

Clearly not all of these techniques can be applied to every case, however, there is always room for more than two techniques to be used. Perfect practice makes perfect.

Recall v process questions

First, let us make a distinction between **recall** and **process** questions. We often, during the course of an interview, wrong-foot ourselves, by failing to understand the sort of question we have put to the suspect, in terms of his having enough time to answer. When we put a question to a suspect certain mental demands are made of him; either there is very little demand, in that all he has to do is to listen to the question in order to answer it, or the demand is such that an answer appears not to be forthcoming, so we repeat the question, or, ask it in another way.

A recall question is precisely that. It requires little mental effort on behalf of the suspect and an immediate answer follows.

Question: 'Who led Germany during World War II?' **recall**
Answer: 'Adolf Hitler.' immediate response.

If we then ask a process question, a question that demands a mental exercise on behalf of the interviewee, which is cerebral, intensive and time consuming, we have to wait, thus:

Question: 'Who is the President of the United States?' **recall**
Answer: 'Bill Clinton.' immediate response

Question: 'Why?' **process**
Answer: '...' long pause.

No immediate answer here. There is a long pause while the interviewee thinks through the mental process. He has to analyse the question, formulate an opinion - his opinion will have to be evidenced and justified. When a mental demand is made on an interviewee, give him time to think it through and formulate his answer. If there is insufficient time, he will reply 'Don't know' or 'Beats me'. In any case he will respond in the negative. There are other dangers with process questions. The young find them particularly difficult to deal with. Their ability to analyse, predict, judge, evaluate etc, is reduced to their limited frames of reference, so that the following exchange can daily be heard throughout the land:

Question: 'What did you do at school today son?'
Answer: 'Nothing daddy.'

Children know that adults do not give them enough time to answer process questions, so they reply in the negative. If you actually want a reply allow time.

The intellectually disadvantaged and the unsophisticated take even longer to answer a process question. Interviewers recognise this and respond by asking simple questions, closed questions, leading questions and, with a view to being helpful to the interviewee, we can prompt them to the suggested answer. Beware of this course. Such people are highly suggestible, and it needs no gift of formal training to bring them round to our way of thinking. Such a circuitous route is fatally flawed. In fact, it is obliquely akin to child abuse.

Finally, there are the situationally disadvantaged. How often, (custody officers, night duty detectives, brace yourselves), have we booked a prisoner in for being drunk and disorderly/incapable, and on suspicion of, say wounding. Twenty minutes later, we interview him regarding the assault. The narrative of the custody record looks like this:

Date	Time	Occurrence
10.5.97	2230	*Drunk and disorderly. Detention authorised to secure and preserve evidence and to obtain evidence by questioning. Placed in Cell 2.*
10.5.97	2315	*Out to DC Smith regarding interview re suspicion of wounding.*
10.5.97	0040	*I, Andrew Smith, DC999, hereby certify that I have complied with PACE and the codes of practice.* *Replaced in Cell 2.*

You do not need to know that Annex C to Code C of the Codes of Practice states that urgent interviews with drunks, can only be carried out in defined emergencies, and then only with the authority of a superintendent. So far as the above custody record is concerned, the light at the end of its tunnel has just been switched off.

Summaries

Summaries are for clarification. If there is one thing that stymies the defence solicitor, or his clerk, when listening to a client's taped interview, it is the summary of each topic. I speak to many solicitors, and I have friends (ex-policemen), who clerk for solicitors and barristers, who are of one voice when they speak of the effect of hearing a topic on tape being summarised. They say that after an agreed summary, between policeman and client, most defences are closed to them.

The more summaries, the more the defence is painted into a corner and the greater the chance of the solicitor or barrister recommending his client to move his eggs from the not guilty basket into the guilty, but strong mitigating circumstances, basket.

Summaries clear up points of ambiguity, vagueness and uncertainty. If a matter has more than one possible interpretation, is in any way oblique or obscure, or hints at the ambivalent; then what is certain is that the defence will argue the most innocent interpretation. That, when his client said: 'They are cooking apples' he did not really mean what the policeman believed - that some people were cooking apples - no, 'What my client meant by this remark your worships, was that the apples in question were cookers. I can understand the officer's mistake but it was open to the officer to clear this matter up at interview. Now, your worships, if the officer made this simple mistake, which he manifestly failed to clear up, let us see what other mistakes he may have made and what other failures he may be guilty of.'

How many times have you witnessed those sorts of remarks - just a few! The most important matters to clear up in summaries are those which deal with *mens rea* - the guilty state of mind. We must clarify the issues such as:

Intent, Knowing or believing, Dishonestly
Maliciously, Negligently, Wilfully

While the defendant may have had these ideas in his mind at the time of the alleged offence, we must get him to agree, out loud, that that is what was actually in his mind. The mens rea that accompanies the criminal act must be voluntary in the sense that it is a product of the will of the defendant, and must be seen to be so.

The Bentley case

The need for summaries was never more strongly argued than in the Bentley case.

On November 1952, Derek Bentley climbed on to the roof of premises in Croydon; with him was a 16-year-old, Christopher Craig. The evidence clearly suggested that they were engaged in an act of burglary. They were spotted on the roof and the police were called. The two were quickly cornered on the roof and, following a struggle, Bentley was seized, but quickly managed to free himself. Craig, produced a revolver. Bentley cried: 'Let him have it, Chris!' Craig immediately shot one of the officers. Other police officers arrived, one of whom, PC Miles, was shot dead by Craig. Following an abortive suicide attempt, Craig was arrested, and the two stood trial for murder.

Bentley, whose part in this affair was to have said to Craig, 'Let him have it, Chris!', was hanged on January 28, 1953, at Wandsworth Prison. The actual killer, Craig, was too young to be hanged. He served a term of life imprisonment, was released, and retired into obscurity. Forty years on, arguments still rage over this *cause celébre*. 'Let him have it Chris!' meant… what? Did it mean, hand over the gun, or, did it mean, shoot the bastard?

Before deciding for yourself, know this. Bentley had been rejected for military service as being 'mentally sub-standard'. So, what was in his mind? The police assumed that he had meant, 'shoot'. The defence argued that he had meant, 'hand over the gun'. Who was right? The jury took the view that he had meant shoot, and, according to law, he paid the highest price for his words - his life.

This is perhaps the best illustration we will find, on a point of ambiguity. In the absence of a summary, where both parties agree as to what was said, together with its meaning, defence lawyers will naturally argue the meaning that favours their client. During summaries, establish without doubt the fact that the criminal act was done voluntarily, in the sense that it was a product of the will of the defendant.

The 'Y' Factor

At the end of the interview, it is critical to have the suspect play the 'Y - card' - WHY did he do it? This is crucially, fundamentally important. What was his motive? Outrage, self-defence, hunger, revenge, or some imbalance that he had to redress? How does he justify his acts, what was his rationale for behaving as he did? Once this question is explored and exposed, the suspect boxes himself out of the 'not guilty' corner and irrevocably into the, 'guilty, but you can see why I did it' corner.

Solicitors and barristers, however clever, however articulate, just cannot cope if their client has played the 'Y' card. The defence may argue that their client did not commit the crime; it is all a dreadful mistake; it may be a case of mistaken identity, or perhaps purely circumstantial. But how do they cope if their client has disclosed his reason, rationale or motivation - the 'WHY' he committed the crime. If you can tease or pry from the suspect his reason why, then magistrates, juries and judges find it simple enough to bring in a conviction as they understand that the suspect had reason or justification (in his eyes) for his behaviour. The reason why is the cherry on the cake. The suspect salves his conscience by way of justification, not according to law, but according to his frames of reference. What he did may be an offence known to law, but the suspect does not find it offensive - it was right for him.

'Motive explained' deals a knock-out blow to the not guilty plea and naturally gives birth to mitigation.

Ambiguities - the case for summaries

What was said	What the police believed was said	What the defence will argue was meant
'It looked a bit iffy'	He knew or believed the goods to be stolen	The goods were not of merchantable quality
'Let him have it'	Shoot the bastard	Hand over the gun
'OK, I did it'	I'm guilty of this offence	While my client did the act in question, he did not understand the act was wrong
'Cut it Dave'	Stab him Dave	Cut it out Dave

Tape recorded interview procedure [Code E]

The rules concerning the tape recorded interview are such that special constables should never attempt a tape recorded interview on their own. In their own interests they should accompany a regular officer.

Recording and sealing master tapes

Two tapes are used during the course of the tape recorded interview. One tape is known as the master tape and must be sealed before it leaves the presence of the suspect. The second tape is used as a working copy. These tapes are used in a twin deck recorder and operate simultaneously. Tapes allow 45 minutes' recording time. The purpose of sealing the master tape in the presence of the suspect is to establish his confidence that the integrity of the tape is preserved.

Interviews to be tape recorded

Tape recording shall be used at police stations for any interview:
- (a) with a person who has been cautioned for an offence which is either indictable or triable either way;
- (b) which takes place as a result of a police officer exceptionally putting further offences to a suspect after he has been charged with or reported for an offence;
- (c) in which a police officer wishes to bring to the notice of a person, after he has been charged with, or reported for the offence, any written statement or the content of an interview with any other person.

Tape recordings are not required for offences under certain sections of the Terrorism Act 1989 or Section 1 of the Official Secrets Act 1911. Custody officers may authorise an officer not to tape record an interview where there is a failure in equipment or where it is clear from the outset that no prosecution will ensue.

The interview

When the suspect is brought into the interview room the police officer shall, without delay but in the sight of the suspect, load the tape recorder with clean tapes and set it to record. The tapes must be unwrapped or otherwise opened in the presence of the suspect.

The police officer shall then tell the suspect formally about the tape recording. He shall say:
- (a) that the interview is being tape recorded;
- (b) his name and rank and the name and rank of any other police officer present except in the case of inquiries linked to the investigation of terrorism (in these cases shoulder numbers shall be used);

(c) the name of the suspect and any other party present [solicitor];
(d) the date, time of commencement and place of the interview; and
(e) that the suspect will be given a notice about what will happen to the tapes.

The police officer shall then caution the suspect in the following terms:

'You do not have to say anything. But it may harm your defence if you do not mention when questioned something which you later rely on in court. Anything you say may be given in evidence.'

Minor deviations do not constitute a breach of this requirement provided that the sense of the caution is preserved. The police officer shall remind the suspect of his right to free and independent legal advice and that he can speak to a solicitor on the telephone at any time.

Significant statement or silence

The police officer shall then put to the suspect any significant statement or silence ie failure or refusal to answer a question or to answer it satisfactorily which occurred before the start of the tape-recorded interview, and shall ask him whether he confirms or denies that earlier statement or silence or whether he wishes to add anything.

A 'significant' statement or silence means one which appears capable of being used in evidence against the suspect, in particular a direct admission of guilt, or failure or refusal to answer a question or to answer it satisfactorily, which might give rise to a court or jury drawing a proper inference.

Ambush defence - special warnings

Prior to the enactment of the Criminal Justice and Public Order Act 1994, sections 36 and 37, suspects could hide behind the shield of silence or make 'no reply' to questions put. If charged with an offence the suspect could then 'spring' a defence in court to which the police would cry 'ambush' on the grounds that the 'defence' was either known to the suspect at the time of interview or a 'defence' had clearly been manufactured since the time of the interview. The new Act sought to clarify this position.

When a suspect who is interviewed after arrest fails or refuses to answer certain questions, or to answer them satisfactorily, after due warning, a court or jury may draw a proper inference from this silence. This applies when:
(a) a suspect is arrested by a constable and there is found on his person, or in or on his clothing or footwear, or otherwise in his possession, or in the place where he was arrested, any objects, marks, or substances, or marks on such objects, and the person fails or refuses to account for the objects, marks or substances found; or

(b) an arrested person was found by a constable at a place at or about the time the offence for which he was arrested, is alleged to have been committed, and the person fails or refuses to account for his presence at that place.

For an inference to be drawn from a suspect's failure or refusal to answer a question about one of these matters or to answer it satisfactorily, the interviewing officer must first tell him in ordinary language:
(a) what offence he is investigating;
(b) what fact he is asking the suspect to account for;
(c) that he believes this fact may be due to the suspect's taking part in the commission of the offence in question;
(d) that a court may draw a proper inference from his silence if he fails or refuses to account for the fact about which he is questioned;
(e) that a record is being made of the interview and may be given in evidence if he is brought to trial.

Statements made - not on tape

If the suspect indicates that he wishes to tell the police officers about matters not directly connected with the offence of which he is suspected and that he is unwilling for these matters to be recorded on tape, he shall be given the opportunity to tell the police officers about these matters after the conclusion of the formal interview.

Conclusion of interview

At the conclusion of the interview, including the taking and reading back of any written statement, the time shall be recorded and the tape recorder switched off.

The master tape shall be sealed with a master tape label and treated as an exhibit in accordance with the force standing orders. The police officer shall sign the label and ask the suspect and any third party present to sign it also. If the suspect or third party refuses to sign the label, an officer of at least the rank of inspector, or if one is not available the custody officer, shall be called into the interview room and asked to sign it.

The suspect shall be handed a notice which explains the use which will be made of the tape recording and the arrangement for access to it and that a copy of the tape shall be supplied as soon as practicable if the person is charged or informed that he will be prosecuted.

Police interview rooms throughout the country have a standard model of tape recorded interviews procedure placed on or near the interview table. The model is shown overleaf.

144 The Special Constable's Manual

Tape recorded interviews procedure model

PACE 1984 Codes of Practice/Notes of Guidance
General
Use one side of tape only. This allows 45 minutes of recording time. Have you enough tapes for the duration of your interview? Unseal each tape in the presence of your suspect. Load the tape recorder and set to record. Wait for audible alarm to cease.

INTRODUCTION	CAUTION THE SUSPECT INTERVIEW THE SUSPECT	CONCLUSION
A	**B**	**C**

Note that later versions of this model may give additional guidance, further sub-dividing the categories into A - E. However the principle and information required remains the same

CHAPTER 9

FILE SUBMISSION

Chapter contents

Preparation, process and submission **146**
Manual of Guidance **146**
    The 10 sections of the *Manual*...............................147
    File submission - time limits 148
    File types 149
    File unique reference number 151
    File content checklist 152
        Custody remand file 152
        Abbreviated file 152
        Full file.. 152
        Files for summary trial/committal..................... 153
Case procedures **154**
    Advance disclosure... 154
    Discontinuance 155
    Mode of trial guidelines 156
    Record of tape-recorded interview 158

Preparation, process and submission

Special constables are at a disadvantage compared to their regular counterparts when it comes to the preparation, processing and submission of files, by virtue of the fact that they are not in the station on a day-to-day basis. It is doubly important therefore that there is a full understanding of such matters as pre-trial issues and the time limit guidelines on the submission of files.

In November 1989, a working group on pre-trial issues was established comprising representatives of the Crown Prosecution Service, Police, Home Office, Justices' Clerks' Society and the Lord Chancellor's Department. This group looked at four specific issues namely:
  (a) the quality and timeliness of police files;
  (b) delays in processing cases in the criminal justice system;
  (c) arrangements for warning witnesses; and
  (d) the provision of case result and antecedent information;

and submitted its report and recommendations in November 1990.

Its first recommendation stated that the police should introduce common national standards for the preparation and presentation of prosecution files; every file should be assigned a unique reference number for adoption by each agency which makes use of the file.

In arriving at this recommendation the working group referred to the need to create nationally standardised forms to be completed by the police and which would form the basis of the prosecution file submitted to the Crown Prosecution Service (CPS). References were also made to a standard order of these forms within a file and the time limits within which files are to be presented and processed by the police and the CPS in offices and training centres throughout the country.

The proposed manual would set out such matters as the standard content of the police files. The manual was intended to meet the need identified by the working party and its aim was to set out for the use of the police and CPS, nationally agreed guidelines for the preparation of files of evidence in terms of their content, format and timeliness of submission.

This manual is now in being and is known as *The Manual of Guidance* for the preparation, processing and submission of files and can be found in charge offices and police stations throughout England and Wales.

Manual of Guidance

The Manual of Guidance comprises 10 sections as follows:

1. Youth offenders. This section deals with the philosophy of the prosecution (or otherwise) of youth offenders and deals with broad statements of principle.

2. Pre-file submission. Deals with:
(a) police bail - to return to a police station;
(b) charge and police bail - to court;
(c) summons.

The section lays down time guidelines in relation to case progress between the police and the CPS.

3. File submission. This section deals with:
(a) file types - general;
(b) advice file;
(c) initial custody remand file, and breach of bail conditions;
(d) the full file;
(e) the abbreviated file;
(f) files for summary trial or committal;
(g) other files.

4. Witnesses. This section deals with witness availability. How to deal with witnesses, information the witness should receive from the police, warning/de-warning witnesses, and how to act as a witness liaison officer.

5. File supervision. This section deals with the supervision of files and is particularly important to special constables who have a supervisory role.

6. CPS - file actions. This section deals with matters the Crown Prosecution Service has to address, including reviews of files, giving advice to police, time guidelines, youth offenders, advance disclosure and discontinuance.

7. Forms - guidance notes. This section deals with the actual essential detail required to be put on the forms which are incorporated in Section 8 of the Manual. Specifically it deals with:

(a) File front sheet.
(b) File content check list.
(c) Defendant details form.
(d) Case disposal information form.
(e) Initial remand application form.
(f) Custody remand application form.
(g) Custody remand (update) form.
(h) Breach of bail conditions form.
(j) Charge sheet/summons.
(k) Witness list.
(l) Witness non-availability form.
(m) Exhibit list.
(n) Confidential information form.
(o) Summary of evidence.
(p) Record of tape recorded interview.
(q) Compensation claim form.
(r) Previous convictions/cautions.
(s) Other offences taken into consideration form.
(t) DVLA printout.
(u) Further evidence/information form.

8. Copy forms. This section contains copies of all the forms used in prosecution cases. They are numbered:
Form MG 1: File front sheet.
Form MG 2: File content check list.
Form MG 21: Custody remand (update).

Special constable supervisors should be in possession of all these forms in order to advise and guide officers in their sections on the production of prosecution files. The forms may be found in the custody suite.

9. Mode of trial guidelines. This important section is dealt with later in this chapter.

10. List of offences. This section deals with types of offences: indictable only, either-way offences and imprisonable, summary offences.

File submission - time limits

Section 3 of *The Manual of Guidance* deals with the time guidelines for file submission and, if used as intended, the guidelines will encourage the application of a minimum standard. However, regard should be had to force policies formulated to meet local needs and difficulties. Custody officers should be consulted where there are local variations.

Initial custody remand file

Should be available to the CPS lawyer at the court building or other locally agreed reception point at least **one hour** before the court commences.

Breach of bail conditions file

Should be presented to the CPS lawyer at the court building or other locally agreed reception point at least **one hour** before the court commences.

The full file

In custody. The period between a defendant's initial appearance in custody and mode of trial and/or plea should be **14 days**. Within this period the file should be prepared and submitted.

On bail. The period between the defendant being charged and the submission of a full file to the CPS should be **three weeks**.

Summons. In most cases the full file will be in existence prior to the laying of the information. In such circumstances the full file should be submitted to the CPS as quickly as possible and in all cases certainly no later than **14 days** prior to the first listing of the case in the magistrates' court.

The abbreviated file

In custody. The period between a defendant's initial appearance in custody and mode of trial and or plea should be **14 days**. Within this period the file should be prepared and submitted.

On bail. The period between charge and the submission of a file to the CPS should be **14 days**.

Summons. In some cases the file will be in existence before the information is laid. In such circumstances the file should be submitted to the CPS as quickly as possible and in all cases certainly no later than **14 days** prior to the first listing of the case in the magistrates' court.

Summary trial

In custody. As a general rule the period between the entry of a plea in the magistrates' court and the date of trial should be reduced to an absolute minimum. The period between the entry of a not guilty plea and the submission of a full file to the CPS should be **seven days**.

On bail. Except in simple or urgent cases, trial dates in the magistrates' courts will not normally be fixed until a full file of evidence and a detailed witness availability list is in the possession of the prosecution. In such cases the period between the entry of a not guilty plea and the date for which the trial date is to be fixed should be **four weeks**. The full police file should be delivered to the CPS within **three weeks** of the adjournment to fix the trial date.

In simple or urgent cases which are adjourned from the plea date direct to a trial date (ie where there is no pre-trial review), the file for summary trial should be submitted to the CPS within **two weeks** of the adjournment.

Committal

In custody. In cases in which the defendant is charged with an indictable only offence, the file for committal should be submitted to the CPS within **three weeks** of the defendant's first appearance.

In cases where the defendant is charged with an offence triable either way, the file for committal should be submitted to the CPS within **three weeks** of the election or direction for trial by jury.

On bail. In cases where the defendant is charged with an indictable only offence a file for committal should be submitted to the CPS within **four weeks** of the date of charging.

In cases where the defendant is charged with an offence triable either way the file for committal should be submitted to the CPS within **four weeks** of the election or direction for trial by jury.

File types

For the purposes of the *Manual of Guidance* the file types are categorised as follows:

(a) **Advice files.**

(b) **Custody remand files.**

(c) **Plea files:**
   (i) the **full file** which may be:
      (1) an assault file,
      (2) a file for summary trial,
      (3) a file for committal, or
   (ii) the **abbreviated file**.

(d) **Other files.**

In cases for which proceedings have been instituted, a police officer will commence the preparation of one of these files for the first court appearance. It is important that the type of file required is identified before charge as the time allotted to its completion governs the length of time for which the defendant is bailed to the first court appearance (see overleaf).

FILE TYPE – FIRST SUBMISSION

Bail and Summons Cases Only

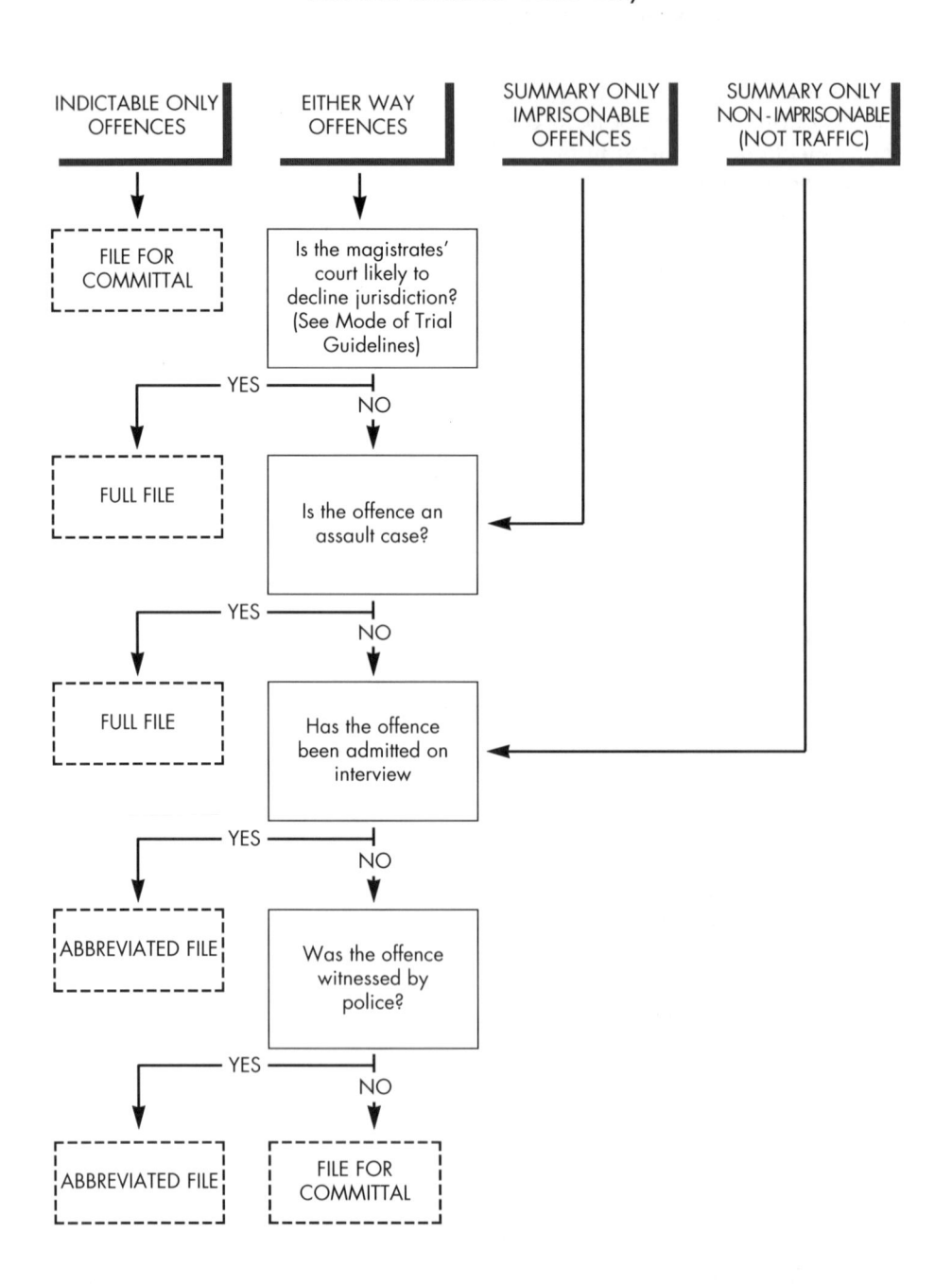

INDICTABLE ONLY OFFENCES → FILE FOR COMMITTAL

EITHER WAY OFFENCES → Is the magistrates' court likely to decline jurisdiction? (See Mode of Trial Guidelines)
- YES → FULL FILE
- NO → Is the offence an assault case?

SUMMARY ONLY IMPRISONABLE OFFENCES → Is the offence an assault case?
- YES → FULL FILE
- NO → Has the offence been admitted on interview?

SUMMARY ONLY NON-IMPRISONABLE (NOT TRAFFIC) → Has the offence been admitted on interview?
- YES → ABBREVIATED FILE
- NO → Was the offence witnessed by police?
  - YES → ABBREVIATED FILE
  - NO → FILE FOR COMMITTAL

The full file

Must be submitted where one or more of the following applies: the defendant or one of the defendants:

(a) has been charged with an assault;
(b) has been charged with an indictable only offence;
(c) has been charged with an offence triable either way, the circumstances of which make it likely that the magistrates will direct that it be heard at the Crown court;
(d) has elected trial;
(e) is likely to deny an either-way offence to be tried summarily or a summary only offence. The appropriate test to apply in deciding whether a case is likely to be denied is: 'has the defendant admitted the offence, or, if not, has the commission of the offence been witnessed by a police officer?';
(f) has entered a plea of not guilty in a case to be heard by the magistrates.

Confusion often arises as to whether an offence is triable only summarily (only at the magistrates' court), either-way (either at the magistrates' court or a Crown court), or on indictment only (only at a Crown court). In order to discover which mode of trial is appropriate for each offence the manual must be consulted (Appendix C).

The abbreviated file

A file which is not a full file. However the CPS have the right to ask for a full file where a Crown Prosecutor considers that all the witness statements are required to undertake an effective review.

The advice file

A file where, in advance of any decision to initiate proceedings, a file may be sent to the CPS seeking advice on:

(a) whether there is sufficient evidence to commence proceedings and whether it is in the public interest to do so;
(b) the choice of charges; or,
(c) for any other reason where it is considered appropriate that legal advice should be sought before proceeding further.

There is no settled list of contents for an advice file but it should contain sufficient information to allow the CPS to consider all the elements upon which advice is sought. The **time guideline** for an advice file is the period between receipt of the file by the CPS and the tendering of advice, which should be two weeks.

Unique file reference number

Every file submitted to the CPS should be assigned a unique reference number by the police regardless of the number of defendants. This should take the following form:

1 = Force PNC Code; 2 = division/sub-divisional reference (if the file is an advice file the reference number should be preceded by the letter 'A'); 3 = case number – maximum five digits; 4 = year.

File content checklist

Section 7 of *The Manual of Guidance* contains the forms used in submitting files together with a checklist for each type of file. When submitting a file check that all the information required for that particular type of file is attached to it.

Custody remand file

(1) File front sheet.
(2) File content checklist.
(3) Defendant details.
(4) Copy charge/summons.
(5) Summary of evidence.
(6) Confidential information.
(7) Remand application form.
(8) Breach of bail form.
(9) Statement by victim (copy).
(10) Other statements taken (copies).
(11) Record of interview (statements, contemporaneous notes, tape recordings).
(12) Previous convictions (defendants).
(13) Cautions (defendants).

Abbreviated file

(1) File front sheet.
(2) File content checklist.
(3) Defendant details.
(4) Copy charge/summons.
(5) Summary of evidence (to be typed).
(6) Confidential information.
(7) Witness list.
(8) Witness non-availability.
(9) Statement by victim (copy).
(10) Other statements taken (copies), where available.
(11) Exhibit list.
(12) Record of interview (statements, contemporaneous notes, tape recordings) - to be typed.
(13) Copy exhibit document.
(14) Previous convictions (defendants) - to be typed.
(15) Cautions (defendants) - to be typed.
(16) Offences taken into consideration.
(17) Compensation forms.
(18) Copy photographs.

Full file

(1) File front sheet.
(2) File content checklist.
(3) Defendant details.
(4) Copy charge/summons.
(5) Summary of evidence - to be typed.
(6) Confidential information.
(7) Witness list.
(8) Witness list updated.
(9) Witness non-availability.
(10) Witness non-availability updated.
(11) Statement of victim (copy) - to be typed.
(12) Statements from all witnesses copy - to be typed.
(13) Exhibit list.
(14) Exhibit list updated.
(15) Record of interview (statements, contemporaneous notes, tape recordings) - to be typed.
(16) Copy exhibit documents.
(17) Previous convictions, defendant - to be typed.
(18) Cautions, defendant - to be typed.
(19) Offences taken into consideration.
(20) DVLA printout.
(21) Compensation form.
(22) Copy of photographs.

Files for summary trial/ files for committal

Both files for summary trial or for committal are identical except that the committal trial file requires four items to be typed in addition to the typing requirements of the summary trial file, ie (1) witness list; (2) witness list updated; (3) exhibit list; and (4) offences taken into consideration forms.

(1) File front sheet.
(2) File content checklist.
(3) Defendant details.
(4) Copy of charge/summons.
(5) Summary of evidence - to be typed.
(6) Confidential information.
(7) Witness list - to be typed.
(8) Witness list updated - to be typed.
(9) Witness non-availability.
(10) Witness non-availability updated.
(11) Statement of victim (copy) - to be typed.

continued

(12) Statements from all witnesses (copies) - to be typed.
(13) Exhibit list - to be typed.
(14) Exhibit list updated.
(15) Record of interview (statements, contemporaneous notes, tape recordings) - to be typed.
(16) Copy of exhibit documents.
(17) Previous convictions (defendant) - to be typed).
(18) Previous cautions (defendant) - to be typed).
(19) Other offences taken into consideration - to be typed.
(20) DVLA printout.
(21) Compensation forms.
(22) Witnesses previous convictions - to be typed.
(23) Copy interview tapes.
(24) Copy photographs.
(25) Original statements.
(26) Other - specify.

While these checklists might seem daunting, the *Manual of Guidance* contains copies of all the forms and it is in the interest of special constable supervisors to have copies of these forms readily available for perusal by officers.

So far as the completion of the forms is concerned, each form is self-explanatory and it is a matter for each officer to complete each section of the form conscientiously. Each and every question contained on the forms should be answered and in any case where a question appears to be not applicable, the words not applicable should be entered.

Case procedures

Advance disclosure

In many cases the defendant has the right to see an outline of the prosecution evidence before the case comes to trial. The best test of the cases which require advance disclosure is: **'Is this offence triable either way?'** If the answer is YES then the defendant may see an outline of the case against him.

Certain confidential information may be held back and touches on such matters as:

(1) Others arrested and interviewed, but not charged.
(2) Persons cautioned for the same offence.
(3) Have any witnesses refused to make statements?
(4) Could any witnesses be classed as accomplices?
(5) Comments on the strength and weakness of witnesses.
(6) Previous convictions of witnesses.
(7) Previous convictions of defendant with similar MO.
(8) Is offence prevalent in locality?
(9) Details of evidence not included in summary of evidence.
(10) Vulnerable witness or any special witness requirements or considerations.
(11) Any other information bearing on offence/decision to prosecute.

This list is not exhaustive. The full list of confidential information which is not subject to advance disclosure is contained in the *Manual of Guidance* which should be consulted in every case.

Advance disclosure will be prepared automatically in cases of files involving offences triable either-way. Either-way offences include those listed below. However it should be noted that there are other such offences which are not listed:

(a) assault occasioning actual bodily harm;
(b) affray;
(c) burglary;
(d) cruelty to children;
(e) damaging property;
(f) deception (obtaining by);
(g) drugs (controlled);
(h) forgery;
(j) going equipped to steal;
(k) grievous bodily harm;
(l) gross indecency (against female);

(m) handling stolen goods;
(n) indecency (gross, between males);
(o) indecency with child;
(p) indecent assault;
(q) making off without payment;
(r) offensive weapon;
(s) prostitution – (living on earnings of);
(t) theft;
(u) trade description offences;
(v) violent disorder;
(x) wounding.

The matter of advance disclosure is one for the CPS only. In the main the CPS edits files before advance disclosure to ensure that the defendant is not supplied with witness addresses. Advance disclosure documents which have been prepared will automatically be kept on the file in readiness to be handed over at court unless:

(a) the CPS is aware of a request for advance information from the defence; or
(b) there has been no such request but the CPS is aware of the name of the solicitor who represents the defendant; or
(c) the CPS receives notification from the magistrates' clerk's office that legal aid has been granted in the case to a named firm of solicitors.

In the circumstances at (b) and (c) above, advance information will be sent automatically, even where no request has been made.

Discontinuance

When time permits, the reviewing CPS lawyer should confer with the police before any decision is made to terminate a case. Whenever a decision is made to discontinue in a case, the CPS should send a written memorandum setting out the reasons for the discontinuance of the proceedings to the officer in the case via the supervising officer.

Mode of trial guidelines

When magistrates are deciding on whether to deal with a case themselves or to commit to the Crown court, it is of more than mere interest to police officers to know what considerations work on the magistrates' minds in making their determinations. Appendix A to the *Manual of Guidance* gives officers an insight into the guidelines laid down.

In a recent practice note, the Lord Chief Justice set out guidelines to help magistrates decide whether or not to commit 'either-way' offences for trial in the Crown court. The guidance applies to defendants aged 18 and above. In general, except where otherwise stated, either-way offences should be tried summarily **unless** the magistrates consider that the particular case has one or more of the features set out below **and** that their sentencing powers are insufficient.

Mode of trial? - features to consider

Burglary - dwellings
(a) Entry in the daytime when the occupier (or another) is present;
(b) entry at night of a house which is normally occupied whether or not the occupier (or another) is present;
(c) the offence is alleged to be one of a series of similar offences;
(d) when soiling, ransacking, damage or vandalism occurs;
(e) the offence has professional hallmarks;
(f) the unrecovered property is of high value*.

Burglary - non-dwellings
(a) Entry of a pharmacy or doctor's surgery;
(b) fear is caused or violence is done to anyone lawfully on the premises (eg night watchman, security guard);
(c) the offence has professional hallmarks;
(d) vandalism takes place on a substantial scale;
(e) the unrecovered property is of high value*.

Theft and fraud
(a) Breach of trust by person in position of substantial authority, or in whom a high degree of trust is placed;
(b) theft or fraud which has been committed or disguised in a sophisticated manner;
(c) theft or fraud committed by an organised gang;
(d) victim is particularly vulnerable to theft or fraud, eg elderly or infirm;
(e) the unrecovered property is of high value*.

DSS fraud
(a) Organised fraud on a large scale;
(a) the frauds are substantial and carried out over a long period of time.

Handling stolen goods
(a) Dishonest handling of stolen property by a receiver who has commissioned the theft;
(b) the offence has professional hallmarks;
(c) the property is of a high value.

* High value in this context means at least £10,000.

Mode of trial? - features to consider (cont)

Violence

Grievous bodily harm/wounding and assault occasioning actual bodily harm:
(a) the use of a weapon of a kind likely to cause serious injury;
(b) a weapon is used and serious injury is caused;
(c) more than minor injury is caused by kicking, head-butting or similar forms of assault;
(d) serious violence is caused to those whose work has to be done in contact with the public, eg police officers, bus drivers, taxi drivers, publicans, shopkeepers;
(e) violence to vulnerable people, eg the elderly and infirm.

Note: These considerations also apply to domestic violence.

Public order

Offences of violent disorder should generally be committed for trial.

Affray
(a) Organised violence or use of weapons;
(b) significant injury or substantial damage;
(c) the offence has clear racial motivation;
(d) an attack on police officers, ambulance crew, fire crew and the like.

Violence to and neglect of children

(a) Substantial injury;
(b) repeated violence or serious neglect, even if the harm is slight;
(c) sadistic violence, eg deliberate burning or scalding.

Indecent assault

(a) Substantial disparity in age between victim and defendant, and the assault is more than trivial;
(b) violence or threats of violence;
(c) relationship of trust or responsibility between defendant and victim;
(d) several similar offences and the assaults are more than trivial;
(e) the victim is particularly vulnerable;
(f) the serious nature of the assault.

Unlawful sexual intercourse

(a) Wide disparity of age;
(b) breach of position of trust;
(c) the victim is particularly vulnerable.

Drugs class 'A'

Supply/possession with intent to supply - these cases should be committed for trial.
Possession - these cases should be committed for trial unless the amount is small and for own use.

Drugs class 'B'

Supply/possession with intent to supply - these cases should be committed for trial unless there is only small scale supply for no payment.
Possession - these cases should be committed for trial when the quantity is substantial.

continued overleaf...

Mode of trial? - features to consider (cont)

Reckless driving

(a) Alcohol or drugs contributing to recklessness;
(b) grossly excessive speed;
(c) racing;
(d) prolonged course of reckless driving;
(e) other related offences.

Criminal damage

(a) Deliberate fire-raising;
(b) committed by a group;
(c) damage of a high value;
(d) the offence has clear racial motivation.

Criminal damage offences which do not amount to arson and where the value of the property damaged or destroyed is **less** than £2,000 must be tried summarily.

Record of tape recorded interviews

1.

When an officer tape records an interview with a suspected person, it will be the usual practice for the officer to prepare a record of the interview on the record of taped interview form.

2.

It will not be necessary to prepare a record of interview where the interview produces no evidence and there is no other evidence on which a prosecution can be considered or if for any other reason no case file is to be submitted.

3

The main purpose of the record of interview is to provide a balanced, accurate and reliable summary of what has been said. The record should be typed.

4

It should contain sufficient information to enable the Crown Prosecutor to decide whether a criminal prosecution should proceed, whether the proposed charges are appropriate, what lines of defence to expect and what mode of trial is appropriate.

The record will also be used:

(i) to exhibit the officers' witness statement;
(ii) to enable the prosecutor to comply with the rules of advance disclosure;
(iii) for the conduct of the case by the prosecution, the defence and the court where the record of interview has been accepted by the defence.

5. Before the interview

Before starting an interview, interviewing officers must remind themselves of the main elements of the offences they believe to have been committed. This will enable officers to be clear - when framing questions and directing the course of the interview - which points it is necessary to be able to prove, by evidence, if a prosecution is to be sustained.

6.

Officers should check that the recording machinery is in working order, that they know how to operate it, and that they, or any other officer present at the interview, can see the time counter on the recording machine.

Record of tape recorded interviews (cont...)

7. The interview

In order to ensure that the interview flows smoothly and yet that particular parts of it may easily be recorded verbatim afterwards, either the interviewing officer or, if present, a colleague should note during the interview the counter times at which anything was said which might later need to be retrieved for verbatim recording or in order to check the accuracy of a third person report.

Information which is likely to need to be retrieved for either of these purposes is as follows:
(a) any admissions and the questions and answers leading up to them (verbatim in all cases);
(b) statements or questions about intent, dishonesty, or possible defences. Matters such as knowledge of key facts, presence at scene of crime on other occasions, or assertion that others were involved should also be noted (main salient points);
(c) factors which might make the offence be considered more serious, eg vulnerable victim, use of excessive force, abuse of influence/position of responsibility (aggravating factors);
(d) matters which might tell in favour of the suspect (mitigating circumstances) eg illness, unemployment, regret.

8. After the interview.

A written record will normally be prepared. This must include verbatim all admissions relating to the offence or offences under investigation and the questions and answers leading up to them.

These will include ambiguous admissions (eg one of the main elements of the offence may be missing - 'I took the bicycle but I knew Jimmy would have let me use it' - and qualified admissions (eg raising a potential defence - 'I did stab him, but it was only because he ran at me with the meat axe when I was carving the bread').

9.

When any admission is made to an offence which is not the immediate subject of investigation but which might be taken into consideration, the tape counter time(s) should be noted and a brief description given in the record of interview.

The record should contain sufficient information to enable the Crown Prosecutor to assess whether the offences charged adequately reflect the gravity of the defendant's conduct and how the case might best be presented in court. Examples might be:
(a) (counter time) unlawful taking, red Escort;
(b) (counter time) burglary, petrol station, High Street;
(c) (counter time) burglary, dwelling house, night time.

10. Complex and straightforward cases.

Most tape recorded interviews will fall into two broad categories although there may be some area of overlap between them. For ease of reference, these two categories are described as 'complex' and 'straightforward'.

Complex cases are defined as those in which:
(i) the suspect, or one of the suspects, has been charged with an indictable only offence; or,

Record of tape recorded interviews (cont...)

(ii) the suspect, or one of the suspects, has been charged with an either-way offence, the circumstances of which make it likely that the magistrates will direct that the case be heard at the Crown court (in cases of doubt reference should be made to the National Mode of Trial Guidelines, Annex B); or,

(iii) the suspect, or one of the suspects, has been charged with an allegation of assault; or,

(iv) the suspect is likely to deny the offence; this should be assumed in all cases in which the suspect has not admitted the offence and its commission was not witnessed by a police officer.

All other cases are likely to fall within the straightforward category.

11. Complex cases.

In the cases defined as complex, not only the admissions offences but also the main salient points must be recorded verbatim.

These will include statements or questions about intent, dishonesty or possible defences, as well as matters such as knowledge of key facts, presence at scene of crime on other occasions, or assertion that others were involved.

The issues of bail and alternative pleas or charges should not normally be discussed in the context of an interview but, if they are, this must be recorded verbatim.

The remaining matters mentioned above (ie aggravating factors and/or mitigating circumstances) may be summarised in the third person, with relevant tape counter times recorded in the margin of the written record.

12.

In deciding whether or not to record parts of the interview verbatim, officers should bear in mind the duty of the Crown Prosecutor to make an independent decision as to whether prosecution is justified. There will be some cases which are so complicated that a record of interview will not be the best method of supplying the information to the CPS and, eventually, the court.

In such cases (of which murder may be the most obvious example) a transcript of the interview under caution will be required.

13.

A decision to provide a transcript must be made at superintendent level or above due to the resource implications. Such a decision should, if possible, be made when the suspect is charged, thereby preventing any waste of resources by preparing a record of interview which will not be used.

14.

The CPS will require the transcript before a decision whether or not to continue the prosecution can be made.

15.

In cases where a transcript is made, a brief summary of the interview may also be needed for police purposes. This will be a matter for senior officers to decide in the light of all the circumstances.

16. Straightforward cases.

The majority of tape recorded interviews will fall into the straightforward category. In these cases, it will usually be appropriate for the record of tape recorded interviews to be written largely in the

Record of tape recorded interviews (cont...)

third person provided that any admissions and the questions leading up to them are recorded verbatim.

17.

While it is not possible to be precise about the circumstances of all straightforward interviews, it is unlikely that records of interview in such cases will take much more than one side of a sheet of paper.

18.

In all cases the record will include the time and date of interview, a note of its duration, the full name of the defendant and the names and rank (where appropriate) of all persons present, and the fact that a caution was given.

19.

Whenever direct speech is referred to in the record the identity of the speaker and the tape counter time should be indicated in the margin.

20.

Where reported speech is used, the time of salient points, such as mitigating factors or expressions of remorse, should be noted in the margin.

21.

The tape recording of an interview does not preclude a suspect from electing to make a written statement under caution.

Such a statement should be taken while the tape is running, the statement should be recorded on the exhibit list.

The record may be shorter if, in the officer's opinion, the written statement under caution accurately summarises what the suspect said during the interview.

22.

Supervising officers should make checks of records of taped interviews and corresponding tapes to ensure consistency in fairness and balance.

23.

In cases where a person being interviewed answers 'no comment' or maintains a silence throughout the interview, there will be no need to prepare a record.

The fact that the interview took place will be referred to in the officer's statement making reference to the silence of the accused or consistently answering 'no comment'.

24.

When it is necessary for an officer to submit a statement of evidence, reference will be made to the fact that, following a taped interview, a record was prepared and this will be an exhibit produced by the officer preparing the record.

In cases where two officers are involved in an interview, the record will be prepared by one officer and one officer only will refer to it in his/her statement. The second interviewing officer will merely state that he/she was present at the interview and will make the usual reference to tape exhibit.

CHAPTER 10

PATROLLING A BEAT

Chapter contents

Patrolling a beat 164
Equipment 164
Paperwork 164
Local knowledge 165
    Hospitals 165
    Other emergency services 165
    Private emergency services 165
    Vulnerable premises 165
    Keyholders 165
    Public houses 165
    Traffic lights 166
    Neighbourhood Watch 166
    Alarmed premises 166
    Garages 166
Intelligence gathering 167
    Informal intelligence gathering 167
Plain clothes duty 168
    Warrant cards 168
    Identity 168
    Assault 168
    Radios 168
    Appropriate clothing 168
    Non disclosure of identity 168
    Special equipment 169
    Note taking 169
    Arrests 169
    Target indication system 169
        The colour clock code 169
        The counting code 170
Off-duty arrests 170
    Jurisdiction 170
    When to get involved 171

Patrolling a beat

Only 20 per cent of patrolling a beat has anything to do with the physical presence of a police officer on the ground making the patrol. The knowledge that the officer has in his head makes up the other 80 per cent. The officer who patrols a beat with which he is unfamiliar, or where his local knowledge is lacking, reduces his value by as much as 80 per cent because the contribution that he is making is a physical one only. The patrolling officer has to have enough information (either in his head, or have access to relevant information) to answer whatever may be asked of him - whether by members of the public, or his colleagues and the communication centre.

Substantially, there are two types of beat: rural and urban. The only real difference in patrolling each is the size of the area to be patrolled and the time it takes to cover each. The sort of information the officer has to have to hand is almost the same in both cases. We deal here with the urban beat which most officers have to become familiar with.

Equipment

The first question that arises before going out on the beat is one of the equipment the officer must have with him:
  (a) radio, tuned to the correct channel and with a fresh battery;
  (b) handcuffs should be carried as well as the key to the handcuffs;
  (c) truncheon, side-handled baton or ASP (carried as discreetly as possible);
  (d) a map of the actual beat as well as a town map should be carried;
  (e) information book containing;
    (i) colleagues' call signs;
    (ii) radio call signs;
    (iii) PNC codes (vehicle/persons checks etc);
    (iv) locations of bleeper alarms;
    (v) local information.

Paperwork

In addition to (a) and (e) above, the officer, depending on force policy, will be required to carry sufficient **paperwork** to deal with street offences he may happen upon or be sent to deal with.
  (a) HO/RT 1;
  (b) accident booklet;
  (c) VDRS;
  (d) fixed penalty booklets;
  (e) local intelligence (sighting) reports;
  (f) excise offence report (CLE 2/6);
  (g) other forms common to the force of which the officer is a member.

Local knowledge

The patrolling officer is only as good as the information he has to hand or has access to. During the course of a patrol the sort of questions he may be asked by an inquiring public, or indeed that he will have to ask himself, will touch on such matters as:

Hospitals

The locations of hospitals on his beat as well as the services/facilities that each provide. Is the hospital a cottage hospital and therefore open during office hours only or is it open for 24 hours?

Does the hospital provide accident and emergency care? Which hospitals have been designated to receive patients in the event of a major disaster?

Other emergency services

The locations not only of the fire brigade and ambulance headquarters but also the policy response to set incidents. For example, an officer might think twice about calling the fire services out to a minor petrol spillage on a road if he knows that the minimum response that that particular brigade has to that type of incident is to despatch two tenders!

If the beat is near water (of any sort) how does he notify the respective water authority of a sudden emergency? In the case of rivers, the officer ought to be aware of the locations of life-belts for use in an emergency.

Private emergency services

Members of the public will often inquire how they are to recover their disabled vehicle or how help may be sought in these circumstances. The officer should not only be aware of the existence of the many private emergency services, AA/RAC/and others, but also the procedure for calling these services out and, most importantly, the information they will require from the disabled motorist, the membership number being the most important.

Vulnerable premises

Premises may be vulnerable by virtue of their nature, ie, post-offices, banks etc.

However there are other premises which may give rise to concern in the short term: vacant houses/premises where the owner is away on holiday for example, or where there are temporary building works, resulting in security being below par.

Keyholders

Lists of keyholders for public or vulnerable premises are kept at police stations as a matter of routine. The patrolling officer should be conscious of this and the more important premises - time permitting - should be visited by him during his patrol.

Not only should he make contact with the occupants and make himself known, but also check the accuracy of the information on the keyholders held by the police and update that information where necessary.

Public houses

Patrolling officers should be prepared to enter public houses and speak to the licensee as a matter of routine. This helps the officer to identify with the licensee so that when the officer has to attend the public house as a matter of duty, he enjoys some sort of rapport with the licensee.

The officer should also know what to look for when entering a public house. The licensee's name, for example, must be displayed above the door. If entering after hours, has the officer the necessary power to do so? What sort of licence is in existence for that particular public house, and where the officer is entering because he believes that there is after hours drinking in progress, has the licensee been granted an extension?

These facts should be known before entering public houses if the officer is not to disadvantage himself. Where is the car park for that particular public house? The number of vehicles in the car park can speak volumes as to the number of persons in the building, especially after hours.

Traffic lights

From time to time traffic lights have to be switched off, this occurs at times of:
(a) sudden emergency, traffic accidents etc;
(b) pre-arranged, carnival route or processions;
(c) during busy periods when officers have to engage in traffic control themselves.

The patrolling officer should make himself aware of the existence of keys to traffic lights on his beat and the procedure when switching the lights off altogether in order to engage in traffic control himself, or switching the lights to manual control in order to allow the officer to interrupt the pre-set timing of the lights and take over himself during busy periods.

Neighbourhood Watch

Many areas of the country are now covered by Neighbourhood Watch schemes. Patrolling officers should be aware if there is such a scheme operating in their area of patrol and if so who is the local co-ordinator. Where there is such a scheme a visit to the co-ordinator will prove invaluable in promoting communications and is always a good source of information.

Alarmed premises

Patrolling officers should be aware of which premises on their beat are alarmed but also the type of alarm, be it audible/silent/delayed. This information will dictate the response type adopted by the investigating officer, ie, silent approach or otherwise.

Garages

The types of garages on the officer's beat should be known and in particular what services they offer. Where the public are asking for information concerning their disabled vehicle the officer dealing will have to know if the garage is able to turn out after hours, and whether it is capable of a suspended tow, rigid tow and the like.

Additionally, the officer should be aware that in most police areas there is a call-out system in operation for garages. Such information can be gleaned from the communication centre.

Intelligence gathering

The officer engaged in patrolling a beat is best placed to gather intelligence of what is actually happening on the ground in relation to criminal activity. Before patrolling his beat the officer should visit the local intelligence officer and acquaint himself with the current crime trends which fall under a number of headings.

Persons wanted/missing

This will include the locations of warrants and missing person files.

Disqualified drivers

There will certainly be a list of disqualified drivers, stating names, addresses, vehicles used and to which they have access and also their place of employment.

Active criminals

Names and addresses together with photographs of criminals who are known or suspected to be active and also their associates.

Target criminals

These include the more prolific criminals who are known to be constantly active to a point whereby they can be described as professional criminals.

Ongoing operations

This will include information of police activity (both overt and covert), which the patrolling officer can give attention to or, if the operation is covert, actively avoid.

In order to update information held by the local intelligence officer, patrolling officers should submit the form, local to their force, containing details of any activity spotted, or information received on the above persons. A mere sighting of an active criminal for example, might tend to prove that he was in the area of a crime which is subsequently reported.

Informal intelligence gathering

Informal intelligence gathering is more commonly referred to by regular officers as 'T-stops'. The object of the exercise is to befriend locals on the beat, in particular shopkeepers and, while enjoying a cup of tea in the back of the shop, listen to what they have to say. Invariably they will disclose much of the activity of the locality at a time when the police were absent. This source of information has proven to be invaluable on innumerable occasions. It should be remembered that locals take time to form a rapport with the local bobby and information should not be expected immediately.

Information gained is of little value unless it is reported back to the local intelligence officer who is able to make it available to all officers who might benefit from it. Special constables should make themselves aware of the procedure and the forms used in communicating with the local intelligence officer.

Plain clothes duty

Increasingly, special constables are being used for plain clothes duties in matters of covert observations/operations and in evidence gathering exercises. There are very definite rules to be observed when engaged in plain clothes duty with which all officers should be familiar.

Warrant cards

Warrant cards should be carried at all times and officers should be in a position to produce the card for inspection on demand.

Warrant cards should never be handed over for inspection and should remain in the firm grip of the officer during production.

Identity

When an officer who is engaged in plain clothes duties has to disclose his identity, this should be done with authority and before the production of the warrant card (or at the same time).

This affords the officer protection from what otherwise might be an assault on his person. Time should not be wasted in the production of the warrant card when the officer can disclose who he is merely by telling the person to whom he is speaking.

Assault

Where an officer is assaulted during the course of his duties while in plain clothes, the person committing the assault cannot be charged with assault on police (although he may be charged with other offences), unless he knows that the person whom he is assaulting is in fact a police officer.

It is vitally important therefore to state identity and office clearly, thus invoking the protection of section 51 of the Police Act 1964 (assault on police) and at the same time reducing the chances of assault.

Radios

Communications are the essence of plain clothes duties and officers so involved should always carry a radio or be in a position to make communication to others when there is a need.

Appropriate clothing

Appropriate clothing for one plain clothes duty may be wholly inappropriate for another. The best form of camouflage is to be dressed in a manner that is suited to the environment being observed, so that a suit may be appropriate for keeping observations in a city building, and leather jacket, jeans, motor cycle boots and earrings may be appropriate for keeping observations in a transport cafe.

Where two or more officers are engaged in plain clothes duty, ideally their dress should be similar in order to create the illusion of togetherness.

Non-disclosure of identity

It sometimes happens that officers engaged in plain clothes duties are required to gather evidence following arrests. For example, where officers are keeping observation on late-night drinkers, a police raiding party may enter, report some offenders and arrest others.

Where the identity of the police observation team is not disclosed, that team is then in a position to gather evidence of post-raid discussions, eg the licensee who tells the late drinkers that the licensee bought all the drinks for his 'friends' and that they are therefore not committing offences! Such information is often vital.

Special equipment

Special equipment is available in police forces for issue to officers engaged in plain clothes duties, eg binoculars, night-sights, voice-activated tape-recorders and a wealth of other really useful equipment.

Inquiries with the local intelligence officer will reveal what equipment is available.

Note taking

During the course of plain clothes duties it is often the case that notes have to be made. Where the note taking is unavoidable and where the production of a pocket book would compromise the officers, then consideration should be given to making notes on papers other than pocket books - cigarette packets, news-papers, whatever is to hand.

The difficulty that then arises is incorporating the original notes into evidence that can be presented to a court.

When the officers find time to make up their pocket books, they must mention that original notes were made at the time and produce those notes as an exhibit to the statements of evidence which they subsequently prepare.

Arrests

S 89 Police Act 1996

Plain clothes arrests should be handled with discretion. It is sometimes the case that suspects who are suddenly confronted by what they had believed to be a member of the public will be likely to panic.

Ideally there should be at least two officers making the arrest who should at once identify themselves. Officers should also have access to transport.

Target indication system

(See following page)

Target indication system

It is often difficult to communicate the location of a target to other officers on plain clothes observation duty. Since the Second World War, the target indication system has been used for operational communications. This works well when the target is in either an open area or a building.

The colour clock code

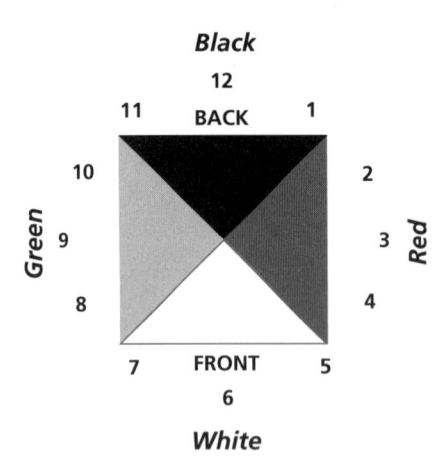

The counting code

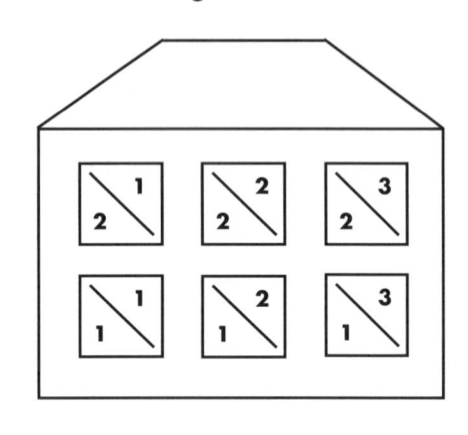

Counting code

On each elevation of a building levels are counted upwards from the first level which is visible. Openings and objects of tactical importance are given numbers from left to right. Where targets leave buildings or there is movement in the area, this should be described in relation to their movement towards a clock number or a colour.

Observation colour coding

Use the horizontal clock with position 6 selected as FRONT. Never use 'left' or 'right', 'front' or 'back'. Use the colour coding shown to describe the side observed or the subject of message.

Off-duty arrests

Jurisdiction

The first question which should arise in the mind of the special constable contemplating making an off-duty arrest is one of jurisdiction. Jurisdiction is dealt with in detail in Chapter 1 but can be summarised briefly:

Own force area

When an officer is in his own force area he has all the powers of a constable, therefore making off-duty arrests presents little problem in relation to the question of powers of arrest.

Areas contiguous to own force area

If an officer is outside his own force area but in a force area which is contiguous to (boundary touching) his own force area, then again he has all the powers of a constable.

Outside own force area or area contiguous to it

When an officer is outside his own force area and also the area contiguous to it then his powers of arrest as a constable cease to exist. The only powers that the special constable is able to exercise are the same as the public, the citizen's powers of arrest. Officers should make themselves familiar with the citizen's powers of arrest where they know they might be travelling beyond those areas in which they enjoy the powers of a constable.

When to get involved

The second question that arises in relation to off-duty arrests is the question of when to get involved. There are times when the question answers itself, for example where an off-duty special constable observes uniformed officers having difficulty in making street arrests. In cases such as these there is a clear duty to help the officers. If a special is about to involve himself in this type of situation he should make it very clear to all the persons he is approaching that he is a police officer. This is particularly important as he may be mistaken by the police as being a person seeking to help those persons being arrested. Prior to becoming involved therefore the special constable should call out in a loud voice, 'I am a police officer'.

The 'when' to get involved, while off-duty, becomes an increasingly difficult question to answer and must necessarily be governed by the prevailing circumstances. Before deciding to make an off-duty arrest certain questions should first be answered

(1) Does the officer know the offender? Perhaps the offence can be pointed out and the offender reported for summons.
(2) Should the offender be followed until such times as the officer can summon assistance or call the police by telephone?
(3) Is the officer physically able to cope with the offender(s)? What is their demeanour, have they been drinking, are they in violent mood, armed, or hostile? It is often counter-productive to approach such persons as the officer may well not only by assaulted, but also lose the suspects.
(4) Will it be enough, for example, to take the index number of an offending car, or the description of the suspect?
(5) If the officer is with his family, or perhaps with a child, what will he do with the child if he involves himself in an arrest?
(6) Where an arrest is to be made, how will the officer transport his prisoner to the nearest police station?

If the above questions can be answered satisfactorily, the fundamental question still remains: When to get involved? To look at the matter clinically the officer might consider the consequences of not getting involved. As a special constable there is a duty placed on the officer of protecting life and property, and keeping the peace. This is balanced by the idea of discretion, in that the officer is expected to exercise prudence in each individual situation. The conflict therefore between duty and discretion may be answered by the question: 'If I do not get involved, will I be guilty of neglect of duty?'

Clearly the question of when to get involved is very vexed and not readily answered. It is a matter for each individual to consider for himself in the light of:
(a) Duty.
(b) Discretion.
(c) Can an arrest realistically be made?
(d) Is there another way?

As with all other arrests which are made in plain clothes, officers should be in a position to produce their warrant cards as proof of identity and the words, 'I am a police officer' should be used at the beginning of any conversation. Officers who make or attempt to make off-duty arrests are often commended by the courts and receive chief constable's commendations in recognition of duty, courage, observation and commitment. The prospect of off-duty arrests is something that each individual should give thought to prior to being overtaken by events.

CHAPTER 11

PRACTICAL POLICING

Chapter contents

Reporting offenders................. 174
    Points to consider............174
Notice of intended prosecution
    176
    The warning 176
Warrants.................................... 177
Street collections....................... 179
Dangerous dogs 180
Seizure of stray dogs 180
Children - police protection..... 180
    Care proceedings..............181
Pocket book rules...................... 181
Lost/found property................. 183
Domestic disputes 186
Domestic violence 188
    Information to be recorded 188
    Children 189
    Other agencies 190
    Specialist units 190
Neighbour disputes.................. 191

Landlord/tenant disputes 191
    Unlawful eviction.............191
    Excluded lettings -
        notice only 192
    Harassment......................192
    Squatters 192
    Suggested procedure -
        WRAPPeR 193
Actions at the scene of crime.. 193
Index of modus operandi 195
Crime reports 195
    Recording the crime.........195
    Amendments....................196
    No crime..........................196
Victims 196
    Compensation 197
    Civil action 197
    Criminal Injuries
        Compensation Board ... 197
    Motor Insurers' Bureau ... 198
    Victims as witnesses 198

Reporting offenders

Where an offence has been committed and it is your intention to report the offender, the purpose of the reporting procedure is to bring the facts to the attention of the court in a way that is admissible. If your manner of dealing with the incident is flawed then it is unlikely to come before the courts. Your force may have a particular form for reporting offenders, if so it is best used at the time because it encourages you not to forget detail, in addition, notes made at the time are contemporaneous and can therefore be read from whilst giving evidence at court. It is important to ensure that you have gathered all evidence that is available at the time as it probably will not be available after the event. Consider the following points when reporting offenders.

Offence or offensive

Has the individual committed an offence **known to law**, or is his behaviour simply offensive?

This is when your knowledge of the law is tested and it is best to have a number of 'bread and butter' type offences well within your knowledge. This will allow you to be pro-active and therefore in control, whereas if you stumble across an incident which is beyond your knowledge, you will become reactive and not enjoy the same control. **Know your law.**

Offender

The personal details of an offender should be sought, that is, enough to bring him before a court: full name, address, age, date of birth, occupation. If a motor vehicle is involved, then details of engine size, the type, class, and index number should be gathered. The vehicle excise licence should be checked as should driving documents and, if necessary, a HO/RT1 issued. If the offender is a juvenile, then the names and address of parents or guardian will be needed as well as his school.

If you are unable to identify an offender sufficiently to bring him before a court then consider your arrest powers under section 25 of the Police and Criminal Evidence Act 1984.

The scene

From your evidence you should be able to reconstruct the scene for the benefit of all in court: day, date, time and location of the incident. Be precise about locations, eg, 'outside number 25 High Street'.

Witnesses

The names and addresses of all witnesses to the incident should be gathered at the time. Where the offence is reported by a member of the public then this information is usually on record, but in any case, ask at the scene: 'Did anyone witness this incident?' Arrangements can be made to collect statements from witnesses at the time or later.

Cautions

In order to ensure that your evidence is admissible in court it is essential that a caution is issued to the alleged offender the moment you believe you have grounds for suspecting him of committing an offence.

Having cautioned, some forces ask, **'Do you understand?'** and note any replies but this is **not** a requirement of the caution.

Interview in the street

Code C 11

Having cautioned the alleged offender there will probably be two courses of action left to you. If the offence is a simple street offence, depositing litter, pedal cycle lighting offence or the like, then the offender need only be reported and an offence report submitted.

If you feel a need to conduct an interview on the streets then be aware of the Codes of Practice governing this situation:

(a) An accurate record must be made of each interview with a person suspected of an offence, whether or not the interview takes place at a police station.
(b) The record must state the place of the interview, the time it begins and ends, the time the record is made (if different), breaks in the interview and the names of all those present. It must be made on the forms provided for this purpose or in the **officer's pocket book** or in accordance with the Code of Practice for the tape recording of police interviews with suspects.
(c) The record must be made during the course of the interview, unless in the investigating officer's view this would not be practicable or would interfere with the conduct of the interview. It must constitute either a verbatim record of what has been said or, failing this, an account of the interview which adequately and accurately summarises it.

If an interview record is not made during the course of the interview it must be made as soon as practicable after its completion.

Written interview records must be timed and signed by the maker. If an interview record is not completed in the course of the interview the reason must be recorded in the officer's pocket book.

Unless it is impracticable the person interviewed shall be given the opportunity to read the interview record and to sign it as correct or to indicate the respects in which he considers it inaccurate.

Seizure of evidence

Where there is physical evidence which, if not seized may be lost to the court, then it should be seized and a receipt issued. This is likely to occur when dealing with such offences as fraudulent excise licences, unlawful street collections (badges/collecting tins), offensive weapons etc.

Defences

Most offences known to the criminal calendar have in-built defences to protect the unwary and naive. Once an offence has been established then it is important to negate any defence at the time, otherwise the defence may be brought up at a subsequent court hearing.

Simple offences like defective lights on a motor vehicle being driven at night have the in-built defence of 'the lamp became defective during the journey in progress'. It would be prudent therefore to inquire when the driver last checked his lights.

Handling stolen goods, for example, requires the alleged offender to 'know or believe' the goods to be stolen, so simply being in possession may not be enough to obtain conviction.

Ask questions, negate defences.

Pocket books, joint notes

Where two or more officers deal with an incident which is written-up jointly, this fact should be recorded in all their pocket books and each officer should sign the other's books to that effect.

Notice of intended prosecution

If the offence requires a notice of intended prosecution, then issue it verbally at the time or arrange for a notice to be served within 14 days.

Notice of Intended Prosecution

> **S 1 Road Traffic Offenders Act 1988**

A prosecution for certain offences will not succeed unless it is proved that the defendant was informed within certain time limits of the intention of the police to prosecute him. The warning must be given in respect of the following offences:
  (a) Driving a motor vehicle recklessly, without due care and attention or without reasonable consideration.
  (b) Reckless or careless riding by cyclist (in which case the notice has to be sent to the alleged offender).
  (c) Speeding (including speed unlawful for a particular vehicle type).
  (d) Failing to conform to a direction given by an officer engaged in the regulation of traffic.
  (e) Disobeying certain traffic signs.
  (f) Leaving a vehicle in a dangerous position.
  (g) Aiding and abetting the commission of any of the above offences.

The warning

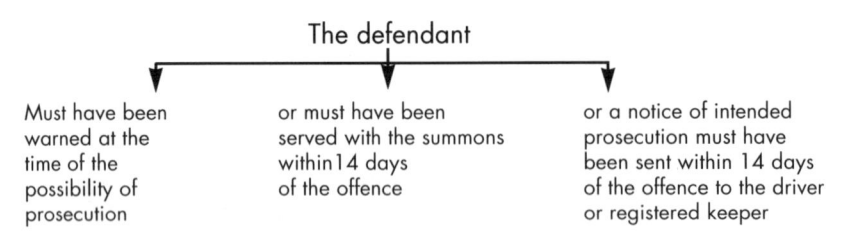

The defendant

- Must have been warned at the time of the possibility of prosecution
- or must have been served with the summons within 14 days of the offence
- or a notice of intended prosecution must have been sent within 14 days of the offence to the driver or registered keeper

Date of offence. When determining the 14 days within which the notice must be sent, the date of the commission of the offence is excluded.

The notice. The written notice must specify in relation to the offence:
  (a) time;
  (b) date;
  (c) location;
  (d) offence;
  (e) vehicle type.

Service. The notice is considered to be served if it was sent by registered post or recorded delivery to the last known address of the registered keeper.

Frustrated service. If the prosecution use reasonable diligence to discover the name and address of the driver or registered keeper but fail to do so within the time limits for service, this is not a bar to prosecution. Nor is it a bar to prosecution if the accused by his own conduct contributes to the failure.

Verbal notice. Where the driver is given notice at the time of the offence it should be couched thus: 'You will be reported for consideration of the question of prosecuting you for . . .' then tell him precisely the nature of the offence, speeding, leaving a vehicle in a dangerous position, etc. It is the practice of most forces to send a written notice even though a verbal warning was given at the time.

Errors in notice. The notice is intended to give an idea of the offence with which the defendant will be charged and to guard against the possibility of his being taken unawares. The test of the validity of the notice is whether the defendant is in any way prejudiced in his defence by the defect.

Accidents. If an accident occurs of which the defendant is aware then the prosecution are exempt from complying with the provisions of this section. This is designed to relieve the police of having to serve numerous notices whenever a series of multiple accidents occur on a motorway.

Warrants

A warrant is a written authority, signed by a magistrate, directing the person named therein to carry out the purpose for which the warrant is issued. In the main, warrants empower the police:
  (a) to arrest a person and bail him to a court;
  (b) to arrest a person and bring him before a court;
  (c) to arrest a person and commit him to prison;
  (d) to search premises and to seize evidence.

The procedure governing the issue of a warrant is now standardised by the Police and Criminal Evidence Act 1984, which states that if, on application made by a constable, a justice is satisfied that there are reasonable grounds for believing:
  (a) that a serious arrestable offence has been committed; and,
  (b) that there is material on premises specified in the application which is likely to be of substantial value (whether by itself or with other material) to the investigation of the offence; and,
  (c) that the material is likely to be relevant evidence; and,
  (d) that it does not consist of or include items subject to legal privilege, excluded material or special procedure material; and,
  (e) that any of the conditions specified below applies:
    (i) it is practicable to communicate with a person entitled to grant entry to the premises, but it is not practicable to communicate with any person entitled to grant access to the evidence;
    (iii) entry to the premises will not be granted unless a warrant is produced;
    (iv) the purpose of the search may be frustrated or seriously prejudiced unless a constable arriving at the premises can secure immediate entry to them;
    (v) the justices may issue a warrant authorising a constable to enter and search the premises. The constable may seize and retain anything for which a search has been authorised.

Warrants (cont...)

Serious arrestable offence. These offences, which are set out in the Police and Criminal Evidence Act 1984, include:
(a) treason;
(b) murder;
(c) manslaughter;
(d) rape;
(e) kidnapping;
(f) incest with a girl under 13;
(g) buggery with a boy under 16 or with a person who has not consented;
(h) indecent assault which constitutes an act of gross indecency;
(j) causing an explosion likely to endanger life or property;
(k) intercourse with a girl under 13;
(l) possession of firearms with criminal intent;
(m) causing death by dangerous driving;
(n) hostage taking, hijacking, drug trafficking and torture.

Any other arrestable offence. Any other arrestable offence is serious only if its commission has led to, or is intended, or is likely to have led to, any of the following consequences:
(a) serious harm to the security of the state or to public order;
(b) serious interference with the administration of justice or with the investigation of offences or of a particular offence;
(c) the death of any person;
(d) serious injury to any person;
(e) substantial financial gain to any person; and,
(f) serious financial loss to any person.

Serious financial loss. A loss is serious for the purpose of this section if, having regard to all the circumstances, it is serious for the person who suffers it.

Injury. Injury includes any disease and any impairment of a person's physical or mental condition.

Commitment or bench warrant. This type of warrant is issued by magistrates in relation to a person whom they have already dealt with by way of a fine and who has failed to pay part or all of the fine.

The warrant contains directions that the person be arrested and taken to a prison, unless the fine is paid before then.

When executing such a warrant consideration should always be given to the resource implications. A person arrested on Saturday afternoon may have to be held in police cells until Monday to await escort to prison.

Arrest warrant. Where magistrates are satisfied by evidence on oath that a person is a witness to criminal proceedings and that that person has failed to respond to a summons, the magistrates may issue a warrant for his arrest, requiring him to be brought before the court at a time and place specified in the warrant.

If the warrant is issued for the arrest of a person for an offence, then the warrant need not be in possession of the arresting officer. The warrant however, must be shown to the arrested person as soon as possible after his arrest. All other warrants must be in possession of the officer who executes them.

Warrant possession. Where an officer executes a warrant for arrest it should be shown to the arrested person but never handed over to that person. Always keep the warrant in your possession.

Street collections

Charities Act 1992

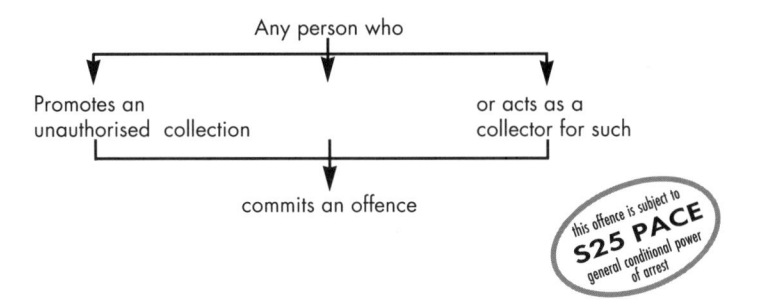

Any person who → Promotes an unauthorised collection / or acts as a collector for such → commits an offence

this offence is subject to S25 PACE general conditional power of arrest

Collection. A collection means an appeal to the public by means of visits from house to house to give, whether for consideration or not, money or other property. A collection may be made by envelope if authorised by the Secretary of State.

The promoter. The promoter must issue to each collector:
(a) a certificate of authority;
(b) a prescribed badge; and,
(c) a collecting box or receipt book indicating the purpose of the collection and a distinguishing number.

The collector. The collector must:
(a) sign the certificate and badge and return them when the collection is completed;
(b) not be under the age of 16 years;
(c) not importune or annoy people;
(d) only collect money which is placed in the collection box, or issue a receipt for it.

Exemption. Where the collection is confined to a single household or public house and is under the control of the occupier, the Act does not apply.

Street collections. Where collections are made in a street or public place they must be in accordance with regulations made by the council of that district (the Common Council in the City of London, or the Commissioner in the Metropolitan Police District).

Control. Before a collection may be made there must be in existence:
(a) a certificate of exemption issued by the police,
(b) a licence issued by the district council, or
(c) an order of exemption issued by the Secretary of State.

Police powers. A constable may require a person whom he believes is acting as a collector, to declare his name and address, and to sign his name. Failure to comply is an offence.

Arrest. This is not an arrestable offence, however, where offences are being committed by bogus collectors then arrest under section 25 of the Police and Criminal Evidence Act 1984 should be considered. Bogus collectors may commit offences of criminal deception, fraud, going equipped to steal etc, under the Theft Act 1968.

Procedure. Offences under this Act are usually committed in high streets crowded with shoppers. Where offenders are suspected checks may be made against their name and address and the name and address held by the promoter of the collection. Signatures may be checked against the certificate of authority and badge issued by the promoter.

Dangerous dogs

> S 3 Dangerous Dogs Act 1991

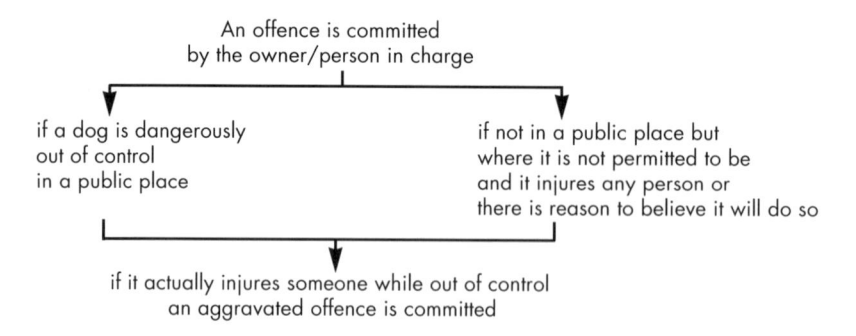

An offence is committed by the owner/person in charge

- if a dog is dangerously out of control in a public place
- if not in a public place but where it is not permitted to be and it injures any person or there is reason to believe it will do so

if it actually injures someone while out of control an aggravated offence is committed

Note: A dangerous dog (currently Pit Bull Terriers, Japanese Tosas, Dogo Argentinas and Fila Brazilieras) may be seized by a constable if it is in a public place and not muzzled and kept on a lead.

Dangerous. 'Is dangerous' is not confined to meaning dangerous to mankind, so that the danger may face sheep, cattle, etc. However, the courts recognise that it is in the nature of dogs to chase rabbits and other small animals therefore it would probably not be an offence against the Act if a dog chases, injures or destroys a pet rabbit or cat.

Transfer of ownership. No order can be made against the person who was the owner of the dog when it was dangerous and not kept under proper control before the hearing, if by the time of the hearing, the dog has been transferred bona fide, to another person's ownership.

Seizure of stray dogs

> S 3 Dogs Act 1906

This Act allows the police to:
(a) seize;
(b) detain; and,
(c) sell or destroy any stray dogs.

This is a useful section when a suspected owner of a dangerous dog refuses to admit ownership.

Children - police protection

> Children Act 1989

Orders for the emergency protection of children are dealt with under the Children Act 1989. Section 46(1) of the Act gives powers to constables to remove and accommodate children in cases of emergency, ie where a constable has reasonable cause to believe that a child would otherwise be likely to suffer significant harm he may:
(a) remove the child to suitable accommodation and keep him there;
(b) take such steps as are reasonable to ensure that the child's removal from any hospital, or other place in which he is then being accommodated, is prevented.

Having taken a child into either police protections (a) or (b) above, the constable concerned shall:
- (a) inform the local authority for the area where the child was found of the fact and the reasons for it;
- (b) give details to the local authority where the child is ordinarily resident;
- (c) inform the child (if he is able to understand):
    - (i) of the steps that have been taken and the reasons for taking them; and
    - (ii) of any further steps to be taken in relation to him;
- (d) take such steps as are reasonable to discover the wishes and feelings of the child;
- (e) ensure that the case is inquired into by an officer designated by the chief officer of police (duty inspector);
- (f) where the child is taken into police protection, ensure that he is moved to accommodation provided by the local authority;
- (g) inform:
    - (i) the child's parents;
    - (ii) inform every person who is not a parent of the child but who has parental responsibility; and,
    - (iii) inform any person with whom the child was living immediately before being taken into police protection;

of the steps taken, the reasons for them and proposed further steps to be taken in relation to the child.

A court may subsequently make a care or supervision order in respect of the child. No child may be kept in police protection for more than 72 hours.

Care proceedings

Section 31 of the Children Act 1989, outlines the circumstances where a care or supervision order may be made in respect of a child; that is to say, where he is suffering, or likely to suffer, significant harm. A family court may make an order if the significant harm, or likelihood of it, is attributable to the care given to the child, or likely to be given to him if the order were not made, not being what it would be reasonable to expect a parent to give to him; or he is beyond parental control.

Pocket book rules

Pocket books are issued to both regular and special constables alike. The purpose of them is to enable an officer to make notes at the time, or as soon as is practicable afterwards, of incidents or occurrences he deals with. The pocket book is an official document and is the property of the issuing force. It may be used in court to refresh the officer's memory of his evidence, or indeed be read from verbatim when dealing with conversations that have been recorded.

Pocket book rules (cont...)

The court officials may wish to examine pocket books and the defence often do.

Pocket books are serial numbered and are issued against individual signatures. Pocket book issue books record who the book was issued to, the date and also the number of the book. Every page in the pocket book is individually numbered. When the pocket book is complete it must be retained in a safe place, usually for a period of seven years.

There are rules concerning the writing-up of pocket books:

Hieroglyphics

Do not use shorthand or difficult or indecipherable writing. Plain English will do nicely.

Author

Write your name, rank and force number on the outer-sheet of the cover.

Standard form

Prior to your tour of duty, write the day and date, which should be underlined. Forces differ but this is usually followed by your tour of duty and lighting-up times. Surnames should be in capitals.

All incidents attended should be written up in detail either at the time, or as soon as practicable afterwards. If the entry is written up afterwards then this fact should be recorded together with the time of entry. At the end of the tour of duty a line should be drawn below the last entry.

Accuracy/brevity

Never sacrifice accuracy for brevity. Above all, the entries should be accurate and truly reflect the incident reported upon.

Errors

Where mistakes are made in writing up the pocket book, do not eradicate, alter or erase the mistake. Simply put a straight line through the mistake in a way whereby the entry can still be read. Next to the line, state that a correction has been made and initial the entry. If the mistake is discovered after further entries have been made, simply refer to the page and line where the mistake took place stating the fact, followed by the correction. Again, a line should be drawn through the mistake and your initials should follow.

Where two or more pages are turned by mistake and entries made in the subsequent pages, upon discovery a diagonal line should be put through the omitted pages followed by an entry:

'OMITTED IN ERROR'

and this should be initialled.

Collaboration

Where two or more police officers attend the same incident, witness the same scene, or are present at an interview, it is natural and acceptable that they collaborate in making up their note books. Clearly, the officers must all be of the belief that what is recorded is a true and accurate reflection of the incident. They should record the fact that there was collaboration and each sign the other's pocket book.

Checking

It is normal practice for supervisors to check pocket books on a regular basis, certainly once every week. Pocket books must be kept up to date as it is the practice of many supervisors to ask to see (and sign) pocket books during meetings on the streets.

If a pocket book is not up-to-date the officer may well be disadvantaged if he then has to record an incident. The effects of allowing a pocket book to lapse are cumulative.

Covert operations

Where an officer is engaged in a covert operation, in particular plain clothes observations in a public place, it would be counter-productive to produce a pocket book and make notes.

In cases like this, notes may be made on any piece of paper. When the pocket book is finally written up, this fact will be recorded in it and the piece of paper kept as the original evidence for production in court as an exhibit.

Loss

The loss of a pocket book should be reported at once and a temporary pocket book will be issued.

Lost/found property

Reports of property which has been lost should be recorded in the appropriate book at the local police station. While each force differs in the book used, the books all contain more or less the same information. Lost property books are serial numbered and contain an index at the front. When checking a lost property book, time will be saved by starting with the index which will look something like this.

INDEX

Serial No	Brief description of property	officer	finalised
B 24451	Visa Trust Card	3901	
B24452	two keys on ring	1033	
B24453	Black leather purse	2332	
B 24453	Notebook in name IAN MITCHELL	3349	found

Having checked the index, the actual report itself may be examined and should contain the following information:

Report of Property Lost
B 24453

Made at .... Police Station

At .... am/pm   on .... 19 ....

Time and date of loss ....

Place lost..

Full description of article(s) ....

....

Name and address of loser ....

.... Telephone number ....

Rank, number and signature of officer receiving report ....

.   ...

Cross reference

When a report is received that property has been lost, a check should be made in the found property book, prior to making an entry in the lost property book.

A check of the lost property book should also be made when found property is handed into the police station.

Location

It may be that a member of the public will report the loss of property at a police station which is some distance from where the loss occurred.

In cases like this, inquiries should be made with the police station in the area of the suspected loss. It may be prudent to fax a copy of the report to that other police station.

Property found

Reports of property which has been found should be recorded in the appropriate book at the local police station. Again, each force differs in the type of book used, but substantially the information contained in the books is the same. The index will be much the same as the index used for the lost property book, and this is always a good place to start.

The keeper

Finders should be encouraged to retain found property unless, of course, this is likely to cause undue inconvenience to the finder or loser, eg where the finder is leaving the district in which the property was found. However the following items should be retained by the police:

(a) items bearing the name and address of the owner or other means by which he/she can be traced;
(b) postal orders;
(c) items which, on account of their nature or value, it may not be lawful, safe or wise to leave in the possession of the finder;
(d) government property (eg service equipment, confidential documents, official passes, etc);
(e) items which may be the subject of or connected with crime, in particular pedal cycles;

Form 398   **FOUND PROPERTY RECORD**   Serial No: ....
(To remain in book)   **20851**
(Prefixed by Divisional Letters)

PART I
Description of Property ....
....
....
....
.... Total Cash £ ....

Date and Place Found .... How Reported: ....
.... (eg in person/phone etc)....................
Finder (BLOCK LETTERS) .... Tel. No: ....
Address:...
Retained by   Finder*   *Delete as Appropriate
           Police*

<u>If Retained by Police</u>
I understand that no claims on my behalf in respect of unclaimed property   Signature of
will be entertained after the period specified on the reverse of this form.   Finder: ....

<u>If Retained by Finder</u> - Please Complete section Marked # below.
                       Yes*
Lost Property Book Checked   No*   Place of Storage ....
                                (If Retained by Police)
Date: .... Station: .... Officer Recording/Receiving
....(Name and No.)

PART II   Record of any movement or transfer of property from original place of storage, e.g. to other store or for despatch to owner etc. (not transfer to HQ)

Officer Receiving			
Time/Date			
New Location or Reason			

PART III   **DISPOSAL**
FINDER
If Retained by / Returned to Finder: I, ...hereby acknowledge to have received the articles listed above. I undertake to return them or their value in the event of the lawful owner claiming his/her right to the property, subject to any deduction of payment made endeavouring to find the real owner.
Signed:.. Given up by: ....Date: ....

OWNER
Restored to Owner (BLOCK LETTERS) .... Tel No: ....
Address:..
Signature: .... How verified: ....
Date: .... Given up by (Name and No.) ....

POLICE
Collected from Station by (Name and No.) ....
Received / Divisional / Sub Div. Office ....
To Credit and Debit Account £ ....
Receipt No. ....Signature ....Date..................
To Sale Room ....Signature ....Date..................
Unsaleable and destroyed ....Signature ....Date..................
Other means of disposal (specify) ....Signature ....Date..................

Date Checked		Finalised	
Initials, Rank & No			

(f) items found by members of the Special Constabulary when on duty;
(g) items found by regular members of the force on or off duty.

Copies of record

It is usual for forces to make three copies of the found property record. Where this is the case they are distributed as follows:

Original. To remain in found property book.

2nd copy. To remain attached to the found property.

3rd copy. Sent to finder. This copy usually informs the finder what will happen to the property if it is not claimed within a certain time.

Time limits

A realistic time limit is laid down by each force as to when (if at all) the property may be claimed by the finder, if not previously claimed by the loser. In this case six weeks is about the norm.

Property not claimed by either the owner or the finder may be disposed of by the police authority. Here eight weeks seems to be the norm.

Retention by finder

Where property is retained by the finder he has a duty to keep that property until the time limit laid down by the force expires. At the conclusion of that time limit the finder who wishes to keep the property should sign a written undertaking to this effect:

I .... hereby acknowledge to have received ....

I undertake to return them or their value in the event of the lawful owner claiming his/her right to the property, subject to any deduction of payment made in endeavouring to find the real owner.

Public relations

Many police officers take the view that lost and found property takes up inordinate time and that this time could be spent on more important issues. The reality is that property returned to owners by the police has a tremendous public relations value.

The record

Allowing for force differences, Found Property Records look substantially like the one shown on previous page.

Domestic disputes

Domestic disputes by their very nature are emotional, vocal and sometimes violent. The role of the police officer attending a domestic dispute is to restore order and then to discover the underlying cause which gave rise to the dispute, and try by way of advice or by invoking the law to remove the cause, thereby removing the fuel whereby it might re-ignite.

It is wise to attend domestic disputes with regular officers in the first place, in order to get a feel for the situation and an insight into the factors which affect them. Every domestic dispute is different in terms of social factors, relationships, proximities of opposing factions, alcohol and violence, and each case has to be treated on its merits.

Entry by invitation

When attending a domestic dispute in a single household, entry is usually by way of invitation. Often one of the occupants will have telephoned the police and will be eager for them to arrive, or else a neighbour has summoned the police because of noise and the fear of damage or injury.

Where there is entry by invitation, any or all parties to the dispute may order the police off the premises and, if there are no grounds for suspecting a breach of the peace, then the police must leave the premises.

If however, one of the parties orders the police from the premises and the other wishes them to remain, then the position of the police becomes increasingly fragile.

The law states that the police are entitled to remain on the premises if they fear that a breach of the peace may occur or it is likely that there will be a renewal of a breach of the peace.

Entry by force

Where the police attend a domestic dispute and are not allowed access to the premises then, unless they fear a breach of the peace, they have no power of entry.

If it is clear to the officers attending the premises that a breach of the peace is ongoing, having regard to raised voices, smashing glass and other noises that attend these matters, then they have the right to enter the premises by force if necessary.

Before exercising the power, officers would be prudent first to ask for entry by stating who they are, demanding entry and the reason for making the demand. If this is refused, then before causing damage to property to effect the entry, try the door first - it may be open!

Damage to property

If property has to be damaged while effecting an entry to quell a breach of the peace, then, time permitting, the damage should be minimal. Rather than knock a door completely from its hinges, it may be possible to break a small window, through which a hand can be put to unlock a door.

Time however, may be of the essence and damage necessarily caused.

However it does nothing to help the situation if damage is left unrepaired. Where the premises are council owned, most councils will send someone out to repair the damage. If the premises are privately owned then the force carpenter may be able to help, but in any case steps should be taken to repair the damage.

Assistance

Where matters are such at the scene of a domestic dispute as to require police officers to make a forcible entry, then consideration should be given to summoning assistance before the entry is effected. The police control room should be given a precise location of the dispute prior to the entry.

Arrest

Having entered the property, by invitation or otherwise, if the officers find that the situation has degenerated to a point whereby offences of assault/damage are in progress, then the immediate remedy (short term as it is) might be to effect the arrest of the protagonist and remove him or her from the scene in order that calm be restored.

Common law powers apply here and the arrested person may be kept in police cells prior to being put before the court to agree to be bound over to keep the peace and be of good behaviour.

Advice

Not all domestic disputes result in a breach of the peace and arrest. Many disputes are, quite simply, noisy, merely involving families in heated discussions. This is the time for police officers to act as professional consultants.

The problem may be drink-related, there may be a problem with overcrowding, poor accommodation, drugs, illness in the family, or a partner having an affair which has been discovered. In these cases the officers have to be in a position to give accurate advice as to where help can be sought from other agencies.

Domestic violence

Officers attending domestic violence incidents should be aware that not only have they a duty to bring order to the existing situation, they also have a responsibility for ensuring that the matter is properly recorded and, if there is a need to inform other agencies of the problems, that they have sufficient detail to do so. It may be that the household is known to the police and other agencies. Equally it may be that the police attend on one occasion not realising that the family are well known to social services or that the children are on the at risk register.

As much detail as possible should be collected at the scene and the matter reported to the local domestic violence unit at police headquarters. The names of these units vary from force to force. Most forces have a standard form which should be completed and submitted following attendance at a domestic incident, and again these forms differ, however they include the same sort of information.

Information to be recorded

> **The victim**
> (a) Full name including aliases;
> (b) date of birth;
> (c) address;
> (d) access to other addresses;
> (e) injuries;
> (f) relationship to assailant;
> (g) hospitalised yes/no;
> (h) alcohol involved;
> (i) drugs involved;
> (j) doctor's name.

Questions should be asked of the victim to elicit whether or not the incident is a 'one-off' or an on-going domestic problem. Advice should be offered concerning other agencies which can help the victim. Where the assailant lives in the same premises as the victim it is particularly difficult to point to the agency which might best offer support. It may be that the victim would benefit from a talk with his/her doctor; the parties can be persuaded to visit a marriage guidance bureau, or indeed apply for an injunction to the courts. In any case advice can always be given to the victim as to where help can be found.

The assailant
- (a) Full name including aliases;
- (b) date of birth;
- (c) address if different;
- (d) relationship to victim;
- (e) alcohol involved;
- (f) drugs involved;
- (g) reported for summons;
- (h) arrested yes/no.

Children

Children are particularly vulnerable in domestic violence situations and it is important that anything that can be done for them should be done. A good starting place is to physically see each child in the household. This is not always easy and may require good negotiating skills, in order to check that they are all there and that they are all well.

If the officer attending the scene believes that a child is likely to suffer significant harm then under the provisions of the Children Act 1989 the officer is empowered to remove the child to suitable accommodation. The provisions of this Act seek to strike the proper balance between speedy and effective help to children at risk and unwarranted interference in family life.

Section 46(1) of the Act empowers a constable who has reasonable cause to believe that a child would otherwise be likely to suffer significant harm to:
- (a) remove the child to suitable accommodation and keep him there; or
- (b) take such steps as are reasonable to ensure that the child's removal from any hospital, or any other place in which he is being accommodated, is prevented.

The child is in police protection when these powers have been exercised. Having exercised these powers the duty inspector becomes a 'designated officer' who is charged under the Act to inquire into the case.

Information to be recorded in cases where children are present in the household includes:

children
- (a) full name;
- (b) date of birth;
- (c) relationship to victim/assailant;
- (d) injuries;
- (e) location of children during the incident;
- (f) did the children observe the incident;
- (g) were the children involved in the incident.

Other agencies

The officer attending the scene of a domestic incident should consider whether or not to inform other agencies of the incident or to advise the parties involved to seek support from other agencies.

> **Other agencies include:**
> (a) Solicitors.
> (b) Doctors.
> (c) Social workers.
> (d) Marriage guidance bureaux.
> (e) Women's refuge.
> (f) The Samaritans.
> (g) Council housing department.
> (h) Alcoholics Anonymous.
> (i) Drugs helplines.

Simply attending a domestic dispute and bringing order to bear is often not enough. The officer attending should take the view that he is in the best position to provide, or arrange for provision of, an after-care service. People need to be helped to help themselves.

Specialist units

All forces now have specialist units to help deal with domestic violence. They come under all sorts of different names but amount to the family and child protection unit. These units consist of trained staff who are highly specialised in their fields and have a great deal of police experience. Among other things they offer are:

Trauma suites

Trauma suites provide an environment in which victims can recover from their ordeal and where they can talk confidentially to caring officers. Statements of evidence can be taken in these sympathetically decorated rooms where there are usually toys for children to play with.

Doctors and scene of crime officers can attend the suite rather than the victim attending a police station which is usually cold and unaccommodating. Trauma suites are designed to bring an air of safety and normality back into the victim's life.

Videotaped interviews

When a child or vulnerable person is the victim of a crime, forces now have the facilities to have any interview recorded.

The officers who are actually involved in the interviews are trained in interview techniques, as is the videotape operator.

The interviewers have useful devices such as anatomical dolls to help children explain what happened to them in sex-abuse cases. The child or vulnerable person will have someone with them who is a member of the family.

Cameras are unobtrusively placed in two or more points in the room where the interview takes place, and the main console recording the interview is placed in an adjacent room. Remote earpieces are used by officers watching the interview from the adjacent room to speak to the interviewer without any others in the room hearing.

These videotaped interviews may be used as evidence in court, although it is usually enough for the assailant to see the interview to bring about admissions.

Agency co-ordination

These specialist family units receive reports from other agencies regarding persons at risk. In most forces officers attending domestic violence incidents are required to make out a report of the circumstances of the incident and forward it to the family unit for attention. Officers wishing to know if a family is 'known' can enquire at the family unit and gain much useful information regarding what to expect to find at known addresses and also which agencies are already involved with the family.

Neighbour disputes

Without doubt, feuding neighbours are quite the most difficult people to deal with, be it over quarrels about boundary fences or the behaviour of their children. Again, advice should be given (usually to contact their solicitors), and the peace should be preserved. Caution must be exercised when dealing with feuding neighbours as they are often tempted to use the police as a vehicle to advance their own causes.

Neighbour disputes often give rise to complaints against the police, because the very nature of the dispute is such that both parties can never be satisfied. It is particularly important when dealing with this type of dispute to make full notes in **pocket books**.

Landlord and tenant disputes

> **Protection from Eviction Act 1977**

Harassment and illegal eviction of a 'residential occupier' are criminal offences under the Protection from Eviction Act 1977. Prosecutions are normally brought by a district council.

Unlawful eviction

This is defined as an eviction (or attempted eviction) of a person entitled to occupy accommodation without the correct legal procedure being followed. In most cases this legal procedure requires serving a valid notice to quit and obtaining a possession order from the county court.

Landlord and tenant disputes (cont...)

Those covered by legal protection are:

Tenants (whether they have a written agreement or not).

Licensees (whether they have a written agreement or not).

Occupants of bed and breakfast accommodation (provided it is not short term and can be described as the occupant's 'residence').

Excluded lettings - notice only

The following cases do not require a possession order to evict and are called excluded lettings:

Eviction by resident landlord - only if the landlord lives at the same premises as the tenant and shares living accommodation with the tenant (eg, living room, bathroom, wc, kitchen, but not hall, stairs etc) and the landlord has lived there since the tenancy began.

Holiday accommodation.

Rent-free accommodation - but not if the tenant provides some service in lieu of rent or is employed at a wage reflecting the provision of accommodation by the landlord. In such cases the landlord is only required to give reasonable notice to the occupant (normally the period of the tenancy equals the notice required, eg rent paid weekly requires one week's notice). These procedures must be followed even where the tenant is alleged to be in the wrong for eg rent arrears.

Harassment

Harassment is defined as the carrying out of acts by a person which are likely to interfere with the peace or comfort of a tenant or the persistent withdrawal of services (eg gas, electricity etc) when the person intends, knows or has reasonable cause to believe that the acts would cause a tenant to leave his home or stop doing things a tenant should normally be able to do.

Squatters

Until recently, squatting was usually a matter for the civil courts, but when section 73 of the Criminal Justice and Public Order Act 1994 came into force it became an offence for any person who is on premises as a trespasser, having entered as such, to fail to leave after being required to do so by or on behalf of a 'displaced residential occupier of the premises' or a 'protected intending occupier of the premises'. A constable in uniform may make an arrest in these circumstances without warrant.

> **Suggested procedure - WRAPeR**
>
> **Warn** landlord he may be committing a criminal offence if he illegally evicts or harasses a tenant. Give him examples of the meaning of harassment.
>
> **Refer** both landlord and tenant to the tenancy relations officer of the local council whereby advice may be sought with a view to resolving their dispute.
>
> **Advise** landlord not to withhold tenant's possessions in lieu of unpaid rent; claims for rent should be dealt with by the county court. The tenancy relations officer is able to advise the landlord on the procedure to be adopted.
>
> **Persuade** both landlord and tenant to put things back as they were until further advice is sought.
>
> **Record** any accusations, admissions etc and all evidence of illegal eviction, harassment or attempts by the landlord. Behaviour and admissions made by the tenant should also be recorded and the whole matter reported on statement of evidence forms to the local council. The local council is empowered to bring proceedings before the magistrates' court when the reporting officer will be required to give evidence.

Action at the scene of a crime

Police officers attending the scene of a reported crime, do so as evidence gatherers. It is their duty to preserve and protect the scene. Evidence can be obtained from witnesses, fingerprints, footprints, blood, semen, saliva, marks and a host of other sources. The actions of the first officer at the scene often dictate whether or not the outcome of the investigations will be successful.

Preserve the scene

Where the report of a crime is received by telephone, the caller should be asked not to touch anything and await the attendance of police officers. Upon arrival at the scene, officers should, while disturbing things as little as possible, make careful notes of what they find. Rough sketches in pocket books can be useful at this stage.

Where it is clear at the outset that there is scope for fingerprints to be found, it is often prudent, if the police are not wearing gloves, for them to put their hands in their pockets in order to avoid smudging existing fingerprints or adding fingerprints which subsequently have to be eliminated by fingerprint officers.

In the case of serious crime, the first officer at the scene, having satisfied himself that there is nothing he can do immediately, should call out senior officers and then remain at the scene and ensure that no unauthorised person enters the area. Preservation of the scene is vitally important at this stage.

Protecting the scene

Where the crime is serious, say homicide, it is important that the first officers at the scene ensure that there is no movement by unauthorised personnel into the protected area. A log should be kept of all movements of personnel to and from the scene; names, times, and purpose of visit should be recorded.

Entry/exit

In cases of burglary the point of entry is usually fairly obvious. It should never be assumed that the point of entry is also the point of exit, therefore the search should continue in order to establish both points.

Time of offence

The exact time of an offence is often unknown, however the victim should be able to say that it occurred between X and Y o'clock. This is most usual in vehicle crime. Mr Smith parked his car at home at 8 pm and found it to be missing at 6.45 am the next day.

Scenes of crime

On arrival at the scene of the crime officers should ask themselves 'is there any scope for scenes of crime officers?'. If the answer is yes then the earlier the scenes of crime specialist attends the crime the better. Scenes of crime specialists are highly trained persons who are aware of the potential of gathering evidence from articles which appear at first sight to be innocuous.

Dog handler

When a crime is committed in an isolated location, or during the course of the night when the streets are empty, then consider calling a dog handler to the scene. Where this is to be done then the movement of persons at the scene should be restricted in order that the scent is not contaminated.

Stolen property

The property stolen should be listed in detail and circulated to other officers as quickly as possible. If the property is identifiable then it can be placed on the property index at the criminal records office. Equally, if the property is unusual, or by its nature it is likely to be 'fenced', then consideration should be given to making inquiries at known outlets, eg scrap-metal dealers.

Modus operandi

Criminals tend to commit the same type of crime and, more importantly, they use the same method or MO. Cheque fraudsters rarely turn to shoplifting just as robbers do not go in for cheque frauds. This can be most useful, in particular, if the MO is an unusual one, eg removing the ground floor windows of dwelling houses at night.

A check with Method Index at the criminal record office might well throw up a suspect who is a specialist in this method of burglary.

Video cameras

Increasingly, video cameras are being installed in shopping precincts, garages, night clubs and other public places. It should always be remembered that the offence and perhaps the culprit may have been video-taped before, during, or after the incident. It is particularly useful when dealing with a drive-off to find that the whole episode has been recorded on video.

Footprints

Where footprints are found in outside areas they should be covered to await photographing or being cast. A dustbin lid can be found most useful in this respect.

Door to door inquiries

Door to door inquiries in the immediate area of the crime might produce a witness, or someone who can cut down the time range of the offence. Consideration should be given to speaking to postmen, milkmen, dustmen, paper boys etc, if appropriate.

Index of modus operandi

Each criminal records office maintains a register of the means used by criminals to commit crime. The means used is indexed under up to 10 points on the register. The more that is known about how the crime was committed, the greater chance there is of identifying the culprit by comparing how he committed the crime in relation to other crimes committed in the same fashion.

---

10 points covering method:

(1) Classword. The class of person or property attacked, (churches, museums etc).

(2) Entry. The point of entry to the premises (skylight, window, through roof).

(3) Means. The means used to effect the entry (smash and grab, con-trick).

(4) Object. The motive for the crime or property stolen (sex, jewellery etc).

(5) Time. The hour, day and date as well as the occasion, ie, public holidays, nights.

(6) Style. The criminal's alleged trade or profession.

(7) Tale. The story told by the criminal accounting for his presence at the scene of the crime.

(8) Pal. Was there more than one person involved in the crime, if so how many?

(9) Transport. How did the criminal arrive at and leave the scene of the crime?

(10) Trade mark. Was there anything peculiar or unusual done at the scene of the crime, use of toilet, consumption of food?

Crime reports

Recording the crime

Forces differ in the actual paperwork used in recording crimes, however all crime reports contain the same information. When attending the scene of a crime the officer in charge of the investigation is responsible for submitting the record of the crime and should therefore gain enough information at the scene to enable him to submit a crime report upon return to the police station.

Crime reports comprise
(a) Offence, ie burglary.
(b) Day, date, time, place.
(c) Reported: day, date, time place.
(d) Name and address of person reporting.
(e) Name and address of victim, date of birth, sex, occupation.
(f) Details of offence (how was it carried out).
(g) Property stolen (identifiable/non-identifiable).
(h) Property recovered.
(j) Persons suspected/wanted.
(k) Persons cautioned/reported/arrested.
(l) Whether the scene was attended and by whom.
(m) The officer in charge of the case.
(n) Further inquiries to be completed.
(o) Date by which inquiries should be complete.

Amendments

If there is a necessary amendment to a crime report, a further crime form should be submitted, cross-referenced to the original report.

No crime

In cases when a crime is reported and subsequently found to be erroneous - eg a reported theft of a pedal cycle, which in fact had been borrowed by a neighbour - then the original report may be marked 'No Crime'.

Victims

Officers who are the first to attend the scene of a crime involving injury, damage or loss are often asked by the victims what remedies are open to them in relation to such matters as compensation and bringing the offender(s) to justice. They often want to know about the procedures at court and obtaining, compensation or the mechanics of how the victim appears at court and gives evidence. It is important that officers who attend crimes and meet victims are in a position to advise on the courses of action open to them and how they might be helped.

The Victim Support organisation aims to provide support and advice for all victims of crime and to increase knowledge and awareness of the effects of crime. This is a registered charity with its head office in Cranmer House, 39 Brixton Road, London SW9 6DZ, telephone 0171 735 9166, and with agents in all main towns and cities. Victims should be encouraged to seek help from this organisation where they have suffered loss or injury or require help when attending court as a witness.

Compensation

Persons who have suffered injury, loss or damage as a result of crime, may qualify for compensation. Three possibilities are open to them:
    (a) a compensation order may be made against the offender;
    (b) they may take civil action; and,
    (c) they may apply for compensation through:
        (i) the Criminal Injuries Compensation Scheme; or,
        (ii) the Motor Insurers' Bureau.

Compensation against an offender who is convicted by a court **may** be awarded by the court in favour of the victim of his crime. The victim may not apply for compensation but the CPS will be aware of the loss, damage or injury and will make the court aware of the circumstances as it affects the victim.

Compensation may cover such items as:
    (a) personal injury;
    (b) losses because of theft of, or damage to property;
    (c) losses because of fraud;
    (d) loss of earnings while off work;
    (e) medical expenses;
    (f) travelling expenses; and,
    (g) pain and suffering.

When a compensation order is made by the court against an offender, the compensation is paid by the offender to the court and the court pays the victim direct.

Civil action

If a victim wishes to take a civil action against the offender in respect of loss, damage to property or personal injury, he should be advised to see his solicitor or seek help from the Citizens' Advice Bureau.

Criminal Injuries Compensation Scheme

When a victim suffers personal injury as a result of a crime of violence he or she may be entitled to compensation from the Criminal Injuries Compensation Board. This is so whether the offender has been caught or not.

Victims should be given a copy of the leaflet 'Victims of Crimes of Violence' which is available at police stations, Victim Support agencies or through the Citizens' Advice Bureau. The minimum payment from the Scheme is currently £1,000, so minor injuries which would attract compensation of a lower amount will not be eligible for a payment.

Motor Insurers' Bureau

Where a victim suffers injury or loss or damage to property as a result of a road traffic accident, compensation will normally be payable under the insurance arrangements. However, where the offender is untraced or uninsured compensation may be available through the Motor Insurers' Bureau.

The Bureau may consider claims for:
- (a) personal injury or loss or damage to property caused by an uninsured driver (including injury, loss or damage caused by an identified driver of a stolen vehicle where the rightful owner is uninsured);
- (b) personal injury (but not loss or damage to property) caused by an untraced driver (including injury caused by an untraced driver of a stolen vehicle).

Further information may be obtained from:
   The Motor Insurers' Bureau
   152 Silbury Boulevard
   Central Milton Keynes MK9 1NB
   Telephone: 01908 240 000.

Victims as witnesses

The Crown Prosecution Service will help and support victims who have become witnesses and the CPS has undertaken to:
- (a) before trial, ask the court to set as convenient a date as possible for witnesses, and tell the witnesses what to expect in court;
- (b) in cases involving the death of a victim, CPS staff will meet the victim's relatives if they wish, to discuss the basis of the CPS decision;
- (c) at trial, they will introduce themselves to witnesses wherever possible, and try to ensure that they are not kept waiting too long;
- (d) they will do all they can to have the necessary information on compensation, and remind the courts to hear evidence on the issue if necessary;
- (e) tell the court that unjust mitigation is not accepted by the prosecution, and ask the court to hear evidence on the issue if necessary;
- (f) after the trial, make every effort to explain the outcome to the victims, pay expenses within five to 10 working days, and make emergency arrangements if necessary; and
- (g) where there is an appeal, tell the police of developments so that they can inform victims or their families, and tell the police in cases of death or sexual crime, if possible before it appears in the media.

CHAPTER 12

THE PNC AND RADIO PROCEDURE

Chapter contents

The Police National Computer **200**
    Who can use the PNC 200
Name inquiries **200**
    CRO number..200
    Wanted/missing information.................................200
    Disqualified driver 201
    Driving licence number 201
    Warning signal codes 201
Vehicle inquiries... **201**
    Codes 202
    Chassis numbers 202
    Requests from the public.......................................202
    Vehicle report types... 203
The Data Protection Act 1984... **203**
    Criminal liability 204
    Caution 204
Radio procedure **204**
    The phonetic alphabet 204
    Standard radio codes... 205
    Personal radios - quick reference guide 205
    The ten code.. 206

The Police National Computer

As the Police National Computer (PNC) is accessed by all UK forces, users must appreciate that a standard phraseology must be employed when interrogating the data base.

Who can use the PNC

(a) Regular police officers;
(b) special constables on duty in connection with incidents occurring when they are on duty;
(c) civilians, PNC operators or those nominated by reason of their job description;
(d) traffic wardens - but only those issued with a unique PNC number and only vehicle checks are allowed.

Name inquiries

If the user wishes to check out an individual person, certain information is required by the PNC operator which is given in this order: NASCH:

N Name (full name including middle names);
A Age, this means date of birth;
S Sex;
C Colour (see ethnic appearance codes below);
H Height.

So far as colour is concerned, Home Office guidelines offer seven ethnic appearance or identity codes. These are given over the radio as IC**1** or IC**3** etc:

1 Nordic European;
2 Mediterranean European;
3 Afro Caribbean;
4 Asian;
5 Oriental;
6 Arab;
7 Unknown.

Most people fit somewhere in these codes and the use of the codes saves time spent on the airways. Having fed this data into the PNC a check will reveal:

(a) CRO number

The criminal record office (CRO) number if the person checked has a criminal record. This will allow the officer to check details of the person and indeed give access to his file if needed.

(b) Wanted/missing information

Where the person checked is wanted or missing the PNC will give detailed information of the circumstances giving rise to the fact. Before this information is passed to the requesting officer, and to maintain security, the code 10/8 (see page 206) will be given to ensure that the information passed is not heard by the person being checked out.

(c) Disqualified driver

If the person checked is disqualified from driving this information will be passed together with the court disqualifying, when disqualified and for how long. Again this information should be preceded by the code 10/8.

(d) Driving licence number

If required, the officer making the inquiry can ask for the driving licence number of the individual checked.

The information passed to the PNC under the head NASCH may result in a high volume of persons matching those details being held on computer. Where this is the case further information will have to be fed into the computer to narrow down the parameters in order to identify the individual, ie:

(a) Marks or scars;
(b) tattoos;
(c) place of birth;
(d) facial hair;
(e) accent.

In addition to the CRO number, wanted/missing, disqualified driver and driving licence number, the PNC is able to alert the officer checking of **warning signals** which may be known. Again this information should be preceded by the 10/8 code before being passed over the air.

Warning signal codes

(a) firearms;
(b) violent;
(c) mental;
(d) alleges (makes false allegations);
(e) ailment (ie, Hepatitis 'B', Aids);
(f) drugs;
(g) weapons;
(h) escaper;
(j) explosives;
(k) contagious (diseases);
(l) male impersonator;
(m) female impersonator.

This information will come up on the PNC display under a code which will be read by the operator and passed to the officer making the check in plain language:

Finally, the PNC, when employed on a names check, is able to give further information on impending prosecutions, a conviction history and summary and aliases used by the checked person.

Vehicle inquiries

If a vehicle registration mark (VRM) is known the registered keeper may be found from the PNC. Before this information is passed to the inquiring officer a code must be given to the PNC operator together with the vehicle's location.

Code 1   Vehicle stopped in street.
Code 2   Moving vehicle.
Code 3   Abandoned/parked/unattended vehicle.
Code 4   Vehicles involved in road traffic accidents.
Code 5   Vehicle subject to investigation.
Code 6   Administrative check.
Code 7   Child access inquiries.
Code 8   Inquiry on behalf of authorised agency.
Code 9   Update/confirm/broadcast (varying information).
Code 10 Other audit checks.

Having received this information, the PNC is able to provide the following information to the officer:
(a) registered keeper of the vehicle;
(b) date first registered;
(c) make of vehicle;
(d) type of vehicle;
(e) class of vehicle;
(f) colour of vehicle;
(g) chassis number of vehicle;
(h) status of tax (current/expired).

If there is only partial information concerning the vehicle registration mark this may be entered and the computer is able to check a maximum 999 options. This facility is most useful in detecting hit and run drivers. Where there is a multiple inquiry (eg vehicles checked in a car park) the computer is able to check up to 15 vehicles at a time.

Chassis numbers

The vehicle chassis number or vehicle identification number can be checked on the computer. This is particularly useful when dealing with vehicles on false number plates or where the vehicle is burnt out. When the chassis number and the make of the vehicle are known then all 40 million records at the Driving and Vehicle Licensing Authority (DVLA) will be searched and will display full details of the vehicle concerned. When the make of the vehicle is unknown then only stolen vehicles will be checked.

PNC checks - requests from the public

When inquiries are received from members of the public as to whether a vehicle is recorded as stolen, the only information which is to be provided to the inquirers is whether or not the vehicle is in fact recorded as stolen. No information shall be provided about the name or address or other details of the registered keeper. Disclosure of any such information is a breach of the Data Protection Act 1984.

If the vehicle is not recorded as stolen, the inquirers must be advised to make their own full inquiries about the history of the vehicle as the absence of any record on the PNC is not conclusive evidence that the vehicle is not stolen.

Vehicle report types

Listed below are the types of reports concerning vehicles which may be placed on the PNC. In all these cases the reports remain logged into the PNC for a specific length of time only. Times vary and PNC operatives should be consulted in each case:

Los   Lost or stolen, or obtained by deception.

Fou   Found, apparently abandoned, or repossessed by a finance company.

Inf   Information about the use of the vehicle. This must be fact. If current driver details are required, you must state why the information is required. The inquirer must be informed that a provisional report stays on the computer for six weeks only and if required longer then a hard copy must be sent to PNC.

Cor   Correction to the vehicle's description, as displayed on the PNC. These can only be entered by hard copy to the PNC bureau.

Rem   Removed, by or on behalf of the police, may be street to street or to police custody.

Res   Restricted, report is of a sensitive nature and must not be disclosed over insecure channels. Can only be entered by hard copy to PNC bureau.

See   Seen or checked at particular locations, or times which may assist in investigation of a specific crime or crimes.

The Data Protection Act 1984 and the PNC

Before dealing with the Police National Computer (PNC) it is necessary to have a sound understanding of the Data Protection Act 1984, as the two matters are inextricably linked. The PNC contains, amongst other things, information about people, and the Act affects the way the police use information about people. The Act applies to both the PNC and to police computers which have access to the PNC. It also applies to operators and users of the PNC, and indeed all computers.

The Act requires that all personal data held on computers:
(a) is collected fairly and lawfully;
(b) is held only for lawful purposes;
(c) is used only for lawful purposes and is only disclosed to people shown on the registration;
(d) is adequate, relevant and not excessive;
(e) is not held longer than necessary;
(f) is kept secure.

Special constables have access to the PNC only when they are on duty in connection with incidents occurring when they are on duty. Abuse of the PNC may make the individual responsible liable to a fine and/or imprisonment.

Offences under the Act include:
   (a) knowingly or recklessly using, obtaining, disclosing, procuring the disclosure of or transferring personal data other than as prescribed;
   (b) knowingly or recklessly disclosing personal data without the authority of the person to whom computer bureau services are provided.

In short, under the Act special constables may incur liability where they knowingly or recklessly use, obtain or disclose information in a way contrary to the purpose for which it is kept. The force in which they serve may also be liable to a penalty.

Criminal liability

Nottinghamshire Constabulary suspended an officer after he pleaded guilty to charges of misusing the PNC. It was alleged that the officer passed information from the computer to a relative concerning the registered keeper of a motor vehicle. An officer in Essex was jailed for one year (with eight months suspended), at Chelmsford Crown Court for breaking the Official Secrets Act by passing information from the PNC to a private detective who received a similar sentence. Both were ordered to pay £700 costs.

Caution

Caution must always be exercised when dealing with data in relation to the PNC. Where officers are in doubt about disclosing information – seek advice.

Radio procedure

The phonetic alphabet

When using radios the identification of sounds is sometimes difficult for the receiver, particularly in areas of poor reception. Clarity of information can be improved by the use of the phonetic alphabet. Phonetics is the identification, description and classification of sounds used in articulate speech. These sounds are codified in the international phonetic alphabet which is a highly modified version of the Roman alphabet.

Before using a radio this alphabet should be committed to memory. It is particularly useful when spelling difficult names over the airways and passing vehicle registration details.

The phonetic alphabet

A	alpha	J	juliet	S	sierra
B	bravo	K	kilo	T	tango
C	charlie	L	lima	U	uniform
D	delta	M	mike	V	victor
E	echo	N	november	W	whisky
F	foxtrot	O	oscar	X	x ray
G	golf	P	papa	Y	yankee
H	hotel	Q	quebec	Z	zulu
I	india	R	romeo		

Standard radio codes

Code	Meaning	Remarks
'over'	End of transmission reply expected	Channel still in use
'out'	End of transmission, no reply expected	Channel is then open for further traffic
'roger'	Message received and understood	Acknowledgement of information

Personal radio - quick reference guide

Aerial — Ensure that the aerial is tightly screwed in at all times to prevent loss in use. Turn radio on by rotating volume control clockwise. Turn off by rotating volume control anti-clockwise. Where an earpiece is in use, avoid prolonged use of maximum volume.

Receiving — Turn radio on and select desired channel using channel selector and LCD display. Place mode select switch in centre position.

Transmit — Switch radio on and select desired channel. Monitor the channel for activity. When the channel is clear press PTT switch on remote microphone and speak clearly, release to change to receive mode.

Battery — LED indicates continuous red for normal transmissions. LED flashes red to indicate a low battery. The battery is installed and removed by a sliding movement.

Scanning — The radio is capable of being programmed to receive transmissions on channels other than that selected. Do not attempt to engage this facility without clear instructions from a supervisor.

The ten code (not used by all forces)

10-1	On watch	Use when booking on the air at start of tour or when resuming after any period off air.
10-2	Make landline contact	Telephone a specific place/person.
10-3	Return to station	If required to return to place other than usual station, the place should be named.
10-4	Temporarily off the air but can be contacted	Use when going off the air at place where you can be contacted by telephone. This code should only be used for refreshments or at the scene of an incident when you can be contacted.
10-5	Temporarily off the air, cannot be contacted	Use when going off the air, eg at the scene of an incident or for refreshments when you cannot be contacted.
10-6	Any messages?	Use after having been away from vehicle or returning to radio transmissions.
10-7	Message not understood - try again	Use to avoid long explanation. It should not be necessary to amplify.
10-8	Confidential message to follow	It is important that all officers on the channel either switch off their loud speakers or turn down the volume if members of the public are within earshot.
10-9	Police officer requires urgent assistance	May be used either to or from control. This code must only be used where an officer is in personal danger, not because he urgently wants to search a building or he is about to do something.
10-10	Off watch	Use at the end of tour of duty.
10-20	'Blocked'	This information will only be communicated via secure channels. Contact your PNC terminal. Patrols receiving this code should do nothing to indicate to the occupants of vehicles that they or the vehicle are of interest to the police.
10-99	Risk of person being armed or violent use caution	This code is used to warn patrols that the person being interrogated may be armed or violent. The code is issued in order that the suspect is not alerted to the nature of the warning. Other officers hearing this code should be alert to what is going on and make a particular note of the location of the incident.

CHAPTER 13

SUMMARY OF POWERS

Chapter contents

Powers of arrest 208
Arrest - definition 208
Common law - citizen's power
....208
Police arrest 208
Arrestable offences...................208
General arrest conditions 209

Powers of search 210
Stop/search.............................210
Prohibited article.....................210

Procedure 211
Gowise 211
Entry and search leading to arrest
....211
Search after arrest 212
Search of prisoner's premises ...212
Premises 213
Seizure of property from
premises 213
Search in public.......................213

Powers - traffic 213
Disqualified drivers 213
Documents / name, address
date of birth 313
PSV driver and conductor.......214
PSV passenger 214
Testing motor vehicles on roads
....215

Goods vehicles operator's
licence 215
Tachographs 215
Removal of vehicles.................215
Traffic regulation 216
Breath test 216
Arrest......................................216
Powers of entry........................217
Road checks 217

Powers - firearms 217
Trespassing with a weapon 217
Carrying in public place..........217
Trespassing with firearm..........218
Require production 218
Stop and search 218
Production of certificate..........218

Powers - miscellaneous 219
Mentally ill people 219
Scrap metal dealers................. 219
Licensed betting office 219
Licensed premises................... 219
Drugs - stop and search.......... 219
Fires....................................... 220
Public meetings 220
Exclusion orders - football...... 220
Alcohol at sporting events 220

Powers of arrest

Arrest - definition

Arrest involves the taking of a person's liberty to answer an alleged offence. Arrest consists in the seizure or touching of a person's body with a view to restraining him. However, the use of words may amount to an arrest if they are likely to bring, and do bring, to the attention of the person the fact that he is under compulsion and he submits to the compulsion. Such force may be used as is **reasonable** in the circumstances but use of force which is unreasonable in the circumstances will make the arrest unlawful.

Common law - citizen's power

At common law any person may arrest without warrant where:
   (a) a breach of the peace is committed in his presence; or,
   (b) a breach of the peace has been committed and it is reasonably believed that a renewal of it is threatened; or,
   (c) it is reasonably and honestly believed that a breach of the peace will be committed in the immediate future although one has not yet been committed. An idle threat will not suffice.

Police arrest (assault or obstruct police) — Police Act 1996

A police officer may arrest any person who assaults or resists or wilfully obstructs him in the lawful execution of his duty under circumstances likely to cause a breach of the peace.

Arrestable offences — S 24 PACE

Arrestable offences are defined in section 24(1) of PACE as:
   (a) an offence for which the sentence is fixed by law (eg murder - life imprisonment);
   (b) an offence for which, on first conviction, a person aged 21 years or over may receive at least five years' imprisonment;
   (c) certain offences specified by the Act creating the offence (eg going equipped to steal);
   (d) attempting, aiding and abetting, inciting, procuring or conspiring to commit any of the above offences.

The powers of arrest for 'arrestable offences' by a police officer are:
(1) A police officer may arrest any person:
   (a) who is in the act of committing an 'arrestable offence';
   (b) whom he has reasonable grounds for suspecting to be committing an arrestable offence.

(2) When an arrestable offence has been committed a police officer may arrest any person:
   (a) who is guilty of the offence;
   (b) whom he has reasonable grounds for suspecting to be guilty of the offence.
(3) A police officer who has reasonable grounds for suspecting that an arrestable offence has been committed, may arrest any person whom he has reasonable grounds for suspecting to be guilty of the offence.
(4) A police officer may arrest any person:
   (a) who is about to commit an arrestable offence;
   (b) whom he has reasonable grounds for suspecting to be about to commit an arrestable offence.

The powers under (1) and (2) may also be exercised by any person.

General arrest conditions   S 25 PACE

When a police officer has reasonable grounds for suspecting that any offence (other than an arrestable offence):
   (1) has been committed or attempted; or
   (2) is being committed or attempted;

he may arrest the relevant person whom he has reasonable grounds to suspect of:
   (a) having committed or attempted to commit the offence; or,
   (b) being in the course of committing or attempting to commit it;

if it appears to him that the service of a summons is impracticable or inappropriate, because:
   (i) the name of the person is not known to the police officer and cannot be readily ascertained;
   (ii) there are reasonable grounds for doubting whether a name given by the person is correct;
   (iii) the person has failed to give a satisfactory address for service of a summons, or there are reasonable grounds for doubting whether an address given by the person is a satisfactory address for this purpose;
   (iv) there are reasonable grounds for believing that an arrest is necessary in order to prevent that person:
      1. causing physical injury to himself or any other person,
      2. suffering physical injury,
      3. causing loss of or damage to property,
      4. committing an offence against public decency,
      5. causing an unlawful obstruction of the highway;
   (v) there are reasonable grounds for believing that an arrest is necessary to protect a child or other vulnerable person from that person.

An arrest in respect of an offence against public decency is only authorised where members of the public going about their normal business cannot reasonably be expected to avoid the person to be arrested.

An address for service of a summons is a satisfactory address if it appears to the police officer:
   (a) that the person will be at it for a sufficiently long period for it to be possible to serve the summons on him; or,
   (b) that another person specified by the first person will accept service of the summons for the first person at that address.

Powers of search

Stop/search

S 1 PACE

A constable may detain and search any person or vehicle (including ships and aircraft) and anything which is in or on a vehicle, if he has reasonable grounds for suspecting that he will find stolen or prohibited articles. (There is no power to stop or detain a person in order to find grounds for a search.)

A constable may exercise this power:
   (a) in any place to which, at the time when he proposes to exercise the power, the public or any section of the public has access, on payment or otherwise, as of right or by virtue of express or implied permission; or,
   (b) in any other place to which people have ready access at the time when he proposes to exercise the power, but not a dwelling.

But where a person or vehicle is in a garden or yard occupied with and used for the purpose of a dwelling (or on other such land), a constable may not search him or the vehicle unless he has reasonable grounds for believing that:
   (a) the person does not reside there, and is not there with the resident's express or implied permission; or,
   (b) the person in charge of the vehicle does not reside there, and the vehicle is not there with the resident's express or implied permission.

Prohibited article

For the purpose of stop and search under the Police and Criminal Evidence Act 1984, an article is prohibited if it is: **S 1(7) PACE**
   (a) an offensive weapon: 'offensive weapon' means any article;
      (i) made or adapted for use for causing personal injury; or, **S 1(9)**
      (ii) intended by the person having it with him for such use by him or by some other person;
      (iii) including blades and pointed instruments.
   (b) any article;
      (i) made or adapted for use in the course of or in connection with any offence of burglary, theft, taking a conveyance, deception; or, **S 1(7)**
      (ii) intended for such use by the person having it with him or by some other person.

Procedure
S 2 PACE

If a constable contemplates a search, other than a search of an unattended vehicle, he shall take reasonable steps before he commences the search to bring to the attention of the appropriate person:
- (a) documentary evidence that he is a constable (if not in uniform);
- (b) the constable's name and police station (except in cases linked to terrorism, in which case he shall give his warrant number);
- (c) the object of the proposed search;
- (d) the constable's grounds for the proposed search;
- (e) the fact that a written record will be made and that a copy of it will be available upon request at a police station.

GOWISE **G**rounds for search
Object of search
Warrant card
Identification of officer
Station to which attached
Entitlement to a copy of the search record

Entry and search leading to arrest
S 17 PACE

Section 17 of the Police and Criminal Evidence Act 1984 provides that a constable may enter and search any premises for the purpose of:
- (a) (i) executing an arrest warrant in connection with criminal proceedings (eg non-appearance - fail to answer summons),
  - (ii) executing a commitment warrant (issued by a magistrates' court for failure to pay);
- (b) arresting a person for an arrestable offence;
- (c) (i) arresting a person for certain statutory public order offences,
  - (ii) (when in uniform) arresting a person who is trespassing on premises with a weapon of offence;
  - (iii) arresting a person who has used threatening behaviour which causes another person to believe that unlawful violence will be used against him;
- (d) recapturing a person unlawfully at large and whom he is pursuing;
- (e) saving life or limb or preventing serious damage to property.

Limitations. Except in the case of (e) above, a constable may only enter and search premises if:
- (a) he has reasonable grounds for believing that the person whom he is seeking is on the premises; and,
- (b) in the case of premises which consist of two or more separate dwellings (eg bedsitters) he enters and searches; only,
  - (i) parts of those premises which the person uses in common with other occupants; and,
  - (ii) any dwelling within those premises in which he has reasonable grounds for believing the person he is seeking, may be.

Search after arrest

> **S 32 PACE**

A constable may search any person, arrested at any place other than a police station, if the constable has reasonable grounds for believing that the arrested person may:
- (a) present a danger to himself or to others; or,
- (b) have concealed on him anything;
  - (i) which he might use to assist him to escape from lawful custody; or,
  - (ii) which might be evidence relating to an offence.

A constable may seize and retain anything (other than an item relating to legal advice) found in such searches, if he has reasonable grounds for believing:
- (a) in the case of a search in (a) above, that the arrested person might use it to injure himself or another;
- (b) in the case of a search in (b) above;
  - (i) that the arrested person might use it to escape from lawful custody; or
  - (ii) that it is evidence of an offence or has been obtained through the commission of an offence.

A constable may also enter and search any premises in which the arrested person was when arrested, or immediately before he was arrested, for evidence relating to the offence for which he was arrested. This power may only be used if the constable has reasonable grounds for believing that there is such evidence in those premises (see below for the power to seize items from premises, and the Code of Practice on searching of premises).

If premises consist of two or more separate dwellings (eg bedsitters) a constable's power of search is limited to:
- (a) any dwelling in which the arrest took place or in which the person arrested was immediately before his arrest; and,
- (b) any parts of the premises which the occupier of any such dwelling uses in common with the occupiers of any other dwellings comprised in the premises.

Search of prisoner's premises

> **S 18 PACE**

The Police and Criminal Evidence Act 1984 provides that a constable may enter and search any premises occupied or controlled by a person who is under arrest for an arrestable offence - if he has reasonable grounds for suspecting that there is on the premises evidence (other than items relating to legal advice) that relates:
- (a) to that offence; or,
- (b) to some other arrestable offence which is connected with or similar to that offence.

These powers can only be exercised if authorised in writing by a police officer of the rank of inspector or above.

A constable may conduct a search for reasons as outlined above:
- (a) before taking the person to a police station; and
- (b) without obtaining prior authorisation (inspector's authority);

if the presence of that person at a place other than a police station is necessary for the effective investigation of the offence.

Premises

> S 23 PACE

The term 'premises' means:
- (a) any place;
- (b) any vehicle, vessel, aircraft or hovercraft;
- (c) any off-shore installation;
- (d) any tent or movable structure.

Seizure of property from premises

> S 19 PACE

A constable who is lawfully on any premises under any statutory power, or with the consent of the occupier, may seize anything (other than items relating to legal advice) which he has reasonable grounds for believing is:
- (a) evidence of an offence; or,
- (b) has been obtained in consequence of the commission of an offence.

Such items may only be seized where this is necessary to prevent their concealment, alteration, loss, damage or destruction.

Search in public (removal of clothing)

> PACE Code A

A constable conducting a search in public may not require a person to remove any clothing other than the outer coat, jacket or gloves. The co-operation of the person to be searched should be sought in every case. Where there are reasonable grounds to require that additional items of clothing be removed, this should be done out of public view.

Powers - traffic

Disqualified drivers

> S 26(2) Sched 2 PACE

A constable in uniform may arrest without warrant any person driving a motor vehicle on a road when he has reasonable cause to suspect him of being disqualified.

Production of documents and power to demand name & address and date of birth

> Ss 164/5 Road Traffic Act 1988

(1) A police officer may demand the production of a driving licence and the name and address of any person who:

(a) is driving a motor vehicle on a road; or,
(b) is reasonably believed by that officer to have been driving a motor vehicle when an accident occurred owing to its presence on a road; or,
(c) is reasonably believed by that officer to have committed an offence in relation to the use of a motor vehicle on a road; or,
(d) is supervising a provisional licence holder who is driving a motor vehicle on a road; or,
(e) is reasonably believed by that officer to have been supervising a provisional licence holder in circumstances as at (ii) or (iii) above.
(2) A police officer may demand the production of a plating certificate, certificate of insurance and test certificates from any person in circumstances as in paragraphs (i), (ii) and (iii) above.

The person required to produce documents may do so:
(a) on demand; or,
(b) within seven days of the demand at a police station specified by that person;
(c) in the case of an insurance certificate following a personal injury accident, within five days of the accident and at a police station specified by him.

A police officer demanding production of a driving licence may require a person to state his date of birth if:
(a) the person fails to produce the driving licence forthwith; or,
(b) he has reason to suspect the licence;
   (i) was not granted to that person; or,
   (ii) was granted to that person in error; or,
   (iii) contains an alteration made with intent to deceive; or,
   (iv) contains a driver number which has been altered, removed or defaced;
   (v) where the person was supervising a learner driver and the constable suspects him of being younger than 21.

PSV driver and conductor

A driver or conductor when acting as such shall, if requested by a police constable, give particulars of his name, the name and address of the person by whom he is employed and, in the case of a driver, of his licence.

PSV passenger

A passenger committing an offence against the regulations may be ejected by:
(a) the driver;
(b) an inspector;
(c) the conductor; or,
(d) on request of any of the above, by a police officer.

Testing of motor vehicles on roads

Road Traffic Act 1988

A constable may require that a motor vehicle be tested forthwith:
- (a) after it has been involved in a road accident (in which case he may detain it for that purpose);
- (b) if in his opinion the vehicle is so defective that it would be dangerous for it to proceed.

Section 69 of the Act gives an authorised constable the power to issue an immediate prohibition notice if, after inspection, it appears that defects in the vehicle would present a risk of injury to any person if it were driven.

Goods vehicle operator's licence

A goods vehicle operator's licence is required for every goods vehicle exceeding 3.5 tonnes RPW which is used for the carriage of goods:
- (a) for hire or reward; or,
- (b) in connection with the operator's trade or business.

The licence can be either restricted (for use in operator's own business) or standard (for hire or reward) - national or international.

The holder of a GV operator's licence shall produce it for inspection by a police officer on demand and may do so at his operating centre, head office, principle place of business, or at a police station nominated by the holder. It must be produced within 14 days of the demand.

The holder of a PSV operator's licence may also be required to so produce the licence as above except that there is not the option to produce it at a police station.

Tachographs

Transport Act 1968

A police officer has power at any time, to detain and enter any vehicle required to have a tachograph fitted. He may demand the production of, and inspect and copy, any record. If an officer has reason to believe that the record chart has been fraudulently altered he may seize the chart.

Removal of vehicles

Removal and Disposal of Vehicles Regulations 1986

(1) A police officer may require certain persons to remove a vehicle which is on a road. They are the owner or the driver or the person in charge.
(2) A police officer may require a vehicle to be removed when:
- (a) it is broken down on a road or is at rest on a road or is in such a condition that it is causing an obstruction or is likely to cause danger; or,
- (b) it is at rest on a road in contravention of a parking restriction or prohibition.
(3) Should a person refuse to move the vehicle or not be available, a police officer may:

(a) remove the vehicle himself; or,
(b) cause it to be removed by another person.
(4) Other vehicles may be removed by an officer if they appear to be abandoned on a road or on land in open air, whether they are broken down or not.

Traffic regulation   Ss 35 and 37 Road Traffic Act 1988

(1) Any person driving a motor vehicle or riding a pedal cycle on a road shall stop on being required to do so by an officer in uniform.
(2) When an officer is engaged in the regulation of traffic;
    (a) the drivers of all vehicles must obey his signals;
    (b) pedestrians must stop if signalled to do so by a police officer in uniform.

Breath test - power to require   S 6 Road Traffic Act 1988

When a police officer in uniform has reasonable cause to suspect:
(a) that a person driving or attempting to drive, or in charge of, a motor vehicle on a road or public place, has alcohol in his body, or has committed a traffic offence while the vehicle was in motion; or,
(b) that a person has been driving or attempting to drive, or was in charge of, a motor vehicle on a road or public place with alcohol in his body and still has alcohol in his body, or has committed a traffic offence while the vehicle was in motion;

he may require that person to provide a specimen of breath for a breath test. The breath test may be taken either at or near the place where the requirement is made.

If an accident occurs owing to the presence of a motor vehicle on a road or public place, a police officer may require any person whom he has reasonable cause to believe was:
(a) driving; or,
(b) attempting to drive; or,
(c) in charge of;

the vehicle at the time of the accident, to provide a specimen of breath for a breath test. This test may be taken at or near the place where the requirement is made or, if the officer thinks fit, at a police station specified by the officer.

Arrest   S 6 Road Traffic Act 1988

A police officer may arrest without warrant, any person (if not a patient at a hospital) lawfully required by him to provide a specimen of breath for a breath test if:
(a) the specimen is positive; or,
(b) the person has failed or refused to provide a breath specimen and the officer has reasonable cause to suspect alcohol in his body.

A police officer may arrest without warrant any person whom he has reasonable cause to suspect is or has been:

> **S 4 Road Traffic Act 1988**

(a) driving; or,
(b) attempting to drive; or,
(c) in charge of a motor vehicle on a road or other public place while unfit to drive through drink or drugs.

For the purpose of arresting a person under the above power, a police officer may enter (if need be by force) any place where that person is or where the officer reasonably suspects him to be.

Power of entry

> **S 6 Road Traffic Act 1988**

If an accident occurs owing to the presence of a motor vehicle on a road or public place and a police officer reasonably suspects that it involved injury to another person. Then for the purpose of:

(a) requiring a breath test; or,
(b) making a subsequent arrest;

the police officer may enter (if need be by force) any place where that person is, or where he reasonably suspects him to be.

Road checks which must be authorised

> **S4 PACE**

Authority in writing from a superintendent or above is required for a 'road check' to ascertain whether a vehicle is carrying any of the following categories of person:

(a) a person who has committed an offence (**which must be a serious arrestable offence**) other than a road traffic or vehicle excise offence;
(b) a person who is a witness to such an offence;
(c) a person intending to commit such an offence; or
(e) a person who is unlawfully at large (**arrestable offence**).

Powers - firearms

> **S 8 Criminal Law Act 1977**

Trespassing on premises with a weapon of offence

A constable in uniform may arrest without warrant anyone who is, or whom he reasonably suspects to be, in the act of committing the offence. For the purpose of arresting a person for this offence, a constable in uniform may enter premises in accordance with the terms of section 17 of PACE (see above).

Firearm - carrying in public place

> **S 19 Firearms Act 1968**

A police officer may arrest any person who without lawful authority or reasonable excuse has with him in a public place either:

(a) a loaded shotgun; or,
(b) any other loaded firearm (except an air weapon); or,
(c) any unloaded firearm with suitable ammunition for that weapon (but not if that weapon is a shotgun or an air weapon).

Note: Carrying a loaded air weapon in a public place is a summary offence.

Trespassing with firearm

`S 20 Firearms Act 1968`

Trespassing with a firearm or shotgun or imitation firearm in a building, without reasonable excuse, is an arrestable offence.

Power to require production

`S 47 Firearms Act 1968`

A constable may require any person reasonably suspected of having any firearm with him in a public place or in a building or on land as a trespasser and without good reason, to hand over the firearm for examination.

It is an offence to fail to hand over the firearm for examination.

Firearms - stop and search

`S 47 Firearms Act 1968`

When a constable has reasonable cause to suspect that any person:
(a) has possession of any firearm in a public place; or,
(b) is trespassing in a building or on land with a firearm; or
(c) is committing or about to commit an offence under section 18 of having a firearm or imitation with intent to commit an indictable offence;

he may search that person and any vehicle involved, and may detain the person for that purpose.

Note: A constable may enter any place to exercise this power.

Production of certificate

`S 48 Firearms Act 1968`

A constable may demand from any person believed to be in possession of a firearm or ammunition, to which s 1 of the Act applies, or a shotgun, the production of the appropriate certificate. If the person fails to produce the certificate or to allow it to be read or to prove that he is exempt from the requirement to hold a certificate, the constable may seize the firearm, ammunition or shotgun and demand the person's name and address.

It is an offence for a person:
(a) to refuse to give his name and address; or,
(b) to fail to give his true name and address.

Powers - miscellaneous

The mentally ill

S 136 Mental Health Act 1983

If a police officer finds in a place to which the public have access a person who appears to be suffering from a mental disorder and who appears to be in immediate need of care or control, the police officer may if he thinks it necessary:
- (a) in the interests of that person; or
- (b) for the protection of other persons;

remove that person, to a place of safety (which may be a police station).

Scrap metal dealers

Scrap Metal Dealers Act 1964

A police officer may enter at all reasonable times any specified place of business of a person registered with the local authority as a scrap metal dealer. He may inspect metal, books or receipts and take copies of any entries.

Licensed betting office

Betting, Gaming and Lotteries Act 1963

An officer may, at the request of a member of the staff, assist to expel any person who is drunk, violent, quarrelsome, disorderly or under 18 years of age, using only such force as is necessary.

Licensed premises

Licensing Act 1964

(1) A police officer may enter licensed premises (other than premises covered only by an occasional licence) at any time during permitted hours and during the first 30 minutes after the end of any period forming part of those hours. This power is intended for routine supervision.

(2) A police officer may enter premises for which an occasional licence is in force during the hours specified in the licence.

(3) A police officer may enter licensed premises at any time outside permitted hours if he suspects an offence is being or is about to be committed against licensing laws.

(4) A police officer shall on demand of the licensee, his agent or servant, **help** to expel from those licensed premises any person who:
- (a) is drunk, violent, quarrelsome, or disorderly, or whose presence would subject the licensee to a penalty under the Act;
- (b) the officer reasonably suspects of having entered in breach of an exclusion order.

Drugs - stop and search

S 23 Misuse of Drugs Act 1971

A police officer may, when he reasonably suspects a person to be unlawfully in possession of a controlled drug, detain and search such a person or suspected vehicle, and seize anything which may be evidence of an offence.

Fires

A police officer may, without the consent of the owner or occupier, enter and if necessary break into, any premises or place: in which a fire has or is reasonably believed to have broken out; or, which it is necessary to enter for the purpose of extinguishing a fire. The senior police officer present at the scene of a fire may regulate the traffic as appears to him to be necessary for fire fighting purposes.

Note: Always ensure that the fire brigade has been called before entering the premises.

Public meetings

> Public Meetings Act 1908

If a police officer reasonably suspects any person of committing the offence of acting in a disorderly manner with intent to prevent the business of the meeting being carried out or he may, at the request of the chairman of the meeting, require that person to give his name and address.

Exclusion orders - football

> Public Order Act 1986

A constable who reasonably suspects that a person has entered premises in breach of an exclusion order may arrest him without warrant. An exclusion order is made by a court against a person who has been convicted of certain football-related offences and prohibits those subject to them from entering premises for the purpose of attending prescribed football matches.

Control of alcohol at sporting events

> Sporting Events (Control of Alcohol etc) Act 1985

During the 'period' (two hours before the start and one hour after) of a designated sporting event (includes association football matches, internationals (including schoolboy ones) and rugby internationals at Murrayfield):

(1) A constable may arrest without warrant any person he reasonably suspects is committing or has committed any offence relating to the control of alcohol at sporting events.
(2) A constable may enter any part of a designated sports ground.
(3) A constable may stop and search a PSV or search a railway passenger vehicle if he has reasonable grounds to suspect that any offence involving the carrying of alcohol is being or has been committed.
(4) A constable may search any person whom he has reasonable grounds to suspect is committing or has committed any offence under the Act.

Note: Any search must be carried out in accordance with the PACE codes of practice.

(5) A constable in uniform may require any person having control of a bar in the ground to close it if he believes it is necessary to prevent disorder.

Note: This power should not be exercised by a probationer constable acting on his own.

CHAPTER 14

CRIME PREVENTION

Chapter contents

Neighbourhood Watch **222**
    History 222
    Setting up a Neighbourhood Watch scheme 222
    Success or failure of Neighbourhood Watch 223
Crime prevention **224**
    Casing the joint 224
    Target hardening 224
    Target concealment or removal 224
    Reducing the pay-off 224
    Dwelling security 225
    Property marking and identification 227
    Intruder alarm systems 228
    Security lighting 228

Neighbourhood Watch

Any - and every - community has the ability to reduce local crime with a Neighbourhood Watch scheme. The important aspect is that every scheme is based within a small community where the concept of being a good neighbour can be exploited with a view to the reduction and prevention of crime through public awareness and liaison with the police.

People often feel that dealing with crime is best left to the police, but prevention and reduction of crime can be achieved much more widely if the police have the help of extra ears and eyes and the willingness of members of the public to report suspicious behaviour.

If neighbours are vigilant, are aware of their own environment, and transmit detailed and accurate information to the police, then criminals can be discouraged. Vigilante groups however are not part of Neighbourhood Watch. Patrolling the streets and arresting people is the task of the police.

History

Neighbourhood Watch - also called Community Watch and Home Watch - started in the United Kingdom in 1982, following the success of such schemes in the US. Mollington in Cheshire was the first village to set up a scheme in this country.

In the US at the time, Neighbourhood Watch had been active for some years and had proved highly successful in two respects, reducing crime and also reducing the fear of crime. To start with, the schemes were designed to persuade people to mark their property clearly and conspicuously and to fit suitable door and window locks. From this developed a public awareness of the problems and possible methods of reducing crime.

Setting up a Neighbourhood Watch scheme

Inquiries from the public about Neighbourhood Watch usually arise from one of two occurrences. First, if they have recently been burgled or, secondly, when their house contents insurance is due for renewal and they see the magic words 'five per cent discount if in a Neighbourhood Watch scheme'.

If you, as a special constable, are asked to set up a scheme, you will have to decide how large an area the scheme will cover. Are there identifiable boundaries, such as a cul-de-sac, part of a street, etc?

Find out if a resident would host the initial meeting. If not, or if the scheme is too large, is there a local community hall or school?

Having booked up the meeting-place, and arranged a suitable date and time (weekday evenings are often more convenient than weekends), leaflet drop every household which will be in the scheme with that information. Giving people two weeks' notice is generally acceptable.

Turn up on the day in plenty of time, possibly in the company of the community beat officer if available. Do not forget to take sufficient crime prevention and Neighbourhood Watch leaflets, Incident Report Cards, window stickers, and Contact Person's Manuals. You may be able to borrow a videotape or two from the crime prevention department - check whether you will need to take a television and video-recorder. Welcome people to the meeting, show one or more videotapes, and explain the concepts, aims and potential success of the scheme. By the end of the meeting, it is vital that you have the name and address of at least one person who is prepared to act as contact person (or co-ordinator).

Next day, advise the Crime Prevention Department of the name of the new scheme and the contact person.

The success or failure of Neighbourhood Watch

Neighbourhood Watch schemes are only as successful as the amount of effort put into them by their members. It is vital that members take collective responsibility for problems in their area, and show potential criminals that they are being watched, which if necessary will lead to the police being called. Sometimes members think that by merely placing a sticker in their window and a sign on a lamp-post, then crime will automatically go away and knock elsewhere. These schemes tend to have a lack of neighbourliness and little or no community spirit.

However, schemes flourish where residents frequently hold social gatherings, such as barbecues and coffee mornings, and social cohesion is developed. These schemes exist where residents take a keen interest in what is going on in the neighbourhood, in recognising each other, their families and friends and cars. In this way, when a stranger or different car is observed in the locality, residents' suspicions are aroused.

Successful schemes are very often part of an identifiable community, which either existed prior to the scheme or has resulted from it. Schemes should have at least one co-ordinator (or contact person) and should be able to organise themselves with as little help as possible from the police, although they are encouraged to keep in regular formal or informal contact with their community beat officer or crime prevention department.

Once the initial 'honeymoon' period is over, it is important for the police to keep an eye on events from a distance, perhaps offering to hold postcoding sessions or a crime prevention talk, to stop the scheme from folding too soon.

Crime prevention

Casing the joint

Before offering crime prevention advice to householders, think about how the property looks from a burglar's view:
- (a) Are any doors or windows open?
- (b) Are ladders available?
- (c) Do drainpipes run alongside windows?
- (d) Are there flat roofs?
- (e) Is there anywhere, such as the rear of the property, which is not overlooked and from where a burglar could operate unseen?

Do not forget that the burglar's enemies are **time**, **noise** and **exposure to view**.

Target hardening

Target hardening is the placement of barriers between the criminal and his target. This could involve door and window locks, laminated glass, intruder alarms, lighting, trimming and thinning of hedges, lowering of walls and fences.

In this way the criminal will be forced to:
- (a) take more time to commit his crime;
- (b) make more noise to commit his crime;
- (c) look more conspicuous while committing his crime.

If any or all of these can be increased, then the criminal may well start to wonder whether or not the crime is worth the risk.

Target concealment or removal

If the potential target is hidden from sight, then the intending burglar will not know whether there is any point in spending time breaking into the property, and may well move on to another property with targets more obviously on show. Similarly, if it is shown to the burglar that there is nothing to take (eg shops leave the cash register drawers open showing that they are empty), then a criminal will see that a crime is not worthwhile.

Reducing the pay-off

Targets are less attractive to the thief if he knows that he will have difficulty disposing of them, or if he will not be able to put them to good use. Therefore, property marked in some way will connect and identify the criminal with that crime. In this way goods may be just not worth stealing.

However, it is vital that the criminal knows that the property has been identified.

Dwelling security

The perimeter

The perimeter of a property is the first line of defence against an intruder, or conversely his first line of concealment. Therefore, any fences, walls, hedges and shrubbery should be kept as low as possible, and well-trimmed so that the burglar can be observed at all times.

Any gates which give access to the side or rear of a house should be flush with the building line, so that anyone scaling the gate would be visible to neighbours and passers-by.

Where possible, all entry points (doors, windows and outbuildings) should have the potential of being viewed by neighbours/passers-by.

Exterior lights

Consider the use of exterior lights — are there any areas that are in darkness at night-time? In addition to ordinary lights switched on/off by the householder, there are now available dusk-to-dawn lights and various sensor lights. All these ensure that a burglar will be illuminated should he approach the property.

House construction

Look at the shell of the house (ie the walls, roof, external doors and windows). The shell needs to be secure so that a target within cannot be reached.

Do flat roofs or drainpipes give access to windows?

Is it possible to climb onto a roof and drop through a skylight?

Remember - this does not mean can you shin up drainpipes or crawl across tiles - it means could someone else do it? Many burglars are young, slim and agile.

Outbuildings

Sheds, garages and other outbuildings should be kept locked - often they house ladders and tools which may be used to break into the owner's home. Most sheds can be secured with padlocks or lockable bolts if mortice locks are inadequate. Garage doors need to be secured by more than the standard key - again, padlocks will offer good security.

Tools

All tools should be stored out of sight and ladders should not be kept on garage roofs or hanging at the side of sheds.

Doors

Many criminals make their way into a house via an insecure door, which may have been left open or unlocked for a few minutes while the householder is in the garden, or while he has popped to a neighbour's or the shops.

Doors tell thieves when the house is empty: letters in letterboxes or visible through glazed doors, notes stuck on the door declaring 'Back in an hour', keys hanging through the letterbox, milk still on the doorstep, all advertise that no-one is at home.

Many people do not distinguish between a lock that is meant for privacy and a lock that can give a real measure of security. Doors which can be locked and/or bolted from the inside are more secure than the final exit door, which can only be locked from the outside. Therefore, the final exit door should be the door most easily seen from the street.

The lock on the final exit door should be a deadlock, either a five-lever mortice deadlock or a rim automatic deadlock. This means that the door cannot be opened without a key. The door itself is recommended to be of solid timber, and fitted with good strong locks. Many existing doors can be improved: half-glazed doors may be strengthened with strong plywood over the lower panels to prevent them from being kicked in.

However, the door frame must be securely fixed to the building itself. Remember - a lock is only as good as the frame to which it is attached.

Door viewers, designed to be installed at eye level, allow the householder to see who is outside without opening the door. These are easy to install, requiring just one small hole to be drilled in the door.

Door chains and limiters allow the door to be opened a few inches, so that one can see who is outside and view ID cards when necessary. However, neither is an extra lock and they will provide only limited protection when the door is partly opened.

Doorstops, which are fitted to the bottom of the door, are operated by pressing a lever with one's foot which brings the base of the stop onto the floor, wedging it in place. The doorstop, which is suitable for internal and external doors, is easily fitted with just a screwdriver. It is a very simple device to operate and allows the householder to decide how much access to give visitors.

Windows

A large number of burglaries are committed through windows, although it is very rare for burglars to actually climb though a smashed pane of glass. Most of the entries are gained by burglars climbing through an open window or reaching through a small open window to open a larger one. Sometimes the putty or beading is removed making it easy to remove the glass. Most domestic windows use cheap glass which is thin, whereas it would be preferable to install stronger laminated glass, although expensive.

Stand outside your house and imagine that you are locked out. How are you going to get in? Can you break a pane of glass to reach a lock?

Would it be possible to climb up to get in through an upstairs window?

Think - if you can do it, then so can a burglar.

Many opportunist thieves climb through a tiny gap - if you can get your head through, a burglar can squeeze inside. A thief will look upon an open or unlocked window as an easy target. With a properly locked window, a thief would have to break enough glass to allow his whole body through. This is a noisy, time-consuming and hazardous task which would deter most criminals. If a thief sees a security device giving protection to both fastener and stay, usually he will go away.

Accessible windows, such as those on the ground floor or those which may be reached from flat roofs, drainpipes or ladders, should be fitted with window locks. Stronger locks should be used on those windows which are unobserved. If the burglar realises that he cannot get into the house without making a lot of noise, or taking a lot of time, he may well decide not to bother.

There are now available locks to fit most types of window, whether made of metal, wood or UPVC or of the sash, sliding or casement design.

Security grills

These are an excellent deterrent as they are a visible physical barrier over the most vulnerable part of any building. They are trouble-free and give continuous protection even when a window is open. Security grills are made from aluminium or steel and usually fit on the inside. A wide variety of designs and finishes are now available.

When fitting security grills, however, always plan for a fire escape — most manufactured grills will have a quick-release locking system available which allows the grills to be removed quickly in case of fire.

Louvre windows

These are particularly vulnerable and difficult to secure because the glass slats can be lifted out easily. Gluing the slats to the frames with epoxy resin adhesive will make it far more difficult for the burglar. There are also special locks available.

When considering the security of a property, the best method is to work from the outside towards the target.

Property marking and identification

Property marking is encouraged for two reasons. First, items obviously marked in some way will be dangerous for a criminal to handle and harder to dispose of, so he may think twice before stealing them. Second, if stolen property is later recovered, it can be returned without delay to its rightful owner. Every year hundreds of thousands of pounds' worth of property is recovered by the police, but cannot be returned to its rightful owner due to lack of identification.

All property should be postcoded, not only expensive items. Remember, items of sentimental value cannot be replaced, and the burglar is only interested in making easy cash, however small.

The correct way to identify property is with the owner's postcode, plus either the house number or the first three letters of the house name. Various methods of marking property are available, depending on the type of property to be marked:

Ultra violet marking

Use an ultra violet pen to invisibly mark metal, pottery, wood and canvas. The mark fades in time and may be rubbed off by repeated washing or polishing, therefore it should be renewed regularly. An ultra violet light source is required to check the mark.

Ceramic marking

Ceramic marking pens leave a permanent mark on any glazed surface, such as pottery and porcelain, without cutting the surface. However, the monetary value of the item may be reduced by the marking.

Engraving or etching

This is carried out by using a hand engraver or an electric engraving tool. It can be used on most hard surfaces where it will leave a permanent and visible mark.

Punching

Heavy metal items, such as tools and lawn-mowers, may be marked with a hammer and set of punches.

Photographic evidence

It is well worth taking colour photographs of property, especially jewellery and other items too difficult or delicate to mark. The photograph should include a ruler to give an indication of the size of the item.

Serial numbers

Keep a note of all serial numbers and other identifying marks of electrical goods etc.

Intruder alarm systems

An intruder alarm is a visible deterrent to potential burglars. These days, with systems being relatively inexpensive to install, owning a burglar alarm does not indicate wealth.

The criminal will realise that, once the alarm is set off, an audible bell will advise neighbours that something is amiss and the police will duly attend. If the alarm does not act as a deterrent, and the burglar gains entry, he will know that his time inside the property is limited as the police will be on their way.

'Perimeter protection' detectors will set off the alarm when an attempt is made to force open a window or door. 'Trap protection' is where detectors are located inside rooms and will be activated when the burglar enters the room. These detectors will be either internal door contacts or passive infra red.

There are several types of intruder alarm system on the market. They will all have an audible siren or bell, whilst the more expensive ones will either dial the police or the alarm company central station.

It is recommended that advice and quotations are sought from three companies, which should all fit to British Standards Institute level.

Security lighting

The use of security lighting, both inside and outside the house, is an inexpensive deterrent to the burglar. Few burglars will attempt to break into a property if they believe it to be occupied. Therefore, by installing internal night lights which switch themselves on and off at irregular intervals, or which activate when certain sounds are received, the burglar will be put off entering that house. External lights with sensors are also effective.

CHAPTER 15

PATH TO PROMOTION (SUPERVISORS)

Chapter contents

Post profile **230**
    Responsibilities 230
    Skills required 231
Seeking promotion **232**
    Mentors 233
    Personal development 233
Setting up a section **233**
    The individual 234
    The team 235
    The organisation 235
    Conflict 236
    Supervision of files 236
    Assessment reports - a model 237
    Availability and duties worked........................... 237
Recruiting **238**
    Disqualified categories 238
    Requirements for selection 239
    Conditions of service 241
Disciplinary procedure **242**
    Past and present 242
    The Police (Conduct) Regulations 1999.................243
        Code of Conduct 243
    Working Group recommendations 245
    Legal representation 245
    Complaints and discipline - the law 242
        Dismissal 246
        Suspension or retirement............................ 247
Operation orders **248**
    IIMAC 250
Specialist units.. **252**
    Criminal Investigation Department (CID)............252
    Road Traffic Department 254
    Support Group (Task Force) 255
    Lower profile units..256

Post profile

Post profile	
Post	Special Constabulary
Rank/grade	**Section Officer**
Duty area	Where appointed
Responsible to	Area Commander via the Special Constabulary Sub-divisional officer
Responsible for	Special Constables in appointed section

Responsibilities

(1) To be responsible for officers within his/her appointed section in relation to all matters concerning administration, operational duties and discipline.

(2) To ensure that the special constables in his/her section attend training courses, parades and perform the minimum hours of duty required.

(3) To keep a record of performance of duties by special constables in his/her section, including dates, times and number of hours worked.

(4) To ensure that special constables are fully kitted with the issued uniform and equipment and that each officer has in his/her possession while on duty, all forms and necessary paperwork to discharge his/her duties properly.

(5) To ensure that special constables within his/her section are fully conversant with the geographical area they are responsible for policing and that they have a good working understanding of operational procedures and administrative systems.

(6) To be responsible for the welfare of special constables within his/her section and to ensure that the number of hours worked do not conflict with domestic or civilian employment arrangements, and to monitor the types of incidents special constables attend with regard to debriefings following stressful incidents.

(7) To ensure that special constables within his/her section are subject to lateral development and receive training commensurate with their needs, and to develop the potential of each officer in relation to improved skills, performance and attachment to specialist units.

(8) To be able to report on each special constable within his/her section in relation to his/her present performance and to make recommendations for further training, specialist unit attachments and matters concerning career development.

(9) To identify special constables within his/her section who have the potential for re-grading and to develop those officers' skills and abilities in anticipation of re-grading. To that end consideration should be given to such officers deputising as section officer.

Skills required

The postholder should:

(a) possess the ability to supervise, motivate, train and develop officers in his/her section;

(b) possess a good working knowledge of the law and procedures;

(c) possess a high standard of inter-personal skills and in particular should be able to communicate well, both verbally and in writing;

(d) be familiar with disciplinary procedures operating within his/her force and be aware of the channels of communication concerning these procedures;

(e) possess an ability to take charge of briefings and be conversant with the contents of an operation order and be prepared to produce such an order when appropriate;

(f) be prepared to act on his/her own initiative, taking command where appropriate, and to deploy officers and resources when necessity dictates, at the same time assuming responsibility for decisions made and actions taken;

(g) possess the necessary drive and enthusiasm to instill in others a sense of purpose and commitment. Demonstrate qualities of leadership that promote high morale in officers, and by example, ability, knowledge and professionalism, create a team who have objectives which are realistic and achievable;

(h) groom himself/herself in order to deputise for his/her immediate senior officer by making himself/herself familiar with his/her duties and responsibilities and develop a more global perspective in relation to what is to be achieved and how best to deploy officers and resources.

Seeking promotion

If a special constable is seeking promotion he must make the decision-makers aware that he has that ambition. In the absence of selection procedures the decision makers cannot know who is seeking promotion and who is not. Before seeking promotion the special constable should ask himself the question 'if promoted, can I do the job?'. If the answer is no, then time needs to be spent bridging learning needs to a point whereby the answer to the question is yes.

Many regular officers are promoted to the rank of sergeant because they are good constables, but they do not always make good sergeants. It follows therefore that the special constable who believes himself to be an excellent special has to ask himself, will I be a good supervisor? This is an important distinction because promotion should bring challenge and the reward of job satisfaction, when in fact it may well bring regret to the person promoted who turns out to have little aptitude for the job. Three issues arise from this:
(a) do you want promotion;
(b) have you the aptitude for the job; if so,
(c) tell people, bring it to the attention of the decision makers. Do not wait in the hope that 'you know' that it will happen sooner or later - help make it happen.

While every force is different, it is the duty of supervisors, both special and regular, to assess the ability of the applicant to perform satisfactorily the duties of the rank to which the officer aspires. To this end, the ambitious special constable can help himself by deputising for his supervisor when the opportunity presents itself. Arrange to take over the duties of the supervisor in order to 'live with' the experience of supervision for a while and to let others see that you can do the job. In assessing the abilities of the candidate supervisors will have regard to criteria such as:
(a) aptitude for command and discipline;
(b) influence on colleagues;
(c) organising ability;
(d) initiative;
(e) integrity;
(f) general police knowledge and efficiency;
(g) experience;
(h) tact and behaviour in dealing with the public; and,
(j) special qualifications.

It should be noted that experience does not figure very high on the list of attributes sought from the candidate. While experience is more than useful to the constable on the street, when promoted there are ten or so other officers who will look after the streets, the newly promoted special constable will then have a greater responsibility in terms of organising ability, influencing colleagues etc. Experience therefore, while useful, is no longer as near the top of the list as it once was.

Mentors

Officers seeking promotion should seek out a mentor, a regular or special supervisor or manager, and come to an arrangement whereby the mentor will guide the candidate to achieving his ambition by way of a structured plan. The idea of mentoring is that of having a 'friend' who will ensure that the candidate knows what lies ahead of him, what is expected from him, and who will help him realise his ambition. In seeking out a mentor, the candidate should find:
> (a) a volunteer, someone who is prepared to spend the time and energy involved in mentoring;
> (b) a person who has the energy to guide and shape the candidate and who will not only encourage but actively take steps to test the resolve of the candidate;
> (c) someone whom he can trust implicitly. There should be a meeting of minds, a chemistry between the two, in a sense they should be soulmates.

The job of the mentor is to guide the candidate, to shape and prepare him for his new role as supervisor. It is his job to ensure that the candidate has a 'voice' and that he is afforded the opportunities to facilitate his ambition. The two should find sufficient time to sit and talk over what they plan to do and then to reflect on what has in fact happened. These counselling periods are of the utmost importance.

Personal development

Not everyone seeks promotion, nor has everyone the aptitude for it. Officers who consciously decide not to climb the career ladder should not be labelled under-achievers; this is certainly not the case. However those who do not wish for promotion need to have their skills, abilities and talents developed just as does the embryonic section officer. This is known as 'lateral promotion', whereby development is not in terms of promotion on an upwards scale but promotion on a broad horizontal scale. Everyone needs to be developed.

Setting up a section

Newly promoted section officers will almost certainly be required to set up a section, or take charge of an existing section of up to 10 special constables. The need for grades/ranks has already been discussed in the introduction and it is a fact that most forces in England and Wales have a rank structure in the Special Constabulary. Having been promoted, the question will arise: 'What happens now?'

The first line supervisor has many responsibilities which may be summarised thus:
> **the individual;**
> **the team;**
> **the organisation.**

The individual

Supervisory officers have a duty of care towards their subordinates and it is important that they know as much about each individual in the team as is comfortable for both the supervisor and the team member. With as many as 10 officers in the team it is impossible to keep information stored in the head and it therefore naturally follows that some sort of filing system be started in order to record necessary information without being intrusive.

It is strongly recommended that any file kept on officers is kept with each officer's knowledge and approval and that the file is open to view by that officer at any reasonable time. Hidden agendas create suspicion and should be avoided. A simple model which might be adopted would include:

Personal file

Name .... Rank/Number

Home address...

Tel (Home) ....(Work)

Is this officer prepared to be telephoned at his/her place of work   YES / NO

Civilian occupation ....

Years' service ....   Seeking promotion   YES / NO

Specialist qualifications ....

....

Training needs/Other information...

....

Next of Kin ....

If the officer is relatively new or is seeking promotion, and therefore will need to be reported on, a model assessment report appears at the end of this section. It may be that an assessment should be kept on all officers under command of the first line manager, that is a matter for each individual. Where an assessment is being made on officers then the assessment should be open and the officer not only made aware that there is an ongoing assessment but also be allowed sight of the assessment. The assessment is for the benefit not only of the supervisor, but also the individual as well as the organisation. **Be open.**

Supervisors should actively seek out their subordinates when they are on duty and engage them in conversation. Find out from them any difficulties they are experiencing with a view to remedy. Discover what expectations/fears/anxieties they may have and be prepared to be their friend, in the professional sense, by offering advice, help and support.

The team

Supervisors are as good as their team. It is a matter for the supervisor to instill in each individual that they are an important member of a team and that each individual has a contribution to make to the team effort. Where there is high morale in a team problems take care of themselves because each individual is highly motivated and is therefore reluctant to let the team down, a sense of collective responsibility exists. Thought should be given to such matters as:

Regular meetings of the team

The meetings should ideally be at a specific venue at a regular time with an agenda, be it formal or informal. The supervisor should encourage discussion, ensuring everyone gets their say. Above all be open.

Irregular meetings of the team

A social get-together whereby both specials and their partners can mix in an informal atmosphere and exchange banter and learn something about each other, thus creating stronger bonding of the team, in a sense making a 'family' of the team.

Special projects

Thought should be given to what special projects the team is capable of taking on as a collective. Something which they 'own' and 'drive' themselves. Setting up, say, a Neighbourhood Watch scheme, keeping plain clothes observation in areas where there are problems, in fact anything which makes a contribution to the force but at the same time keeps the team together with a common purpose.

The organisation

The organisation is in many ways like a large wheel, containing a great many cogs; the team leader is in charge of one cog and it is a matter for him to ensure that it is well oiled and works with the minimum of supervision.

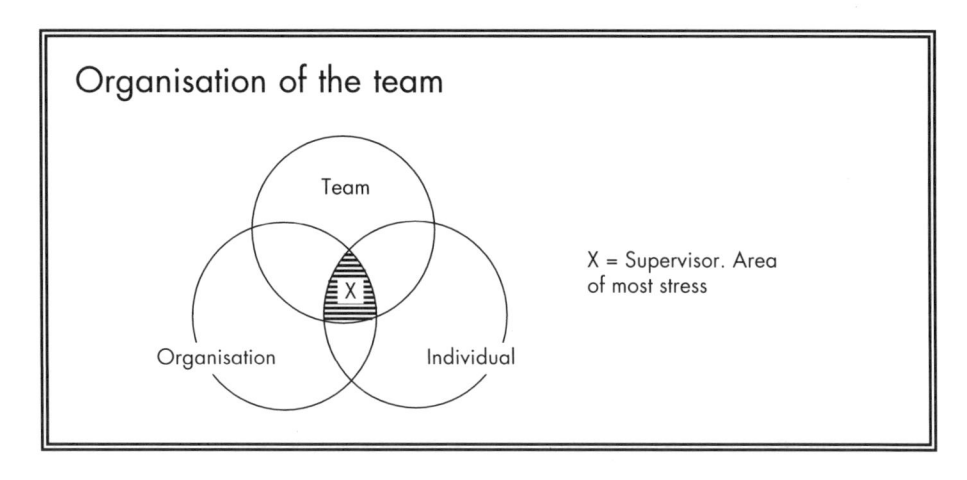

Organisation of the team

X = Supervisor. Area of most stress

Organisational needs create pressure on the team, team needs create pressure on the individual and the pressures from all sources focus on the team leader who has to keep everyone happy. The team leader has to be able to enjoy helicopter vision, to see the global picture of needs and attend to all with the minimum of fuss.

First line supervisors are the eyes and ears of the police force, its executive arm, its cutting edge. There is no room here for namby pamby apologism. The supervisor has not only to be decisive and make sometimes unpopular decisions, he has at the same time to be encouraging, supportive and, above all, understanding of everyone's needs. Without doubt the first line supervisor's job is perhaps the hardest job to undertake in the Special Constabulary but the rewards in terms of job satisfaction are enormous.

Conflict

It sometimes happens when there is a promotion that someone, somewhere who is passed over is miffed for reasons that do not stand serious scrutiny. It is important that these people are befriended and their help sought, and that they are encouraged to make a contribution rather than be left to stew on what they believe to be an injustice. Where they are not befriended they may become alienated and distance themselves from the team goals. This is counter-productive and self-defeating.

Behaviour breeds behaviour; such people should be sought out and actively encouraged to be team players, use their talents and skills and give them areas of personal responsibility whereby they can demonstrate their qualities and professionalism and thus be as worthwhile to the team as the supervisor himself. These people need to be shown that they are as equal as the others and are valued.

Supervision of files

Supervisors can reasonably expect to be approached by members of their sections for advice on such matters as how to put a prosecution file together. There is little credibility in the reply, 'you had better see a regular officer!' In order to promote professionalism in the group the supervisor will do well to be aware of the contents of the *Manual of Guidance* for the preparation and submission of files which is held in every police station. His section would be very well served if he were to copy all the forms that are required and have them readily available for use by his section and also to be mindful of the time limits imposed on each type of file.

The ability to instill this knowledge in the members of his section is perhaps the most singular contribution the supervisor can make in advancing the professionalism of his section members. (See assessment report.)

Assessment report

	A	B	C	D	E	F	
Always immaculately turned out							Always dirty or untidy
Interested in all aspects of work							Lacks/loses interest in his work
Extremely fluent and effective							Limited vocabulary and inarticulate
All facts correct and well set out							Unable to obtain facts and express them
Attends training regularly							Fails to attend training
Gets through a vast amount of duties							Does as little as possible to get by
Can handle people efficiently							Has difficulty in handling people
Held in high regard by all							Rubs colleagues up the wrong way
Full of confidence with justification							Very self-conscious
Comprehensive knowledge of law							Inadequate knowledge of law

A = Excellent; **B** = Very good; **C** = Good; **D** = Adequate; **E** = Poor; **F** = Unsatisfactory

Availability and duties worked

Regular officers responsible for duty sheets and the deployment of members of the Special Constabulary cannot be expected to speak to 10 individual officers concerning their availability to come on duty and it will necessarily therefore fall to the first line supervisor to be in a position to inform regular officers of the availability of the specials under his control. To that end it is useful to circulate members of the section with a pre-planned pro forma inviting them to state when they will be available for duty. This of course will not meet the needs of short term emergencies, but will go a long way in helping to provide a record of medium term availability. Such pro formae contain information such as that shown in the diagram overleaf.

> **Availability for duty**
>
> To ....
>
> Please note below duties you are prepared to work during the course of ..*month*....
>
> | Date | Tour of duty | Number of hours |
> |------|--------------|-----------------|
> | ...... | ...... | ...... |
> | ...... | ...... | ...... |
> | ...... | ...... | ...... |
> | ...... | ...... | ...... |
>
> and return to me together with the number of hours you worked during ..*previous month*
>
> Date ....   Signed ....

This form will act as a hard copy note of willingness to work on specific dates at specific times and also record hours worked each month which can be checked at a glance. It makes the individual officer personally responsible for what he says he will do and what he says he has done.

Recruiting

Special constable supervisors and managers will, from time to time, be required to sit on recruiting panels and judge the merits of applicants for entry into the Special Constabulary. Where this is the case the officers on the panel will have to have a clear formula to help them establish what they are looking for in the applicant. During the course of a recruiting interview they will have to address such issues as:
- (a) persons disqualified from being a special constable;
- (b) minimum requirements for selection;
- (c) equal opportunities;
- (d) skills to be tested;
- (e) aptitude for the job.

Disqualified categories

Certain persons, by reason of their profession or calling, are disqualified from entry into the Special Constabulary and therefore this question should be the first to be addressed. The Home Office Working Group of 1996 made particular recommendations regarding this subject (See Chapter 20 'Changes to terms and conditions of service'). These recommendations as supported by the Standing Committed on the Special Constabulary will soon be made the subject of Home Office regulation or guidance.

Disqualified categories include:*

1. private detectives, private inquiry agents, bailiffs, security officers, and members of private police forces or security organisations/companies;
2. the holder of a justices' licence under the Licensing Act, or the manager of licensed premises, also husbands/wives of licence holders/managers, unless approved by the chief constable;
3. a justice of the peace;
4. clerks to the justices and clerks of the court;
5. a member of a police authority;
6. a serving member of Her Majesty's armed forces;
7. volunteer members officers and other ranks of the Territorial and Army Volunteer Reserve **(see note Chapter 20 re former TA members)**;
8. the Royal Observer Corps;
9. the Merchant Navy;
10. the fire service;
11. the medical, nursing and midwifery professions **(see proviso within Working Group recommendations Chapter 20)**;
12. the ambulance service;
13. traffic wardens;
14. school crossing patrols;
15. persons engaged for gain in promoting

* **In addition to the above, the Working Group recommended that, as for regulars, those taking an active part in politics (with an expectation that this may include standing for or serving as a Member of Parliament) should not be eligible for the Special Constabulary. The Standing Committee also considered that civilian front office staff in police stations who deal with suspects should be ineligible.**

Armed services reserves - Certain members of the armed services reserves may be enrolled subject to clearance by the service authorities as 'available for peacetime service only'. These include those members who are designated as reserves, volunteer reserves, special reserves, pensioners and those on the retired list. Clearance must be obtained from the Manning and Records Branch of the appropriate service in each case.

Requirements for selection

(Also see 'Model Selection Procedure Form' in relation to transfers (Chapt 20)

While there are nationwide variations concerning the qualifications required to join the Special Constabulary, the basic requirements are:

Age - The minimum age is 18 years. **However, note that the Working Group recommendation is 18 and a half to bring specials into line with regular officers and will be made statute in 1999/2000.**

Eyesight - Distance vision:
both eyes together $v = 6/6$;
one eye $v = 6/6$; other eye $v = 6/12$.

Most forces accept applicants who wear spectacles or contact lenses, provided the acuity of unaided vision is not less than $v = 6/18$ in one eye and $v = 6/24$ in the other and is correctable with vision aids to the standard above.

Applicants must also be able to distinguish principal colours by means of the Ishihara test.

Health - A candidate must be in good mental, bodily and dental health, and be of good physical fitness with a satisfactory correlation of height and weight measurements.

Nationality - Applicants must be British subjects, citizens of the Irish Republic or Commonwealth citizens whose stay in this country is not subject to any restriction.

Education - Candidates will be subject to an entry by examination. Certain persons may be exempt from this requirement.

Equal opportunity - Forces are committed to being an equal opportunities employer and are determined to ensure that no job applicant:
(a) receives less favourable treatment on the grounds of gender, marital status, colour, race, nationality, ethnic or national origins; or,
(b) is disadvantaged by conditions or requirements which cannot be shown to be justified.

They also seek to ensure that applicants are not victimised or sexually harassed in accordance with the Codes of Practice issued by the Commission for Racial Equality and the Equal Opportunities Commission. The following issues should not affect the applicant:
(a) gender;
(b) marital status;
(c) colour.

Skills to be tested - The recruiting panel will address the areas of skills, abilities and aptitudes they believe necessary for appointment. Many forces have a prepared marking guide. In the absence of such, recruiting officers may wish to look at the model for selection (see opposite).

Conditions of service - While there are force differences, the panel should ensure that the applicant is able to fulfil the conditions of service as laid down by the chief constable. A typical list of such conditions can be found opposite.

Model for selection

NAME OF APPLICANT..
NAME OF ASSESSOR ....

	A	B	C	D	E
Appearance					
Fluency of speech					
Motivation					
Initiative					
Practical ability					
Judgement					
Confidence					
Knowledge of force					
Discretion					

Remarks: including aptitude for the job

Grades: **A** = Immediately acceptable; **B** = Acceptable; **C** = Adequate but acceptable; **D** = Not YET acceptable; **E** = Unacceptable.

Conditions of service

Also see chapter 20 - Changes to Terms and Conditions of Service.

While there are force differences, the usual conditions of service which apply to special constables are:

(1) The chief constable may enroll such persons as he thinks fit with a view to their appointment as special constables. All applicants will be required to take an entrance exam.

(2) Only persons who are British or Commonwealth Citizens (whose stay in the UK is not subject to restrictions), aged over eighteen and a half years and under 50 years, of good character, healthy and physically fit are eligible for appointment, and every person must declare before appointment, whether or not he or she has previously served in a regular police force or in any special constabulary.

(3) As a special constable you will be required to agree to serve for a minimum period - see the local training officer for particular requirements for your force.

(4) You must notify any change of address.

(5) You will be required to attend at the police station to which you are attached whenever you are summoned on any occasion of public emergency, but the chief constable when requiring your services will make arrangements so as to cause the least possible interference with your ordinary occupation.

(6) When on duty you will take your instructions from the officers of the regular police force, who act under the direction of the chief constable.

(7) All clothing, accoutrements and documents supplied to you remain the property of the police authority. You are responsible for keeping them in good order and for giving them up when so required by the chief constable.

(8) Unless otherwise directed, when you are called for duty you must wear the clothing and accoutrements supplied to you, and you must have your warrant card in your possession.

(9) You may resign (subject to paragraph 3 above) on giving one month's notice in writing to the chief constable, but a shorter period of notice may be accepted at the chief constable's discretion;

(10) The chief constable may require a special constable to retire on such date as he may specify because of age, disability, or instead of dismissal.

Disciplinary procedure

Past and present

In the recent past special constables have been at a disadvantage in relation to their regular counterparts where matters of discipline are concerned. No rules governing procedures in matters of discipline have been in place for the Special Constabulary to protect its members from arbitrary behaviour and the excesses of local persons in authority.

This absence has contributed to excessively high turnover rates, making it increasingly important that specials are protected in the same way as regular officers. Natural law demands that an alleged offender should know the nature of the charge against him, that he should be heard and, should he be convicted, have the right to appeal to a higher authority. Special constables should not be 'required' or 'invited' to resign at the whim of local police chiefs.

Clearly a national package having the force of law embodied in statute is required for specials to enact the checks and balances which save regular officers from abuse of authority.

The 1996 Home Office Working Group on the Special Constabulary made several recommendations regarding disciplinary procedure for specials (see the Working Group Recommendations in Chapt 20 'Changes to terms and conditions of service').

The substance of the recommendations concerning discipline was that:

> **'It is a view that since special constables carry the same powers as regular officers and frequently undertake the same duties, involving direct contact and potential conflict with the public, similar levels of accountability with regard to complaints and discipline should apply. It is recommended that special constables, like regular officers should be bound by Regulation to carry out all lawful orders and at all times punctually and promptly perform all appointed duties and attend to all matters within the scope of their office as constable.'**

At the time the Working Group made these recommendations, the legislation governing regular officers was under review. The Working Group therefore based its recommendation upon what was believed would be the outcome of that review. This included a recommendation that a Code of Conduct be adopted for specials based on that to be devised for regulars.

This review of the regulars' disciplinary procedure was completed in 1998, becoming statute on April 1, 1999, in the form of the Police (Conduct)

Regulations 1999. At the time of going to press (July 1999) a consultation document will be drawn up by the Home Office before the end of the year.

This document will consider both the Working Group recommendations and the Police (Conduct) Regulations 1999 with a view to bringing complaints and disciplinary procedures into Regulation for the Specials Constabulary in 2000.

The Police Conduct Regulations 1999

By virtue of section 50 of the Police Act 1996, the Police (Conduct) Regulations 1999 make provisions for the conduct of members of police forces and the maintenance of discipline. They establish procedures for cases in which a member of a police force may be dealt with by dismissal, requirement to resign, reduction in rank, reprimand or caution. (By virtue of regulation 3, the Regulations do not apply to chief constables or other officers holding a rank above that of superintendent.)

The Regulations revoke (with savings) the Police (Discipline) Regulations 1985 and provide new procedures for dealing with conduct which fails to meet the standard set out in the new Code of Conduct. It is expected that the pending new Regulations for the Special Constabulary will enforce a similar Code of Conduct for specials.

Code of conduct

Schedule 1 to Regulation 4(1) Police (Conduct) Regs 199

Honesty and integrity
1. It is of paramount importance that the public has faith in the honesty and integrity of police officers. Officers should therefore be open and truthful in their dealings; avoid being improperly beholden to any person or institution; and discharge their duties with integrity.

Fairness and impartiality
2. Police officers have a particular responsibility to act with fairness and impartiality in all their dealings with the public and their colleagues.

Politeness and tolerance
3. Officers should treat members of the public and colleagues with courtesy and respect, avoiding abusive or deriding attitudes or behaviour. In particular, officers must avoid favouritism of an individual or group, avoid all forms of harassment, victimisation or unreasonable discrimination, and avoid overbearing conduct to a colleague, particularly to one junior in rank or service.

Code of conduct (cont...)

Use of force and abuse of authority
4. Officers must never knowingly use more force than is reasonable, nor should they abuse their authority.

Performance of duties
5. Officers should be conscientious and diligent in the performance of their duties. Officers should attend work promptly when rostered for duty. If absent through sickness or injury, they should avoid activities likely to retard their return to duty.

Lawful orders
6. The police service is a disciplined body. Unless there is good and sufficient cause to do otherwise, officers must obey all lawful orders and abide by the provision of Police Regulations. Officers should support their colleagues in the execution of their lawful duties, and oppose any improper behaviour, reporting it where appropriate.

Confidentiality
7. Information which comes into the possession of the police should be treated as confidential. It should not be used for personal benefit, nor should it be divulged to other parties except in the proper course of police duty. Similarly, officers should respect as confidential information about force policy and operations, unless authorised to disclose it in the course of their duties.

Criminal offences
8. Officers must report any proceedings for a criminal offence taken again them. Conviction of a criminal offence may in itself result in further action being taken.

Property
9. Officers must exercise reasonable care to prevent loss or damage to property (excluding their own personal property but including police property).

Sobriety
10. While on duty officers must be sober. Officers should not consume alcohol when on duty unless specifically authorised to do so, or it becomes necessary for the proper discharge of police duty.

Appearance
11. Unless on duties which dictate otherwise, officers should always be well turned out, clean and tidy while on duty in uniform or in plain clothes.

General conduct
12. Whether on or off duty, police officers should not behave in a way which is likely to bring discredit upon the police service.

Addition to specials' Code of Conduct - The Working Party recommended that the proposed Code of Conduct for Specials should include a clear statement that a regular officer has authority over a member of the Special Constabulary whatever the rank or grade of either party.

> ### Notes to the Code of Conduct
>
> a. The primary duties of those who hold the office of constable are the protection of life and property, the preservation of the Queen's peace, and the prevention and detection of criminal offences. To fulfil these duties they are granted extraordinary powers. The public and the police service therefore have the right to expect the highest standards of conduct from them.
>
> b. This Code sets out the principles which guide police officers' conduct. It does not seek to restrict officers' discretion: rather it aims to define the parameters of conduct within which that discretion should be exercised. However, it is important to note that any breach of the principles in this Code may result in action being taken by the organisation, which, in serious cases, could involve dismissal.
>
> c. This Code applies to the conduct of police officers in all ranks while on duty, or while off duty if the conduct is serious enough to indicate that an officer is not fit to be a police officer. It will be applied in a reasonable and objective manner. Due regard will be paid to the degree of negligence or deliberate fault and to the nature and circumstances of an officer's conduct. Where off duty conduct is in question, this will be measured against the generally accepted standards of the day.

Working Group recommendations for specials' regulations

Although the emphasis is that legislation for Specials should be based on that for regulars, the Working Group nevertheless made specific recommendations for the proposed Regulations for Specials which are outlined in Chapter 20.

> ### Procedure for specials prior to Regulation
>
> Prior to the enactment of the specials' conduct regulations, the Home Office recommends that forces seek to base their disciplinary procedures for Specials on the Working Group Recommendations as cited above, subject to any obvious differences in the Police (Conduct) Regulations 1999.

Legal representation

In November 1998, The Standing Committee on the Special Constabulary agreed that free legal advice and representation will be made available to all specials. This will mean that should any special find himself in difficulties he will have instant access to a solicitor or barrister and to representation either in a court of law or at a disciplinary hearing. However, as the Home Office, who will pay for this provision, has to tender the contract to insurance companies, it is likely to be April 2000 before this cover is made available.

Complaints and discipline - the law

Relevant legislation for Specials currently in force

Section 51 of the Police Act 1996 states:
(1) The Secretary of State may make regulations as to the government administration and conditions of service of special constables.
(2) Without prejudice to the generality of subsection (1) above, regulations under this section may make provision with respect to:
  (a) the qualifications for appointment of special constables;
  (b) the retirement of special constables;
  (c) the suspension of special constables from their office as constable;
  (d) the allowances payable to special constables.

Dismissal

The law touching on the question of dismissal of special constables is found in section 27 of the Police Act 1996:
(1) The chief officer of police of the police force maintained for any police area may, in accordance with regulations under section 51, appoint special constables for that area.
(2) Subject to such regulations under section 51, all special constables appointed for a police area shall be under the direction and control of, and subject to dismissal by, the chief officer of police.

Arbitrary dismissal

Section 51 of the Police Act 1996 clearly places the power of dismissal of special constables in the hands of chief officers of police. This means the chief constable himself.

However caution must be exercised here in that chief constables devolve powers of all description to local commanders and it might very well be that the local commander whom you serve under is so empowered.

When a local commander requires a special constable to resign and he is not empowered to do so, then without doubt he would be guilty of abuse of authority which is in itself a breach of the Code of Conduct.

All officers, be they regular or specials, must be protected from such excesses and must not allow themselves to be hoodwinked or cajoled into premature resignation.

'Invitation' to resign

Officers who are 'invited' to resign may well feel that they have a sufficiency of knowledge and wit to defend themselves. However, to do this often gives them 'a fool as a client'. If an officer is 'invited' to resign he must do nothing - **take advice**.

In the first instance the question has to be asked, 'Does the officer making the "invitation" have the power to make it?' or, 'is he acting *ultra vires* (beyond his powers)?'. In order to check his credentials and diffuse what must be a difficult situation, the special constable in this position should ask for time to reflect upon the matter. This is the time to take advice from others as to the *bona fides* of the offer.

Taking advice

Each police district has a regular officer who is a Police Federation representative, and who is well versed in the disciplinary procedures for regulars.

This officer is the best person to speak to concerning disciplinary matters. He will be aware of the powers of the local police chief and will be able to advise on powers concerning discipline and dismissal. It is important to be in a position to inform the representative of the full facts of the case and in order to facilitate this then ideally the allegation made against the special constable should be in writing.

Discipline friend

The Home Office Working Group of 1996 recommended that members of the Special Constabulary have a right to seek advice of a 'friend' in disciplinary matters. This can be anyone who has the welfare of the officer in mind.

It is a good idea to seek out a 'friend' who is able to act as a mentor and who has the necessary knowledge to help guide the special during what can be a trying time. The special constable should not hesitate to ask the 'friend' to be present during any interviews concerning the matter under investigation. There is no reason why a regular officer cannot act as a 'friend'.

Regulars and specials as co-defendants

When regular and special constables form part of the same complaint or allegation, there has been a tendency in many forces to treat the special constable as a witness in the first place, rather than a defendant. This is because, as the special has not been covered by the conduct regulations, the burden of proof is greater for the regular than it is for the special constable. It is always wise in these circumstances to seek advice at the earliest opportunity. The special constable who is involved in a complaint or allegation may, if he is told that he is to be treated as a witness rather than a defendant, drop his guard and feel that he has nothing to fear.

In reality, if he has made a witness statement, that very statement may be used to justify his suspension from duty or even his dismissal. Great caution must be exercised during such proceedings and advice sought at all times.

However, given the current Home Officer recommendations and pending legislation, this situation is likely to be increasingly infrequent.

Interviews

Special constables who are interviewed by complaints departments are, by their very nature, anxious to clear the matter up and answer all questions put by the interviewers.

Interviews on tape or a contemporaneous note taken at interviews are, frankly, best avoided. The spontaneity of the situation is such, that unless the special constable is very knowledgeable about both the law and disciplinary regulations, then he might well disadvantage himself by making unguarded disclosures.

The best advice when called to an interview concerning discipline is to ask for a list of questions to be asked, or a written report of the allegation and also for time to reply. Take advice and then make a written reply. While this might sound defensive, it is a course of action which limits the opportunity of ambush. The first rule of holes states 'if you are in one, stop digging'.

Suspension or retirement

This is provided for by Regulations 2 and 3 of the Special Constables Regulations 1965 which state:

Suspension
`Reg 2`
(1) When a report, allegation or complaint is received from which it appears that a special constable may have been remiss or negligent in the discharge of his duty or otherwise unfit for the same, the chief constable may suspend him from his office as constable until such time as either:

(a) it is decided that no action need be taken in his case in consequence of the report of allegation; or
(b) any such action has been taken.
(2) A chief constable may delegate his powers under this Regulation to the deputy chief constable or to a member of the police force acting in the place of the deputy chief constable.

Retirement | Reg 3 |

(1) A special constable may retire subject to his having given to the chief constable a month's written notice of his intention to retire or such shorter notice as may have been accepted by the chief constable. Provided that a special constable may not, without the consent of the chief constable, give notice for the purpose of this regulation, or retire in pursuance of a notice previously given, while suspended under these regulations.
(2) The chief constable may require a special constable to retire on such date as he may specify -
(a) on account of age (see Chapt 20 'Changes to terms and conditions of service');
(b) on the grounds that he is disabled to perform the ordinary duties of a special constable and the disablement is likely to be permanent;
(c) or as an alternative to dismissal, where he has been remiss or negligent in the discharge of his duty or otherwise unfit for the same.

Operation orders

Some forces are becoming more imaginative in their use of supervisory grades of the Special Constabulary and are encouraging them to produce their own operation orders for events controlled by specials. These are usually weekend events, where it is expected that large numbers of members of the public will be gathering together for a common purpose.

Most forces use the IIMAC form of operation order, which is described here. It is well within the capability of any sound section officer to produce his own operation order and there is no reason why a supervisor should not seek permission to do so.

I - information;
I - intention;
M - method;
A - administration;
C - communication.

Where there is an incident which is either spontaneous, or the occurrence of which was unforeseen, clearly it is impossible in those circumstances to produce any meaningful written order. However, where the incident is

A routine Operation Order cover

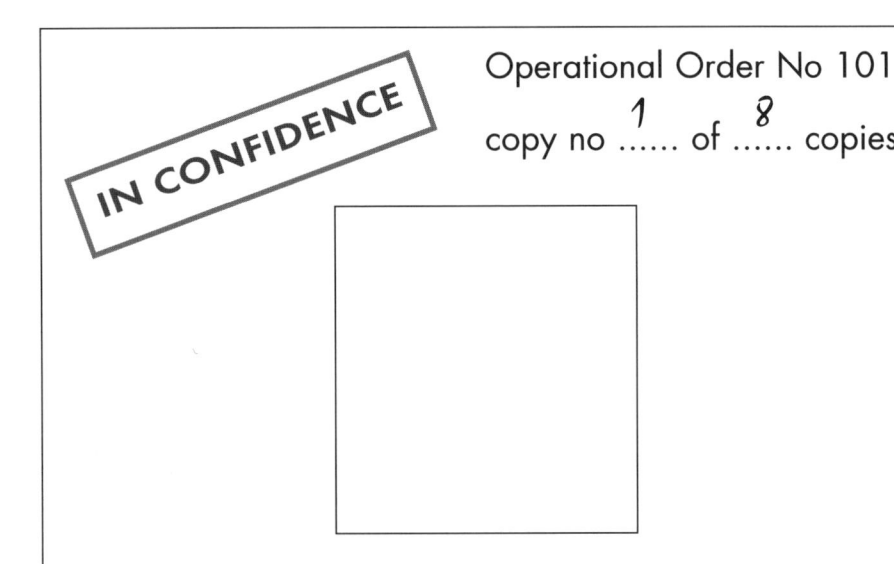

IN CONFIDENCE

Operational Order No 101
copy no ...1... of ...8... copies

BLANKSHIRE CONSTABULARY

OPERATION **'FORFEIT'**

IN CONFIDENCE

copy no	
1	INCIDENT COMMANDER
2	GROUND COMMANDER
3	APS JONES
4	TASK FORCE 1
5	TASK FORCE 2
6	TASK FORCE 3
7	CHIEF SUPERINTENDENT
8	CONTROL ROOM

pre-planned, and there is sufficient warning of its occurrence, then thought should be given to preparing an operation order formalising the position of the police. This will include all information known about the occurrence, the stated police intention, how the police intend to implement their stated intention, command, control, administration, communications etc.

The Operation Order should be sufficiently flexible to deal not only with what is known of the event, but likely and anticipated difficulties which might be experienced. The Operation Order is the plan for the expected as well as the unexpected, and, of course, the routine. Provision must be included for the human element in the widest sense as well as for the task undertaken.

Before embarking on the production of an Operation Order, it would be wise to look at the type of Operation Order that is in use within your force, because not all forces are the same. However, whatever type of Order your force issues it will contain the same information, the difference is in layout. Remember that all Orders of this nature should be in confidence as they lay out the specific police intention touching on an event in the future. It is prudent therefore to ensure that copies go to specific individuals on a 'need to know' basis, and that spares should be jealously guarded. Each copy should be given a number (eg copy number 7 of 17 copies), with each copy addressed to a specific addressee, in order to maintain the confidentiality of the document.

IIMAC

Information

The information part of IIMAC deals with all information that is known or can be gathered about the event before it happens. It deals with such matters as locations, dates, times, places.

In essence it would read: 'It is known that a steam rally event is scheduled to take place at [location], on [date], starting at [time], and ending at approximately [time]. In keeping with other years, it is expected that some 3,000 people will attend this rally where there will be displays of some 50 steam engines. This rally has in the past been of low profile from a policing/public order point of view and is expected to pass without incident.'

Intention

Record here what is in the mind of the police and make it global in its observations.

This section therefore might read:

'This rally will be policed substantially by the Special Constabulary, with the assistance of three regular officers.

The intention is to:
(a) provide controlled traffic points at the entrance and exits to the event;
(b) keep a uniformed but low police presence at the event during the course of the day;
(c) deal early and positively with any incidents of public order;
(d) pay regular visits to the beer tent and discourage drunkenness;
(e) establish a Command and Control point near the entrance to the arena by use of the police caravan;
(f) keep in close contact with the event organisers in order to anticipate any problems which might occur.'

Method

This part of the order deals with the nuts and bolts as to how the order will be put into effect.

It will touch on such matters as:
(a) briefing, location and times;
(b) transport arrangements;
(c) refreshments;
(d) tours of duty;
(e) specific duties for each officer;
(f) lost/found property;
(g) lost children arrangements;
(h) use of megaphone for announcements;
(i) location of police HQ (tent/caravan);
(j) operational commander - SDO;
(k) ground commander - section officer;
(l) Uniform and equipment.
(m) arrangements for arrested persons;
(n) transportation of arrested persons;
(o) use of police vehicles.

This list is by no means exhaustive. It should touch on all those matters relating to how you will carry out your intention.

Administration

The administrative side of the order deals with all matters touching on administration. This will include lists of personnel, individual times for refreshments and tea breaks, maps of the areas to be policed, names of the organisers. emergency telephone numbers, locations of specific items of equipment, emergency call out schemes, etc.

Communications

Under this head will be specific instructions as to call signs, base station, land-line numbers for control rooms, call signs for dedicated consoles and personal radio issues together with channel numbers.

Further information

Each Operation Order will be different, its nature and size being dictated by the nature of the event to be policed. In order to ensure that the operation order can be improved if the event is an annual one or is likely to be repeated, it is important to have a de-briefing of all participants, to go over the order and the day's events with a view to upgrading information and amending the order accordingly. Sketch plans are especially useful, in particular for those officers who are not familiar with the location or the terrain, giving details of such things as the police post, toilets, entry points and exits, car-parking, beer tent etc. These need not be to scale and need only represent a generalised impression of the area. Sketch plans can be added as an appendix to the order.

Operation Order numbers and names may be obtained from your district administration officer or from the operation order department, if there is one. Each page in your Operation Order should be numbered consecutively in order to alert officers should one go adrift.

Orders should be flexible so as to take account of the unexpected and therefore should not be drafted or couched in language that leaves no room for the initiative of individual officers.

Experience of Operation Orders has taught me that the weather can cause more problems than people. You should have the most up-to-date information on the weather that is available because it can cause only 10% of the expected number of people to turn up if there are storms and, equally, increase the numbers dramatically if the weather is especially favourable. Pay particular attention to the effects of wet weather if the event is to be held in a field. How might this affect car parking, are there facilities for recovering disabled vehicles which are bogged-down and what about the exits and the effect mud might have on the highway? You will probably not think of everything, but this will help you think of most things.

Specialist units

The special constable who is seeking to advance his career in terms of skills, abilities and knowledge in order to become more professional, can do no better than have himself attached to specialist units. Once the officer is satisfied that he is able to deal effectively with routine street incidents it is right that his abilities should be developed by giving him an insight into in depth policing at specialist level.

Special constable supervisors and managers have a particularly important role to play in this respect as the officer on the ground probably does not command sufficient clout to arrange for attachments himself.

While each force is different, and many have their own systems in operation, a section officer should be in a position to identify those officers in his section who are ready for development and should report to senior management with a view to specialist attachments being arranged. Again, it is a matter for section officers to inquire into local policies and procedures within their force to discover what is available to further develop their officers. Where no procedures exist then it is a matter for section officers to lobby senior management in order to implement suitable procedures.

Criminal Investigation Department (CID)

(a) Undertake and assist in the investigation of crime.

(b) Become aware of the use of informants, surveillance techniques and other covert intelligence-gathering means.

(c) Interview witnesses to crime, record statements and gather and prepare evidence for the prosecution which is admissible in court.

(d) Interview suspects in accordance with the provisions of the Police and Criminal Evidence Act 1984.

(e) Develop an interview technique which is ethical and, in particular, become skilled in dealing with suspects who are hostile, resistant or who remain silent during interview.

(f) Become aware of current patterns and trends of crime and develop an awareness of the motivation of the professional criminal fraternity.

(g) Become familiar with the latest criminal legislation including case law, policies and procedures and of sources of information.

Drug Squad

(a) Undertake and assist in the investigation of controlled drug offences and look at measures for the prevention of controlled drug offences and the detection of offenders.
(b) Become familiar with the specialist and dedicated team of officers whose aim is to investigate and prevent drug abuse, with a special emphasis on identifying and detecting suppliers and distributors of controlled drugs to unauthorised persons.
(c) Gather information and intelligence relating to drug matters and associated crimes and look at any information and intelligence gained with a view to analysis and dissemination to other officers.
(d) Cultivate and develop informants.
(e) Advise colleagues and members of the public on all matters concerning drug abuse and maintain a close liaison with chemists and other agencies concerned with drugs.
(f) Become familiar with the procedures involved in the gathering of information sufficient to swear out a drug warrant at court and be aware of the legislation concerning its use and time limitations.
(g) Develop skills in relation to searching persons, vehicles and addresses where drugs are likely to be found and where drugs are most likely to be hidden.
(h) Be aware what help is available to drug users and be in a position to offer professional help when the opportunity presents itself.

Scenes of Crime

(a) Become aware of the scope and resources of the scenes of crime department.
(b) Increase knowledge as to where scientific evidence is likely to be found and the expected nature of that evidence.
(c) Become familiar with the procedure concerned with the gathering of fingerprint evidence, types of fingerprint, the anatomy of a fingerprint and points to prove for court purposes.
(d) Become familiar with the nature of photography in dealing with crime, suicides, serious and fatal road traffic accidents.
(e) Be aware of the types of powder and other substances which are employed in marking property and in the setting of 'traps' where crime is suspected but particularly difficult to prove.
(f) Become familiar with the method of operation of criminals and in particular identify modus operandi common to certain types of crime;
(g) Become familiar with the requirements of the Police and Criminal Evidence Act 1984, in relation to taking intimate samples and non-intimate samples from suspects in police detention.
(h) Become familiar with the duties of an 'exhibits officer' concerning collection, labelling, production and exhibiting evidential property;
(j) Become familiar with covert surveillance equipment, in particular the use of voice-activated tape recorders, cameras and night sights.

Stolen Vehicle Squad

(a) Undertake and assist in the investigation of thefts of motor vehicles;
(b) Become aware of criminals who specialise in motor thefts or who undertake to 'ring' (steal and change identity) motor vehicles for others.
(c) Become familiar with the use of the police national computer in relation to vehicles which have been stolen. Gain knowledge of the nature of number plates and the use and abuse of chassis numbers.
(d) Become aware of the procedure in relation to examining vehicles which have been scrapped and then re-registered.
(e) Become familiar with the favoured types of vehicle that are stolen, the favoured locations from which they are stolen and favoured areas of disposal.
(f) Become familiar with the tools and equipment used by criminals when stealing vehicles, how these tools work and which types of vehicles are most vulnerable to the tools used.

In addition to the above squads forming part of the Criminal Investigation Department, there are other dedicated specialist squads too numerous to mention here in any detail but which include:

Fraud Squad
Financial Investigation Unit
Cheque Squad
Crime and Robbery Squad
Special Branch

and many others relating to the local needs of each force.

Proposed National Crime Squad

Opportunities for specials may be widening as the National Crime Squad (NCS) is considering approaching the Home Office with a view to setting up its own Special Constabulary.

This follows a successful NCS anti-drugs operation which involved Hertfordshire Special Constabulary. The National Crime Squad approached the force for the assistance of its Special Constabulary because the surveillance aspect of the inquiry required substantial manpower over a lengthy period. For over two years the specials carried out surveillance and videoed a number of targeted gang members importing and distributing drugs.

The Hertfordshire operation may well have set a precedent and the specials involved demonstrated the diligence and professionalism of the Special Constabulary. Should an NCS Special Constabulary become reality, different terms and conditions of service may have to be adopted for specials serving within it.

Road Traffic Department

(a) Assist and undertake inquiries into all aspects of crime and in particular to focus specialist attention on matters concerning the use of roads by the public and uphold legislation in relation to motor vehicles and drink drive law;
(b) Gain knowledge of the types of specialist vehicles available to traffic officers and the training officers have to undergo in relation to their use.
(c) Become familiar with the habits of the travelling criminal.
(d) Increase awareness of how to search vehicles and be able to identify a vehicle on false plates or which has been 'ringed'.
(e) Increase knowledge of traffic legislation, especially in relation to special types of vehicles, foreign vehicles and abnormal vehicles.
(f) Become aware of the actions at the scene of a road traffic accident, types of accidents (eg serious/fatal) and the demands which each make.
(g) Become aware of the specialist equipment carried by traffic vehicles in relation to testing and inspection of vehicles - speeding offenders, video recording and equipment used to effect release of persons from disabled motor vehicles.
(h) Become aware of the transportation of hazardous chemicals on roads and the HAZCHEM scheme and emergency procedures.
(j) Increase awareness of the use of armed response vehicles (ARVs), and their rules of deployment, arming, use, containment and arrest procedure.
(k) Become aware of procedures adopted when following stolen vehicles, or vehicles whose occupants are engaged in crime, the motorway 'rolling stop', check points, road checks and commentary over the air when following.

Again, there is much more to learn from the road traffic department than is outlined here and space forbids further comment, however the resources in terms of highly trained officers and specialist equipment are such that any attachment to this unit will improve an officer's knowledge to a point where he will be a much more useful person when patrolling the streets with the knowledge of what he is able to summon from the traffic department to help him in his duties.

Support Group (or Task Force)

(a) Increase awareness of the reasons for public disorder and how the police measure the response.
(b) Become aware of the methods used for gathering intelligence of suspected public disorder and where to look for indicators of covert potential disorder, eg 'rave parties' etc.
(c) Become aware of the concept of the police support unit (PSU), its make-up, equipment, training and terms of reference, as well as interforce call out procedures.
(d) Become aware of the police tactics in relation to planned events where public order may become a problem, eg sporting events, in particular football matches.
(e) Increase awareness of anti-terrorist tactics and crime scene search training where attention to detail is paramount.

(f) Familiarise self with underwater search training techniques, officers' specialist training, fitness requirements and equipment available for use. How best to search an area, safety techniques and call out procedures.
(g) Become aware of firearms and bomb response training, equipment used, tactics, containment, target identification systems, rules of engagement and arrest procedures, the procedures adopted in searching premises and the criteria used concerning evacuation of buildings.

Lower profile units

In addition to seeking attachments to specialist units where permissions have to be sought from the appropriate authority, there are many specialist units both inside and outside the police station where attachments can be agreed locally without fuss. These units are not high profile and at first might seem unattractive in terms of career development.

Enquiry office

The enquiry office is actively avoided by many police officers due to the nature of the complexity of the job because of the number of different enquiries that are likely to be made and the expert knowledge needed to handle the enquirers.

However, a week in the enquiry office will provide the officer with a good working knowledge of firearm and shotgun law; an ability to check driving documents with speed and expertise; familiarity with lost and found property procedures, and he will generally feel at ease in dealing with the public and offering help. The enquiry office is a specialist department in itself and any officer would receive a good grounding from this attachment.

Traffic wardens

Arrangements may be made locally with the senior traffic warden with a view to attachment in order that the attached officer may learn about parking offences, wheel clamping, tow-away procedures and the powers exercised by traffic wardens. An insight will be gained into such matters as excise licences and the procedure for reporting offenders who are with their car and the procedure when the vehicle is unoccupied. The Fixed Penalty system would be explained in detail as would the art of actually issuing a ticket in a way that causes the issuing officer the least discomfort. The matter of placing cones, their lawful use, time limitations on use, colour, size and other matters would be learned in a hands-on environment.

Traffic wardens are an invaluable source of information by virtue of the fact that they spend the whole of their duty time on the streets.

CHAPTER 16

EVIDENCE

Chapter contents

Statements of evidence 258
    Statement taking.. 258
    Witness statement... 259
    Hearsay evidence 261

Statements of evidence

Section 9 of the Criminal Justice Act 1967 allows your statement of evidence (you being a witness to an event) to be tendered in evidence, and it shall be admissible in evidence to the same extent as oral evidence, if:
  (a) the statement purports to be signed by the person who made it;
  (b) the statement contains a declaration by that person to the effect that it is true to the best of his knowledge and belief and that he made the statement knowing that, if it were tendered in evidence, he would be liable to prosecution if he wilfully stated in it anything which he knew to be false or did not believe to be true;

and before the hearing at which the statement is tendered in evidence, a copy of the statement is served on each of the other parties and none of the other parties or their solicitors, within seven days, serves a notice objecting to the statement being tendered. This allows your statement of evidence to be read out in court without you having to appear - in cases in which the evidence you are giving is not contested.

It is important therefore to make your statements on proper statement of evidence forms which can be found at all police stations. If the statement refers to an exhibit, the defence must be given the opportunity to inspect it. Exhibits may be included in the statement so long as they are exhibited on an exhibit label. A statement of evidence is shown opposite, outlining the facts of a simple case, showing you the standard format of your statement, how to fill it in and how to exhibit an article.

Statement taking

Statements should be true, accurate and fair, in logical order of events (chronological), relevant and complete, legible and neat. The two main purposes of a statement are:
(1) if necessary to be used as a source of evidence in any subsequent proceedings,
(2) to provide sufficient information so that a decision can be made concerning the possible prosecution or otherwise of an alleged offender.

When writing a statement

Do

(a) be accurate and truthful;
(b) include relevant information;
(c) keep to a chronological sequence;
(d) be legible and neat;
(e) include the points to prove;
(f) use plain, clear English;
(g) include sufficient detail.

Do not

(a) use inaccuracy, conjecture, fabrication;
(b) include irrelevant information;
(c) use muddled sequences;
(d) include opinion (unless you are an expert);
(e) use jargon.

Chapt 16: Evidence 259

Witness Statement

Form MG 11

Statement of .... Ray Harris ....

Age if under 21 ..... over 21 ..... (if over 21 insert 'over 21')

This statement (consisting of ...2... pages each signed by me) is true to the best of my knowledge and belief and I make it knowing that, if it is tendered in evidence, I shall be liable to prosecution if I have wilfully stated in it anything which I know to be false or do not believe to be true.

Dated the ...1st... day of ...MAY... 19 99

Signature ....

I am a Special Constable of the Avon & Somerset Constabulary, stationed at Canonsgrove, near Taunton. At 1435 hours on Wednesday 1st May 1996, I was on foot patrol, in uniform in High Street Canonsgrove, when I saw the defendant, whom I now know to be Richard Jones, walking in the direction of Taunton town centre. Mr Jones was shouting and swearing and was waving his hands about.

As I approached him he fell over. I assisted him to his feet. I could smell alcohol from his breath, his speech was slurred and his eyes were glazed... He was drunk.

I said 'How far have you to go?'

He replied 'It's got nothing to do with you copper.'

I said 'You've had enough to drink, can you get home safely.'

With that, Mr Jones pushed his hand into his right hand trouser pocket and produced an item which he struck out at me with. The item was metal, dark brown in colour and seemed to be the size of his fist. The blow missed and I tried to restrain Mr Jones. He shouted:

'Come on you bastard, let's see how tough you are.'

I said 'I'm arresting you for being drunk and disorderly.'

I then cautioned Mr Jones and placed him in handcuffs. At this point I

Signature .... Signature witnessed by ....

6 92

Form MG 11
Continuation sheet No 2

Continuation of Statement of Ray Harris

noticed that he dropped the metal object which I had earlier seen in his hand. I picked the object up and found it to be a knuckle-duster which I labelled and which contains my signature. I summoned transport and took Mr Jones to Taunton Police Station where he arrived at 1501 hours and was placed in the custody of Sergeant Williams.

At 2200 hours on Wednesday 1st May 1996, at Taunton Police Station, I charged Mr Jones with being drunk and disorderly and with being found with an offensive weapon. I cautioned him and he replied 'I'm sorry.' He was then bailed to appear before the Taunton Deane Magistrates.

Signature .... Signature witnessed by ....

FOR COURT USE ONLY	CJ ACT 1967
REGINA v ...R Jones............	MC ACT 1980 S 102
EXHIBIT no	MC RULES 1981 R 70
Signed...................................	
Justice of the Peace/Clerk to *Barchester* (Magistrates' Court)	I IDENTIFY THE EXHIBIT DESCRIBED OVERLEAF AS THAT REFERRED TO IN THE STATEMENT MADE AND SIGNED BY ME
DATE *1st July 1999*	

	SIGNATURE	DATE
FOR POLICE USE ONLY POLICE FORCE *Blankshire Constabulary* DIVISION ... *'L'* DESCRIPTION OF ITEM *1 x brown metal knuckle duster (offensive weapon)* IDENTIFYING MARK ... *RH/1* LAB REF	*R Harris*	*1/5/96*

Hearsay evidence

Hearsay is evidence of what a witness has heard another person say. It is generally inadmissible, but there are exceptions which include:
 (a) statements made by the accused;
 (b) statements made in the presence and hearing of the accused.

'If in doubt, put it in the statement.'

This is a recommendation from the Crown Prosecution Service.

CHAPTER 17

STAFF APPRAISAL

Chapter contents

Preparing reports 264
Assessment criteria 264
Ratings 265
    Potential gradings 265
    Rating criteria 266
    Supervisory ranks - rating criteria 270

Preparing reports

Writing reports on your colleagues is an everyday experience in the police force if you happen to be a section officer or above. Reports may be written with a view to making recommendations for promotion, or touching on matters of discipline; or recommending a particular course of action in relation to postings, attachments to various units, or simply the annual staff appraisal report. In any case, report writing is perhaps the single most important matter a supervisor will be asked to undertake, and it must be remembered that reports you write on your colleagues very often say more about the author than the colleagues reported upon. It is important that everything said in such a report can be supported by evidence. Having feelings 'in your water' won't do, or saying that you 'just know' this or that to be so, is insufficient.

The good report writer follows a particular line and touches on those matters which are relevant to the object of the report. If, for example, you are preparing a report based on recommendations for promotion of a junior colleague, then the report would be incomplete if it did not mention:
  (a) leadership potential;
  (b) acceptance of responsibilities;
  (c) organising ability;
  (d) effectiveness of control; and,
  (e) assessment of people.

These matters are the main criteria in making recommendations and failing to report in some detail on each would disadvantage the potential supervisor and also you, the author of the report. In order to prepare a report which is fair and just, and therefore ethical, it is best to try and prepare a pen-picture of the individual concerned in a way that allows him to be identified as an individual. A bland report which can describe half a dozen people is quite useless and self-defeating.

I have set out in this chapter a formula which will help you prepare reports on any matter which is likely to touch on the qualities of the individual. It is set out in three parts:
  (a) descriptions of characteristics and rating;
  (b) criteria for supervisory ranks; and,
  (c) eight reports ranging from excellent (should be promoted at once) to substantially below a level of acceptance and requiring resignation.

Assessment criteria

When reporting on a colleague, it is important to have a clear idea of the matters which are relevant to the report. Outlined opposite is an ideal, but not exhaustive, list of qualities looked for in most reports that you will have to pen in relation to a colleague.

Assessment criteria

> Professional knowledge.
> Powers of expression, both written and verbal.
> Practical ability and judgment.
> Initiative.
> Appearance and bearing.
> Relationship with colleagues.
> Relationship and attitude to public.
> Temperament and stability.
> Problem solving.
> Organisation of work.

Criteria for supervisory ranks…

> Leadership and leadership potential.
> Acceptance of responsibilities.
> Organising ability.
> Effectiveness of control.
> Assessment of people.

Ratings

When reporting on colleagues there clearly has to be a grading system especially when writing recommendations for promotion. It is a fact of life that there has to be a priority system that ensures that the best man or woman gets the job. The report has to be objective and be based on the same system for everyone. Subjectivity results in giving good reports to the people we like and poor reports to people we cannot warm to. If you can provide evidence for what you have to say, then this will keep you in the area of objectivity and as a result your reports will be fair and just. In deciding what rating to apportion to an individual, look below and decide roughly where you rate him or her (based on evidence), and then look at the subsequent report to see if it fits. The probability is that it will fit roughly in with your feelings, you need only amend slightly the report you find under that rating.

The ratings are:

1. Top assessment
2. Very good assessment
3. Above average assessment
4. Average assessment
5. Adequate assessment
6. Fair assessment
7. Poor assessment
8. Lowest assessment

see following pages

Potential gradings

'A' An outstanding candidate fit for immediate promotion.
'B' Fit for immediate promotion.
'C' Requires a broadening of experience in present rank.
'D' Requires more experience in present post.
'E' Unlikely to progress further in rank.

1. Top assessment

Professional knowledge. Possesses an exhaustive knowledge of police law, practice and procedure, together with a profound understanding of the principles of police work. Keeps himself completely informed of current service developments.

Power of expression. Consistently outstanding, well balanced thoughts presented and expressed clearly and concisely. A fluent, persuasive speaker whose words and manner never fail to convince. Effective in formal and informal surroundings.

Practical ability and judgement. Is completely positive and resourceful in the performance of his duties, is invariably able to apply his knowledge and understanding of police work to whatever tasks confront him.

Initiative. Exceptionally constructive/resourceful.

Appearance and bearing. Always smartly dressed and immaculately groomed. Impressive bearing, makes strong impact on others.

Relationship with colleagues. Maintains an excellent relationship with colleagues. Is considerate of feelings of others, has helpful and constructive attitudes and makes marked contributions to resolving common problems.

Relationship with public. Maintains exemplary standards of courtesy, helpfulness and compassion while remaining fully committed to his duties. Firm but exercises authority with tact and good humour.

Temperament and stability. Very well balanced, remains calm even under stress, is determined and resolute in everything undertaken. Possesses a high order of moral courage in carrying out a determined course of action. Commands great respect but is not dogmatic or inflexible.

Problem solving. Shrewd, penetrating and possessing an outstanding ability to analyse complex problems swiftly to achieve sound, unshakable and often striking solutions. Adaptable and possessing a rare combination of good sense and original thought.

Organisation of work. Organises all tasks most efficiently, prioritises time management of resources and personnel.

2. Very good assessment

Professional knowledge. Possesses a high level of knowledge of police law, practice and procedure and an excellent grasp of the principles of his professional knowledge. Makes active efforts to keep abreast of current service developments.

Power of expression. Always produces very good, clear, concise reports which are based on evidence. A very good speaker who holds attention easily with well formulated ideas and judgements.

Practical ability and judgement.. A first class officer well able to apply his knowledge and understanding of his professional duties in the vast majority of situations met in the course of duty.

Initiative. Shows outstanding initiative and ability when faced with unusual problems.

Appearance and bearing. Maintains high standards of dress and grooming and his bearing makes positive impact on others.

Relationship with colleagues. Is well regarded by colleagues and his general attitude is considerate and helpful, making a positive contribution to working relationships.

Relationship with public. Is most courteous, helpful and considerate in his attitude to the public, is mindful of his duties and pursues his objectives with firmness and good humour.

Temperament and stability. Is determined and resolute with considerable moral courage. Vigorous and self assertive, well respected.

Problem solving. Is shrewd and has an analytical ability of high order. Solves unusually difficult problems. Adaptable and achieves solutions which are well reasoned and often show evidence of original thought.

Organisation of work. Consistently shows a good degree of organising ability and is most adept at time management.

3. Above average assessment

Professional knowledge. Possesses good all round knowledge of police law, practice and procedure and an understanding of principles appropriate for his duties. He has good knowledge of current service developments.

Power of expression. Usually produces very good written work, a good speaker who usually expresses himself very well.

Practical ability. Most adept in dealing with tasks confronting him. A sound officer well able to deal effectively with unusual situations.

Initiative. Usually adept when dealing with unusual problems.

Appearance and bearing. Presents a very good appearance and creates a good impression.

Relationship with colleagues. Enjoys a good relationship with colleagues who generally hold him in high esteem.

Relationship with public. Has a good attitude to the public, can display a sense of humour while retaining his authority and is polite and helpful.

Temperament and stability. Possesses self-control. Possesses qualities of resolution and determination. An officer of vigour and moral courage.

Problem solving. Has a shrewd and analytical mind, achieves sound, well reasoned solutions to problems. Adaptable and brings undoubted intelligence to bear on issues of practical importance.

Organisation of work. Is an efficient organiser and is well able to manage resources and personnel.

4. Average assessment

Professional knowledge. possesses an all-round working knowledge of his professional duties and keeps up-to-date with current service developments.

Power of expression. Usually produces good written work and has no difficulty in expressing his views.

Practical ability. Displays considerable ability in dealing with all routine police duties. Applies himself to the practical aspect of his job.

Initiative.. Displays ability to deal with unusual problems.

Appearance. Maintains acceptable standards of dress and grooming and bearing. Fairly impressive.

Relationship with colleagues. Generally achieves good working relationships with colleagues. Usually makes a contribution when called upon to do so.

Relationship with public. This officer's attitude and relationship and approach to the public is sound.

Temperament. Well balanced and calm in most situations. Displays determination in the performance of his duties.

Problem solving. An intelligent officer who has genuine ability to appreciate, analyse and solve a variety of problems confronting him in the course of his police duties.

Organisation of work. Often shows a good degree of organisation of work. Is usually able to prioritise his time and resources.

5. Adequate assessment

Professional knowledge. Possesses a requisite knowledge of police law, practice and procedure. Has an efficient knowledge and understanding of professional matters relating to his area of work plus some knowledge of current developments in the service

Power of expression. Reasonably good on paper but is inclined to pay insufficient attention to detail.

Practical ability. A good working police officer who thinks and acts correctly on his own initiative in most situations.

Initiative. Thinks and acts correctly on his own initiative.

Appearance and bearing. Of reasonably good standard on most occasions. Some room for improvement.

Relationship with colleagues. Generally achieves a working relationship with colleagues but occasionally rubs them up the wrong way.

Relationship with public. This officer does not always approach the public in a manner which is calculated to obtain the most positive response from those with whom he is dealing.

Temperament and stability. Approaches work in a determined manner, some tendency to be dogmatic and inflexible.

Problem solving. Possesses analytical ability and sound common sense which he is able to employ effectively in the performance of routine police duties.

Organisation of work. Capable of planning the more routine tasks. Time and resource management not always sound.

6. Fair assessment

Professional knowledge. Knowledge of police law, practice and procedure is inadequate in some aspects. Has not yet achieved sufficient grasp of principles. Does not have a sufficient knowledge of current service developments.

Power of expression. His precise meaning sometimes gets lost. Inclined to be ambiguous. Finds some difficulty in verbal communication, ill at ease.

Practical ability. Achieves an acceptable general standard but does not always act as effectively as the situation demands.

Initiative. Achieves an acceptable general standard using initiative but not always correctly.

Appearance and bearing. Fails to maintain acceptable standards, unimpressive. Much room for improvement.

Relationship with colleagues. Has some difficulty in appreciating the points of view of others. Does not take into account the feelings of others resulting in some friction within the group.

Relationship with public. This officer does not maintain satisfactory standards in his relationship with the public and elicits negative responses.

Temperament and stability. Usually copes but needs reassurance at times. Approaches problems with a degree of determination. Occasionally inconsistent.

Problem solving. Displays adequate ability in the performance of the majority of routine duties.

Organisation of work. Incapable of planning more than one task at a time. Often fails to see the overall plan.

7. Poor assessment

Professional knowledge. Knowledge of police law, practice and procedure is inadequate in most cases. Has consistently failed to grasp the principles of the job. Has little knowledge of current trends and service developments.

Power of expression. Has difficulty putting his thoughts into writing. Inarticulate and dull, has difficulty in commanding attention.

Practical ability. Tends to act without sufficient consideration of implications. Occasionally his actions are ill-advised.

Initiative. Rarely shows initiative.

Appearance and bearing. Very untidy. Is unkempt, rarely groomed and does nothing to improve himself.

Relationship with colleagues. Rarely appreciates the points of view and feelings of others.

Relationship with public. This officer maintains a poor relationship with the public, consistently eliciting negative responses.

Temperament and stability. Some-what irresolute and easily distracted from his purpose.

Problem solving. Has some difficulty in applying his mind to practical problems. May act inappropriately at times.

Organisation of work. Even routine tasks are often beyond his ability. Organisation of time and resources is often wasteful.

8. Lowest assessment

Professional knowledge. Has inadequate knowledge of police law, practice and procedure. Has little or no grasp of, or interest in, the principles of the job or knowledge of current service developments.

Power of expression. Unable to express his thoughts on paper. Unable to express himself in verbally.

Practical ability. Has little or no practical aptitude for police work.

Initiative. Lacking in original thought.

Appearance and bearing. Slovenly.

Relationship with colleagues. Does not achieve good working relationships with others. Rubs people up the wrong way. Relationships are counter-productive.

Relationship with public. This officer gives nothing to his relationship with the public. He is often uncivil.

Temperament and stability. Goes to pieces under pressure. Lacks determination, resolution and moral courage. Possesses occasional dogmatism and inflexibility of a weak character.

Problem solving. Thinking shallow and concentration weak. Has narrow and inflexible approach to problems leading to incomplete judgments. Slow to react, has difficulty solving even simple problems.

Organisation of work.. Incapable of planning even the simplest task. No concept of time or resource management.

Supervisory ranks

So far as supervisory ranks are concerned, in particular when reporting on officers who are seeking to become section officers, there are other criteria to be considered in addition to the general criteria considered above. When reporting on these officers you should pen-picture a general outline using the criteria described and also address those matters that are common to the qualities looked for in supervisors, managers and also leaders. Again, using ratings (1) - (8), I outline below the sort of report which you will be expected to write, (always evidenced) and, above all, objective.

Remember, nothing should be hidden and there should be no hidden agenda. You should always take the view that this report will be read out to the officer concerned and may be subject to appeal. The best rule of thumb is to be prepared to read the report to the officer concerned yourself. This will ensure fairness and justice and will shape your remarks in terms which will be acceptable to the officer.

1. Top assessment (supervisors)

Leadership/potential. Inspires great confidence in others and provides an excellent example. Others respond readily to his directions in all circumstances. They seek, accept and respect his advice in all difficulties.

Acceptance of responsibilities. A consistently outstanding and inspiring leader who is rarely placed at a disadvantage and enthusiastically approaches all tasks with which he is presented in an outstandingly efficient manner.

Organising ability. An excellent organiser possessing considerable foresight and ability to plan for the unexpected as well as the routine. His planning always provides for the human element in the widest sense as well as for the tasks undertaken.

Effectiveness of control. Directs and controls the activities of others effectively under all circumstances. Always commands obedience of subordinates who readily entrust this supervisor with all relevant information to assist him to make high quality decisions. Excellent judge of others, being able to assess and employ their talents to obtain optimum efficiency.

Assessment of people. An exceptionally shrewd judge of character who has analytical ability of a high order.

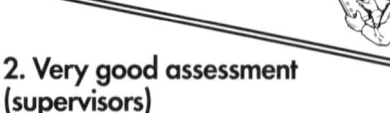

2. Very good assessment (supervisors)

Leadership/potential. Inspires a high level of confidence in others and provides a good example. Others respond well to directions and seek and accept and respect advice in most circumstances.

Acceptance of responsibilities. Takes the lead when the situation demands. Is never reticent – will always come forward.

Organising ability. A most capable organiser who appreciates the long-term consequences of projected courses of action.

Effectiveness of control. Directs and controls under most circumstances. Commands high levels of obedience from subordinates who entrust him with relevant information to assist the decision-making process. An unusually good judge of character.

Assessment of people. A shrewd judge of character who shows deep personal insight.

3. Above average assessment (supervisors)

Leadership/potential. Inspires confidence in others and maintains sound standards. Others will accept his direction and his advice commands a significant degree of respect.

Acceptance of responsibilities. Accepts responsibility. Is prepared to take the lead if the situation demands it.

Organising ability. Generally a very good organiser and planner. Usually appreciates the long-term consequences of his action.

Effectiveness of control. An effective controller of subordinates whose directions are habitually followed and whose decisions are based on sound intelligence provided by subordinates when required.

Assessment of people. Reliable in character assessment. Sometimes shrewd, showing an analytical mind.Average assessment (supervisors)

4. Average assessment (supervisors)

Leadership/potential. Inspires some confidence in others and maintains sound standards. Others will accept his direction and his advice commands respect.

Acceptance of responsibilities. Usually willing to accept responsibility. Sometimes takes the lead when the situation demands it.

Organising ability. A satisfactory organiser, sometimes appreciates the long-term consequences of his action.

Effectiveness of control. Exercises an effective level of control over the activities of subordinates.

Assessment of people. Usually assesses people accurately. Occasionally shows an ability to be analytical.

5. Adequate assessment (supervisors)

Leadership/potential. Maintains acceptable standards of conduct and, where directions are given, these are normally followed. Others do not actively seek advice but his views command some respect.

Acceptance of responsibilities. Sometimes willing to accept responsibility but shows some reluctance when faced with problems.

Organising ability. Personally well organised but tends only to see the short term advantage of courses of action. Not always sufficiently flexible when planning.

Effectiveness of control. Occasionally fails to exercise an effective or appropriate level of control.

Assessment of people. Occasionally makes errors of judgment but can usually be relied upon.

6. Fair assessment (supervisors)

Leadership/potential. Does not always command respect of others. His own standards vary occasionally. His advice is often unsought, overlooked or discarded.

Acceptance of responsibilities. Accepts responsibility only when told and then very reluctantly.

Organising ability.. Not very well organised personally and fails often to see completely the consequences of his action.

Effectiveness of control. Does not exercise control over the activities of subordinates. Excessively harsh or weak in his dealings with others. Little capacity to judge the performance of others.

Assessment of people. Frequently misled in his judgment of people. Does not probe and question.

7. Poor assessment (supervisors)

Leadership/potential. Does not inspire confidence of others. Standards variable and drives rather than leads if opportunity arises. Inconsistency leads to his decisions lacking credibility.

Acceptance of responsibilities. Reluctant to accept responsibility and is often placed at a disadvantage.

Organising ability. A muddled thinker, works without system, lacks any real vision.

Effectiveness of control. Seldom competent when placed in control. Lacks direction and purpose. Little motivation results in inertia.

Assessment of people. Easily taken in. Relies on subjective judgments resulting in constantly being disadvantaged.

8. Lowest assessment (supervisors)

Leadership/potential.. Exercises little or no influence over others. Has low standards of discipline and is not an effective leader. Inconsiderate and has little or no interest in the welfare or efficiency of others.

Acceptance of responsibilities. Avoids responsibility where possible. Actively uninterested in sharing responsibility.

Organising ability. Has little or no or-ganising ability. Lacking in foresight, and tends to be bogged down by irrelevancies.

Effectiveness of control. Incapable of exercising control. Wastes time and resources.

Assessment of people. Cannot be relied upon for accurate assessments. Readily taken in.

CHAPTER 18

STRESS AND BURNOUT

Chapter contents

Introduction to stress **274**
    The fight or flight response 275
    Vulnerability 275
Recognising stress **276**
    Signs of tension 276
    Change in lifestyle 276
    Stress indicators 277
Minimising burnout and stress responses **277**
Seeking help **279**
    Self help 279
Burnout **280**
    Structured programmes 280
        Tutor constables 289
        Assessments 280
        Solo patrol 281
        Training programme 281
        Final assessment 283
Special to regular **283**
    Gaining insight 283
    Improving position 283
    The unsuccessful candidate 284
    Best advice 284
Post-traumatic stress **285**
    Post traumatic stress disorder 286
        Characteristics 286
        General symptoms 287
        Defusing 288
    Critical incident stress debriefing 289

Stress

Introduction

Stress and burn-out are major factors which account for illness in the service, often resulting in the premature retirement of both regular and special constables. In many ways stress is like metal fatigue; where a person or thing is pushed too hard for too long there is bound to be a breakdown. This has been discussed by Charles Cowe, Chief Commandant of Northumbria in *Special Beat* where he states, 'Specials give too much too soon'. He says, 'they start off by doing three or four night duties a week and burn themselves out and then leave the force'.

The number of mature recruits joining Northumbria has dropped considerably in recent years and many others are leaving. This decline in mature members is leaving the force short of experienced officers. The argument is advanced that new recruits should be 'fed in' to duties more gradually, in order to prolong the life of the officer in the service. This applies equally to special constables who have many years' service and it is a matter for supervisors to ensure that officers are not doing too much in terms of hours worked and, more importantly, attending stressful incidents without being properly debriefed afterwards.

Supervisors should be aware of officers attending incidents which give rise to shock or fear. Road traffic accidents involving death and injury leave clear impressions on the minds of those officers who have to attend them. Occasions of public disorder and street violence create fear in the minds of the officers involved and leave a lasting impression of negativity, which can become self-defeating. It is important that officers be given the opportunity to talk over with someone how they feel about a given situation. There is much truth in the saying 'a problem shared is a problem halved'. Supervisors not only need to be able to identify a problem when they see it, they need also to know where to turn to for help.

What follows is an in-depth look at the factors which cause stress, which if left unchecked may result in burn-out. There is advice on where to look for help and what that help is likely to be. Special Constabulary supervisors should be very familiar with what follows in order that they can deal effectively with problems before they become disasters. Failure to identify and deal with stress can have damaging effects, not only on the individual, but also the team as well as the organisation.

Most people work at least an eight-hour day. If you are a member of the Special Constabulary it is quite possible that at least once a week you are performing not only your regular daily tasks but are spending part of your 'free time' carrying out police duties.

Western society is founded on the work ethic. We often put up with long working hours and silently suffer uncomfortable working conditions. Promotion is seen as an emblem of success rather than a means of fulfilment and self-esteem is linked to earning power. Work-related stress is increasingly recognised as a major cause of illness and mental breakdown.

On a positive note, the work we do gives us a sense of belonging and purpose. It defines our role, strengthens our sense of identity and gives us responsibility. Being a special can provide satisfaction and fulfilment, offering challenges and experiences outside our everyday lives.

Stress and the fight or flight response

Stress has been with us since the beginning of time. A natural response to challenge or stimulus, it aids our continuing survival and can generate action, whether it be in a life threatening situation or to meet an approaching deadline. The fight or flight response is the body's answer to challenge or danger. It consists of a complex chain of bodily and biochemical changes involving the interaction of the brain, nervous system and a variety of hormones. As a result of these biochemical responses, the body goes on 'full alert'. Because our nervous system cannot differentiate between various sources of stress the body's response is identical whether we are in a life threatening situation or caught in a traffic jam! The fight or flight response is quite normal provided it was necessary in the first place, and we can use up the energy that has been created.

When the response is inappropriate or lasts too long it may start to generate harmful stress and nervous tension. If this happens over a long period of time the result may be overload, exhaustion and, ultimately, ill health.

Vulnerability

It is estimated that more than 40 million working days are lost in Britain each year due to the effects of stress. Illnesses related to stress costs medical and social services an average of £55 million per year. 'Stress burnout' has become an established medical term. Stress is not only a problem for those with a hectic life style but also for people who suffer excessive monotony, boredom or frustration because of insufficient stimulus. The common factor amongst those suffering stress burnout is the feeling of life being 'out of control'. There is no single solution to the stress problem, what is stressful for one person may not be for another. The ultimate responsibility for our well-being rests first and foremost with ourselves. In order to remain in control we must develop a healthy and stress-proof life style.

Recently a growing awareness of the importance of a balanced diet, the need for exercise, the dangers of smoking, alcohol, drugs, pollution and ecological imbalance have provided a renewed interest in holistic well-being. This concept is based on the ancient Greek ideal of the unity of mind and body whereby balance can be restored by treating the whole person. We cannot separate our physical health from our mental well-being, they are interdependent. The balance of mind and body is also affected by the way we communicate and relate to other individuals and the environment in which we live.

Virtually everything in life is potentially stressful to someone. Your vulnerability will depend on your response to the event and your ability to control it. Unavoidable major life crises face all of us at some time or another.

Recognising stress

If you are going to cope with stress effectively you must become aware of your own stress responses. Very often we fail to notice the effects of stress. Our bodies and minds are very adaptable. As we appear to cope with the pressures around us the greater the temptation to drive ourselves beyond our capabilities. Stress distorts our perception so that we do not realise what is happening. If the process is allowed to continue the end result may be fatigue, exhaustion and eventually complete breakdown. The more stressed we are the less chance we have of realising it.

Signs of tension

The human body is designed to deal with stress up to a certain level, if this level is exceeded then the body ceases to function smoothly and becomes overworked, leading to physical and/or mental exhaustion. Different parts of our bodies may become stress targets and symptoms may arise in a variety of combinations. Symptoms will vary for each individual depending on which organ or system is the weakest link in our physiological make-up.

Change in lifestyle scale

Our health and survival are based on the body's ability to maintain a balance of all the physical and mental processes. The body is constantly adjusting to change. Too much change in our lives can overtax our adaptive resources which may lead to illness. The 'change in lifestyle scale' was devised by American doctors T H Holmes and R H Rahe. It gives over 40 positive and negative life events which have been valued according to the amount of adjustment needed to cope with them.

Scoring over 300 points in one year greatly increases the risk of illness, 150-299 reduces the risk by 30 per cent. A score of less than 150 involves a slight chance of illness. The point scoring ranges from death of a spouse at 100, to loss of job at 47, death of a friend at 37, child leaves home at 29, trouble with employer at 23, small mortgage taken out at 17, holiday at 13 and Christmas at 12. Many people would experience a particular event as being more or less stressful than the Holmes-Rahe scale, for instance Christmas can be very traumatic in some families while a child's leaving home might be a cause for celebration and/or relief. It all depends on the individual.

Illness is not an inevitable result of change. Your personality and your ability to cope largely determine how well you react.

Stress indicators

Physical symptoms

Chronic stomach upsets
Skin problems
Irregular breathing
Asthma
Muscular aches and pains
Headaches
Backpain
Sleeplessness
Migraines
Sexual disorders

Nervous reflexes

Biting nails
Clenching jaw
Grinding teeth
Tapping feet
Clenching fists
Drumming fingers
Hunching shoulders
Touching hair

Emotional responses

Anxiety
Frustration
Hostility
Helplessness
Restlessness
Depression
Anger
Hopelessness
Irritability

Behaviour

Aggression
Emotional outbursts
Over reactions
Doing several things at once
Disturbed sleep patterns
Leaving jobs undone
Talking too fast or too loud
Out of character behaviour

Minimising burnout and stress responses

Diet

A varied and well-balanced diet is essential to healthy living, ensuring the mind and body are encouraged to function at their optimum levels. What makes up a balanced diet is open to debate but it should consist of fresh fruit, vegetables, salads, grains and whole foods. Refined and processed foods, animal fats, dairy produce and sugar should be kept to a minimum. Some foods may influence our moods and emotions. Alcohol for example makes most people relaxed, but too much can reduce your body's ability to withstand stress and affect your physical well-being.

Exercise

Like food, this is something you should enjoy that will do you good. It is important to find an activity that suits you as an individual, fitting in with your personal schedules and physical capabilities. It is better to exercise regularly for short periods rather than exercising infrequently or irregularly.

Relaxation

Ideally, to keep ourselves as fit as possible it is important to alternate periods of physical tension with regular times of relaxation. The amount of unconscious or hidden tension in our bodies means that few people could honestly claim to be completely relaxed for most of their waking hours.

A good night's sleep should help us to relax but even those who have good sleeping patterns may find this is not sufficient to eliminate all the stress in their lives.

Many people do not realise how unrelaxed they are and ignore the build-up of strain and tension in limbs, joints and muscles. After a period of time this stored up tension will start to affect the way you feel and function, making your body less efficient. The effects of this may be physical aches and pains, headaches and migraine.

There are a variety of relaxation techniques that can be learnt, from simple exercises that can be carried out easily during your working day to more complex exercise systems such as aerobics, yoga, martial arts and calisthenics.

Information is obtainable from libraries, book shops, gyms or further education colleges.

Routine and variety

Too much routine dulls the mind and saps energy. Conversely, being faced with a multitude of tasks and responsibilities can lead to disorganisation, muddle and confusion. Either way the end result may be stressful. It is important to strike a balance to maintain efficiency and enjoyment in your life. Be positive!

Time management

Whatever we do, time is a precious commodity. Fitting commitments and leisure activities into your waking hours can create time shortages.

The longer and more demanding our work schedules the greater the risk of becoming a victim of stress.

Trying to cram too many activities into a day means that jobs pile up or are completed late. Deadlines loom, tempers are lost, we feel anxious and often in a state of panic. Work suffers, relationships and home life become fraught and resentment builds up as there never seems to be enough time to relax and enjoy the company of friends and family.

This situation will ultimately affect the amount of general satisfaction we get from life.

It is important that you plan your time carefully:
(1) take into account your capabilities;
(2) fit in your proposed work schedules;
(3) build in time for relaxation and leisure.

This will ensure that your commitments are compatible with your home life. It is often in the area of relationships and home life that tension can build up gradually and unknowingly because one of the partners has not given this the priority it deserves.

Seeking help

If you identify signs of stress within yourself or notice that a colleague, friend or family member may be suffering from stress-related symptoms help is available from various sources.

(1) First, you could see your doctor. A check-up is important and will often put your mind at rest in that symptoms you may be experiencing can be explained and treated. Many GPs run their own 'stress awareness' groups or employ counsellors to help people resolve their difficulties.
(2) Help may also be available through a welfare or occupational health unit at your place of work.
(3) Various organisations and self-help groups such as Relate, Alcohol Advisory Service, Mind, etc are trained to help with specific problems. Make contact with whichever of these organisations is most appropriate.
(4) Talk things over. If you have a problem release some of the tension by discussing things with someone you feel you can trust.
(5) If you notice someone else appears to be very anxious or tensed up be a good listener and give him or her the opportunity to talk to you about what is worrying them.

Self-help

(1) Exercise regularly.
(2) Plan your work so than you use your time and energy more efficiently.
(3) Take a break. No matter how busy you are a short break, standing back from things if only for a few minutes, often provides a new outlook on old problems.
(4) Relax. Set aside a few minutes every day to take time out for yourself.
(5) Be realistic. Set yourself achievable goals. Many people expect too much of themselves.
(6) Be positive.
(7) Avoid too many changes coming at once.
(8) Plan your time.
(9) Take control of your life.

From time to time we will all experience stress of some sort, life would be very boring and mundane if we never experienced challenges and change. The first step towards solving a problem is recognising that it exists. Try to keep things in perspective, seek help early and go for prompt professional advice to keep minor troubles from developing into major problems.

Burnout

Many special constables resign prematurely from the service, due mainly to having given too much too soon, resulting in burnout. This problem can be addressed by specials' supervisory ranks creating a structured programmed aimed at introducing new - and not so new - recruits to their duties in a measured and balanced way, thus saving the enthusiastic special from himself.

There is further unnecessary wastage from the Special Constabulary resulting from boredom; not because the officers are too tired to find meaningful work, or because nothing excites their sense of curiosity, but because there is often no structured programme which gives direction and a sense of pace and drive to their activities. We all owe a duty of care to ensure that our recruits are not burnt-out or bored-out.

Structured programmes

It is a matter for each section officer when a new special is appointed to his section to look at the needs of that particular officer. His needs, expectations and anxieties should be explored and a programme prepared for his induction to the travail of the streets. In the first instance he should be under the supervision and care of a special constable who has enough experience to look after the interests of the recruit. Regular officers each have a tutor constable who performs his function during the early months of the recruit's service to a point when he is deemed fit to perform duty on his own.

Tutor constables

New recruits should be attached to a tutor constable of the Special Constabulary for a period not less than six months, during which time, the tutor can best report to the section officer when the recruit is able to perform duty on his own.

The tutor should be a person who is able to make objective assessments of the progress of the recruit and address any difficulties that may arise. The tutor should have a structured introduction package aimed at helping the recruit to 'land on his feet running' when he first performs solo duty. To that end it would be useful for the tutor to arrange for the recruit to perform duties designed to give as much information and knowledge to the recruit as is possible in the time.

Assessments

The tutor constable should, at the end of six months, be in a position to recommend that the officer is fit for solo patrol, or recommend further tutoring. His assessment should be based on considerations such as:

(a) reliability;
(b) moral and physical courage;
(c) willingness to learn;
(d) ability to cope with stress;
(e) communication skills;
(f) relationship with colleagues/ public;
(g) knowledge of procedures;
(h) confidence;
(i) negotiating skills.

Solo patrol

The object of the structured programme overseen by the tutor constable is to ensure that when the recruit is finally asked to perform duty on his own, he is fit to do so. Some forces have a training programme for recruits and some form a tutorship, but not all. In the absence of such a programme in your force the section officer may wish to introduce a programme that is suitable for his district.

Training programme

Location	Purpose
Police station	Initial introduction to section officer and tutor constable. Meet as many special constables as possible. Issue of locker, map, forms and documents. Check uniform and equipment. Discuss needs, expectations and anxieties. Visit police station offices during the quiet hours.
Police station	Visit operational areas of the police station including front office complex, examine books in inquiry office. Visit custody suite and cells. Visit communication centre and study maps of boundaries and become familiar with call signs.
Foot patrol	Introduction to geography of area, meet people, visit pubs, clubs, schools and other places of police interest or where difficulties may arise. Get used to using personal radio, call signs and the PNC. Stop vehicles and check driving documents. Issue HO/RT 1.
Foot patrol	Patrol beat. Attention to vacant and vulnerable premises. Locate places of police interest, hospitals, garages, hotels, betting shops. Attend alarms and deal with street incidents. Talk to people, develop communication and negotiating skills. After each incident discuss the distinction between arrestable offences and section 25 of PACE, how the situation arose.

continued overleaf...

Training programme... cont

Location	Purpose
Foot patrol (nights)	Work part of a night duty (2200-0200) and get the feel for nights as well as the different activities that night brings. Discuss drink/drive laws and licensing difficulties likely to be encountered. Get used to dealing with yobs and minor public disorder problems. Again, develop communication and negotiating skills.
Mobile patrol	Become familiar with marked police cars, equipment carried, car radios and in particular accident and emergency equipment carried. Drive the boundaries of the district and become familiar with coded procedures that are applicable to mobiles.
Public disorder	Attachment to either a public disorder vehicle or a location where disorder is likely to occur; football match, sporting fixture. Become familiar with diffusing difficult situations, domestic disputes etc. Watch and practice restraint and arrest techniques. Practice stop and search powers. Gain an insight into the workings of conveying arrested persons to designated police stations and the procedures in the custody suite.
Police station	An evening with the section officer and tutor constable assessing how things are shaping up. How does the recruit feel he is doing? Look again at his needs, anxieties and expectations and see if the issues are being properly addressed. Now is the time for soul searching and open and frank discussion. Now is the time to discuss the way ahead and, if necessary, prepare an action plan to deal with matters arising.
Police station	Paperwork. Become familiar with the Manual of Guidance concerning prosecution files, time limits on submission, minimum requirement of proofs of evidence. Ensure there is a firm understanding in the mind of the recruit of where all the paperwork goes after it leaves his possession.
Police station	Consideration should now be given to posting the recruit to a regular section of officers. Local policies dictate what procedures have to be adopted but at this stage it would be prudent to introduce him to the regular sergeants and inspectors with whom he may be required to work.

Final assessment

It is now a matter for the section officer and tutor constable to assess if the recruit is able to perform solo duty. If the answer is yes, then no doubt he will go on to make a valuable contribution to the organisation. If the answer is no, it may be that a further period of tuition is required backed up by an action plan. If the answer is still no then it will no doubt have dawned on the recruit as to why and he will take the action necessary in all the circumstances. It is at this stage that officers charged with the duty of making assessments have to be open and, above all, frank. A recruit who is allowed to go on when he clearly shows that he has insufficient aptitude for the job, will not only be unhappy, he will cause difficulties for the team and the organisation.

Particular attention should be addressed to the questions of:
(a) ability to cope with stress;
(b) communication and negotiating skills;
(c) willingness to learn;
(d) relationships with colleagues and the public;
(e) moral and physical courage.

Special to regular

Many people join the Special Constabulary because they feel it to be worthwhile in itself and to make a valuable contribution to the society we live in.

Those with an eye on the regular police service either:
1. join with a view to gaining an insight into the police force - they feel that they wish to be a police officer and that by joining the specials they will be in a better position to judge if that is what they really want; or
2. feel that they might improve their chances of being accepted into the regular force if they are special constables.

Gaining insight

For those joining the specials to gain an insight into the workings of the regular force it is common that their 'insight' either promotes their wish to join or, having seen the reality of the job - stress, violence, working shifts, etc - their initial enthusiasm wanes to a point where they are happy to continue as a special. There is nothing sinister or wrong with joining for this reason as it settles the mind of the embryonic police officer that he made the right decision either way.

Improving position

Those joining the specials because they feel that, by being a member *per se*, they will be better positioned to enter the regulars should know that there is no evidence to support or contradict the proposition either way. Joining the Special Constabulary is emphatically not a back door into the regular force.

It is understandable that specials who believe they have gained useful experience and acquitted themselves well in the Special Constabulary should feel that this must stand them in good stead. Indeed, this is a topical issue. *Special Beat* in several recent issues has featured letters from would-be regulars who feel that their experience as specials is being overlooked by the recruiting departments.

Many forces are providing more feedback to candidates on their interview performance (see *Special Beat* Vol 9 No 1, 'If the hat fits'. However, as quoted in *Special Beat,* forces are at pains to emphasise that all candidates are treated as external candidates on the day; that selection standards are more rigorous for regulars, and that the realities of full time shift work are very different from a few hours of volunteer duty. However it is also clear that it is up to specials at the interview to ensure they give examples of the experience they have gained.

The best that can be said to someone who feels that his chances of selection to the regular force may be improved by becoming a special, is that he should, in the first instance, join a force which is actually recruiting regular officers! There are a great many regular officers who have in the past been special constables, but they are outnumbered by a factor of 50 to one by those who have not.

The unsuccessful candidate

When a special constable applies to join the regular force and is unsuccessful, resignation as a special should not be the first consideration. Should he then apply to another force, inquiries will quickly reveal that he has been a special constable, applied to become a regular, failed, and then resigned as a special. This applicant would not be applying from a position of strength. The best advice is for this officer to remain in the Special Constabulary and apply to other forces.

Best advice

Officers who have applied, unsuccessfully, to join the regular force, often cannot be consoled and leave the Special Constabulary. This is a great waste and supervisory specials will ask themselves what arguments they can advance to the unsuccessful special to keep them from resigning. The truth of the matter is that where the force in which he serves continues actively to recruit, then the likelihood of his remaining in the specials is heightened; equally, where there is a fall-off in recruiting, so the likelihood of resignation increases. By remaining in the Special Constabulary the potential recruit must increase his chances of selection because he becomes a more attractive proposition as he gains in service, attends courses, achieves promotion etc. This is a real improvement of position. **Stick with it - keep trying.**

Post-traumatic stress

Traumatic incidents can extend far beyond the atrocities of war and terrorist activity. Over the last few years many traumatic events have left behind a trail of disasters. Recent air crashes, rail accidents, ferry disasters, football- ground deaths and London Underground fires remind us that the general population is not immune to the possibility of post-traumatic stress.

Trauma is a word which was used in Greek surgical terminology to mean an injury stemming from the penetration of the body. Psychological trauma is defined as an event of such deep emotional intensity that it breaks through the ego's defences and floods it with uncontrollable anxiety. An event such as this is outside the normal range of ordinary human experience. In every day policing, trauma is an all too frequent occurrence.

A stress reaction may occur whether an incident is relatively minor or amounts to a major disaster. It is important to remember that no event is inherently stressful. The stress comes from our response to the event, which to some extent will be determined by our personal perceptions and previous experience in similar situations. In the context of police work it is possible to divide traumatic incidents into three main groups:

1. **The shooting incident.**

2. **The horrifying incident.** Road traffic accidents, child abuse, suicide, rape, fire, stabbing, actual bodily harm. This type of incident may be traumatic not only for the victim but also for those involved in determining the factual details surrounding the event.

3. **The life threatening incident.** Life threatening incident traumas are those in which a police officer feels personally involved or threatened. The individual's perception of the event will have a great effect on his/her response to it. When attacks like these occur they may not only affect those directly involved in the incident but other staff as well. Examples of this may be those who prepared the duty rosters, or colleagues who perhaps were off sick at that time and felt they should have been dealing with the incident instead. These members of staff may suffer enormous guilt, emotions which need to be expressed and worked through.

Post-traumatic stress (PTS) is the development of characteristic symptoms following a psychologically distressing event. Not everyone involved will suffer the symptoms but what needs to be emphasised is that to be affected is normal and the reactions that some of us may experience are normal. PTS is the normal reaction of normal people to abnormal events.

Post-traumatic stress disorder

PTS can influence the feelings people have about themselves. It can interfere with all their relationships, both at work and at home with partners and families. Health may break down and sometimes more disturbing symptoms may appear. If PTS symptoms persist or intensify over a period of four to six weeks, a condition called post-traumatic stress disorder (PTSD) may emerge. It has been known for symptoms to emerge months and even years after the traumatic incident, these symptoms may vary between being mildly disturbing to incapacitating.

Acute. With onset between six weeks and six months after the incident, usually lasting less than six months.

Chronic. Where the course of PTSD lasts longer than six months.

Delayed. Where the onset is delayed more than six months after the event.

Characteristics of post-traumatic stress disorder

PTSD would have been defined in bygone years as combat fatigue or battle shock. Some psychiatrists will confirm that this shows similarities to grief and bereavement responses. Three major types of PTSD are recognisable.

Re-experiencing (flash-backs)

The event can be re-experienced days, months or years later. These reactions may be triggered by, for example:

Sight - TV, video, photographs, media reports, people.
Sound - police sirens, bangs, crashes, voices.
Smell - petrol, rubber, disinfectant, dampness, sweat, food.
Taste - food, water, petrol, alcohol, sweat.
Touch - rubber, metal, skin, dampness, water.

'Out of the blue' reactions may occur with no apparent trigger.

Avoidance

This may cause someone who has been involved in a traumatic incident to avoid anything or anyone that might remind him of the incident. He may also try to avoid thoughts, feeling or situations. There may be loss of concentration, loss of feeling and emotions. This can severely disrupt relationships, marriages and careers.

Sensitivity

There may be an increased sensitivity to noise, the slightest sound may cause the individual to 'jump'.

There may be problems in coping with normal everyday life at work and at home. Some sufferers may isolate themselves, others may have outbursts of anger or violence.

Difficulty in sleeping may exacerbate all these problems, concentrating for any length of time may become a problem and the sufferer may be over-vigilant, expecting something unpleasant to happen at any time without warning.

General symptoms

Symptoms may occur months or even years after a traumatic event but can also occur during or immediately following it. To experience some sort of physical or emotional reaction immediately following an incident should be seen as a normal response. These symptoms should gradually diminish over the following days and weeks. Some people may not experience any of the following symptoms and this too should be regarded as normal for them.

Denial

Denial can be strong. It can be particularly so in males who are involved in a service such as the police where the macho image is a strong part of the normal 'police culture'.

Feelings

(1) Sense of pointlessness - 'Why bother? Why go on?'
(2) Increased anxiety and sense of vulnerability.
(3) Depression and sadness.
(4) Intrusive thoughts and images.
(5) Shame, anger, regret, guilt, bitterness.
(6) Survivor guilt - 'Why did I survive when they didn't?'
(7) Sense of isolation.
(8) Strong feeling of identity with those involved in the incident.
(9) Fear of enclosed or open spaces.
(10) Fear of being in the same situation again.
(11) Fear of crowds or groups of people.
(12) Sympathy for any aggressors - 'The Stockholm Syndrome' - resulting from being taken hostage or prisoner.

Behaviour

(1) Inability to concentrate or make simple decisions.
(2) Impulsive actions - excessive spending, moving home, changing job or life style, ending or creating new relationships.
(3) Irritability, anger or violence.
(4) Sleep disturbances, dreams and nightmares.
(5) Isolation.
(6) Incessantly talking about the event - keeping a diary.
(7) Physical effects.

(8) Illness - headaches, stomach and chest pains. Non-specific symptoms and feeling generally unwell.
(9) Listlessness and feeling tired.
(10) Increased sensitivity to noise, people, work, home etc.
(11) Excitement and hyperactivity.
(12) Increased smoking or drinking.
(13) Possible use of drugs.

Life belief

There can also be changes in values or beliefs and re-adjustments in relationships. There may be detachment from a previous relationship and way of life or a new, clinging need and sense of dependency. Some people will discover a new faith or lose an existing one. Others may deepen already held beliefs, whether religious or not.

During a crisis basic beliefs are called into question or even completely distorted. The responses to an event will be determined by the nature and extent of the incident, by previous experiences, coping mechanisms already learned and by the individual's own inner resources - or the lack of them.

Most people have three basic life beliefs:

(1) invulnerability;
(2) meaning and purpose;
(3) self-respect and self-esteem.

On the positive side, an officer may find after dealing with a traumatic experience that he or she has:

(1) a deeper appreciation of life;
(2) a sense of achievement;
(3) an increased sense of value.

Police officers, by the nature of their job, may be involved in dealing with incidents which may cause them to experience unusually strong emotional reactions. These reactions have the potential to interfere with their ability to function either at the scene or later. A major disaster is one type of critical incident but it does not have to be of this magnitude to be classified as a critical incident.

In recent years, following research carried out by J T Mitchell of the USA and Dr Atle Dyregrov of Bergen, Norway, it has been recognised that a support system must exist for those who have been involved in a critical incident. This includes the helpers and carers as well as the victims. Support can come from other workers who may be at the scene of the incident but can also be given by supervisors, and psychiatric and counselling support teams.

Currently, individual police forces vary quite considerably as to the amount of support they offer to officers who have dealt with a very traumatic situation. Some forces are being very pro-active and educating their staff about the importance of defusing and debriefing. They are also able to offer psychological debriefing via their own welfare or occupational health unit. For officers who find themselves suffering from the aftermath of trauma and have no help available through the job, the alternative is to seek help through their doctor. However, even then some GPs may have very little knowledge of PTS thus making diagnoses and treatment rather hit and miss.

Defusing

Immediately following an incident, before the individual or team go off duty, it is vital that a defusing or 'demobilisation' is carried out. This is best undertaken by a member of the group who was at the scene or by an immediate supervisor. The process need take no longer than ten to fifteen minutes, its primary aim being to check out how everyone is feeling and if they are now feeling calm enough to travel home. This time is also used to reassure them that any unusual or unpleasant feelings they may experience are a normal reaction to experiencing an abnormal event and their symptoms should gradually subside over the next few days. Officers should be reminded that if they find memories of the incident becoming more intrusive into their everyday lives over the next few weeks that they should seek help. If a more formal debriefing session is required (not to be confused with 'operational debriefing') officers can be notified of when and where this is likely to take place. The defusing time may also be used by those present as an opportunity to discuss what has happened and express how they are feeling. In many instances defusing occurs naturally and spontaneously.

For most situations that occur in everyday policing this informal defusing is sufficient to allow officers to 'off-load', and to reduce the likelihood of on-going or long term problems from the incident. Supervisors and colleagues should be especially vigilant of officers who have been exposed to a serious incident while alone and would benefit from the opportunity to talk through their experience with a sympathetic colleague or friend who is a good listener. Many officers will be able to go home and talk through the events they have witnessed and share their experience with partners, friends or family. Some officers will not have this support readily available. For individuals in this situation it is particularly important they are reassured and given the opportunity to talk about what has happened to them before they go off duty. Following a traumatic incident those who were involved should be monitored over the next few weeks by their supervisors to ensure they have fully recovered and are not suffering any unpleasant or uncomfortable effects. People who bottle up their feelings immediately following a serious incident have an increased risk of developing a serious post traumatic stress reaction at a later date.

Critical incident stress debriefing (CISD)

When an officer has gone through a traumatic experience or an individual is observed to have experienced a very strong emotional reaction to something he has dealt with, CISD is a very effective way of relieving the build up of post trauma stress symptoms. Research has shown that if CISD is carried out shortly after an incident the likelihood of individuals going on to develop a serious long term stress reaction is reduced by up to 80 per cent. CISD is **not** a counselling session and is totally separate from the operational debriefing.

CISD can be carried out individually or in a group. If several officers are involved they should, whenever possible, be debriefed as a group. For large-scale incidents officers will need to be divided into manageable sized groups, usually with the colleagues they work alongside. In some incidents this could mean a multi-disciplinary approach, ie fire, ambulance and police personnel being debriefed together.

The aim of CISD is to reduce unnecessary psychological after effects. Ideally CISD should take place 48 to 72 hours after the incident finishes. It may still be effective if there is a delay but the longer the debriefing is left the less useful it is likely to be. The importance and benefits of CISD are now widely recognised by police welfare departments and occupational health units throughout the United Kingdom. Many police forces have their own trained debriefers who can be available at short notice to deal with staff who have been involved in a traumatic incident. CISD can be effectively carried out by any person who has been properly trained to use the techniques. Confidentiality must be agreed by the group with no notes being taken. Follow up reports are made.

CISD involves moving people through the incident from beginning to end. During the session each person will be invited to share not only what their particular role was but also how they felt, what they saw, heard and smelt, impressions they gained, their emotions, physical symptoms anxieties and concerns. Further support is offered as required. The intention of the debrief is to 'normalise' the effects of trauma and reduce the possibility of deeper symptoms emerging at a later stage. When group debriefing takes place, it is also effective in encouraging peer support. Each member of the group is invited to participate, reassuring and encouraging anyone who is anxious about how the incident has made them feel to share their concerns.

Group CISD sessions enable everyone to be dealt with in the same way, no individual is made to feel less capable than their colleagues or identified by management as someone who 'has problems' following an incident. CISD should be regarded as a pro-active safety net. It is often impossible to say who is going to develop unpleasant psychological symptoms following an incident. The effects of a specific trauma may not be obvious for weeks, months or years.

Post traumatic stress disorder

Where there has been exposure to an event which is outside the range of normal human experience many people will experience some sort of reaction. This is a perfectly normal response to an abnormal situation. For most people any unpleasant symptoms will subside over the following weeks and they will continue with life as before. If any of the following symptoms develop or get progressively worse then help should be sought.

Symptoms

Flash backs, nightmares, avoidance, poor sleep patterns, mood swings, irritability, phobias, guilt, emotional numbness, relationship problems, poor memory, loss of concentration, hypervigilance, exaggerated startle response, violent outbursts, joint and muscle pains, nervousness, depression, anxiety. These symptoms may be evident within a short while of the incident or in some cases will occur a considerable time after the traumatic event. Being equipped, trained and prepared for a major incident reduces the likelihood of officers developing long term post trauma reactions. However, PTSD may develop because the individual has been subjected to a series of traumatic events and has reached the point of 'overload.' Example: a traffic officer may have had to deal with one too many fatal road accidents and now feels he can no longer cope with that situation.

Another scenario could be the police officer who has suffered several potentially serious assaults in a relatively short space of time and realises he has begun to feel very frightened and vulnerable when dealing with situations where he may possibly be injured or assaulted again. Developing PTSD is not a sign of weakness or lack of moral fibre and could affect any officer at any time in their service. By implementing Defusing and Debriefing techniques the possibility of developing Post Trauma Stress Disorder is significantly reduced.

CHAPTER 19

USEFUL INFORMATION

Chapter contents

Expenses **292**
    Basic allowances 292
    Other allowances/expenses 293
Sick pay/pensions **293**
    Death or permanent disability 293
    Permanent partial disability 293
    Injuries 294
Pay for specials **295**
Uniform and equipment **296**
The Ferrers trophy **297**
Associations and further sources of information **300**
    The Black Police Association 300
    European Police Information Centre (EPI-centre) .. 300
    International Police Association (IPA) 301
    Magazines 301
        Special Beat 301
        Police Review 301
    Further reading 302

Expenses

The 1965 Special Constables Regulations stipulate that a special 'may be reimbursed any out of pocket expenses reasonably incurred by him in the execution of his duty or paid an allowance in lieu of such reimbursement'.

The allowance system

Basic allowances

There are three basic allowances are payable to specials:
1. refreshment;
2. boot, and
3. tights/stockings.

1. Refreshment/subsistence allowance - The Home Office circular which lists all expenses explains that the refreshment allowance (from September 11, 1989 onwards) is payable to a special 'who incurs expenditure to obtain a meal'. The rates (which change regularly) are the same as for regular officers.

The Home Office position is that the allowance can only be paid in reimbursement - it should not be paid as an 'attendance' allowance. However, the wording of the regulation suggests that the entire allowance is paid, irrespective of how much the special spends on the meal.

Under the Police Regulations, regular officers can claim the meal allowance if they work for two hours beyond their normal duty time. Most forces take this to mean that specials can claim the meal allowance if they do duty for more than two hours.

However, the rules for special constable allowances are not explicit and some forces have re-interpreted payment of expenses.

For instance, in 1992, West Midlands ruled that a special constable's normal tour of duty, including travel to and from the police station, was five hours. Using the 'two hour' rule, the force decided this meant special constables could not receive the refreshment allowance until they had worked seven hours. Naturally, this almost entirely eliminated specials' expenses claims. The most seriously disadvantaged officers were those who worked mid-week football matches straight after a day's work, and the move by the force lead to a 'work to rule' as specials boycotted football games.

However, not all forces have paid their specials the refreshment allowance. Indeed, in some of the larger forces, the practice varies between divisions.

2. Boot allowance - Payable annually in arrears.

3. Tights and stockings allowance - This is payable on a *pro rata* basis under regulation 55 of the Police Regulations according to the average number of hours worked by women specials in a force.

Under new Regulations - based on the recommendations of the Home Office Working Group 1996 and the Standing Committee on the Special Constabulary November 1998 - the reimbursement of out-of-pocket expense or lost remuneration as a result of duty will will be mandatory. At the time of going to press (July 1999) it is envisaged that these Regulations will be in force by the latter half of 2000. Prior to this the Home Office recommends that forces follow the Working Group recommendation

Other allowance/expenses

Travelling expenses. Travel costs to and from duty may be paid as a direct reimbursement of public transport costs or as an allowance. A mileage allowance can be paid under the same circumstances in which it would be paid to a regular officer. Some larger rural forces with poor public transport facilities regularly pay a mileage allowance.

Other out of pocket expenses. The situation has been that other out of pocket expenses not covered by a statutory allowance 'may be paid by the force at the discretion of the chief constable'. The most common of these are telephone and postal costs and uniform cleaning. However as mentioned above - as recommended by the Working Group and to be made statute, 'the reimbursement of out-of-pocket expense or lost remuneration [see below] as a result of duty will will be mandatory'.

Reimbursement of lost income. If a special is required to work by his force during his normal work time, he will be paid an allowance equal to his actual daily loss of earnings in his private employment. This normally refers to attendance at court, but would also include duties at national or local emergencies. However, the allowance can be paid for attendance at compulsory duties only. It is not available for specials who perform duty at work-time operations where this attendance is voluntary.

Sick pay/pensions

On paper, specials who are injured or killed on duty would appear to be well provided for by sick pay and pension regulations. However, loopholes have in the past left some injured officers living on minimal state benefits.

Death or permanent disability

The Special Constables Regulations 1965 apply should a special be permanently disabled so that he is incapable of *any* kind of employment, or dies within 12 months because of injuries received on duty. In such cases, there is a gratuity of five times the annual pensionable pay of a regular officer payable to the special's dependent(s). There would also be a pension entitlement on the same basis as that for a regular constable under the 1987 Police Pension Regulations.

In the event of death or a serious disabling injury, a pension is payable to specials which will be based on the pensionable pay of a regular constable up to a maximum of 14 years' service. This provision will be brought within the new Regulations currently being drafted by the Home Office (at the time of going to press (July 1999)) and should be in force by late 1999 early 2000).

Permanent partial disability

The Home Office definition of partial disability is that an injured officer cannot carry out the duties of a special constable nor can he continue in his ordinary employment (but is not incapable of *any* employment). In this case, the special is entitled to a gratuity and pension on the same basis as would be paid to a regular constable with the same length of service up to a maximum of 10 years.

If a special is disabled but that disability does not prevent him carrying on with his job, then he is not eligible for these awards.

If the special is unemployed, the pension and gratuity will still be payable if his ability to perform his usual job is affected.

Injuries

New Regulations covering compensation for loss of earning due to injury sustained on duty will be in force late 1999 / early 2000. These will be based on the recommendations of the Home Office Working Group 1996 and the Standing Committee on the Special Constabulary November 1998.

Under these new Regulations, should a special constable - as a result of injury or illness sustained as a result of his Special Constabulary duties - be on sick leave without pay from his regular employment, it will be mandatory for the police authority to provide his full pay for the first six months and then half pay for the second six months. At the discretion of the chief officer, full pay may also be given for the second six months.

In the past injury has proved a thorny area of sick pay and pension entitlement. The situation prior to the recommendations has been that:

> Home Office guidance states that there is 'no provision' for a special who is unfit beyond 28 weeks but is expected to make a full recovery. This is the grey area between injury and permanent (partial) disability which has caught out some specials in the past and left them living on state sickness or state unemployment benefit.

The new recommendations and Regulations will go some way to redressing this in providing for the mandatory and further discretionary payment by the Police Authority for the second six months.

However injuries sustained on duty will still cause problems because the Regulations, not wishing to seem unfair to regular offices, have followed current provisions for regulars which is based on compensation for actual loss of earnings. There is no provision for expenses incurred due to injury, or for injury *per se*.

> A special could still end up out of pocket, as expenses incurred as a result of the injury, such as child care or medical treatment, cannot be reclaimed.

> More importantly, a special who loses his job (but is expected to make a full recovery) cannot be paid sick pay at the same rate as if he were still in employment. Neither can an unemployed special be paid under this provision because there is no 'actual' loss of earnings. Any claim that the injury prevented the special from getting a job would refer to a loss of 'notional', not actual, earnings.

> Akin to the situation regarding permanent partial disability (above), a Special cannot be compensated for injury or disfigurement sustained on duty, even if permanent, if it will not affect his ability to carry out his work - an example would be losing the end of a finger.

Private insurance cover against injury on duty

Because of the perceived inadequacy in some areas of the regulations, some forces have taken out group insurance cover for their reserve officers. However, the Home Office's official position is that police authorities are not empowered to do so because there are already statutory provisions for injured specials. The effect of this restriction, the Home Office says, is that any personal accident insurance contracts are not enforceable in law. It also advises specials to check with their own insurers that they remain covered while performing police duties.

However, a ruling from the Association of British Insurers in 1992 said that specials should not pay surcharges on their life insurance policies. This followed complaints from the Association of Chief Police Officers (ACPO) that some specials had been refused cover and told that mortgage polices might be affected. The ABI said regular officers did not attract uprated premiums and specials were considered 'standard risks'. Permanent health insurance though, which guarantees payment of loss of earnings during long-term illness, might be uprated.

Industrial injuries benefits

Specials who are injured on duty are entitled to claim State Industrial Injuries Disablement Benefit, which is explained in booklets NI2 and NI6 available from DSS offices. This follows the case of a Merseyside special who was injured during the 1992 Grand National but refused benefits because he was 'not classed as an employed earner'. As a result, guidelines were issued to DSS officers clarifying that specials are eligible for sliding scale weekly payments.

Pay for specials

The idea of paying special constables has been around for some time. Some were paid during the Second World War and the idea of an annual 'bounty' payment has been mooted at regular intervals since then, although there was no support when the topic was raised in 1967, 1981 and 1987.

However, bounty payments became a fact for one force between 1991 and 1993. This came about as part of the Home Office's recruitment campaign for specials, which began in 1991. The aim was not only to reward the commitment of serving specials but also act as an incentive to join the service and deter those already in from leaving. It was also hoped the money would lead to the completion of more duty time. Under the proposed bounty, officers completing 250 hours in a year would receive £400. A 1991 amendment to the 1965 Special Constables Regulations - which previously prohibited payment to specials - empowered police authorities to pay the bounty.

The Home Office intended the payment to be tax free, along the lines of the bounty paid to the Territorial Army, and four forces agreed to run trials on this assumption. However, the Inland Revenue intervened, stipulating that any payment made to specials would be liable to income tax. Taxed bounty payments would then have altered the status of specials from volunteers to employees, which meant that the allowances most frequently claimed by specials - refreshment allowance and travel to and from duty - would also be taxable. Not only this, but specials who did not receive the bounty because they did less than 250 hours, would still have their allowances taxed. After the Inland Revenue's decision the four pilot forces withdrew from the scheme.

Dorset was the only force to take up the offer and its two-year experiment (backdated to October 1991) then became the official Home Office pilot project. Specials paid the tax on the bounty at source, but the police authority met the tax due on allowances. In October 1994, an internal report said that the payment had not improved recruitment or retention levels, nor had it resulted in more hours (duty time had increased, but this could have been due to other factors) and Dorset decided to discontinue the bounty, which had cost the police authority £108,000 over two years, and spend the money earmarked for the third year on better equipment for the specials.

In the light of the Dorset evaluation, the Home Office decided not to make the bounty mandatory for all forces. However, as the amendment to the 1965 Special Constables Regulations remains in force, and there are no plans to repeal it, any police authority can pay specials if it wishes to, and introduce the bounty at any time in the future.

Uniform and equipment

Uniform issued to specials has varied over time and between forces. Until 1990, specials everywhere wore flat caps and, in most forces, the 'Special Constabulary' shoulder flash. A few forces used a less conspicuous epaulette flash, but Devon and Cornwall had a 'Special Constabulary Police Reserve' shoulder flash. In 1990, the City of London Police reintroduced the Special Constabulary logo worn until the early 1970s - the letters 'SC' surmounted by a crown and worn on the epaulette. The Met soon followed suit and a handful of forces, including Gwent, Bedfordshire and Northumbria, have this discreet insignia.

The most significant change in uniform was initiated by the Met which, at the beginning of 1991, switched from flat caps to helmets. The majority of forces in England and Wales now issue their male specials with traditional police helmets.

In the latest move to 'uniformity', Specials in Hampshire removed their shoulder insignia during a pilot project which took place from February to March 1999. The trial was a move to redress the problem of specials being identified as targets in public order situations. One hundred and fifty specials surveyed said they had problems if recognised as a special while out on patrol. Particularly on Friday and Saturday nights they suffered verbal abuse and people refused to believe that they had the power of arrest. Regular officers can identify another officer as a special by the full colour number, but to members of the public they are indistinguishable without the shoulder flash. The results of the pilot will be evaluated by the force's research and development department.

The items and quantity of uniform issued to specials is a matter for each force. Specials are often issued with a smaller quantity of equipment - fewer shirts or blouses for instance - than regulars. There has been some criticism by specials over recent years that they are also likely to be the last to get new or the most up-to-date pieces of kit. However, with the increased use of the Special Constabulary, more and more forces are equipping their volunteers as they equip their regulars (see cover pictures). The majority of specials wear identical uniform to the regulars and receive batons, quickcuffs radios (and CS spray where applicable) after the appropriate training.

The recommendations of the Home Office Working Group are that 'a special constable's uniform should [other than suitable insignia] be identical in design, colour and material to that of a regular officer, with the issue of standard helmets or headgear and the same colour shirts...' (see Chapter 20 for further details of the recommendations).

The Ferrers Trophy

This Trophy is awarded annually to honour the outstanding special constable of the year, and was inaugurated by Lord Ferrers, Home Office Minister of State, in 1993. The award is 'emphatically' not a matter of counting the largest number of hours spent on duty. The award winner is an individual who is judged to have made the most significant contribution to the policing of his or her area. The award is also open to groups of specials.

The Trophy will highlight over the years the great variety of ways in which special constables bring their abilities, talents and qualities to bear in the work of policing.

The award might recognise:
    (a) a particularly skilled piece of policing;
    (b) sustained involvement with a successful community initiative;
    (c) the application of personal skills to resolving a long-standing problem;
    (d) any other personal contribution to policing the community.

Nominations for the Ferrers Trophy 'Special of the Year' are accepted by the Home Office during January of each year and details of the award are sent to all forces. The selection panel comprises HM Chief Inspector of Constabulary, a chief constable and a chief executive from trade or industry.

Ferrers Trophy awards

1993

Winner
SC Debbie Jones
South Yorkshire
Runner up
SDO John Brett
Nottinghamshire
Highly commended
SC Gillian Curtis
Humberside
SC Terrence Dobbins
West Midlands
Div Comm Peter Mould
Hertfordshire

1994

Winner
SDO Phillip Carroll
West Mercia
Runners up
SDO Derek Holden
Lancashire
SDO Jacqueline Price
Leicestershire
Highly commended
CDO Brian Peters
Sussex
SDO Stephen Barron
Dorset
SC Michael Bunce
West Midlands
SC Christine Cockrem
SC Harbans Singh Dogra
West Yorkshire

1995

Winners
SO Val Waite
SC Gale Arnold
North Yorkshire
Runner up
SC Max Deverill
Hertfordshire
Highly commended
SC Samuel Black
West Mercia
SO Judith Bokor-Ingram
Sussex
Div Comm Kevin McGetrick
Hertfordshire
SC George Slack
West Yorkshire
Wrexham team
North Wales

1996

Winner
SC Glenn Michell
Essex
Runners up
SC Helen Bell
Derbyshire
SC Graham Ball
West Mercia

Ferrers Trophy awards (cont...)

1996 (cont)

Highly commended
DO Francis Brown
Cambridgeshire
SC Robert Crossland
Avon & Somerset
DO David Turner
SC Paul Griffin
South Yorkshire
SO David Swan
Suffolk
Unit Officer Hazel Wood
Northumbria
Leicestershire team
Leicestershire

1997

Winner
Div Comm Julie Holmes
West Yorkshire
Runner up
SC Neil Parker
Derbyshire
Highly commended
SO Andrew Fogden
Gloucestershire
SC Philip Whitmore
Nottinghamshire
SO Philip Wright
Norfolk
Weymouth team
Dorset
Partnership Award
SC Jonathan Britton
SC Kerry Hemenway
North Yorkshire
Special Award (posthumous)
SC Tina Chant
Avon & Somerset

1998

Winner
SO Gail Walford
Leicestershire
Runner up
SO Derek Hopkins
Essex
Highly commended
Sp Chief Insp David Burgess-Joyce
Merseyside
SC Simon Venguedasalon
Lancashire
Sc Kay Williams
Kent
SC Michael Dunn
SC Graham Goulbourn
Durham
SC Karen Harding
SC Lisa Root
SC Kathryn Wilson
Hertfordshire

1999

Winner
SO Robert Tomkins
West Mercia
Runner up
SC Katherine Major
Kent
Highly commended
SC Sue Evans
Suffolk
SC Michael Clapham
Thames Valley
Div Commandant Julie Holmes
West Yorkshire
Mid Bedfordshre team
Bedfordshire
Special Award
SC Olwen Taylor
Avon and Somerset

Associations and further sources of information

The Black Police Associations

The Black Police Association (BPA) was founded on a local level. Its beginnings were in the Metropolitan Police during 1993, with this first branch formally established in 1994. Bedfordshire Police, Leicestershire Constabulary and Northamptonshire Police followed suit and, in 1999, there are now 12 Black Police Association branches in the UK.

The first meeting of BPAs and individuals was held at Bramshill in October 1996 and the National Association came into being in November 1998 with Home Office backing and Government support. (There will be a launch on November 29, 1999.)

'The primary object of the National Black Police Association,' says its National Co-ordinator, David McFairlaine, is 'to improve the working environment for ethnic minority staff with a view to enhancing the quality of service to the ethnic minority communities in the UK'.

The National Association has a current programme of visits and presentations to forces around the country (including Scotland and Northern Ireland) to offer support, guidance and encouragement for ethnic minority policing and recruiting strategy. Force policy is a matter for individual forces and the the local branches of the association, but the message from the National Black Police Association is that all forces should do everything within their power to recruit officers from all ethnic minorities.

The association's membership includes special and regular officers of all ranks and grades and also civilian staff. If staff need further information they can contact the national office:
Tel 0171 273 3249 Fax 0171 273 3249
E-mail nationalblackpoliceassociation@yahoo.com

European Police Information Centre (EPI-Centre)

A conference facility for the Special Constabulary has been set up on the Police Scientific Development Branch's (PSDB's) intranet - the European Police Information Centre (EPI-Centre). The purpose of the Special Constabulary conference is to encourage the exchange of information and views on issues relating to special constables. Home Office circulars concerning the Special Constabulary would for example, be accessible via the conference. All Special Constabularies require to obtain access is force agreement and a stand-alone computer and modem.

The International Police Association (IPA)

The IPA is a friendship and travel organisation for serving and retired police officers and members of the Special Constabulary. It has more than 250,000 members worldwide in 60 countries throughout the world. Its aims are to cultivate friendly relations and mutual assistance between members at home and abroad.

The International Travel Form Scheme is a popular feature of IPA. Here members request assistance of fellow members overseas - whether it be simply to meet up, or to recieve help in making arrangements. Another facility which attracts a great deal of interest is the provision of IPA Houses. These include accomodation obtained and maintained by local members for use by visitors at very good rates.

Additional information can be obtained from:
IPA National HQ, 1 Fox Road, West Bridgford, Nottingham NG2 6AJ
Tel 0115 981 3638   E-mail: IPAGB@compuserve.com   or   www.ipa-uk.org

Magazines

Special Beat

Special Beat is written specifically for specials and was launched in January 1991. The magazine is published quarterly and is free to serving members of the Special Constabulary. Both lively and colourful, it contains news, topical issues and features. It covers everything that touches on the lives of special constables and is avidly read by regular officers when they can get their hands on it. Its letters page is particularly illuminating, fielding no-nonsense, no-holds-barred expressions of heartfelt feelings from specials who have something to say and know how to say it. Everything is aired here, the great helmet debate, expenses, the quality and quantity of uniform, disciplinary procedures, rank structure, you name it, they publish it. It is especially warming to see the occasional apology under the heading 'sorry'.

Each issue contains a reply paid card which new specials are invited to complete and dispatch to secure delivery directly to their home address.

Police Review

Police Review magazine has been published weekly since January 1893, and is the most widely read police publication in the country. Its founder, John Kempster, wrote in the first issue:

> 'It must be for the advantage of all concerned that there should be a recognised medium of inter-communication for the public guardians of law and order... it should not be considered in any sense prejudicial to the best interest of the force that one policeman should speak to all his colleagues through the medium of the press.'

Since that time, over 100 years ago, *Police Review* has gone from strength to strength, to a point whereby the magazine is a major tool in lobbying support for the police and giving voice to the officers on the ground. The *Review* has maintained a balance between representing the views of officers on all matters which concern their working life, supporting the increasing professionalism of the police service, assisting the substantial core of customers who are interested in furthering their careers, and - fortunately less frequently than was the case in its early years - providing a platform for officers with a genuine grievance.

The *Review* contains regular features, news, comment, letters, details of new legislation and a wealth of other information including classified advertisements. It advertises books and training services as well as uniform and equipment and other items of special interest to police officers. *Police Review*'s annual subscription is currently (July 1999) priced at £63.75. Payment can be made by credit card (Tel 0171 440 4732) or by cheque made payable to Police Review Publishing Co (Freepost LONDON WC1V 7BR). Alternately you can order *Police Review* through your local newsagents.

Books

For the special who has completed his initial training (and read *The Special Constable's Manual!*) and wishes to expand his knowledge and understanding of chosen subject areas, the following titles provide useful further reading.

Crime Patrol: to recognise and arrest criminals
First edition 1998, Mike McBride. New Police Bookshop: £12.50

Crime Patrol has been written for every officer who wishes to improve his or her patrolling skills and provides an invaluable source of practical advice. *Crime Patrol* explains the motivation and techniques required to intercept criminals and arrest them. It deals in detail with the core skills of observation, field interviewing and searching vehicles and aims to further officers' knowledge of common crime. *Crime Patrol* is issued by several forces to their probationary officers before they commence independent patrol. Probationers and regular PCs have described it as a 'varied source of reference and practical advise' providing 'easy reading', but 'even an experienced PC of 20 years could learn something from it'.

Investigative Interviewing Explained
First edition 1999, Brian Ord and Gary Shaw. New Police Bookshop: £12.50

Investigative Interviewing Explained is an 'easy to read and easy to understand guide' (John Stevens, Deputy Commissioner, Metropolitan Police), written for all officers who wish to develop their core interviewing skills. For specials who wish to further their knowledge of practical interviewing techniques, then *Investigative Interviewing Explained* is the book for them. Using flow charts and examples, it explains in detail the structure and considerations of both witness and suspect interviews, and gives a practical interpretation of the relevant legislation. It has been described by Investigative Interviewing Trainers as 'offering a good coverage of the subject' and a 'a useful source of reference'.

The Beat Officer's Companion
Seventh edition 1999/2000 (currently in production), Gordon Wilson. Police Review Publishing: price tba (likely to be c£19.95).

The Beat Officer's Companion provides a practical and speedy reference to those aspects of legislation likely to be of operational value to the patrolling police officer (with the exception of traffic laws). Diagrams, flow charts and illustrations combine to provide an easily read and understandable interpretation.

The Drug Officer's Companion
first edition 1997, Paul Harper & Steve Dalrymple, Police Review Publishing: £16.35

The Drug Officer's Companion is intended for street level officers and their supervisors. It provides a quick and easy source of reference and the background knowledge vital for successful drugs investigations. 'All police officers have a responsibility to investigate offences relating to the misuse of drugs at street and community level. This book aims to assist officers to carry out that responsibility safely and effectively' (DA Leonard, Chief Constable, Humberside Police).

Street Survival Skills
First edition 1996, Mike McBride. Police Review Publishing: £17.85

The aim of the book is to assist the operational police officer to improve his or her safety. By developing street survival skills, officers will become more confident in handling incidents and be able to act without hesitation to protect both themselves and the public. 'This book reflects and consolidates so much good practice and will become an essential aid to those who consider officer safety. The most important aspect of training is that the operational officer understands, can use, and relates to the advice that is offered. This book does all those things, it is not just a trainer's manual,' (F H J Broughton, Chairman, Police Federation of England and Wales).

Points to Prove
revised fourth edition 1997, Stewart Calligan. Police Review Publishing: £12.75

What are the points to prove? What do the points mean? How are the points proved or disproved. What about supporting evidence? '"Simplicity is an aid to learning." With this statement in mind, I have concentrated on the points to prove for some 75 offences which can be found in the Police Summons and Charges lists and in the Magistrates' Court sheets on most days of the week' (Stewart Calligan).

Taking Statements
revised fourth edition 1997, Stewart Calligan. Police Review Publishing: £9.75

'An essential tool in the everyday collection of evidence is the police officer's skill in recording that evidence on paper. This includes the experiences and observations of witness to an incident, defendants, and the officer's own observations and actions.' The aim of *Taking Statements* is to improve the standard and professionalism of statement taking and fill the gap between theory and practice. Part I of the book deals with the necessity for statements, the law regarding statements, and procedures for unusual statements. Part II provides a ready-made sample collection of the more common types of statement found daily in magistrates' courts.

Summonses and Charges
tenth edition 1995, Jack English. Police Review Publishing: £13.75

The primary objective of this book is to provide police officers with a quick reference to charges which they may require in the course of their daily work. The author has included both charges in the true sense ie those which would be recorded on a charge sheet, and offences which would normally be dealt with by way of summons. To assist speedy reference, the contents of the book have been divided into two parts: the first dealing with all matters other than road traffic, and the second with road traffic matters. Within these divisions the contents table lists alphabetically the Acts of Parliament from which charges have been drafted and the numbers of the charges which refer to each particular Act.

To order any of the books listed:

for New Police Bookshop titles contact Brookland Mailing Services
Unit 5, Parkway Trading Estate, St Werburghs, Bristol BS2 9PG
Tel 0117 9555 215   Fax 0117 9541 485
Email npb@brookservices.demon.co.uk

for Police Review Publishing titles contact the book inquiries department
Tel 0171 440 4703   Fax 0171 4057167 or write to
Police Review Publishing, Celcon House
289-293 High Holborn London WC1V 7HZ

The author would welcome any suggestions for this chapter, whether general information or further reading, which would help contribute to the provision of 'useful information' for Specials. Please contact the Publisher c/o Brookland Mailing Services (details as above) or E-mail; tombarron1033@yahoo.co.uk

CHAPTER 20

CHANGES TO TERMS AND CONDITIONS OF SERVICE

Chapter contents

Recommendation and implementation 306
Home Office Working Group Recommendations......... 307
    Role and purpose 307
    Retention 307
    Leave of absence 308
    Transfers 308
    Employer support 308
    Grading structure.. 309
    Promotion 310
    Special Constabulary insignia 311
    Eligibility for appointment................................... 312
    Age 312
    Requirement to retire 313
    Ineligible occupations 313
    Recruitment.. 315
    Training 317
    Representation 318
    Complaints and discipline................................... 318
    Resignation 320
    IMPORTANT NEW CONDITIONS 321
Health and safety...321
    Hours of work 321
    Rest periods 322
Compensation for injury...322
Legal representation..323
Complaints and discipline..324
Transfers 324
Other conditions of service...334

Recommendations and implementation

The establishment of a Working Group to review the full range of terms and conditions of service of special constables, as well as current deployment and organisational practices was announced on 29 March 1995 by the Minister of State for the Home Office. The Working Group was to examine the totality of the workings of the special constabulary and in particular:

> personnel issues;
> training;
> complaints;
> discipline;
> unsatisfactory performance;
> grievance procedure.

The report and recommendations of the Home Office Working Group was published in August 1996.

Following further review and recommendation by the The Standing Committee on the Special Constabulary at its inaugural meeting in November 1998, the Home Office has undertaken the process of implementing a number of the recommendations on a statutory basis (others being made the subject of guidance). At the time of going to press (July 1999) this process will be ongoing for a further 12 months and should be complete by the latter half of 2000.

In the majority of situations the Regulations will reflect the recommendations of the Working Group. When this is not the case, it is likely to be in concession to the overriding aim to follow as closely as possible the policies for regular officers.

Where Regulation has yet to be implemented the Home Office's general recommendation is for forces to follow the Working Group recommendations

Home Office Working Group Recommendations

A summary of subjects covered and views expressed - August 96

Role and purpose of the Special Constabulary

The Special Constabulary is a voluntary body designed to assist the regular police, drawn mainly from the communities a police force serves. Special constables perform constabulary duties and exercise constabulary powers under the supervision of, and supported by, regular police officers. They should achieve and maintain a level of proficiency which will enable them to assist regular officers in solving local policing problems, and thereby to enhance the overall contribution and effectiveness of their local police force. This may be achieved by working with regular officers on routine duties: by freeing regular officers, in the event of an emergency calling for large-scale police deployment, by taking over their normal functions (such as manning local police stations); or by providing police support at local public and ceremonial events. They are a manifest sign of partnership between the police and the public.

Retention

Every year about 5,000 specials are recruited and a similar number leave.* Many last less than two years. Although there is a level of unavoidable loss to Special Constabularies, it is thought there is a great deal which can be done to reduce losses overall. It is recommended that police forces should be required by Regulation, as they are for regular officers, to keep personal records for each serving special constable, that these personal records are transferred from one force to another if the special constable transfers forces, and that these records form the basis of a certificate to be issued to every special on leaving service.

An annual appraisal system for individual performance development is essential. Any such system should have the following characteristics:
(a) regular, ideally annual;
(b) a record of discussion between the appraisee and the immediate manager, seen and commented on by the appraisee;
(c) reviewed and countersigned by the manager's manager or by another more senior officer;
(d) a review of performance, achievement and objectives, which notes the individual's strength and skills, but also identifies areas for improvement;
(e) performance is reviewed against objectives, key result areas and performance standards as described in a job description;
(f) contains a summary of overall performance over the period;
(g) contains a recommendation about the training and work experience required for immediate job performance and for longer term development.

* In 1998 approximately 2,600 were recruited and 3,600 resigned

Leave of absence

Any person devoting private time to public benefit is likely to face occasions when the demands of paid employment or domestic commitments reduce or preclude such activity. Forces should have policies providing for a quasi 'career break', which would enable voluntary personnel to be freed from work demands of duties as a special constable for a defined period of time without, as at present, being asked to resign their appointment. Such a leave of absence should not be unreasonably denied. On that basis the chief constable should take into account the special constable's record and performance as well as the reasons given for the application. Leave of absence should not be granted if it is likely to exceed one year and the expectation should be that, normally, it will be much less.

Transfers

There is a strong view that a special constable appointed through processes which show that he or she is performing duties of a special constable to the satisfaction of his or her force, should have the right to request a transfer with retained seniority to the Special Constabulary of another force, and this should not unreasonably be refused.

It is recommended this course of action is based on the career needs of the special constable which lie wholly separate from those of regular officers; the present waste of talent and investment due to the absence of transfer systems is intolerable in resource terms. The transferring force should provide appropriate information to the force requested by the special constable. The receiving force should then arrange an interview on a mutually agreed date with the special constable to evaluate any special needs in terms of base location and introduction. Where vacancies exist, special constables who have achieved any particular grade should be allowed to apply to be considered at that level or an equivalent one.

Each force should have procedures and policies to administer transfers and the process of acceptance or rejection should be completed within eight weeks of the request for transfer being received. If there are delays in the system due to attestation dates, induction training or local administrative difficulties, the special constable concerned should be placed at the head of the waiting list. Local supervisors should be asked to take advantage of any opportunities which arise in the interim to allow the applicant to meet future colleagues.

Employer support

It is recommended that arrangements, which should be appropriately funded, are made:
    (a) to raise the standing of the Special Constabulary among employers, specials' peers in the employing organisation and families, and
    (b) to secure the support of employers for those employees who are members of the Special Constabulary.

Efforts should be made at the national level to promote the Special Constabulary and further understanding of the role of specials by preparing materials, lobbying and campaigning, and at the local level committees, run by specials and former specials with the support of the force chief officer, could provide support, contacts and general liaison among employers.

Grading structure

It is recommended that it should be left to the discretion of forces to decide whether the administration of the Special Constabulary is carried out by civilian staff or members of the Special Constabulary themselves. It seems sensible to suggest that a level of operational supervision should be undertaken by Special Constabulary officers. While for a vast percentage of their time, special constables could be properly utilised and well integrated into the regular force by becoming part of the local section of shift and supervised by regular sergeants, there are many occasions when it is quite proper for operations to be run almost exclusively by members of the Special Constabulary, and in these cases operational supervision would be necessary.

Members of the Special Constabulary require their own command structure for management, representation and leadership. There is therefore a need for a grading structure within the Special Constabulary.

Levels of supervision - It is recommended that there should be no more than five grades of special constable overall, with an expectation that few forces would need more than four. These should be:
 (1) special constable;
 (2) section officer;
 (3) divisional/area/district officer;
 (4) force commandant.

Whatever titles are chosen, they will informally be equated to the Special Constabulary equivalent of:
 (1) constable;
 (2) sergeant;
 (3) inspector;
 (4) superintendent.

Grade insignia - It is recommended that the replacement of chevrons and stars with simple bars should continue thus:
 > Section officer .... 1 bar;
 > assistant divisional/area/district officer .... 2 bars;
 > divisional/area/district officer .... 3 bars;
 > force commandant .... 4 bars.

It is recommended that it should be possible to identify the grade of a special wherever he or she may serve round the country. This means that forces which do not have assistant divisional officers should go straight from one to three bars.

Ratios between grades - It is recommended that there should be an approximate ratio of 10 special constables to one section officer. In view of the earlier conclusion that the duties for senior Special Constabulary grades are restricted compared with those of regulars, there should be a strong encouragement to Forces to have only one divisional officer per division. Devolvement of responsibility is recommended, and to enhance the role of section officers who could, in the absence of the divisional officer, act in that capacity. Similarly even in large forces, there should only be one force commandant.

Promotion

One purpose for promotion which is believed to have existed extensively in the past and, to a certain degree, in the present is that of reward. This is not now favoured. Promotion is not the way to reward officers for long dedicated service. Promotion should only take place within the organisation according to both need and merit. This does not mean that the commitment and contribution made by members of the Special Constabulary should be ignored. Forces should be encouraged to explore means of recognising the work of their specials over and above that offered by long service awards.

It is recommended that all vacancies above special constable should be advertised force wide as a matter of principle. Short-listing and appointments should be by individuals trained in interviewing and selection, with processes and decisions monitored to ensure that they conform to equal opportunities processes. Appropriately trained members of the Special Constabulary should be involved as far as possible in the selection process. Feedback should be offered to both successful and unsuccessful candidates to assist their development.

Appointments should be made with regard to the job description and person profile developed for each post. The use of performance appraisal information, as well as interviews, is essential. Forces should be free to use assessment centres if they wish. This will be helpful in identifying the training needs of candidates who, even if successful, are likely to have training needs in supervision and management in order to fulfil their duties.

Appointments to all grades should be for an initial trial period not exceeding a year, with successful completion resulting in permanent appointment. This trial period should be varied only on performance assessment, disciplinary procedures or by internal organisational change.

Special Constabulary insignia

The debate about the general insignia for the Special Constabulary has continued now over many years. Forces adopt a wide range of means of identifying their specials, from the cloth shoulder emblem depicting the words, 'Special Constabulary', metal or cloth epaulettes carrying the same wording, wording which extends to 'Special Constabulary Police Reserve', through to a small discreet metal emblem depicting 'SC' surmounted by a Crown. In some forces, members of the Special Constabulary are denoted by a different numbering system.

The views of members of the Special Constabulary about the disadvantages of being clearly identified as specials in difficult situations in public are well known and do not need repeating here in detail.

While being part of British policing in general, the Special Constabulary is a distinct element and should be proud to be recognised as such. It is more important for its members to be recognisable within the Service than for the public to be able to distinguish between regulars and specials at a distance and at a glance. This does not mean that when in close and extended contact with the public, there should be any continuing confusion as to whether they are specials or regulars. It is believed that a satisfactory distinguishing mark should be the wearing of the letters 'SC' with the surmounting Crown in a way that would fit with normal force practice on uniform dress, and by allotting specials a unique series of collar numbers.

It is recommended that a special constable's uniform should otherwise be identical in design, colour and material to that of a regular officer, with the issue of standard helmets or headgear and the same colour shirts. Some forces are moving away from helmets towards flat caps for regular officers; where this is acknowledged force policy it is acceptable for the policy to continue and the forces to allow the regulars to catch up with the specials rather than incur the expenditure of changing its arrangements for specials.

It is recommended that the quantity of uniform issued should take account of the average hours an individual contributes, and the shifts or duties on which they are routinely deployed. The issue of specialised items of uniform (such as car coats and NATO sweaters) should also take account of such considerations.

Each special should have access to, and be trained appropriately for, personal protective equipment in line with the force policy towards issue to regular officers on similar deployments. It may be that issue should be personal or in sufficient quantities on a pool basis. It is known that there have been cases where specials have been permitted, or even encouraged, to purchase their own items of uniform and equipment. This is a dangerous practice. If an item is needed it should be provided by the force, which can ensure adequate controls over training and certification. It is otherwise envisaged that liability could become a contentious issue, were injury to officers or the public to result from defective or misused equipment.

All specials patrolling alone should have access to a personal radio or cellphone. Again, this equipment could be provided on a pool basis. Where regular officers working in pairs would share a single radio, the force should have discretion to issue radios to specials on the same basis.

Eligibility for appointment

Only the following persons are eligible for appointment to the Special Constabulary:
> British citizens;
> citizens of British Dependent territories;
> British Overseas citizens;
> Commonwealth citizens, or;
> citizens of the Republic of Ireland -
>> (a) who have that status by birth, naturalisation or registration, and
>> (b) whose residence is not subject to restrictions, and
>> (c) who are not subject to immigration control.

Recommendations for eligibility to become a special are based on the following principles:
(a) people willing to volunteer to serve their local police and communities as special constables should be allowed to do so without unnecessary hindrance;
(b) judgements about personal suitability ought, as far as possible, to be left to chief officers;
(c) eligibility to join [or remain in] the force depends upon people having the general health, fitness, and sufficient ability, to make a positive contribution to the policing of their communities;
(d) in general, those appointed as special constables should be trusted not to abuse or misuse their constabulary powers;
(e) where guidance is given that certain occupations are incompatible with service as a special constable, the principles underlying the guidance should be clearly stated and should be equally comprehensible to both recruitment personnel and applicants.

Age

At present the age for recruitment for the Special Constabulary is 18, this is in contrast with their regular colleagues which is 18 and a half. It is recommended that parity should exist and that the age for special constables should be 18 and a half.

It is recommended that there be no other change to the existing age rules, ie, that 50 should be the maximum age of entry to the Special Constabulary, but that the chief officer should have discretion to accept particularly suitable applicants over this age, and that 55 should be the normal retiring age, especially for the lower grades, with more senior grades retiring at 60 (on the assumption that they would be engaged in administrative rather than vigorously physical duties). Chief officers have discretion to extend these retiring ages by up to 5 years in each case.

Requirement to retire

Ultimately a chief officer has the power to require a special to retire on the grounds of age or infirmity. It is recommended that chief officers should issue clear and understandable guidance to all serving specials about what standards of health, fitness and performance are expected, and that decisions on health and fitness, while ultimately a matter for chief officers, should be grounded on the advice of trained medical personnel.

Decisions about a special's ability to make a positive contribution to policing also should be based on clear criteria with an inbuilt right of appeal against the recommendations of junior officers.

Ineligible occupations

Special constables, like regular officers, possess the powers and privileges of a constable for 24 hours a day, and should not be put into a position where they might be pressured to abuse their powers. Persons in paid employment should not be sworn as special constables in order to enhance their employment function, whether by going beyond the bounds of their job description, by going beyond the restricted law enforcement powers considered suitable by parliament for their profession, or by using Special Constabulary status to gain a business advantage over competitors. Equally individuals should not be sworn as special constables if there is a significant chance that this would lead to conflicts of interest, for themselves or for others.

Medical and health professions -

(a) Staff should not find themselves with a conflict of loyalties between their duties as doctors, nurses, etc., and their responsibilities as special constables, such as would arise if patients told them in a clinical context information relevant to a criminal inquiry;
(b) the relationship between patient and health practitioner should not be inhibited, eg, patients who knew that their doctor was a special constable might feel reluctant about giving him/her information essential to their care. This might particularly be the case in a small community with little choice of medical services.

If an applicant to the Special Constabulary can show that their local NHS Trust or Health Authority would not object to their becoming a special constable, they should be considered eligible for appointment.

The fire service - It is recommended that members of a fire brigade (both regular and retained) be eligible to be sworn as a special constable so long as the chief officer was satisfied that he or she could make a contribution despite the obligations to the fire service.

Traffic wardens and school crossing patrols - The Road Traffic Regulation Act 1984 declares that 'a police authority shall not employ as a traffic warden any person who is a constable'. Because, under the same Act, a school crossing patrol is deemed to be in an analogous position to a traffic warden, constables are also excluded from work as school crossing patrols. It is considered that traffic wardens (and school crossing patrols) have been given specific duties by Parliament and that if their attestation as constables were allowed, their law enforcement powers during their hours of duty in their paid work would thereby be greater than Parliament intended.

Employers' police forces - private constabularies - Private constabularies (parks police, police forces maintained by government departments, and any other bodies with constabulary powers) have powers under the law, and Special Constabulary status would enable them to go beyond the confines of existing legislation in respect of their normal employment.

Private security organisations - Private security organisations, bailiffs, private detectives and enquiry agents should continue to be ineligible to be attested as special constables as they may be tempted to use the police uniform or the police organisation to advance their personal business interests, because they would have constabulary powers and police training, or because they would have access to information as police officers that would be denied them as civilians.

Prison officers - Under the Prison Act 1952, prison officers have the full powers of a constable when on duty. If their managers within the prison service and the police service agree, there is no reason why a prison officer should not be attested a special constable when he is not on duty as a prison officer. While they are working as prison officers, the exercise of constabulary powers will be on the prison service's behalf.

Civilian detention officers - The roles of civilian detention officers and custody escort officers seem the subject of continual debate, but even if further enhanced they will be more limited than those of a special constable. It is difficult not to suspect that those who are also special constables have an advantage over their colleagues in handling suspects. Accordingly therefore, it is recommended that those employed in either category should not be eligible to be attested or to serve as special constables.

Political activity - It is recommended that it should be for the chief officer of each force to decide whether a special can be said to be taking an active part in 'politics' but, as with regulars, there should be an expectation that this includes standing for or serving as a Member of Parliament.

Recruitment

National standards or local criteria? It is recommended that all those involved in the recruitment of volunteers into Special Constabularies abide by common standards and practices and that there should be a minimum standard complied with and that this should be clearly stated. Recruitment of specials should be seen to be both speedy and fair.

Manpower plans - To assist recruitment planning, it is recommended that each force should develop and maintain a manpower plan for its special constabulary showing:
- (a) number of applicants;
- (b) numbers appointed (and categorisation of failures);
- (c) promotion patterns;
- (d) number of exits:
  - (i) by dismissal;
  - (ii) by resignation;
- (e) number of applicants required;
- (f) number of appointees required.

It is recommended that forces collect accurate information about the cost of all aspects of the recruitment, training, and management of special constables and about the hours they contribute on various policing activities, as an essential aid to informed decision-taking.

Sources of volunteers - The Home Office has been running a national advertising campaign since 1994 which has proved very successful in encouraging public interest and support. Many volunteers make an application because they know someone already serving. This is a very important source of recruitment. Serving specials should not encourage applications from among their friends unless they have been properly briefed about the criteria for selection and the demands to be placed upon recruits. It is recommended that a determined effort is made to enlist the support of local communities as is done in Leicestershire and the West Midlands.

Encouraging applications - Applicants should be encouraged to find out more about the Special Constabulary by being invited to talk to serving volunteers, before embarking on the process of a formal application.

'Open evenings' are especially productive where potential recruits are invited to attend police stations, ideally with their families, to find out more about Special Constabulary service in their area. This serves two functions. First, it ensures that applicants and their friends or families have a good idea of what is expected and why the application process is necessarily a protracted one. Secondly, it should reduce the number of wasted applications with which recruitment departments have to deal.

Information pack - It is recommended that potential recruits be sent an information pack which might include:
   (a) a letter from the chief officer;
   (b) something about the history of the force, its mission statement of common purposes and values;
   (c) the role of the Special Constabulary and its place within the force;
   (d) duties and responsibilities, including a job description, person profile, eligibility criteria and the minimum hours expected. Estimate of force resource commitment;
   (e) a description of the training;
   (f) a description of the recruitment process and the personal information which will be required;
   (g) a note aimed at employers referring to the benefits of training, experience and personal development which a special could bring to the employer, and warning of the need for time off for court appearances;
   (h) some questions to aid self-assessment;
   (j) a contact point.

Application forms - A limited version of the force application form for regulars, presented in a user-friendly format, seems appropriate. The forms should reflect the following principles:
   (a) they should be as easy to understand and to complete as possible;
   (b) they should explain why information is required;
   (c) they should explain the criteria by which certain confidential information, such as medical history or the details of previous convictions, will be judged;
   (d) they should give the applicant an opportunity for self-assessment.

The whole recruitment process should not take more than 20 weeks, and ideally should be much shorter.

Recruitment criteria - It is recommended that forces and the security service reassess the priority given to security checks for applicants to the Special Constabulary as delays at this stage result in recruits losing interest. As far as possible parts of the recruitment process should run concurrently, so that the application as a whole is not put on hold. References are of little value unless the referee is asked specific questions. The names of applicants for the post should be checked against local and national criminal records. A blemish on the record of an applicant should not as a matter of principle invalidate their application, although, quite rightly, it should trigger careful consideration of their suitability for appointment.

Assessment tests and training centres - There is no reason in principle why applicants for the Special Constabulary should not take the Police Initial Recruitment test (the same as regular officers). Recruits should be expected to achieve the same pass rate. For the purposes of assessing the candidates it is recommended that assessment centres be used by all forces. Candidates should be interviewed by personnel, including a regular officer, who are trained in assessment procedures and recruitment interview skills.

Outcome of applications - After attending an assessment centre, the outcome should be notified to the applicant on the next working day. Where an applicant is rejected, at any stage of the process, the rejection should be handled in as positive a manner as possible. It is recommended that reasons for rejection be given. Where the applicant has been successful, notification by the force should be congratulatory and personal. It should include a formal offer of appointment and the next steps in the process if the applicant accepts. It is not recommended that attestation as a special constable should wait until after basic training as this is not done for regular officers and the contrast in levels of trust can be demotivating to recruits. It is recommended that all special constables should, like regular officers, be required to have their fingerprints taken.

Training

It is recommended that foundation training in every force conforms to common principles, however it is managed. First there should be an expectation that regular officers will be able to recognise elements of their own probationer training in the training of special constables. Secondly, every force considering an application for transfer by a special constable from a different force area (or even division) should expect to be sufficiently confident about the content and level of training already undergone to be able to accredit the applicants transferring from other forces for prior learning. It is recommended that foundation training for specials, like probation training for regular officers should be linked to the development of the 36 Skills and Abilities to at least Performance Level 2 as described in the Police Training Programme. *(See Appendix A.)*

Tutor constables - It is recommended that every trainee special constable should be attached to a tutor constable. This individual may be a regular officer or special constable, but will have been chosen on the grounds of experience, skill, abilities and aptitude. The tutors should receive appropriate training in tutoring to help them carry out their role. It will be important for tutor constables to:
    (a) encourage trainees to think about how particular incidents or situations should be handled and not just impose a solution;
    (b) encourage trainees to explore alternative ways to deal with occurrences and weigh their options before decision making;
    (c) allow the trainees an opportunity to consider why they took a particular course of action;
    (d) give constructive feedback to trainees on how they have performed;
    (e) provide opportunities for the trainees to discuss their own and the tutor's performance, and to plan strategies to deal with any identified problems;
    (f) debrief the trainee about incidents which occurred in the tutor's absence;
    (g) take responsibility for fostering the trainees' capacity for independent judgement and action.

Post Foundation Training - The Post Foundation programme should consist of:
  (a) the on-the-job aspect of training and development, supervised by suitably experienced special constables, regular officers and the training officers;
  (b) classroom-based training undertaken by suitably qualified personnel.

Representation

It is recommended that in every police area there should be regular formal meetings between senior regular officers and senior special constables to discuss issues of common concern, and in turn between the most senior grades of Special Constabulary. Force facilities should be made available for such meetings.

Complaints and discipline

It is a view that since special constables carry the same powers as regular officers and frequently undertake the same duties, involving direct contact and potential conflict with the public, similar levels of accountability with regard to complaints and discipline should apply. It is recommended that special constables, like regular officers should be bound by Regulation to carry out all lawful orders and at all times punctually and promptly perform all appointed duties and attend to all matters within the scope of their office as constable.

Codes of conduct and procedures - It is recommended that a Code of Conduct be adopted based on that currently in development for regular officers, subject to the following amendment:

Lawful orders	The inclusion of a clear statement that a regular officer has authority over a member of the Special Constabulary whatever the rank or grade of either party.

It is recommended that there should be the adoption of a framework for discipline procedures based on that emerging for regular officers, subject to the following amendments:

Non-compliance	These matters should be dealt with, in the cases first instance, by first line managers.
Investigation	Where the supervisory officer considers matters sufficiently serious to justify formal disciplinary investigation, it is recommended that only members of the regular force should investigate special constables. Forces are expected to make sensible arrangements for senior members of the Special Constabulary.
Suspension	It is felt that suspension policies for special constables pending the outcome of an investigation, should not differ in principle from those for regular officers.

Disciplinary hearings	A superintendent of police should sit on a disciplinary hearing for special constables. It is felt entirely proper that a senior special should be invited to give antecedent history, a character reference and, as appropriate, to make recommendations about punishment.
Discipline friend	It is recommended that members of the Special Constabulary have a right to seek advice of a 'friend' in disciplinary matters.
Outcomes	It is recommended that the following outcomes be available in respect of disciplinary hearings: (a) dismissal; (b) requirement to resign; (c) reduction in grade; (d) reprimand (recorded in personal record); (e) caution (not recorded); (f) no action.

Unsatisfactory performance procedures - It is recommended that there should be an unsatisfactory performance procedure for special constables which should apply after they have finished foundation training. It is important that those special constables who cannot or will not perform to satisfactory levels are held accountable and that the procedures agreed on Police Personnel Procedures for managing poor work performance on the part of regular officers be adopted for special constables, subject to the following amendments:

(a) in the same way as the procedures are not applicable to probationer regular officers, nor should they be applicable to special constables until after the end of foundation training;

(b) as for regular officers, it is expected that poor work performance should be identified first by their immediate supervisor;

(c) in formal unsatisfactory performance interviews it is an overriding consideration that the officer conducting the interview is the officer's line manager (regular or special);

(d) officers subject to unsatisfactory performance interviews should have access to a 'friend' either a special or a regular officer;

(e) if a time is set for improvement at the first interview and after that time there is no improvement to an acceptable standard, the person holding the interview should contact the person in the force who has responsibility for the Special Constabulary, with a view to holding a second interview. The same officer should conduct the second interview with advice from the person responsible for the Special Constabulary;

(f) a written communication to a special constable subject to a second interview, should inform him that he has a right to a 'friend' at the second interview;

(g) where there is a hearing following two unsatisfactory performance interviews,

it is recommended that it be presided over by an assistant chief constable and a chief commandant from another force area;
(h) where there is a decision to require the special to resign or be reduced in rank it should have immediate effect from the day the officer is informed in writing;
(j) a special constable should have the right to ask the chief constable to review the decision of the hearing.

Grievance procedure - It is recommended that all special constables should have access to the established procedures made available to civilians and regular officers.

Resignation

It is recommended that forces assign a nominated officer, regular or special, to discuss any voluntary resignation with the special concerned. This would provide an opportunity:
(a) to confirm or understand more fully the reasons for departure;
(b) if appropriate, to set in motion arrangements to relieve pressures or help resolve problems for the special constable concerned, thereby encouraging the withdrawal of the resignation letter;
(c) where resignation is due to a move out of the force area, to facilitate a transfer to another Special Constabulary - to this end, resignation letters should be suspended until a transfer is agreed - forces will need a clear policy for this, appropriately published;
(d) to obtain feedback about the quality of the organisation in which the special constable has been involved.

Important new conditions

Health and safety

Specials are now covered by Health and Safety legislation by virtue of the Police (Health and Safety) Act 1997. The 1997 Act (in force July 1, 1998) applied the Health and Safety at Work etc Act 1974 and subsequent Health and Safety legislation to police officers, including Specials.

Subsequent legislation includes the Working Time Regulations 1998 (in force October 1, 1998), and the Police (Health and Safety) Regulations 1999 (in force April 14, 1999)

The legislation is applicable to anyone holding the 'office of constable'.

Hours of work

The Working Time Regulations apply in cases in which any employee is working more that 48 hours per week. This 48 hours include hours undertaken for one or more than one employer or types of employment. If a person has two jobs, then the hours worked for each will be added together.

For the purpose of the Regulations the Specials' voluntary duty is the equivalent of being employed. It is highly unlikely that a special constable will undertake over 48 hours of police duty in a week, but his tour of duty, when combined with the hours worked in his regular employment may well exceed the 48 hours.

> Forces would be in line with the Working Time Regulations if all new recruits to the Special Constabulary and currently serving specials were asked the number of hours worked as part of their regular employment and the number of hours they work or intend to work as a Special.

> If this will or is likely upon occasion to exceed 48 hours then the Special should be asked to sign a form acknowledging that he has waived his right to the 48-hour limit.

> The Special should also be advised that he may wish to inform his employer that he was undertaking voluntary work over and above the 48-hour limit.

In this circumstance, the Special himself has a responsibility - and both the employer and the force have a duty of care - to ensure that the Special's welfare and ability to undertake his work is not being placed in jeopardy.

Note - Forces are not required to contact the Special's employer.

Rest periods

Regulation 10 of the Working Time Regulations 1998 states that adult workers are entitled to a rest period of not less than 11 consecutive hours in every 24.

However, while the legislation governing the number of hours worked encompasses both everyday and Special Constabulary employment, the legislation for rest periods does not. The Regulation does not prevent a special constable from working or being asked to work a tour of duty until 2am in the morning if he has to be at his regular place of work at 8.30am.

Regulation 10 only affects specials in terms of the tours of duty they undertake for the force, and so it is generally perceived that it will rarely be applicable as specials tend to work only limited hours. Also specials have the discretion to waive this right. However, should a special constable be asked to undertake police work until 2am in the morning and then come back on duty at 6.00am - and does not wish to do so - he could point to the WTRs in his defence.

Note - this is the Home Office position with regard to entitlement to rest periods at the time of going to press, but this entitlement is generally not clear and is pending possible DTI changes.

Compensation for injury

New Regulations are being drafted which will improve compensation for injury and sick pay arrangements and other conditions of service. It is likely that these regulations will be in force late 1999 or early 2000.

In the event of death or a serious disabling injury, a pension is payable to specials which will be based on the pensionable pay of a regular constable up to a maximum of 14 years' service

Should a special constable - as a result of injury or illness sustained as a result of his Special Constabulary duties - be on sick leave without pay from his regular employment, it will be mandatory for the police authority to provide his full pay for the first six months and then half pay for the second six months. At the discretion of the chief officer, full pay may also be given for the second six months.

In one notable instance the Regulations will not follow the Working Group recommendations. The recommendation that a Special should be compensated for injury sustained on duty - resulting in permanent disability, but not one that would not affect his ability to undertake his everyday work - will not be carried. An example of such an injury would be loosing the end of a finger. This is because regular officers are not compensated for injury *per se* - but only for loss of earnings.

Legal representation

If a regular officer has the misfortune to become the subject of:
1. disciplinary procedure;
2. a complaint to answer;
2. civil action;
4 criminal action taken against him;

apart from in certain particular circumstances, the police authority may pay for the cost of his defence.

However Specials are not covered by the Federation, and have no staff association. Although very few cases come to light, when they do, they tend to become the focus of attention due to lack of the cover. The Special, to date, has been on his own.

This is not a matter of Regulation, but the Standing Committee on the Special Constabulary has agreed that free legal advice and representation will be made available to all specials. This will mean that should any special find himself in difficulties he will have instant access to a solicitor or barrister and to representation either in a court of law or at a disciplinary hearing.

As the Home Office, who will pay for this provision, has to tender the contract to insurance companies, it is likely to be April 2000 before this provision is made available.

Complaints and discipline

At the time of the 1996 Working Group recommendations there was an ongoing review of the procedures for regular officers. The Working Group therefore based its recommendations upon what was believed at the time the outcome of the regular review would be. However the review was not completed until 1998, becoming statute on April 1, 1999 in the form of the Police (Conduct) Regulations 1999.

The situation at the time of going to press (July 1999) is that a consultation document will be drawn up by the Home Office before the end of the year. The consultation document will consider both the Working Group recommendations and the Police (Conduct) Regulations 1999 with a view to bringing complaints and disciplinary procedures into Regulation for the Specials Constabulary in 2000.

Transfers

The Working Group recommendations on transfers can be summarised as follows.

1. Breaks in service should be kept to a minimum, and transfers should normally be completed within two to three months.
2. Special constables should not feel obliged to resign from one force before applying for appointment in another.
3. Forces should publish a transfer policy.
4. The transferring force should provide appropriate personnel information to the force to which the officer wishes to transfer.
5. Special constables who have achieved a particular grade should be eligible to apply for a post at an equivalent level, where vacancies exist.
6. Each force should produce a 'Transfer List' which is circulated to other forces giving details of special constables leaving to relocate elsewhere.

The recommendations have been supported by forces with the exception of those regarding the retention of supervisory or management grades (see 'Model Transfer Policy' (post)). Two draft proposals were tendered, one by Norfolk and Cambridgeshire Constabularies and one by Hampshire Constabulary. As a result of these proposals the Working Group has developed a standardised transfer procedure agreed by the National Special Constabulary Conference in March 98 and subsequently approved by the Standing Committee on the Special Constabulary in November 1998.

General points and principles

The 'Model Transfer Procedure' and 'Model Transfer Policy' documents (post) outline in detail the recommended force procedure and policy. General points and principles are as follows.

a. A 'Special Constabulary Co-ordinator' will be appointed by each force.
b. A special wishing to transfer should submit his application to his existing force (see 'Model Application Form' opposite).
c. The personnel departments of both forces should co-operate to adopt uniform procedures, ensure that there are no delays, and demonstrate to the transferring special that his service is valued and that he will be welcomed in his new force.
d. The transferring special will be contacted by the receiving force and invited for interview.
e. To identify training needs the receiving force should request the officer's personal file and last performance and development review, plus a statement of his force's selection criteria and training programme (see Model Selection Procedure and Model Training Policy (post)).

See following pages for all recommended model forms.
(Note - it is recognised that recruitment criteria and procedures can differ considerably from force to force, and that forces may need to consider some revision of the models.)

Special Constabulary
Application to transfer to another force

Section A - *To be completed by applicant*

MODEL APPLICATION FORM

Full name ....

Present address ....

....

Telephone - Home ....Work ....

Date of birth ....Nationality...

New address (if applicable) ....

....

Date due to move to new address...

Name and date of birth of other   ....
persons living at address   ....

                                                              ....

Name and address of employer ....

....

Present force ....

Division / Station..

Present grade ....

Force that you wish to transfer to ....

I agree to my personal record being passed to the force to which I wish to transfer.

Applicant's signature .... Date ....

For official use: Date application received ....

Section B - *To be completed by the force*

Service Record

Date joined Special Constabulary ....
Date and grade of promotions ....
Date received long service awards ....
....

Details of commendations ....
....

Have there been any complaints made against the applicant? ....
Has any disciplinary action been taken against the applicant? ....
(If either answer is YES, please give details on a separate sheet)

MODEL APPLICATION FORM

Training record	Tick box	Date due for requalification
Induction	☐	....
Foundation	☐	....
Post-foundation (continuous)	☐	....
Supervisory (for managers)	☐	....
First aid	☐	....
Defensive tactics	☐	....
Conflict resolution	☐	....
Quickcuffs	☐	....
Baton	☐	....
CS spray	☐	....

Specialist and standard
(eg driving) ....
....

Accreditations ....
....

Comments by line manager (use separate sheet if necessary)

Signature............................ Name (in caps) ....
Rank/Grade .... Date ....

Blankshire Special Constabulary
Transfer Process

This form is to facilitate the transfer of a special constable from one force to another

MODEL TRANSFER PROCESS

1. On receipt of the Transfer Application Form [see previous two pages], the releasing force will complete Section B and forward the form to the receiving force within 14 days.

2. Within 14 days of receipt of the form, the receiving force will acknowledge receipt of the transfer application directly to the applicant and provide the applicant with a contact name and telephone number.

3. Unless there are any *prima facie* reasons for rejecting the application, the receiving force - again within 14 days of receipt - will request the personal record file of the applicant.

4. Within 14 days of this request (as at 3 above), the releasing force will forward the personal record file.

5. On receipt of the personal record file, the receiving force will arrange to interview the applicant at the earliest date convenient for the force and the applicant.

6. If accepted, the applicant should join the receiving force and be attested as soon as possible.

7. The process - from the date of receipt of the application form by the releasing force until the date the applicant joins the receiving force - should not take longer than four months.

8. Any suspension in service between formally resigning from the releasing force until attestation in the receiving force should not be counted as a break in service providing the length of the suspension is not longer than four months.

9 Should the applicant require a formal break in service while transferring between forces, the applicant should be attested as soon as possible in the receiving force which will then consider any request for a break in service.

Blankshire Special Constabulary
Statement of Transfer Policy

MODEL TRANSFER POLICY

Blankshire Police welcomes applications from members of the Special Constabulary of other forces who wish to transfer to Blankshire Special Constabulary.

Where an officer transfers under the arrangements described in this note, they will not be required first to formally resign from their existing force, but will be deemed to have resigned on attestation in Blankshire Special Constabulary.

Special Constabulary Co-ordinator

Applications to transfer are dealt with by the Special Constabulary Co-ordinator, who is located at Police Headquarters and may be contacted on (Telephone, Facsimile and E-mail details).

The Co-ordinator will aim to deal quickly with applications to transfer and any enquires for information.

Transfer procedure

An officer who wishes to transfer to Blankshire Special Constabulary should submit a transfer application to their existing force, which will forward it to the Co-ordinator together with information about the officer's service.

If a vacancy exists, the Co-ordinator will
1. notify the applicant's force, and request a copy of their personnel file; and
2. write to the applicant inviting the officer to respond in order to arrange a convenient time for interview - at the same time the Co-ordinator will provide information about the force and the activities of the Special Constabulary.

The purposes of the interview are:
1. to determine the applicant's suitability;
2. to identify any training needs they might have, and
3. to discuss where the officer will serve and the arrangements for attestation and availability for duty.

continued...

MODEL TRANSFER POLICY

Vetting

As part of the procedures the force will conduct the standard vetting checks for criminal convictions of the applicant and members of their immediate family. All applicants will also be checked in respect of outstanding debts on the EQUIFAX database.

Medical examination

A medical examination will not normally be required. However, applicants will be required to complete a health assessment form, which is assessed by the Force Medical Officer who will request additional information from the applicant's general practitioner if he considers this to be necessary. On the basis of these reports the Force Medical Officer will advise whether the applicant is fit to serve in Blankshire Special Constabulary.

Leave of absence

Blankshire Special Constabulary recognises that where the application is made as a result of a change of home or employment it will often be difficult for the officer to attend for duty. In these circumstances, it will respond sympathetically to any request for leave of absence in the period following attestation. Leave of absence of up to [4] months will not count as a break in service.

During any period of leave the officer will be invited to attend appropriate meetings and training sessions.

Retention of supervisory or management grades

Where an officer who transfers to Blankshire Special Constabulary has held a supervisory or management grade in another force, under normal circumstance they will not be permitted to retain the grade on transfer. They will, however, be eligible to apply for promotion as soon as a suitable post becomes vacant. Their previous supervisory and management service will be taken into account.

Blankshire Special Constabulary
Recruit selection procedure and criteria

MODEL SELECTION PROCEDURE

1. Physical assessment

Blankshire Police does not require applicants for the Special Constabulary to undergo a physical assessment.

2. Health assessment

Applicants are required to complete a health assessment as part of their initial application form. This is assessed by the Force Medical Officer who will request additional information from the applicant's General Practitioner if he is of the opinion that it is necessary. The Force Medical Officer will, on the basis of these reports, advise as to whether or not the applicant is fit for duty in the Special Constabulary. The Force Medical Officer does not conduct a physical examination on potential recruits.

3 Eyesight standards

All applicants are required to take a Keystone eyesight test and must have unaided vision of the standard of 6/[ ].

4. Selection procedure

1. Potential recruits are required to attend a central selection centre at Training and Support Headquarters. There, they are expected to sit the PIR examination and achieve the national pass mark of 230.

2. They are also required to complete a questionnaire which further tests their literacy skills under examination conditions.

3. Successful applicants are then interviewed by the local management team on the division to which they have applied. The selection board is chaired by a regular officer of a rank of not less than Inspector (usually the Divisional Liaison Manager), the Divisional Liaison Officer and a Section Officer who have attended a one-day selection interviewing course.

continued...

MODEL SELECTION PROCEDURE

5. References and vetting checks

a. All applicants and members of their immediate family are vetted for criminal convictions by the Force Disclosure Unit and Special Branch.
b. References are taken up from their current employer or, in the case of an applicant who is unemployed, their last employer.
c. In cases where an employer's reference cannot be obtained, the applicant will be requested to supply referees.
d. All applicants are checked in respect of any outstanding debts on the EQUIFAX database.
e. The same criteria in respect of any disclosures in regard of previous convictions etc are applied to special constables as they would be for applicants for the regular Force.

Further details may be obtained from

    The Force Recruiting Manager
    Blankshire Police
    Police Headquarters.

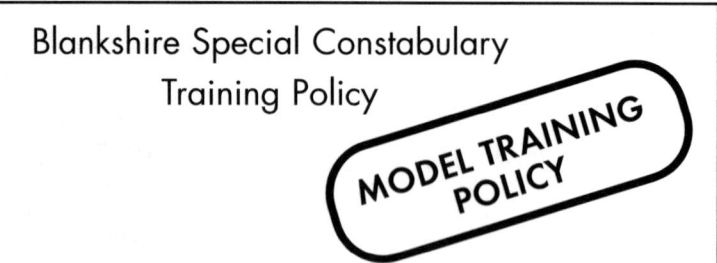

Blankshire Special Constabulary
Training Policy

MODEL TRAINING POLICY

1. Introduction

The following is a summary of the core subjects currently taught on initial training and thereafter. Depending upon the transferee's length of service there may be some variation on the content of previous training packages, although the core subjects have always been broadly similar.

2 Initial training

All recruits to the Blankshire Special Constabulary are required to attend four residential weekend courses at Training and Support Headquarters.

The core subject areas are as follows:

- Pocket note book rules
- Data protection
- Stop search
- Personal safety and infectious diseases
- Court practical
- Property
- First aid
- Caution
- Radio procedures, PNC
- Unarmed defence tactics
- Rigid handcuff training
- Equal opportunities
- Communication skills, questioning, listening and NVCs
- Learning, feedback and debriefing
- Power of arrest
- Arrest/reporting
- Custody procedures
- Road traffic definitions
- HORT/1 and 2 document production
- Driving licence, test certificate and insurance
- Powers to demand driving documents
- Witness statements
- Memory
- ASP baton training
- Attitude and behaviour
- Contamination of evidence
- The PEACE cognitive model
- Public order legislation section 4, 4a and 5 Public Order Act

continued...

MODEL TRAINING POLICY

3. Post- initial training

Following initial training, all Special Constable are required to attend local training sessions which are delivered by Devolved Divisional (Regular) Trainers. These are generally two-hour packages which are conducted on a continuous monthly rolling programme.

The following is a summary of the core subjects covered, although it is by no means and exhaustive list.

Theft	Searching premises etc
Burglary/robbery	Powers of entry
Criminal damage	Assaults
TWC	Drink/drugs driving
RTA	FPT VDRS CLE2/6
Custody procedures records cell block etc	Statutory preventative measures
	SOC (crime scene)
Drugs	

Further details may be obtained from

> The Special Constabulary Co-ordinator
> Blankshire Police
> Police Headquarters.

Other notable conditions of service

Ineligible occupations - The Standing Committee endorsed all the Working Group Recommendations, including those that traffic wardens and civilian detention officers should not be eligible for appointment. The Standing Committee also considered that civilian front office staff in police stations who deal with suspects should be ineligible.

The intention at the time of going to press (July 1999) is to base in Regulation:
> the ineligibility of traffic wardens and school crossing patrols;
> the ineligibility of those involved in political activity;
(following exactly the Regulations for regular officers).

The position of the Fire Service is still to be confirmed but it is expected that regular fire fighters will also be excluded by Regulation. All other groups cited in the recommendations will be subject to guidance but not to Regulation.

Note: Recruiting former TA members for the Special Constabulary - During 1999 the Territorial Army will be significantly downsizing and the Home Office is actively targeting, and encouraging forces to target, former TA members who may wish to continue giving voluntary service to the community through the Special Constabulary.

Recruitment - The Standing Committee on the Special Constabulary recommended that recruitment standards should be broadly in line with those for regular officers. This will include using the Police Initial Recruitment test, looking for the same pass mark as that for regulars, and medical fitness standards. These recommendations however will be a matter of guidance and not Regulation. (See 'Model Selection Procedure Form' in 'Transfers' section (ante).)

Age of joining - The Working Group recommendation of 18 and a half will be made statute.

Retention / personal records - Forces will be required by Regulation, as they are for regular officers, to keep personal records for each serving special constable. The records will be transferable between forces and will form the basis of a certificate to be issued to every special on leaving service.

Expenses - Mandatory reimbursement of out-of-pocket expense or loss remuneration as a result of duty will also be brought within the new Regulations.

Retirement age - The Working Group recommendations were based on retirement ages at the time of the report. The pending Regulations will instead follow whatever changes are implemented by the regular officers' pension review.

Promotion - The recommendation for appointments to all grades to be for an initial trial period not exceeding a year - with successful completion resulting in permanent appointment - will not be made statutory.

Leave of absence - The recommendation for force policies providing for career breaks will not be made statutory.

APPENDIX A

SKILLS AND ABILITES

Appendix contents

Desired character traits 336
Monitoring and performance 337
Communication and relationship with others 338
Investigation 339
Decision making, problem solving and planning............340
Practical effectiveness 341
Written reports 341
Knowledge 342

Desired character traits

	Level 1	Level 2
Punctuality	Fails to recognise importance of punctuality with regard to duty, appointments and paper-work. Fails to complete work on time.	Keeps appointments and submits paperwork on time. Reports punctually for duty at all times.
Pride in appearance	Has no pride in appearance. Poorly turned out and makes little effort to rectify this. Little attention to personal hygiene.	Smart in appearance, has good bearing.
Reliability	Unreliable, needs close supervision. Acts in a less than satisfactory manner when unsupervised.	Can be relied on to work well with minimum supervision. Can be trusted to complete tasks and act in a prudent way when unsupervised
Concentration	Cannot keep mind on what he/she is doing, loses track of what is happening around him/her.	Pays attention to what is being done or said. Is not easily distracted. Capable of applying himself to given tasks.
Morally and physically courageous	Not prepared to maintain own principles. Avoids any situation which involves potential physical danger to self. Visibly shrinks from any confrontation.	Has principles and prepared to adhere to them. Ready to become involved, where necessary, in incidents which involve potential physical danger.
Creativity	Lacks imagination or flair. Always depends on others for ideas	Is prepared to use imagination to suggest different approaches and new ideas. Capable of considering wider dimensions and implications of situations and presents them to others.
Self-motivation	Is reluctant to ask questions. Shows little interest in police work or wider social areas.	Is alert and has an enquiring mind. Shows active interest in police work but not to the exclusion of interests in other social and external activities.
Attitudes towards others	Is selfish, impolite and inconsiderate towards others. Is reluctant to help others. Makes abrasive or insensitive remarks without appreciating the effects on others.	Shows willingness to help others and puts the needs of others before personal needs. Is polite and considerate. Is aware of own effect on others and avoids making insensitive comments.
Professional and personal responsibility	Is dishonest with self and others. Lacks personal integrity and is disloyal to colleagues and the service.	Is honest with self and others. Is trustworthy and loyal to colleagues and the service.

Monitoring and personal performance

	Level 1	Level 2
Self monitoring	Having followed a particular course of action, fails to think about what has been done or said. Does not understand the value of the self monitoring process.	After an event, reflects on the effect it had, own actions and feelings. Seeks performance feedback from others and cross checks data received with own and others' perceptions. Readily accepts and makes use of others' observations.
Stress	Is not aware that stress can effect police officers. Is insensitive to the fact that others might be under stress.	Is aware that stress can be a problem that can affect police officers as well as the people they come into contact with. Is aware that their actions can cause stress in others. Shows sensitivity when dealing with others who may be under stress.
Fitness/health	Fails to achieve the required standard of physical fitness. Lacks motivation and interest, does not recognise the benefits of keeping fit and healthy	Reaches the required standard of physical fitness. Aware of the consequences that failing to keep fit and healthy can have. Aware of contagious diseases and how they can be avoided.
Learning from experience	Fails to draw upon past experience when dealing with situations. Fails to understand the relevance of learning from experiences.	Draws upon past experiences in order to deal with the situation in hand. Recognises the value of learning from experience.

Communication and relationships with others

	Level 1	Level 2
Consideration of the feelings of others	Does not demonstrate an appreciation of others' feelings.	Demonstrates an understanding of the feelings of others when dealing with a given situation.
Non-verbal communication NVC or body language	When dealing with others, uses body language inappropriate for the circumstances.	Has a basic knowledge of body language. Is aware that own body language plays an important part in the way others interpret what is being said.
Oral communication	Does not express him/herself clearly. Cannot get the point across.	Speaks clearly and in a way that those listening can understand. Gets message across. Reports back in a concise and accurate manner. Presents evidence in a clear and concise fashion.
Effective listening	Shows lack of interest in what is being said.	Listens carefully to what is said, demonstrating an understanding of the content and where necessary, relates back a summary, asking questions to clarify as needed.
Self control	Allows personal feelings to show in the way he/she deals with others. Is easily influenced by outside pressure.	Is tolerant towards the behaviour and views of others, even when provoked. Is impartial and fair when dealing with others, resisting outside pressure, personal prejudices and stereotyping.
Use of physical force	Fails to understand the legal limitations of the use of physical force. Ignores those constraints in practice.	Understands the legal limitations of the use of physical force and recognises those simulated and tutor-supervised situations where force may be used. Can exercise the legal constraints in practice.
Relationships with others	Does not get along with colleagues. A loner. Has a negative attitude towards the community.	Develops and maintains a co-operative relationship with others. Accepts proper discipline and is willing to follow instructions. Is a good team member. Recognises role as a member of the community.

Investigation

	Level 1	**Level 2**
Assesses the total situation	Approaches situations with a closed mind. Fails to draw inferences from situations or what people are doing or saying. Fails to observe the obvious.	When approaching situations or handling information, does so with an open and enquiring mind, tackling the problem from different angles. Observant.
Collation and analysis of information	Cannot make sense of information gathered or presented. Confused by all but simple data.	Having gathered information, picks out what is relevant and accurate and uses this to assist in further investigation or in the presentation of reports.
Questioning	Accepts the first answer given without following it up. Cannot formulate logical questions when interviewing. Unable to apply the basic principles of questioning.	Understands the value of pre-planning for any interview. Maintains a series of reasoned questions from contact to conclusion. Seeks to elicit more information by asking relevant questions in order to explore all possible avenues of investigation and follow up points raised by earlier answers or statements.

Decision making, problem solving, and planning

	Level 1	Level 2
Decision making	Identifies problems but allows others to both suggest and implement decisions. Indecisive.	Having identified a problem, makes a decision when alternative solutions are provided. Gives appropriate justification and explanations for own conduct when required.
Planning	Unable to plan and organise work. Gets bogged down in minor detail.	Sets objectives in relation to work load. Plans and prioritises courses of action accordingly.
Flexibility	Maintains a chosen course of action despite changing demands of the situation. Unable to react to new information. Inflexible.	Responds to and modifies judgement and decisions as necessary, in light of changing circumstances and new information.
Dealing with conflict and ambiguity	Can only deal with situations which lack conflict and are unambiguous. Unable to resolve conflict/confrontation between self and others.	When conflict arises, gets a clear understanding of both sides of the story before dealing with the problem. Is able to resolve conflict/confrontation even when personally involved.

Practical effectiveness

	Level 1	**Level 2**
Initiative	Does not recognise the need for initial action to be taken. Responds only to directions given by others. Only willing to take on a minor role in given situations.	Identifies the circumstances where the use of initiative is requited. Demonstrates the ability to take the initiative in simulated and tutor-supervised situations.
Confidence	Lacks confidence in own ability.	Demonstrates under simulated and tutor-supervised situations to be realistically confident in ability to handle a wide range of tasks.
Responsibility	Stands back, allows others to accept responsibility.	Takes responsibility for own decisions and actions when dealing with simulated and tutor supervised incidents and events.
Leadership	Fails to take control of situations where necessary.	Demonstrates the ability to take control of simulated and tutor-supervised situations. Is capable of giving appropriate directions. Understands the importance of working with others for task completion.

Written reports

	Level 1	**Level 2**
Written reports	Reports are poor in content and presentation.	Presents written work neatly and in a clear and accurate manner. Keeps accurate notes and knows how to make relevant use of them. Knows which forms to use for which situation and is careful and accurate in their completion.

Knowledge

	Level 1	Level 2
Knowledge of law	Lacks understanding and application of legal knowledge.	Understands and can apply legal definitions to classroom problems, simulated exercises and under tutor supervision in operational situations. Familiar with basic and frequently recurring tasks operationally which require this knowledge. Takes steps to develop own knowledge. Appreciates the importance of the exercise of discretion.
Knowledge of technical skills	Does not demonstrate practical knowledge in the correct use of police equipment.	Has a sound knowledge of the use of police equipment in operational use, eg radio, telephone, truncheon, hand-cuffs, shield, breath test device. Demonstrates ability to use the equipment under supervised circumstances.
Knowledge of procedures	Fails to demonstrate a sound knowledge of procedures to be adopted in simulated or tutor supervised situations	Demonstrates a sufficient knowledge of procedure to successfully deal with simulated and tutor-supervised incidents. Knows the initial action to be taken at more serious incidents /offences. Knows how the force is organised and the specialists available for assistance. Understands policies and guidelines governing police procedures within the force.
Community awareness	Fails to recognise the role of the police in the community. Is unaware of the issues affecting the community.	Develops a good understanding of the local community through personal interaction with its members. Recognises that there are local organisations, agencies and key people in the community who can assist. Recognises the role the police play in the community and the perception the community has of the police.

Index

Abuse of authority...............244
Accident
road traffic 86-90
Action at scene of crime...193-5
Actual bodily harm 45
Age of joining...............239, 312
Aggravated
burglary 79
vehicle taking.........................76
Aid and abet............................70
Alarm systems......................228
Alarmed premises................166
Alcohol
control of at sporting events ..220
sobriety.................................244
Allowances 292
boots.......................................292
refreshments.........................292
tights and stockings................292
Appointment (to force)
by chief constable...................11
eligibility for.........., 239-240, 307
Appraisal, staff 263-270
Arrest
arrestable offence..14, 178, 208-9
assaulting police 208
assessment of danger...........26-28
batons.......................................20
before arrest............................19
breach of the peace..................44
breath test...........................216-7
case law (use of force) 25-26
caution.....................................20
citizen's..............................14, 208
classification of offences 14
common law powers 14-15
delay in returning to station.....21
entry after................................37
entry and search leading to 211
entry in order to 38
factors to consider before 19
force, use of.........................21-30
general arrest conditions
.... 16-18, 209
information to be given 19
jurisdiction........................12, 171
mode of....................................19
obstruction............................208
off-duty 171
PACE
s24 15
s25 16-19
plain clothes 20
police powers 15, 208
release because no grounds 21
road traffic accident 216-217
search after................30, 37, 212
search leading to......................211
serious arrestable offence..24, 178
stop and search........................210
warrant 177-178
Assaults
actual bodily harm 45
common assault 44
police, on..................................46
 plain clothes duty...............168
unlawful wounding..................45
wounding with intent..............45
Assessment
criteria...................................264
ratings............................265-270
report....................................237
Attempts
to commit offence 46-47
Attestation 11, 328
Authority
abuse of 244
of regular officer............244, 318
Availability for duty.........327-8

Beat, patrolling............164-172
equipment.............................164
intelligence gathering.............167
local knowledge......................165
Bentley case 139
Betting office 219
Black Police Association 300
Blackmail................................81
Books 302-304
Boot allowance 292
Breach of the peace 44
Breath test..........................216
Burglary................................78
aggravated..............................79
Burnout................................280
minimising 277-8

Charging.....................113-115
Charitable collections
.................................68, 179
Children
ages, relevant....................66-68
care proceedings...................181
domestic disputes..................189
offences in relation to 66-68
prevention of cruelty to...........68
police protection.................180-1
CID..252
Code of Conduct.............243-5
Colour clock code
(target indication system)........170
Conditions of service
.........................241, 305-334
Confidentiality 244
Confrontational continuum
.................................23-25
Counsel and procure
to commit an offence...............70
Counting code
(target indication system)........170
Crime, action at scene of
.................................193-5
Crime prevention.............224-8
dwelling security..................225-7
intruder alarms......................228
Neighbourhood Watch.......222-3
property marking...............227-8
security lighting....................228
target hardening....................224
Crime and Disorder
Act 1998 ....70a
Crime reports 195-6
Criminal
Criminal Injuries Compensation
Scheme...............................197
damage..............................69-70
liability (misuse PNC) 204
offences................................244
Critical Incidents Stress
Debriefing.................289-90
Custody suite 101-116
arrested person's rights...........109
authorising detention.........111
charging..............................113
detention conditions..........114
fingerprints and
photographs....................115
questioning........................114
cells 111
Codes of Practice 102
custody officer......................106
designated police stations
.................................105-106
detained persons
free legal advice..................110
property..............................108
review of detention.............115
treatment of 112-3
detention officers.................103

detention without charge
  time limits 116
fingerprints.............................115
free legal advice 110
informing named person 109
insufficient evidence to
  charge 111
interviewing....................119-144
juveniles.................................113
officers at variance 108
photographs 115
property of detained person
 108-9
questioning after charge.........114
review of detention 115
review officer's detention
  conditions..........................116
solicitors 110
urgent interviews....................110
Dangerous dogs...................180
Data Protection Act..........203-4
Death on duty 293
Deception
obtaining property by.........80-81
obtaining services by 83
Defence
negating the....................122-123
Designated police stations
 105-6
Detention
authorising 111
reviews of...........................115-6
without charge (time limit) ...117
Diet..277
Disciplinary procedure
 242-248
advice, taking 246
appearance..............................244
authority
  abuse of 244
  of regular officer.........244, 318
co-defendants.........................247
Code of Conduct 243-5
confidentiality 244
criminal offences 244
dismissal..............................246-8
  arbitrary dismissal................246
  invitation to resign 246
  taking advice......................246
duties, performance of...........244
force, use of............................244
'friend' 247
general conduct......................244
interviews 247
law, the 242
lawful orders...........................244
legal representation 245, 323
past and present 242

Police (Conduct) Regulations
  1999 243
property...................................244
resignation..............................316
  invitation to resign.... 242, 246
retirement................................248
sobriety...................................244
suspension...............................247
taking advice 246
use of force and abuse of
  authority.............................244
Working Group
  recommendations 245
Dismissal 246-8
Disqualified drivers.............213
Documents, driving..........93-95
driving licence 93
endorsements 94
insurance 94
MoT..95
production of....................213-4
Dogs
dangerous 180
seizure of stray 180
Domestic disputes 186-191
agencies, relevant...................190
neighbours..............................191
specialist units....................190-1
violence...........................188-191
Debriefing..................289-290
Disability..........................293-4
Dress, improper 247
Drink/driving....................63-4
breath test 64-5, 216
driving while unfit...................63
Drink offences....................62-5
breath test 64-65, 216
drunk and disorderly...............62
drunk and incapable 62
drunk in charge.......................62
drunk in charge of child...........62
drunkenness 62
Driving licence 92-4
also see documents, driving
Driving offences
also see documents, driving
endorsements 94
notice of intended
  prosecution 176-7
Drugs...................................57-8
squad 253
stop and search 58, 219
unlawful possession 57-8
Duties
availability for 237-8
performance of.......................244
Electricity
abstracting.........................79-80

Emergency services...............165
Endorsements........................94
Enquiry office.....................256
Entry
domestic disputes...................187
fire extinguishing 220
following arrest........................37
Equipment 296-7, 311-2
equipped for stealing...............83
for use on patrol....................164
radio procedure 204-6
**European Police Information
  Centre**
(EPI-Centre) 300
Evidence
hearsay....................................261
interview.................................121
pocket book 181-3
statements..........................258-61
witness statement.............259-60
Exclusion order
football 220
Exercise................................278
Expenses 234, 292
lost income.............................293
out of pocket..........................293
travelling.................................293
Eyesight 239, 330

Fairness 243
Ferrers Trophy...................297-9
File submission 145-58
advance disclosure..................154
case procedure........................154
content check list...............152-3
discontinuance 155
file types.........................149-151
Manual of Guidance..............147
mode of trial guidelines......156-7
preparation 146
submission 146
supervision 236
tape recorded interviews 141-4
time limits..........................148-9
unique reference number......151
fingerprints
in custody...............................115
Fire
police powers at.....................220
services 165, 220
Firearms
carrying in public place.........217
certificate, production of........218
production, power to
  require 218
stop and search......................218
trespassing with weapon
 217-218

Index

Fixed penalty system..........96-7
Football
alcohol....................................220
exclusion orders....................220
Force
use of 244
when making arrests 21-30
Further reading................301-4

Garages 166
Going equipped for stealing
....83
Goods vehicle operators
licence..............................215
GOWISE..............................211
Grades..................4-5, 304-310

Handling stolen goods..........82
Hearsay evidence................261
Help in handling stress
seeking 279
self help 279
History
modern police....................8-11
Special Constabulary................2
Hit and run..........................89
Honesty..............................243
Hospitals..............................165
House-to-house collections...78

Impartiality........................234
Information
confidentiality of....................244
Injuries on duty 294-5
compensation for 294-5
industrial injuries benefit.......295
private insurance 295
Insurance 294
certificate (driver documents)
....94-5
legal representation
cover............................243, 323
private injury cover 295
Insignia..................296-7, 311-2
Integrity 243
International Police Association
(IPA)..................................301
Interviewing....................120-44
confession (case law)..............125
disciplinary proceedings..........247
defence, negating the..........122-3
evaluating............................120-1
evidence..............................121
information evaluating.......120-1
intelligence gathering..............167
offence, proving..................122-3
planning..............................120
pocket book 181-3

questioning......................127-37
classification of 128
counter-productive........128-31
oppressive 127
solicitor, treatment of............124
street, in the 175-6
suspect................................123-4
tape recording................141-144

Jurisdiction 11-12, 171
Juveniles
in custody..............................113

Keyholders..........................165
Knowledge, local................165

Land
aggravated trespass 52
stealing..................................73
trespass..................................53
Landlord and tenant
disputes..............................191-2
harassment 192
procedure, suggested............193
unlawful eviction 191-2
Lawful orders......................244
Legal advice
complaints and discipline..............
detained persons 110
Legal executives................124-5
Leave of absence..........308, 329
Licensed betting office 219
Licensed premises................219
Litter 55
Local knowledge 165
Lost property 183-6
index....................................183
record..............................185-6
report....................................184

Making off without paying..83
Manual of Guidance
(prosecuting)....................147
Mentally ill people
place of safety 219
Modus operandi index........195
MoT certificates..................95

Name inquires (PNC)
....200-1
Named person................109-10
Neighbour disputes............191
Neighbourhood Watch
............................166, 222-3
Note taking
on plain cloths duties............169
Notice of intended
prosecution....................176-7

Observation
colour coding 170
counting code 170
Obtaining
property by deception 80-1
service by deception 83
Off-duty arrests 171
Offences
aid, abet, council or procure to
commit..............................46-7
attempts to commit 70
children, relating to 66-8
criminal 244
Offender
reporting............................174-6
Operation orders 248-51
IIMAC................................250-1
Orders, lawful....................244

Paperwork 164
Pay......................................295-6
Pensions 293-4
Performance of duties........244
Personal file..............234, 324
Phonetic alphabet..............204
Plain clothes duty 168-9
arrests............................20, 169
assault during 168
note taking 169
special equipment 169
warrant cards........................168
Planning the interview........120
Pocket book 181-3
Police areas 9
jurisdiction 11-12, 171
Police (Conduct) Regulations
1999 243-5
Police national computer
(PNC) 200-4
authorised users....................200
criminal liability 204
Data Protection Act 203-4
name inquiries 200-1
phonetic alphabet..................204
public, requests from 202
radio codes 205
vehicle inquiries............201-203
warning signal codes 201
Police protection
children 180
Police Review 301
Police stations
arrival at..............................107
designated 105-6
Politeness............................243
Post-traumatic stress......285-90
defusing 288-9
general symptoms 287

Powers
arrest 12, 16-18
jurisdiction 11-12
summary of 207-220
Premises
alarmed 166
definition of 213
prisoner's 212
seizure from 213
vulnerable 165
Preparation and planning
the interview 120
Prohibited articles 210
Promotion 231, 305
Property
damage to (domestic disputes)
  187
detained person's 108-9
lost/found 183-6
prevent loss or damage (police
  property) 244
obtaining by deception 80-1
trespassing on 53
Prosecution
advance disclosure 154-5
discontinuance 155
Manual of Guidance 147
mode of trial 156-7
preparing file 146
types of file 149-151
Public houses 165-6
Public meetings
police powers at 220
Public order 47-56
affray 49
aggravated trespass 52
intentional harassment, alarm or
  distress 49
litter 55
noise 56
offensive conduct 47
offensive weapons 56
racial hatred 52
raves 53
riot 50
threatening behaviour 48
trespass on land 53
trespassory assemblies 51
violent disorder 50

Questioning
after charge 114
Questions 127-37
art-form 133-5
Bentley case 139
classification of 128
closed 128-31
counter-productive 128-31

leading 128-31
open 132-3
process 137-8
productive 132-3
recall 137-8
summaries 138-9
Y-factor 140

Racial hatred 52
Radios
phonetic alphabet 204
plain clothes duty 168
quick reference guide 205
ten code 206
standard codes 205
Rank
chief commandant 7
divisional commandant 7
regulars 7
section officers 6
structure 4-7, 309-310
sub-divisional officers 6
Raves 53-5
Recruiting 238-41
conditions of service
  .... 241, 305-34
disqualified categories
  .... 238-9, 313-4
model for selection 240
selection requirements
  .... 239-40, 330-1
model form (transfers) 330-1
Regular force
authority over specials ... 318, 244
joining 283-4
relationship with 7, 8
Relaxation 278
Reporting offender 174-8
Resignation 242, 246, 316
Retirement 248, 313, 334
Road checks 41, 217
Road traffic accidents 86-90
action at scene 87-90
arrest 216-7
breath test 216
definition 86
department 254
disqualified drivers 213
documents, production of .. 213-4
driving documents 91-5
fixed penalty system 96-7
goods vehicle operators'
  licence 215
HO/RT 1 91-2
insurance 94-5
licence 92-4
MoT 95
Motor Insurers Bureau 197

PSV driver 214
PSV passenger 214
regulating traffic 216
removal of vehicle 215
road checks 41.217
tachograph 215
testing vehicles 215
vehicle defect rectification
  scheme 98-9
Robbery 77
Routine 278

Scene of crime
action at 193-5
department 253
modus operandi, index of 195
Scrap metal dealer 219
Search
arrest, after 30, 37, 212
arrest, in order to 38
clothes 213
conduct of 35
Criminal Justice and Public
  Order Act 1994 42
drugs 58, 219
entry and 211
PACE powers 32-41
places where allowed 34
police station, other than at 39
premises
  definition of 213
  prisoner's 212
  seizure from 213
public, in 213
records of 36
  copy 36
road check 41
stop and 32-33, 210
terrorism 42
vehicles 41
warrant 40
Section
setting up a 233-7
Security lighting 228
Seizure
search, following 30
Services
obtained by deception 83
Sexual offences 59, 61
gross indecency (indecency
  between men) 60
indecent assault on man 61
indecent assault on woman 59
kerb crawling 61
prostitution 60
rape 59
solicitation by men,
  persistent 61

Sick pay 293-5, 322
Skills and abilities 336-42
Sobriety 244
Solicitor 110, 124
Special Beat 301
Specialist units 252-6
 CID 252
  drug squad 253
  scenes of crime 253
  stolen vehicle squad 254
 enquiry office 256
 National Crime Squad
  (proposal for specials') 254
 road traffic 255
 support group 255
 task force 255
 traffic wardens 256
Sporting events
 alcohol control 220
Squatters 192
Staff appraisal 263-70
 assessment criteria 264
 ratings 265-70
  supervisory ranks 270
Stolen Vehicle Squad 254
Stop and search 32-6, 213
 drugs 219
 premises 213
 procedure 211-3
  GOWISE 32, 211
Stray dogs
 seizure of 180
Street
 collections 179
 interview in the 175-6
 search in the 213
Stress 273-89
 indicators 277
 lifestyle changes 276
 minimising 277
 post-traumatic 285-9
 recognising 276-7
 seeking help 279
 vulnerability 275
Supervisors
 assessing 270-2
 burnout, avoiding 280-3
 conflict 236
 files 236
 mentors 233
 operation orders 248-50
 post-traumatic stress 285-9
 promotion, seeking 232-3
 responsibilities 230
 skills required 231
 teams 235
Support group
 (Task Force) 255-6

Tachographs 215
Tape recorded interviews 141-4
Target indication system 170
Task force 255-6
Ten code 206
Terrorism
 stop and search 42
Theft 72-84
 aggravated burglary 79
 aggravated vehicle taking 76
 appropriates 73
 belonging to another 75
 blackmail 81
 burglary 78
 dishonestly 72
 electricity, abstracting 79
 going equipped for stealing 83
 handling stolen goods 82
 intention 75
 land, of 73
 making off without paying 83
 motor vehicle 76
 mugging 77
 obtaining
  property by deception 80
  services by deception 83
 property, of 73
 robbery 77
 vehicle interference 84
 wild creatures 74
 wild plants 74
Threat
 recognition of 27-8
 signals of submission 22
 threatening behaviour 48
Time management 278
Tolerance 243
Traffic
 lights 166
 officers 90
 regulation 216
 wardens 239, 256, 314
Training
 burnout, avoiding 280
 model training policy
  (transfers) 332-3
 structured programme 280-1
 Working Group
  recommendations 317-8
Transfers 324-33
 Working Group
  recommendations 324
 general principles 324
 model forms 325-33
Uniform 296-7, 311-2
 appearance 244
Unlawful eviction 191-3
 procedure, suggested 193

Vehicles
 accidents 86-90
 aggravated taking of 76
 defect rectification scheme 98-9
 disabled at scene of accident 90
 documents 91-5
 driving licence 92, 93
 endorsements 94
 fixed penalty system 96-7
 HO/RT 1 91-2
 inquiries on PNC 201-3
 insurance 94-5
 interference with 84
 MoT 95
 removal of 215
 Stolen Vehicle Squad 254
 theft of 76
Victims 196-8
 civil action 197
 compensation 197
 Motor Insurers' Bureau 198
 witness, as 198
Violence
 anticipation of 42
 domestic 188-91

Warrants 177-8
Witness
 reporting offenders 174
 statements 258
 victim, as 198
Wounding
 actual bodily harm 45
 common assault 44
 police, assault on 46
 unlawful wounding 45
 wounding with intent 45

'Y factor' 140